Approaches to Teaching the Works of Karen Tei Yamashita

Approaches to Teaching the Works of Karen Tei Yamashita

Edited by

Ruth Y. Hsu

and

Pamela Thoma

Modern Language Association of America
New York 2022

Library of Congress Cataloging-in-Publication Data

Names: Hsu, Ruth, 1957– editor. | Thoma, Pamela S. (Pamela Sue), 1961– editor.
Title: Approaches to teaching the works of Karen Tei Yamashita /
edited by Ruth Y. Hsu and Pamela Thoma.
Description: New York : Modern Language Association of America, 2022.
Series: Approaches to teaching world literature, 1059-1133 ; vol 168 |
Includes bibliographical references.
Identifiers: LCCN 2021010611 (print) | LCCN 2021010612 (ebook) |
ISBN 9781603295406 (hardcover) | ISBN 9781603295413 (paperback) |
ISBN 9781603295420 (EPUB)
Subjects: LCSH: Yamashita, Karen Tei, 1951—Study and teaching. |
Yamashita, Karen Tei, 1951—Criticism and interpretation. |
MESH: Essays. lcfgt | Literary criticism. lcfgt
Classification: LCC PS3575.A44 Z55 2021 (print) |
LCC PS3575.A44 (ebook) | DDC 813/.54–dc23
LC record available at https://lccn.loc.gov/2021010611
LC ebook record available at https://lccn.loc.gov/2021010612

Approaches to Teaching World Literature 168
ISSN 1059-1133

Published by The Modern Language Association of America
85 Broad Street, Suite 500, New York, New York 10004-2434
www.mla.org

CONTENTS

PREFACE

Karen Tei Yamashita's writing has been a dynamic force in the coeditors' lives as teachers, scholars, and individual members of varied collectives endeavoring to comprehend and deal with the perils and possibilities of the present. We came to know each other professionally through our shared respect for this body of writing and have found great satisfaction in working on this volume as full and equal coeditors (our names are listed alphabetically). Together, we first thank the twenty-six teacher-scholars, Karen Tei Yamashita, and the survey respondents for their contributions to the project. We also thank Washington State University's Department of English for its support, and Kara Falknor for her excellent editorial assistance; the College of Languages, Linguistics, and Literature at the University of Hawai'i, Mānoa, for providing us with the grant support to obtain data analysis software; the Asian American forum of the Modern Language Association (MLA) for its early enthusiasm for this project; and the MLA acquisitions editors who worked with us on the project, including James Hatch, Katherine Kim, and most intensely Jaime Cleland. We additionally thank Sally Ball at Arizona State University for her invaluable assistance.

Among the characteristics of Yamashita's oeuvre is its capacity to vividly portray the everyday life of its characters; at the same time, we emphasize here that Yamashita's writing is always anchored in an astute and often prescient apprehension of the larger historical, geopolitical, and hegemonic matrix of relations affecting the mundane. Yamashita's work has been remarkable in its world-making, which the coeditors believe this volume solidly demonstrates. *Approaches to Teaching the Works of Karen Tei Yamashita* offers educators an extensive collection of essays on Yamashita pedagogy—the first of its kind. Further, this volume deals with Yamashita's formalistic innovations in multiple genres: she has written essays, a memoir, novels, poetry, plays, short stories, a film script, and song lyrics, utilizing comics, magical realism, photography, polyvocality, nonlinear chronotopes, and realism, among other textual styles and techniques. Her narratives are set on three continents and draw from personal history and the artistic, cultural, and historical cartographies of Asia (such as China, Japan, and the Philippines), Anglo-European countries (Britain, France, and others), and the Americas (notably, the United States, Brazil, and Colombia). Her teaching has taken many forms and has developed over the course of a distinguished career: in the 1990s, she began as a lecturer and later became a professor at the University of California, Santa Cruz (part 1 of this volume contains Yamashita's essay on her teaching practice); she has also edited anthologies, given numerous interviews and lectures, and participated in classes (in person or virtually, as two essays in part 2 of this volume describe), workshops, and readings.

Yamashita's writing has been adopted in multidisciplinary and interdisciplinary curricula in many countries, has been written about by scholars, is the subject of dissertations, and has been credited as transforming the parameters of Asian American literary and cultural studies from one that is US-centric to one that is hemispheric and transnational; her career as a writer and teacher is in many ways exemplary. In February 2019 the Humanities Institute of the University of California, Santa Cruz, hosted a celebration of Yamashita's contributions as a faculty member on the occasion of her retirement. Although she is now a professor emerita, her career is surely not over. The coeditors encourage educators to read part 1, "Materials," before delving into part 2, "Approaches."

Part One

MATERIALS

A Writer in Motion

Ruth Y. Hsu and Pamela Thoma

A sourcebook for pedagogical inspiration, *Approaches to Teaching the Works of Karen Tei Yamashita* will be useful to educators who want to help students understand and respond to the current and historical conditions that shape our lives. Yamashita's writing explores both the complex causes and the unfolding effects of the seismic transformations of the late twentieth and early twenty-first centuries. As contributor Caroline Rody writes, "[Yamashita's] gigantic canvasses and striking designs, as they accommodate a transnational scope and histories of global migration, become arenas for the dramatic interaction of people of multiple histories, languages, memories, and tastes in food and music who tend to morph into crowds of distinct classes or ethnicities, which then converge in spectacular crowd-meets-crowd scenes." The essays collected in part 2, "Approaches," offer myriad pedagogical routes for reaching critical understanding of Yamashita's "gigantic canvasses" and useful strategies for teaching her "striking designs" in the limitless art of writing.

Educators should thus read the volume for overall pedagogical guidance and for its attention to Yamashita's refashioning of the immigrant tale, the postmodern novel, magical realism, apocalyptic literature, and the picaresque, along with other tropes and conventions. Yamashita's dynamic corpus has also inspired new and influential interpretative frameworks for Asian American literature and American literature alike, such as the hemispheric approach advanced by the scholars Claudia Sadowski-Smith, Claire Fox, and Kandice Chuh; theorizations of form, illustrated in Rody's concept of interethnic literature (*Interethnic Imagination*) and in the early critical recognition of the genre of climate fiction; and even periodization, as with Rachel Adams's concept of "American literary globalism" (250). Matters of formal innovation and newer reading practices are variously represented in the essays collected in this volume. This volume, in other words, is a tool kit, offering educators ideas for refreshing familiar pedagogical approaches to Yamashita's work and newer methodologies reflective of curricular and disciplinary changes. Contributors' essays elaborate how best to inspire students at all course levels to engage deeply with Yamashita's writing, how best to encourage students to develop their analytical skills, and how best to help students participate in humanistic and civic discourse.

In addition to the topical immediacy and formal innovations of Yamashita's works, her oeuvre holds an influential position in American literature. In the decades since the 1990 publication of *Through the Arc of the Rain Forest*, her first published novel, Yamashita's works have achieved eminent status in Asian American and American literary studies—illustrated by the presence of this literature in college curricula in the Americas, in Asia, and in Europe, as the survey results and the essays in this volume demonstrate. Yamashita's novels—*Brazil-Maru*,

Through the Arc of the Rain Forest, *Tropic of Orange*, and *I Hotel*—and her work of creative nonfiction, *Circle K Cycles*, have attracted the robust interest of educators. The prominence of Yamashita's oeuvre is evident in the wide-ranging adoption of her work in interdisciplinary contexts beyond literary studies. In addition to English studies (19.27% of responses), participants in the survey that was conducted to prepare this volume listed American studies (7.22%); Asian American studies (6.02%); comparative literature, philology, and other language and literature disciplines (6.01%); gender and women's studies (2.4%); ethnic studies (1.8%); environmental studies (1.2%); Asian studies (0.6%); and Latin American studies (0.6%), among others, as curricular contexts in which Yamashita's work is taught. In North America, environmental and Latin American studies classrooms were some of the first to adopt Yamashita's works. The significant place that Yamashita's corpus currently enjoys is linked to the academy's concomitant embrace of ethnic literary and cultural texts of the United States in interdisciplinary undergraduate curricula across the social sciences and the humanities, to the establishment of more Asian American studies units, and to the increasing number of Asian American students.

The importance of Yamashita's oeuvre is also connected to the question of what constitutes Asian American literature, in part because Yamashita's writing emerged on the scene just as scholars began to theorize the category in the 1990s, questioning the cultural nationalist basis that had underwritten the field of Asian American studies since its emergence in the academy in the United States in the 1970s. In fact, Yamashita's works have inspired a good deal of the contemporary reframing and development of both Asian American and American literary studies. Accordingly, select contributions to this volume, such as the essay by Lynn Mie Itagaki, describe teaching approaches that incorporate newer reading methods developed within critical ethnic studies, women of color feminisms, comparative racialization studies, critical mixed race studies, and other interdisciplinary contexts that seek to move beyond an ethnic studies rooted in national paradigms. Many of the essays are also indebted to the retheorization of Asian American literary studies undertaken since the transnational turn, or to alternative scalar approaches, such as *planetarity*.

In the materials that make up part 1, and in the essays on pedagogical approaches in part 2, instructors will find useful guidance on Yamashita scholarship. The volume includes a selected bibliography of Yamashita's writing and an extensive works-cited list for a dispersed body of scholarship, all of which will assist educators wanting to adopt Yamashita's works as part of their curricula. While Yamashita has been publishing creative work since the 1970s, the major works under consideration in this volume include *Anime Wong*, a collection of "fictions of performance" or dramatic works that have been theatrically produced for over forty years and that predate the publication of Yamashita's long-form fiction; four novels, namely *Through the Arc of the Rain Forest*, *Brazil-Maru*, *Tropic of Orange*, and *I Hotel*; *Circle K Cycles*, a mixed-genre, multilingual narrative in English, Portuguese, and Japanese; and a memoir, *Letters to Memory*.

This volume focuses on teaching Yamashita's writing in English since the coeditors did not receive survey responses or abstract submissions on teaching Yamashita's works in translation. In the section in part 1 titled "Plays, Memoir, Essays, Interviews, Short Stories, Translations, and Papers," the coeditors provide information on translations of Yamashita's work.

Karen Tei Yamashita was born on 8 January 1951 in Oakland, California, to Hiroshi John Yamashita and Asako Sakai. When Yamashita was a year old, her family moved to Los Angeles, where Yamashita grew up with her younger sister, Jane Tomi. Yamashita attended Carleton College in Minnesota and studied at Waseda University in Tokyo during her junior year. She earned degrees in English and Japanese literature and was inducted into Phi Beta Kappa.

After college Yamashita traveled to São Paulo on a Thomas J. Watson Fellowship to research the history of Japanese immigration to Brazil. She interviewed Japanese immigrants, their descendants, and members of a commune for a study on Japanese Brazilian agricultural life. While there, she also began to write fiction and plays. Remaining in Brazil for a decade, Yamashita married the architect Ronaldo Lopes de Oliveira and had two children, Jane and Jon. Yamashita's research and experience in Brazil had a profound effect, as Helena Grice emphasizes: her "interest in immigration and travel, and the mixing of different cultures, can be traced to this time" ("Karen Tei Yamashita" 339). Yamashita moved to Los Angeles in 1984, worked on translations and screenplays, and soon produced dramatic works such as *Hannah Kusoh: An American Butoh*, *Tokyo Carmen vs. L.A. Carmen*, and *Noh Bozos*, which she has linked in content and style to her third published novel, *Tropic of Orange*.

In addition to the 1974 Watson Fellowship, Yamashita has received prestigious accolades for her creative works, including a Rockefeller Playwrights-in-Residence Fellowship at East West Players in Los Angeles for *Omen: An American Kabuki* and, in 1991, the Before Columbus Foundation American Book Award for her first novel, *Through the Arc of the Rain Forest*, which in 1992 also won the Janet Heidinger Kafka Award. *I Hotel* received the American Book Award, the California Book Award, the Asian/Pacific American Librarians Association Award for Literature, and the Association for Asian American Studies Book Award. It was also a National Book Award finalist. From 2012 to 2015 Yamashita coheld with Bettina Aptheker the University of California Presidential Chair in Feminist Critical Race and Ethnic Studies. In 2017 Yamashita's eminent place in Asian American letters was solidified when she was invited to deliver one of two keynotes at the inaugural Asian American Literature Festival, which took place at and was cosponsored by the Library of Congress, in collaboration with the Smithsonian Asian Pacific American Center and other notable Asian American literary and arts organizations. In 2018 she received a VONA (Voices of Our Nations Arts Foundation) tribute and in 2019 a John Dos Passos Literature Award. For *Letters to Memory* Yamashita received a second Association for Asian American Studies Book Award in 2019. The Karen Tei Yamashita Papers, which document her career, are housed at the McHenry Library at the University of California, Santa Cruz.

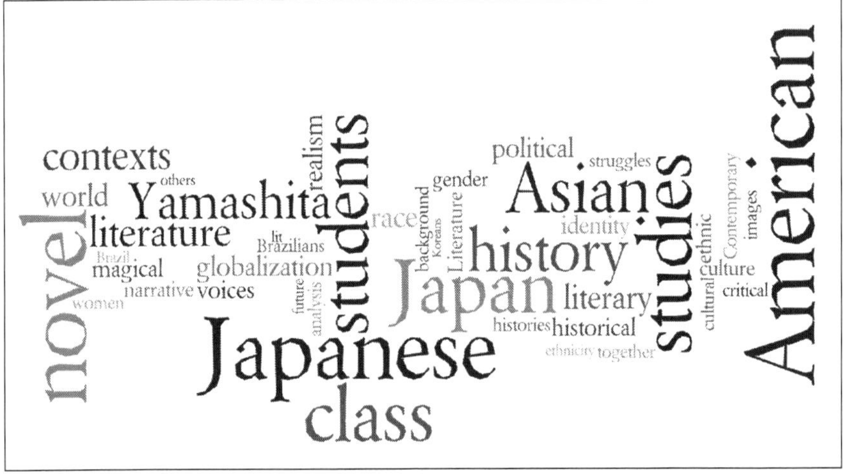

Figure 1. Survey word cloud.

While the widespread teaching of Yamashita's works was confirmed in certain ways by the survey, there were also some surprising absences—or at least they seem surprising given the pedagogical emphases described in the contributor essays. Some of these absences are evident in the word cloud (fig. 1). For example, while words such as *globalization* or *global* were frequently cited by respondents, few used the words *transnational* or *transnationalism*. We might attribute this to a preference for lay language over technical language or jargon while quickly typing responses online, or to the search for new relations to space reflected in the titles of the third and fourth sections of part 2, "Mapping Alternative Spaces" and "New Transnationalisms and Ecocritical Approaches." There was also only negligible reference to *feminism* in the survey responses. As is often the case, the far more general *women* may have been a substitute for *feminists*, or *gender* may have been a stand-in for *feminism*, since *women* and *gender* made more frequent appearances than did *feminists* or *feminism*. Again, we read this as a preference for mundane language, but these apparent slippages are nevertheless noteworthy since so many of the essays we received and those we include here explicitly or implicitly address feminist reading and pedagogical practices. Accordingly, the organization of the essays in part 2 gives feminism the final pedagogical word, as it were, with Aimee Bahng's essay on feminist decolonial science studies rounding out their dialogue.

While it includes only the fifty words most frequently used by survey respondents, the word cloud neatly captures our sense of Yamashita as a writer in motion. It tells its own story, visually and verbally, of works that dynamically travel through time and across space—whether those temporalities and spaces are cultural, geopolitical, conceptual, or narrative. As such, it provides a fitting transition to the overview of Yamashita's storytelling and of the scholarship on her novels that follows.

Novels: Critical Dialogue and Long-Form Fiction

Pamela Thoma

Karen Tei Yamashita's novels have sparked lively dialogue among scholars, kindling critique, propelling analytics, and stretching fields. A review of scholarship might begin with Stan Yogi's 1997 chapter in *An Interethnic Companion to Asian American Studies*, for it acknowledges Yamashita's category-defying dimensions with respect both to the formal qualities of her work and to the author's identity and heritage. Yogi situates Yamashita's writing within Japanese American literature. But this positioning might be accompanied by Rachel Lee's 1999 recognition of the "uneasy fit" between Yamashita's focus on globalization in her first published novel, *Through the Arc of the Rain Forest*, in 1990 and "traditional definitions of Asian American literature" (*Americas* 107). Further, educators might usefully pursue Ursula K. Heise's observation that *Through the Arc*, as well as *Brazil-Maru* and *Tropic of Orange*, has "far stronger affinities with late twentieth-century Latin American fiction" than with ethnic literatures of the United States ("Local Rock" 126).

Because of these evident affinities—including Yamashita's reworking of magical realism, tropes of the telenovela, Gabriel García Márquez's "A Very Old Man with Enormous Wings," and Mário de Andrade's *Macunaíma* (1928)—*Through the Arc* was initially elided in Asian American and American literary studies alike, as was the more realist *Brazil-Maru*, published in 1992.[1] In the mid-1990s in the United States, however, several fields began moving away from implicit or explicit national perspectives and toward discourses of transnationalism as part of the transnational turn. By the time *Tropic of Orange* appeared in 1997, scholars in Asian American and American literary studies were considering alternative disciplinary configurations, such as Pacific Rim studies, and were paying much closer attention to Yamashita's novels, which offered new ways of imagining the world and inspired further reformulation of fields, approaches, and teaching. Jinqi Ling's 2012 *Across Meridians: History and Figuration in Karen Tei Yamashita's Transnational Novels*, the first published monograph devoted to Yamashita's writing, includes chapters on Yamashita's four novels and one on *Circle K Cycles* that detail the specific contributions of these works to an understanding of Asian American transnational social experience and literature. In 2020 Jolie Sheffer published *Understanding Karen Tei Yamashita*, which positions Yamashita among over one hundred other esteemed contemporary

American authors featured in the University of South Carolina Press's Understanding Contemporary American Literature series.

Yamashita scholarship elaborates and mobilizes transnational and diasporic concerns, which lends itself to many pedagogical possibilities. Caroline Rody, for instance, shifted inquiry with *The Interethnic Imagination: Roots and Passages in Contemporary Asian American Fiction*, which recognizes the significance of the larger context of processes of globalization for understanding newly reconfigured interactions among and between ethnicities and peoples. Min Hyoung Song discusses some of the vexing questions that Rody's intervention poses and ventures additional questions in *The Children of 1965: On Writing, and Not Writing, as an Asian American*. More recently, Cyrus R. K. Patell has suggested that Yamashita's novels are well placed in the paradigm of "emergent literature," which draws on Raymond Williams's understanding of the interactions among "dominant," "residual," and "emergent" culture. "What makes literature 'emergent' is the fact that it portrays beliefs and practices that are taken to be 'new' by the dominant culture" (Patell 10) for the cultivation of "cosmopolitan virtue," or a constant and often ironic interrogation of one's own cultural assumptions and truth-claims, with the aim of enacting respect and care for others (15–16). Several published works address Yamashita in relation to writers of color beyond Asian America, especially other women of color writers, including Toni Morrison, Helena María Viramontes, and Leslie Marmon Silko, with particular attention to the authors' treatment of human rights, social justice, or feminist and queer concerns.[2] In *Border Fictions: Globalization, Empire, and Writing at the Boundaries of the United States*, Claudia Sadowski-Smith adopts a hemispheric approach that places Yamashita's works in dialogue with texts that represent borders that the United States shares with Canada and Mexico.

Positioning Yamashita's fiction outside, at the edges of, or in interlocutive relation to established fields and frameworks of literary studies, Yamashita scholarship most frequently draws from and builds on the extranational, and this pattern continues to characterize scholarly commentary well into the twenty-first century (Chuh, "Of Hemispheres" 620). There also has been a gradual shift, Song points out, in reader priorities away from valuing classification toward celebrating complex representations of the "simultaneity of social experience" (*Children* 182). Song cites Yamashita's first published novel, *Through the Arc of the Rain Forest*, as one that "beautifully fulfills the need to pay attention to the social and the ecological, telling the stories of characters from across the world who find enormous material success in the Amazon at the end of one millennium and the beginning of another" (182).

Through the Arc of the Rain Forest *(1990)*

Scholarship on *Through the Arc of the Rain Forest* has been and continues to be vibrant, especially in the field of ecocriticism, in part because ecocriticism was maturing as a field of literary and cultural studies around the same time that the novel was published in the early 1990s, a period that saw renewed public concern for the environment. Like classification schemes, generational genealogies are best used cautiously, but distinctions among the waves of ecocriticism are instructive. For instance, early ecocriticism largely disregarded ethnic literatures of the United States, other than Native American literature (Simal, "Junkyard"), and was deeply skeptical of the global (as opposed to the local) as an analytic, but second and subsequent waves of criticism have had much more to say with respect to Yamashita's first novel.

Early, first-wave, ecocriticism "tended to equate environment with nature; to focus on literary renditions of the natural world in poetry, fiction, and nonfiction as means of evoking and promoting contact with it; to value nature preservation and human attachment to place at a local-communitarian or bioregional level; and to affirm an ecocentric or biocentric ethics, often intensified by some conception of an innate bond—whether biological, psychological, or spiritual—conjoining the individual human being and the natural world" (Buell et al. 419). *Through the Arc* may be read as a parabolic lament about the alienation of people from the natural world, and specifically the destruction by modern human technology and transnational capitalism of the Amazon rain forest, which has long been a popular symbol of environmental degradation (Heise, *Sense* 12).[3] In this vein, interpretations may rely on the novel's magical realist dimensions for reading key mutant or cyborgian elements as a satirical commentary on violations either of the nature-culture bond or of the nature-culture divide: the nonhuman, golf ball-sized narrator sphere that orbits the retired Japanese railroad inspector turned prospector, Kazumasa Ishimaru; the three-armed Jonathan B. Tweep, the American CEO of GGG (a corporation named after George and Georgina Gamble), who incites the stockholder Ishimaru to help monopolize profits from the pillage of the Brazilian rain forest; and the commodities of the Matacão's "bizarre ecology" (*Through the Arc* 168). This new ecology, created from the integration or hybrid mixture of nature and culture, produces spiritual healing through appropriations of Indigenous knowledge and sells a broad range of material and organic goods that the magnetic Matacão bedrock has the capacity, it is discovered, to mimic, despite its origins as compressed nonbiodegradable and plastic waste from the Global North. Frenzied commercial and infrastructural development leads first to dispossession of local inhabitants' land and livelihoods, next to the social alienation of characters, and finally to the depletion of the Matacão. In a final miraculous twist, however, the Amazonian rain forest is revived by a plastic-eating bacterium and a typhus epidemic.

A powerful theoretical lens trains its sights on Yamashita's novel with second-wave and more recent ecocriticism, which began to emphasize environmental justice concerns around the beginning of the twenty-first century, focusing on "the unequal distribution of environmental benefits and hazards across population groups, especially by race and/or class" (Buell et al. 419). Aimee Bahng's 2008 reading of the novel as both Asian American literature and postcolonial science fiction is indebted to and advances these concerns, illustrating the ways in which Yamashita scholarship has mobilized the category of the transnational to accomplish far more. Specifically, *Through the Arc* excavates "the disavowed imperial legacies" of resource development through Indigenous exclusion, exploitation, and displacement, and places "buried histories . . . in critical dialogue with a long line of science fictions that have worked on behalf of European and US empire-building to render the resource-rich jungle available for imperial conquest and expansion" ("Extrapolating Transnational Arcs"123). Bahng's article; a subsequent chapter in her book *Migrant Futures*, titled "Imperial Rubber"; and her contribution in this volume point to illuminating materials on Fordlândia, Henry Ford's early-twentieth-century neocolonial rubber plantation system in Pará, Brazil, and the analog for Yamashita's Chicolandia, the amusement park built from Matacão plastic, on Matacão terrain, and "to introduce the new technology of Matacão plastic to the world" (*Through the Arc* 166). These include images available online in the Henry Ford Archives, secondary source materials on this history, such as Greg Grandin's *Fordlandia: The Rise and Fall of Henry Ford's Forgotten Jungle City*, and a host of possible intertexts for teaching Yamashita's novels, such as Werner Herzog's 1982 film *Fitzcarraldo*.[4]

The concerns of contemporary ecology, and especially the question of what counts as nature, demanded the rethinking of social and ecological relations, specifically the nature-culture divide that had so long animated a preservationist ethos and the recovery of innocent or natural space untouched by humanity in modern ecology. The concept of nature was undermined both by technological and scientific advances that blurred the lines between machine and human, animal and plant, and by a postmodern and specifically poststructuralist understanding of the social and discursive construction of nature. And yet, ecology paradoxically remained a powerful political and philosophical movement. In this context, Molly Wallace's reading of *Through the Arc* in "'A Bizarre Ecology'" tackles the question of "what 'nature' . . . ecologists might be committed [to]" when an external nature is no longer a given or foundation (140). Yamashita's novel points us, Wallace writes, toward a contradictory understanding:

> The clear-cut binary distinction between nature and culture—so central to modernism and modernization—becomes confused; objects enter the novel as subjects; nature is and is not culture; the global and the local are networked; cottage industries become multi-national and multi-nationals capitalize on Amazonian naturopathy. As a model of contemporary nature-culture, *Through the Arc of the Rain Forest* is not only about each side of the modern binary; it is about what goes on in the middle—the hybrids, the wonders and horrors of denatured nature. (147)

The insights of materially oriented ecocritical scholarship in the past ten years especially emphasize Yamashita's deep skepticism and frequently ironic fictional stance toward romantic resolutions and conventional notions of resistance. This is now a pattern, a "textual performance familiar to readers of Yamashita novels, which tend to append apparently unwarranted happy endings—or at least happy sounding endings—to fictional accounts of domination and destruction" (Blyn 205).

Heise has influentially found in *Through the Arc* a complex, antiromantic depiction of localism. Yamashita's "exploration of international ecology and economy, cross-cultural migration, and the transformation of local landscape . . . imply a critique of certain forms of economic globalization" and "question the possibility of reterritorialization as envisioned by environmentalists" who see in it an ethical response to alienating sociocultural deterritorializations from nature or nonhuman surroundings in globalization processes ("Local Rock" 127). Heise observes that an "understanding of global ecology and a global ecological citizenship does not logically follow from an attachment to place" ("Globality" 642). Finally, in *Sense of Place and Sense of Planet: The Environmental Imagination of the Global*, Heise theorizes an alternative ethical vision in "eco-cosmopolitanism," or environmental world citizenship (11–12). The scalar shift and materiality here are important. The combination of Ishimaru and the plastic sphere that orbits him and narrates the story—the combination of human and nonhuman—is an integration that arrives at rootedness through mobility. *Through the Arc* challenges environmentalists "to imagine local environments less as foundations for unalienated existence than as habitats that are ceaselessly being reshaped by the encroachments of the global as well as by their own inherent dynamism" (114).

Following Gayatri Spivak, Song discusses this challenge as it appears in the contemporary novel as a struggle to narrate "becoming planetary"; on a different scale and less imperially universal than the global or globality, planetarity "might be thought of as a different order of connection, an interrelatedness that runs along smooth surfaces, comprises multiples, and manifests movement" (*Children* 192). This is also, then, a challenge to educators and to classrooms, where imagining new habitats and new forms of world-making are not only the work of literature and narrative but also of reading.

Against the grain of postromantic readings, John B. Gamber argues that *Through the Arc* relies on romantic and transcendentalist notions of nature. Revealed especially in its "fixation on birds," the novel asserts "a need for ecological balance via the image of the pastoral, a harmony between nature and culture, a natural culture rooted in the agricultural successes of its Nikkei (or foreign-born Japanese) population" (40). Clearly, Yamashita's art grapples with questions fundamental to contemporary ecocriticism, and this example of dialogue and debate within Yamashita studies indicates scholarship's usefulness for educators who may want to bring such concerns into the classroom, where students can also wrestle with them.

Drawing on material feminisms in an ecocritical third (and fourth?) wave, Matthew Henry's 2018 essay on *Through the Arc*'s interest in the nonhuman relation to the human in several ways picks up where recognition of the interconnectedness of the local and the global as a reconfigured model for ecology leaves off, challenging preoccupations with the Anthropocene.[5] Henry argues that, "[t]hough *Arc* affirms the advent of the Anthropocene, it takes on the additional task of unseating the human as the epoch's sole political actor, a fact exemplified by the novel's omniscient narrator, a whirring sphere of *Matacão* plastic that remains in a fixed position six inches from the head of Kazumasu Ishimaru, a Japanese immigrant living in São Paulo" (568). Here, the novel is read through the interpretive framework of "material narrativity," which presupposes the "entangled, rhizomatic nature of human and nonhuman agency" and offers "alternatives to traditionally anthropocentric interpretations of literature" (568). *Through the Arc*, Henry concludes, "reminds us that by removing ourselves as a species from the center of Anthropocene narratives, by recuperating the alterity of both the human and nonhuman casualties of extractive capitalism, and by calling attention to the agency and human-nonhuman coalitions, we may begin to conceive of a more equitable, sustainable encounter with nonhuman nature" (580).

Ultimately most interested in the possible resistance of contemporary ecologies, Treasa De Loughry provides a detailed and extremely useful contextualization of the novel in Brazil's long history of economic resource booms and its more recent history of neoliberalism. Understood as the now dominant political-economic practices and global political rationality, neoliberalism holds that "human well-being is best advanced by liberating individual entrepreneurial freedoms and skills" and prioritizes deregulation, privatization, and the withdrawal of the state from social provision (Harvey, *Brief History* 2–3).[6] De Loughry points to how the junkyard facilitates the evolution of mutated wildlife and how the niche animals in *Through the Arc* exist through extreme adaptation and mutation. De Loughry writes that, "Although petromodernity and imperialism are here marked by environmental devastation, extra-human natures emerge in the *Matacão* that more properly resist and challenge extractivism" (339).[7]

Brazil-Maru *(1992)*

Yamashita's second published novel focuses on a group of Japanese immigrants and their descendants who in 1925 establish an agriculture-based commune, optimistically named Esperança ("hope"), with the desire to "create a new civilization" (*Brazil-Maru* 6). *Brazil-Maru* has been discussed in relation to the modern Japanese I-novel, and it is evidently concerned with cultural hybridity both in form and in content. It is based on the author's experience living in Brazil, and especially on oral histories that Yamashita conducted while on a fellowship to research the history of Japanese Brazilians. While *The Village Voice* named it one of the best twenty-five books of 1992, there unfortunately is little published scholarship on *Brazil-Maru* (Grice, "Karen Tei Yamashita" 340). Thus, two recently published chapters and a third forthcoming chapter that address *Brazil-Maru* in a sustained fashion are welcome additions to Yamashita scholarship. Chris LaLonde provides a surprisingly rare treatment of humor in an often humorous oeuvre, and Nicholas Birns offers concise contextualizing materials on

Japanese Brazilian immigration and the role of Jean-Jacques Rousseau in the novel. Ruth Hsu's "Rousseau and Emile in Karen Tei Yamashita's *Brazil-Maru*: The Intertexts of Colonies, Utopias, and Freedom" will appear in *De/Colonization in the Americas*.

With respect to transnationalism, Jinqi Ling's "Southward Migration: Empire Building and Transculturation in *Brazil-Maru*" is the most comprehensive contribution to date. It includes a discussion of how Yamashita reinvents Rousseau and provides significant contextualizing material for the novel. Elizabeth Espadas's much earlier "Destination Brazil: Immigration in Works of Nélida Piñón and Karen Tei Yamashita" frames a comparative discussion of two immigrant novels, Piñón's *The Republic of Dreams* (*A República dos Sonhos*) about Galician immigrants, and Yamashita's *Brazil-Maru* about Japanese immigrants, within the country's history of immigration. Brazil was once one of the three most common destinations of intercontinental immigration, receiving about a third of fifty-two million immigrants (voluntary and forced through abduction and slavery) to Latin American between 1824 and 1924 (Espadas 51). Espadas suggests that for many voluntary immigrants national belonging was elusive, with high return migration rates across different immigrant groups, a fact mentioned in Piñón's novel, which is deeply critical, through its affinities with testimonial literature, of the Brazilian state (55), while Yamashita's novel depicts a generational process of assimilation that fragments the ethnic community in the commune of Esperança.

Perhaps the most influential treatment of *Brazil-Maru* is Kandice Chuh's "Of Hemispheres and Other Spheres," which advances "a collaborative and dynamic link among studies of the Americas writ large" (619). Chuh builds on Sadowski-Smith and Claire Fox's efforts to rethink American studies "outside and beyond national boundaries" through a hemispheric approach that complements "other emergent national, regional, and global perspectives in American, Canadian, and Latin American studies" (Sadowski-Smith and Fox 6, 7).[8] Through a reading of *Brazil-Maru*, Chuh explores how Asian American studies and hemispheric studies may be complementary, underscoring that "hemispheric approaches derived through minority discourse and ethnic studies based institutional history of Asian American studies might look quite different from those bearing the legacy of institutionalized American Studies" ("Of Hemispheres" 619). Moreover, this approach shifts the East-West axis of transnational Asian American studies toward a North-South orientation. Yamashita's novel "anticipates the contemporary concerns of hemispheric studies to find ways of grappling with the irregular emergence of modernities across the Americas," and to compel "coordination of efforts among scholars working in specific sites to produce collaborative knowledge" (620).

Importantly, Chuh is careful not to present the hemispheric paradigm as some sort of universally relevant "geographical protocol" or tidy corrective to the national, even when the national is understood to be linked to the global, as she asserts it is in Asian American studies (636). Chuh accomplishes this through highlighting Yamashita's awareness, rendered in the close of *Brazil-Maru*, of displaced indigeneity, or "the infinite other stories existing beyond the bounds of this novel and beyond the trope of immigration, which are as yet unrepresented and perhaps unrepresentable within the economy of visibility marked by national, transnational, or global epistemic frames" (628).

Tropic of Orange *(1997)*

Most well-known of Yamashita's novels, *Tropic of Orange* is frequently treated as a book primarily about globalization, including the literal processes of transnational labor migration or the movement of commodities and capital, as well as the flows of culture and hybrid or diasporic identities, families, and communities.[9] With an ensemble cast of seven main characters, several of whom are immigrants or laborers or both, the novel dramatizes a series of border crossings within the span of one eventful week, depicting what has come to be known as postmodern or late capitalist time-space compression (Harvey, *Condition* 147, 260–307). The novel begins in Mazatlán, Mexico, with much back-and-forth between Mexico and the United States, though movement propels the story to and all around the global city of Los Angeles. Scholars often read the novel as a critique of the 1994 North American Free Trade Agreement (NAFTA), especially because it also spectacularly dramatizes, with the key ingredient of magical realism, the predominantly Indigenous resistance movement of the Zapatista Army of National Liberation, which initiated an uprising the day after NAFTA went into effect. At the center of the story is an apocalyptic orange that draws the Tropic of Cancer to LA and ultimately causes a city-stalling traffic accident on the highway that evolves into a settlement and then ends in militarized violence and death.

Analyzing the contexts of intense change and material effects associated with globalization, Wallace's "Tropics of Globalization: Reading the New North America" finds in *Tropic of Orange* the suggestion that "parts of the 'North' may be becoming the 'South'" (153). The scare quotes around the compass points are significant, for the novel "offers a critique not only of the politics of NAFTA and of globalization, but of the politics of the discourses surrounding these phenomena" (148–49). Wallace's work is connected to T. Christine Jespersen and David Plante's discussion in this volume of strategies for teaching the discourse of neoliberalism. Other contributions on the contexts and meaning of globalization include Rody's "The Transnational Imagination" and Sadowski-Smith's "The U.S.-Mexico Borderlands Writes Back: Cross-Cultural Transnationalism in Contemporary U.S. Women of Color Fiction," which analyzes the gendered dimensions of racialized immigration in *Tropic of Orange*, including the rape of Rafaela Cortes, and links Yamashita's storytelling to that of Chicanx and Native American women writers. Julie Sze has written about *Tropic of Orange* in "'Not by Politics Alone'" and "From Environmental Justice Literature to the Literature of Environmental Justice," offering readings in which gender and race analytics come to the fore, as they do in Chiyo Crawford's "From Desert Dust to City Soot: Environmental Justice and Japanese American Internment in Karen Tei Yamashita's *Tropic of Orange*." Julian Yates's "Orange" offers ruminations on *Tropic of Orange* in a collection of essays on ecotheory, while Kara Thompson's "Traffic Stops, Stopping Traffic" contends that, "By cohering one of its central crises to a spectacular traffic jam, Yamashita conjures an ecology bound up with, and beholden to, racism, militarized violence, and climate change" (95).

A substantial amount of commentary on *Tropic of Orange* focuses on the city, the power relations of urban spaces, and spatiality.[10] Elisabeth Mermann-Jozwiak considers Yamashita's city a postnational space and argues that *Tropic of Orange* "conducts a historical excavation of the city's neighborhoods," which reveals social injustices in "various layers—of past and present inhabitants of the city, of regulations that restricted access to certain areas, and of the distribution of resources and development of infrastructures in those neighbourhoods" (2). Esen Kara reads *Tropic of Orange* in relation to the fields of geography and urban studies, drawing on Henri Lefebvre's influential idea of "the right to the city": "The novel's envisioning [of] an urban revolution based on spatial appropriation and communal participation . . . provides a creative way of realizing the right to the city. The novel rewrites the city as an *oeuvre* in Lefebvrian terms, as a collective work of art, against its designation as a fetishized product" (75).

Providing a detailed review of relevant scholarship that specifically contextualizes *Tropic of Orange* is Xiaojing Zhou's "Mapping the Global City and the 'Other' Scene of Globalization" in *Cities of Others: Reimagining Urban Spaces in Asian American Literature* (258–89). Zhou contends that, "rather than a 'metropoetics,' a broader poetics of space characterizes Asian American city literature. . . . Asian American urban literature produces a counterdiscourse of spatial inscriptions of identities, which naturalize racial exclusion and segregation. At the same time, it explores spatially constitutive formations of subjectivity and the possibilities embedded in the urban environment for interethnic, multiracial 'counterpublics' and 'communal alternatives' for advancing social and environmental justice" (292). As published discussion on cities and the contributions in this volume by Jessica Luck and by Anastasia Lin and John Dees confirm, *Tropic of Orange* invites cartographic methods of analysis that in turn offer an array of pedagogical possibilities, such as plotting character locations with *Google Maps* or using more complex Geographic Information Systems tools for 3D image production that layers data. Methods associated with the spatial turn or literary cartography are typically both geographic and cognitive, not least in this case because the character Manzanar Murakami has a special ability to see all maps at once and draw from them to orchestrate the body politic of LA. An essay by Cristina M. Rodriguez argues that Yamashita offers "a different map, one perceived by the subsets of LA's population that fall through the cracks of the city's grid. *Tropic of Orange*'s unorthodox formal structure, when combined with is narrative surrealism, creates a differential space in the text, transforming the novel into the Los Angeles imagined and lived by its anonymous users and inhabitants" (106).

If the interest in mapping in *Tropic of Orange* suggests a number of compelling opportunities for entry and analysis, a related critical dialogue has alternatively and provocatively focused on the network, which is both a powerful trope in the novel and a structuring formal technique, graphically exhibited in the "HyperContexts" table of contents. The storytelling of *Tropic of Orange* conveys that the network is a key feature of the logic as well as a characteristic machine of societies of control, the successors to disciplinary societies, as Gilles Deleuze, following Michel Foucault, has observed (5–6). Recognizing that *Tropic of Orange* prefigures and complicates the vision of politics of Michael Hardt and Antonio Negri, Robin Blyn argues that

> [e]ffective resistance is not a matter of epistemological reorientation. Rather, in this novel the grounds for challenging neoliberalism are immanent in the ontological condition of the neoliberal network itself. The potential for change, in other words, lies not in what the subject comes to know but in the emergence of a collective subjectivity, a being-in-common, that itself takes the form of a network. Modeled on the World Wide Web, Yamashita's postmodern networks simultaneously figure the world space of neoliberalism and a mode of collectivity endowed with the potential to instigate radical change. (192)

Here, magical realism recedes as a transcendent force, and the novel "attributes the transformation of the globe . . . to the connections forged by a fiber of the neoliberal network itself" (201–11). In an analysis of the ways in which the novel recodes science fiction and noir, Sherryl Vint contends that through speculative techniques the novel makes visible and "traces the obscured networks of globalization" (405). Jina Kim brings the tools of a feminist disability studies approach to the conversation about networks in *Tropic of Orange*, making a crucial contribution that carefully demonstrates, in keeping with the focus of her analysis, how scholars build from and with one another to understand Yamashita's writing. Kim observes that, "[a]kin to Manzanar's mapping practice, *Tropic of Orange* attunes its readers to LA's infrastructures—the oft unnoticed roads, pipes, and labor networks that enable the city to function—in order to highlight *interdependency* as both political and aesthetic value. Interdependence, as understood by scholars in feminist disability studies, suggests a condition of mutual dependence, an ecology of contingent relations, in which dependency can be conceptualized in terms of its mutualistic, symbiotic properties" (2). This analysis of infrastructure—what it is and what it can be—in *Tropic of Orange* points to a growing field, one that suggests exciting exploration of Yamashita's other novels and important social justice pedagogies for the classroom.

Connected to the essays in this volume by Jolie Sheffer, Josephine Lee, Noelle Brada-Williams, and J. Edward Mallot, two analyses of *Tropic of Orange* highlight its commentary on the media. Lynn Itagaki's chapter, "The Media Spectacle of Racial Disaster," in her book *Civil Racism* insightfully explains that

> Yamashita's novel provides the naturalized flow and segmentation of mediatized environments such as television, radio, and the Internet, showing how these environments shape her protagonists' subjectivities—and, thus, the textual narrative and the novel form itself. In addition to Yamashita's intensely detailed focus on the lives of seven memorable characters and their interactions with one another, the novel's structure, like a week of television programming, narrates the complex interplay of globalized media capital and its material effects on those forced outside the US body politic (the nonwhite and non-citizen) and those perceived outside the economy (the non-worker). (183)

Similarly, and also pedagogically suggestive for our media-saturated era, Hee-Jung Serenity Joo's "Flexible Chaos" analyzes Yamashita's use of the disaster movie week media event in *Tropic of Orange* in a discussion of LA disaster film and fiction. An analysis of depictions of race as the main factor in determining the future of LA in Ridley Scott's *Blade Runner* (1982) and Marco Bambillo's *Demolition Man* (1993) supports Joo's argument that while much LA disaster film blames racial diversity for the city's and the nation's demise, "the novel presents transnational late capitalism—globalization—as an incoherent and chaotic system, a disaster in its own right," building as it does from connected forms of racism in the history of imperialism (254). For other films that may be used with and to understand *Tropic of Orange*, see in this volume Mallot's contribution about teaching courses devoted to the road narrative.

I Hotel *(2010)*

Yamashita's fourth novel, *I Hotel*, has been enthusiastically taken up by scholars, especially Asian Americanists, given that it focuses on an intense period of Asian American political activism and a specific campaign to save the International Hotel (I-Hotel) at 848 Kearney Street in San Francisco from gentrification and its mostly immigrant Filipino residents from displacement. This 2010 National Book Award finalist is made up of ten novellas, and in some ways, especially with respect to its graphic elements, *I Hotel* is perhaps the most experimental of Yamashita's novels. A provocative contribution to scholarship is Catherine Fung's "'This Isn't Your Battle or Your Land,'" which focuses on the depiction of Asian American involvement in the Native American occupation of Alcatraz in Yamashita's *I Hotel* and Shawn Wong's *Homebase*. Rather than a comparative discussion of the similar treatment of Native Americans and Asian Americans in the society of the United States, Fung's analysis explores how "political solidarities can emerge in spite of, and because of, difference" (150). Reading a canonical text and a newer novel, Fung considers how these two works might imagine alternative modes of coalition, building on Grace Kyungwon Hong and Roderick A. Ferguson's *Strange Affinities: The Gender and Sexual Politics of Comparative Racialization*.[11]

Expanding intertextual analysis of the political movement that Yamashita depicts to include nonprint cultural forms and narratives, David Palumbo-Liu's "Embedded Lives," a version of which was presented at the Presidential Forum of the 2011 MLA convention, addresses the human right to housing in the wake of the 2008 global economic crisis. Palumbo-Liu considers Yamashita's *I Hotel* alongside Curtis Choy's 1983 documentary film *The Fall of the I-Hotel*, Estella Habal's historical analysis in *San Francisco's International Hotel: Mobilizing the Filipino American Community in the Anti-Eviction Movement*, and *Until Today: Spectres for the International Hotel*, an art exhibit that celebrated the 2005 opening of the Manilatown Heritage Foundation on the Kearney Street site of the I-Hotel. Palumbo-Liu's focus on the right to housing in his analysis of this rich archive is perhaps just as or even more timely in 2021, given the effects on housing of the COVID-19 global pandemic.

Two articles, both published in 2017, create an incisive critical dialogue about *I Hotel*'s engagements with institutionalization and historiography. Lily Wong observes that Yamashita "reanimates a pivotal moment [of historical volatility] before the United States' institutionalization of 'neoliberal multiculturalism' since the late 1970s by dwelling over 'China' before its rise as itself a neoliberal empire after the Cultural Revolution":

> Instead of glossing over the jagged histories that constitute US-Chinese connections—between the 'two Chinas,' the 'Chinese diaspora' and 'Asian America,' as well as between 'Asian America' and 'Third World Liberation Fronts'—Yamashita returns us to sites of historical contention. She offers us a narrative shelter, a scaffold contact zone, in which we are asked to piece together and evolve with the uneven, often antagonistic, histories that intervene in her characters' disparate endeavors for shared livelihood. (737)

In "Queer Genealogies of (Be)Longing" Chris A. Eng considers the ways in which *I Hotel* thematizes the founding of ethnic studies and problematizes a generational model of the history of the field, which "helps us to recognize how concepts commonly used to narrate the history of institutionalization—activist, community, academic, among them—operate within a logic of reproductive futurity" (346).

Connected to essays in this volume by Caroline Hong, Silvia Schultermandl, Jolie Sheffer, Wen Jin, and Ana María Manzanas-Calvo, essays by Lai Ying Yu and Grace Talusan offer discussions of activities involving the classroom creation of an online guide for *I Hotel*. A complement to Manzanas-Calvo's timely essay in this volume is her "'We the People of the International Hotel' and the Hotel State," which investigates how *I Hotel* "fleshes out the ambiguous zone between inclusion and exclusion, a grey area that is not sufficiently explained in the dyad of in/out. Inclusion, the novel illustrates, does not imply belonging . . . but rather a kind of sick hospitality that includes as it excludes" (107). Deep engagement with scholarship on the novels is a rich resource—a critical dialogue—that provides tools for developing approaches to teaching the works of Karen Tei Yamashita, and that promises to take readers into new areas of inquiry.

NOTES

[1] For a discussion of how Yamashita reworks García Márquez and Andrade, see Heise, "Local Rock."

[2] See Rody, "Impossible Voices"; Wald; Sadowski-Smith, "U.S.-Mexico Borderlands"; Delgado, "Trespassing the U.S.-Mexico Border"; and Schultermandl.

[3] See also Jain.

[4] The spelling of *Fordlândia* is inconsistent; while most scholars retain the circumflex over the first *a*, the Henry Ford Museum and Grandin do not.

[5] For alternatives to anthropocentric thinking, see Sagan's discussion of terms such as *capitalocene*, *racial capitalocene*, *Chthulucene*, and *Cyanocene*.

[6] See also Brown, which emphasizes the dominance of the political rationality of neoliberalism in which the state promotes a decidedly self-governing and self-caring subject as human capital that enhances capital. See also Duggan.

[7] For a related discussion of how Yamashita's use of magical realism enables a critique of globalization or late capitalism, see Mallot. See also Entin.

[8] Chuh also refers to Erika Lee's "Orientalism."

[9] I discuss, for example, a border-crossing scene from *Tropic of Orange* at the beginning of a 1999 article that focuses on Asian American transnational feminism in relation to globalization and associated increases in migration and commodity production and consumption (Thoma, "Of Beauty Pageants").

[10] See also the essays by Kase, Maucione, and Pooch.

[11] For further discussion of this historic moment, see Ragain, "Revolutionary Romance," and Jinqi Ling's chapter, "Toward a Critical Internationalism: Nation, Revolt, and Performance in *I Hotel*," in *Across Meridians* (147–88).

Plays, Memoir, Essays, Interviews, Short Stories, Translations, and Papers

Ruth Y. Hsu

Karen Tei Yamashita began writing short stories and plays, and had those plays staged, years before the publication of her first novel, *Through the Arc of the Rain Forest*, which quickly caught the attention of scholars. Yamashita's novels have garnered more academic interest than her earlier short stories, her plays, her essays, and, later, her more overtly experimental prose narratives. This essay provides historical and cultural background for *Circle K Cycles*; *Anime Wong: Fictions of Performance*; Yamashita's essays and interviews; *Letters to Memory*; translations of her writing; her papers at the University of California, Santa Cruz; and *Sansei and Sensibility*, a short story collection published in 2020. Whenever possible, this essay also suggests juxtaposing Yamashita's work with that of other writers in order to broaden and deepen students' understanding of how Yamashita's corpus engages with and energizes a vast literary, intellectual, and cultural canvas.

Circle K Cycles

Circle K Cycles is a mixed-genre memoir about March to August 1997, when Yamashita and her family lived in Seto, near Nagoya, Japan. A Japan Foundation grant supported Yamashita's purpose in traveling to Japan of understanding the experiences of the country's Brazilian community, descendants of the Japanese who began settling in Brazil in the early 1900s. In the ironically titled prologue to *Circle K Cycles*, "Purely Japanese"—the irony doubled by the kanji underneath the English title meaning "nation" or "homeland"—Yamashita explains that "[i]n 1990, the Japanese government had passed a law to allow nisei [persons whose parents are immigrants] and sansei [persons whose grandparents are immigrants] to acquire visas to perform unskilled labor in Japan . . . Japanese descendants who should, it was thought, integrate more easily into Japanese life and society" (13). Yamashita's stay in Japan was also sponsored by Ryuta Imafuku, a central figure in the online magazine *Cafe Creole* (www.cafecreole.net/). *Circle K Cycles* is a mixture of the travelogues that Yamashita wrote monthly for *Cafe Creole* and of other fiction she wrote about the time she spent in Seto.

The book consists of drawings of origami instructions and human anatomy as well as photographs of paved roads, residential streets sans pedestrians, and tongue-in-cheek lists of rules of behavior ascribed to the Japanese, the Brazilians, and the Americans. The lists are likened to house rules that might be hung on a common room wall of a condominium. On the one hand, they indicate the

Japanese desire for orderliness, decorum, and mutual respect. On the other hand, these rules represent the internalized prejudices that the population of one culture might bear toward another. The irony is that rules of behavior are meant to enable different people to live together, to avoid potential friction. These lists, however, remind readers that *oughts* and *ought nots* are steeped in the cultural biases of the rule-makers. In a similar vein, Yamashita's decision to write *Circle K Cycles* in three languages is important for educators to grapple with. First, in the United States as well as in Japan, language—the question of which language is the official one as well as the history and perceived purity of a language—is a stand-in for rules about who should be counted as a natural member of the homeland and about who can never become a natural member despite having learned and despite adhering to all the house rules. Educators wishing to incorporate this book into their course might find pairing it with Sandra Cisneros's *House on Mango Street* productive. Second, language explains, but it can also shut out and shut away, an existential uprooting and sense of estrangement that many immigrants experience. Educators in bilingual schools, or who teach courses on immigration; on language and translation; on ethnic, racial, and national identities; and on gender, labor, and global capitalism will find *Circle K Cycles* to be a rich text. For upper-division courses dealing with the politics of language, reading *Circle K Cycles* with Ien Ang's "Can One Say No to Chineseness," from Ang's transnational memoir *On Not Speaking Chinese*, would be interesting.

Instructors interested in designing a course on narratology or an interdisciplinary course on literature and anthropology may find *Circle K Cycles* particularly useful. Yamashita's narration studiously avoids falling into the trap of pre-Geertz anthropology or becoming an example of an earlier ethnographical approach in the United States, in which the United States assumes the normative role of investigator and the subject of study is the marginalized primitive. *Circle K Cycles*, like most of Yamashita's corpus, avoids this trap by calling attention to itself as a narrative, and to its narrator as an outsider who passes as "pure" Japanese by learning to answer questions put to her by Japanese well enough to pass (12). It is a performative role that does not become more authentic with repetition. Educators might find it helpful to acquaint themselves with narratives on Americans of Japanese descent returning to Japan, most notably David Mura's memoir, *Turning Japanese*.

In *Circle K Cycles*, the portrait of the experiences of the Brazilian community in Japan with the Japanese frequently parallels the experiences of people of color in the United States in relation to Euro-Americans; instructors wishing to juxtapose experiences and sociocultural and political structures of racial identity in the United States and Japan will find the following texts useful: Toni Morrison's *The Origin of Others*, a lucid and lyrical rendition of the process of othering; Michael Omi's *Racial Formation in the United States*, which has assumed canonical status in the social sciences and the humanities; and Yamashita's essay

"A Gentlemen's Agreement." Japanese immigration to Brazil increased after the United States and Japan entered into the informal "Gentlemen's Agreement" in 1907. The agreement stated that the United States would not impose restrictions on the number of Japanese wishing to enter the United States if Japan stopped Japanese immigration to the United States. Ellen D. Wu's book *The Color of Success: Asian Americans and the Origins of the Model Minority* presents a comprehensive historical analysis of the discursive development and deployment of the model minority stereotype. The following studies of the Japanese diaspora to Brazil and of Brazilian communities in Japan will also prove useful to educators: Mieko Nishida's *Diaspora and Identity: Japanese Brazilians in Brazil and Japan* and Yamashita's essay "Writing and Memory: Images of the Japanese Diaspora in Brazil" in *Orientalism and Identity in Latin America: Fashioning Self and Other From the (Post)Colonial Margin*, edited by Erik Camayd-Freixas.

Kandice Chuh's 2006 "Of Hemispheres and Other Spheres: Navigating Karen Tei Yamashita's Literary World" is an incisive examination of *Circle K Cycles* (and *Brazil-Maru*) within the context of the transnational turn in Asian American literary studies. Chuh argues that Yamashita's "creative visions . . . demarcate a circum-oceanic spatial logic characterized by cyclicality and infinite connectivity. Cultural hybridization, intersectionality, and most of all, change—in place, identity, and worldview—dominate" (622). Jinqi Ling's "Subterranean Transnationality: Race, Affect, and Material Form in *Circle K Cycles*" offers an extensive analysis of *Circle K Cycles* in relation to *Brazil-Maru*. Ling's interpretation of the experimental form of *Circle K Cycles* uses Arjun Appadurai's influential concept of "ethnoscapes"—the "erratic flows of identities and populations . . . of an increasingly delocalized and disjunctive global system"—to interpret the centrality in *Circle K Cycles* of figurations of electronic media (63–64). Nathan Ragain's "(Re)Production Cycles: *Circle K Cycles*" in *Karen Tei Yamashita: Fictions of Memory and Magic*, edited by A. Robert Lee, the first anthology of critical essays on the work of Yamashita, engages with this hybrid text through a Marxian lens. To Ragain, *Circle K Cycles* most closely resembles the form of the short story cycle.

In this volume, Ikue Kina's "Encountering Others within Ourselves: *Circle K Cycles* and Ethnic Identity in Okinawa," in the section "Histories and Interventions," is an example of how this memoir can be used in different classroom contexts, including in both lower- and upper-division courses for the English major.

Anime Wong: Fictions of Performance

This collection contains most of Yamashita's dramatic works that have been theatrically produced—nine avant-garde plays—as well as photographs of performers, props, playbills, set designs, drawings of costumes, and musical scores. The play *Jan Ken Pon* was written several years ago, while other plays in *Anime Wong* are from the 1980s. *Anime Wong*'s experimental dramaturgy parodies, mocks, and satirizes the Western exoticization and fetishization of Asian bodies, especially the Asian female body.

Educators wishing to teach plays from *Anime Wong* will benefit from familiarizing themselves with David Henry Hwang's *M. Butterfly*, which criticizes the Western Orientalism embodied in iconic cultural texts like Giacomo Puccini's *Madama Butterfly*. Researching the controversy over Claude-Michel Schönberg's *Miss Saigon*, also based on Puccini's opera, will enlarge the context for *Anime Wong*. Robert G. Lee's *Orientals: Asian Americans in Popular Culture* contains a historical overview of racist constructions of Asians, the Chinese in particular, stretching back to the nineteenth century. Peter X. Feng's *Identities in Motion: Asian American Film and Video* is a helpful study of the figurations of Asians and Asian Americans in film. Anna May Wong (*Anime Wong* is a pun of Anna May Wong) acted in many films while contending with being typecast as either the stereotype of the Oriental seductress and Dragon Lady or the docile, passive ingenue. There is a considerable body of scholarship and video documentaries on Wong. Particularly relevant to *Anime Wong* is Jean-François Staszak's "Performing Race and Gender: The Exoticization of Josephine Baker and Anna May Wong."

An invaluable resource is Stephen Hong Sohn's afterword to *Anime Wong*. The afterword consists of a critical interpretation of the collected plays as well as a description of *Urashima Taro*, a play written by Yamashita when she was still an undergraduate student at Carleton College, and of plays written while she was in Brazil (*Omen: An American Kabuki*; *Asaka-no-Miya*, adapted from a short story of the same title; and *Hiroshima Tropical*). For Sohn, the thematic and formalistic thread that runs through the plays in *Anime Wong* is located not only in the playwright's integrative use of multicultural signifiers, such as Butoh, cyberpunk, and the figure of Godzilla or the cyborg alien; its thread is woven as parody, which "reveal[s] the 'excesses' of particular sedimented discourses and narratives" regarding Western Orientalism, anxieties over ethnic purity and cultural preservation, and the questionable desirability of Japanese American assimilation, among other concerns (365).[1] Sohn's analysis of *Anime Wong*'s final piece, *Jan Ken Pon: A Dance Performance Idea*, is noteworthy, as *Jan Ken Pon* is idiosyncratic, even in comparison to a collection of avant-garde drama and, as such, easily overlooked. The inclusion of *Jan Ken Pon*, reproduced as a series of PowerPoint slides and related commentary, illustrates Yamashita's capacity to be innovative, as, in this case, when she adapts a text from one context to another.

Another important resource is Josephine Lee's essay in this volume, titled "Through the Arc of the Theater: Yamashita Does Asian American Drama," in the section "Belonging and Nonbelonging." Lee often has her students read *Anime Wong* alongside plays by Hwang, Philip Kan Gotanda, Ping Chong, and other Asian American playwrights. Students examine the ways that Yamashita's use of caricature and "surreal exaggeration" undermine the racial and gender stereotyping of Asians and Asian Americans throughout the history of this panethnic group.

Additionally, the following scholarly works will contextualize Yamashita's unique contribution to Asian American drama: Josephine Lee's *Performing Asian America: Race and Ethnicity on the Contemporary Stage*, Karen Shimakawa's *National Abjection: The Asian American Body Onstage*, Celine Parreñas Shimizu's *The Hypersexuality of Race: Performing Asian/American Women on Screen and Scene*, and Rachel Lee's *The Exquisite Corpse of Asian America: Biopolitics, Biosociality, and Posthuman Ecologies*, an incisive theorization of the Asian American body and body parts in terms of biopolitics and late capitalist culture. Although Lee's monograph focuses on prose fiction, her introduction, subtitled "Parts/Parturition" offers a helpful framework through which to understand the ways that the Asian American body is dissected and mediated through an Orientalist, specular regime of display and domination (1–38). For critical approaches dealing with techno-Orientalism, the recently published anthology *Techno-Orientalism: Imagining Asia in Speculative Fiction, History, and Media*, edited by David S. Roh, Betsy Huang, and Greta A. Niu, contextualizes the historical development of techno-Orientalism, includes a comprehensive bibliography, and analyzes various aspects of the latest, globalized phase of Orientalism. To understand the transpacific discursive valence of Godzilla, see Nancy Anisfield's "Godzilla/Gojiro: Evolution of the Nuclear Metaphor" and Philip Brophy's "Monster Island: Godzilla and Japanese Sci-Fi/Horror/Fantasy." Instructors wishing to understand Yamashita's plays within the larger historical development of Asian American drama or to develop a course on contemporary American drama should consult *Asian American Plays for a New Generation*, edited by Josephine Lee and colleagues.

Letters to Memory

Coffee House Press, the publisher of *Letters to Memory*, categorized Yamashita's seventh book as a memoir. *Letters to Memory* incorporates photographs selected from the Yamashita Family Archives (yamashitaarchives.ucsc.edu/); photographs of a letter written by Yamashita's grandaunt in neat, rounded cursive and of a typed list of titles of sermons from Yamashita's father, John, who was a Methodist minister; newspaper articles from 1943; official United States government documents; and a photograph of what is perhaps a shipping label, handwritten with a fountain pen in both English and graceful, fluid kanji. The title of the book includes the word *memory*; there is also a family tree (169–70). *Letters to Memory* is about the searing effects of Japanese American internment during World War II on Yamashita's father's generation and, to an extent, Yamashita's own generation.

Letters to Memory is not simply another literary remembrance of internment; in thematic and formalistic terms, this narrative expands the capacity of conventional memoir to tell the life story of the autobiographical "I." Yamashita refashions that "I," changing it from one that is dominated by an Anglo-European cosmology to one that is constituted through complex multigenerational and transpacific collectives. Although Japanese Canadian writer Joy Kogawa's *Obasan* may seem at first glance tangentially connected to Japanese American internment narratives, *Obasan*'s vivid and lyrical rendering of the Japanese Canadian camp experience is a useful counterpoint to *Letters to Memory*. Educators seeking to acquaint themselves with the corpus of Japanese American internment accounts may also consult Lawson Fusao Inada's *Only What We Could Carry: The Japanese American Internment Experience*, a collection of excerpts of longer accounts of internment. Also germane to *Letters to Memory* are Miné Okubo's *Citizen 13660*, a graphic narrative of the Topaz camp in Utah where Okubo and her family were incarcerated, and Jeanne Wakatsuki Houston and James Houston's *Farewell to Manzanar*, first published in 1975 and reissued in 1995 and again in 2002. There is a filmic rendition of *Farewell to Manzanar*, directed by John Korty. Manzanar is also the name of one of the seven characters in Yamashita's novel *Tropic of Orange*; Manzanar "Ringo" Murakami is reprised in *GiLArex (or Godzilla Comes to Little Tokyo)* in *Anime Wong*. *Citizen 13660*, initially published in 1946 and reissued in 2014, has never gone out of print. For educators interested in designing a course focused on internment in the Americas, see Seiichi Higashide's memoir, *Adios to Tears: The Memoirs of a Japanese-Peruvian Internee in U.S. Concentration Camps*. Ignacio López-Calvo's chapter "Seiichi Higashide's *Adiós to Tears*: Flexible Citizenship, American War Propaganda, and the Birth of Anti-Japanese Hysteria in Peru," from his monograph, *The Affinity of the Eye: Writing Nikkei in Peru*, offers valuable historical context.

Letters to Memory incorporates various archival material in an endeavor to halt the fading of the narrator's memories, and to find answers to lifelong questions, which the narrator's father, a preacher who is otherwise loquacious, refused to address directly. The crucial question to which the narrator seeks answers has to do with forgiveness: Can epic, multigenerational injustices be forgiven? Is healing possible without forgiveness?

Letters to Memory is also a biography of Yamashita's father and an ontological quest through the *Iliad*, the Hindu epics, Ecclesiastes, the story of Ishi and the postmortem studies of his brain, and the beliefs and actions of exemplary revolutionaries, such as Buddha and Gandhi. The narrator has dialogues about charity, love, poverty, death, and laughter, not with John Yamashita, but with fictional interlocutors—with Homer, Ishi, Vyasa, Qohelet, and Ananda, all of whom Yamashita fashioned with the help of family, friends, and colleagues (*Letters* 171–73). Yamashita includes in *Letters to Memory* a selected bibliography listing works by James Clifford, W. E. B. Du Bois, Edward Said, and Howard Thurman, among many others (175–76).

Drawings, documentary texts, and photographs constitute another form of narration, one that complements or transgresses the words on the page. *Citizen 13660* and *Letters to Memory* offer rich possibilities in a course focusing on semiotic analysis of visual or graphic texts. Additional resources providing visual representations of Japanese American relocation and internment include Richard Cahan and Michael Williams's *Un-American: The Incarceration of Japanese Americans during World War II*, which features photographs of the internment by Ansel Adams and Dorothea Lange, and *Displaced: Manzanar, 1942–1945: The Incarceration of Japanese Americans*, edited by Evan Backes. Monica Chiu's "Introduction: Visual Realities of Race," in the scholarly anthology she edited, *Drawing New Color Lines: Transnational Asian American Graphic Narratives*, focuses on the representation of racial identities in graphic narratives.

A history of Japanese American internment is provided in Wendy Ng's *Japanese American Internment during World War II: A History and Reference Guide*. Numerous in-depth and reliable video documentaries and websites on this episode in American history can be found in the National Archives, on PBS, in the Smithsonian, and on the very comprehensive *Densho* website (densho.org/). The National Park Service has a detailed list of assembly centers, internment camps, and other detention facilities, as well as a list of internment camps that have become historic sites.

Educators who wish to teach *Letters to Memory* as part of a genre course on the memoir may wish to consult G. Thomas Couser's *Memoir: An Introduction*, while Nancy Miller's "The Entangled Self: Genre Bondage in the Age of the Memoir" complicates the notion of memoir as a factual recounting of events easily retrieved from a reservoir of faithful memories. Laura King's "Travelling without Moving: Navigating the Liminal Space between Memoir and Fiction" will also be helpful in this respect. Robert F. Sayre's "Autobiography and the Making of America" asserts that the constructed "I" of an autobiography is a quintessentially American articulation of self. *Letters to Memory* reimagines the American self in ways that broaden the definition of *American*. Rocío Davis's *Relative Histories: Mediating History in Asian American Family Memoirs* can be used to historically contextualize *Letters to Memory* within a broader literary and historical topography consisting of Asian American memoirs of family.

Ruth Hsu's essay in part 2 of this volume, in the section "Histories and Interventions," describes teaching *Letters to Memory* in an undergraduate, upper-division, Asian American literature class in an English department at a large, public university. Students enrolling in this course usually have little or no prior exposure to Asian American writing; their knowledge of Asian American history is similarly sparse. The challenge lies in being able to offer sufficient historical and Asian American cultural context in order for students to be able to grapple with the thematic topics in *Letters to Memory*.

Short Fiction

Karen Tei Yamashita's shorter works have been overshadowed by critics' robust early attention to her novels. Yamashita has been writing short stories since the mid-1970s (Sohn 360). One of these earlier stories is "Tucano," published in 1975 in the English- and Japanese-language newspaper *Rafu Shimpo*, based in Los Angeles. In the same year, Yamashita published the Portuguese version in the Brazilian journal *Colonia Bungaku*. "The Bath" won the 1975 *Amerasia Journal* short story contest and, together with "The Last Secretary," is the most well-known of Yamashita's short fiction. "Asaka-no-Miya," which won first place in the James Clavell American-Japanese Short Story Contest in 1979, was rewritten as a play, but it was never fully staged (Sohn 360). "Madama B" is collected in *Anime Wong: Fictions of Performance*. The selected bibliography in this volume lists some of Yamashita's short stories, including, if applicable, when and where they appeared in Japanese or Portuguese.

The most accessible of Yamashita's short stories—"The Bath," "The Last Secretary," "The Orange," and "Madama B"—reveal a writer who is remarkably nuanced in her construction of the inner moods and sensibilities of her characters; she portrays shadows and silences without effacing scene or characters. "The Bath," for instance, can stand much more frequent exposure in classrooms; it can be productively paired with Leslie Marmon Silko's "Lullaby" in terms of the ways that the two stories portray, in evocative and affecting ways, the experiential transitions of youth, adulthood, and old age. "Madama B," included in *Anime Wong*, initially appears to be a short story mistakenly included in a collection of plays. That being said, *Anime Wong* also includes a series of PowerPoint slides, meaning that "Madama B" may be in this collection of performance pieces to help call attention to the constructed nature of genre convention. A course on genre or adaptation may find a comparative analysis of "The Orange," *GiLArex*, and *Tropic of Orange* edifying in terms of Yamashita's formal innovations.

In the section "Mapping Alternative Spaces," Gloria Karam Delbim's essay "*Through the Arc of the Rain Forest*, *Brazil-Maru*, and Other Short Stories in a Brazilian Context" shows how Delbim uses Yamashita's short stories, such as "The Last Secretary," to engage her students with respect to the topics of immigration and Brazilian identity, the impact of global capitalism on Brazil and its environment, and the gendered nature of work in a globalized market.

In the same section, Robin Field's "Troubling Boundaries and Beginnings with 'The Orange,'" describes using "The Orange" as a stand-alone text, rather than as a prelude to *Tropic of Orange*. As Field points out, the first-person narrator, while nameless and genderless, is a Latinx Los Angeleno who details the cultural, economic, and political upheavals that occur as the Tropic of Cancer, entangled in an orange, moves northward, carried in a worker's pocket from Mexico to the global city of Los Angeles in Southern California.

Sansei and Sensibility

Karen Tei Yamashita's seventh book, *Sansei and Sensibility*, published in 2020, challenges conventional categories of genre, which has long been a pattern in her oeuvre. At moments, the stories in this collection take on the character of vignettes. These stories deliver penetrating insights into the existential preoccupations and the sense of place of sansei (third-generation Americans of Japanese descent) in Southern California in the 1980s and 1990s. Yamashita's formal innovations are interwoven with her thematic concerns in this collection and in her other writings.

Educators will find it rewarding when designing syllabi or assignments that incorporate this book to first obtain a basic understanding of Jane Austen's novels and their fine-grain depictions of the social milieu Austen was most familiar with—each story in *Sansei and Sensibility* distills an essential quality of Austen's narration, then refreshes, reinvents, and transports that quality into the mundane society of the fictional characters in the collection. Instructors can design reading and discussion assignments focused on satire, irony, parody, and the nuances of mood by juxtaposing excerpts from Austen's fiction with the stories in *Sansei and Sensibility*. The section titled "Monterey Park" associates elements of Austen's *Mansfield Park* with the significant presence of Asian communities in Monterey Park, a suburb of Los Angeles (133–41). Instructors interested in teaching *Sansei and Sensibility* in courses on spatiality and literature, multiethnic literatures of the United States, American studies, and contemporary Asian American literary studies, among others, might have students read excerpts from the counterhegemonic intervention of Monique Truong's *The Book of Salt*. In terms of narrative technique, educators might have students analyze *Sansei and Sensibility* alongside the linked short story cycles of Charles Chesnutt (Conjure Woman; "*Wife*"), Langston Hughes, and Sherwood Anderson.

Essays

Yamashita's essays fall into two broadly defined categories: commentary on Japanese American identity in relation to the United States and on the Japanese communities in Brazil, with which she maintains connections; and reflections on literature garnered from her many years as a critically acclaimed writer and an award-winning teacher of writing and literature. She is well traveled and reads deeply in many literary traditions, including popular cultural texts in film, music, and graphic narratives. Her essays, somewhat akin to her interviews, reveal a writer who is intensely interested in human beings and the communities they have constructed. A recurring theme in her essays, short stories, dramatic works, and novels is colonialism, its hegemonic discursive tropes and metaphors, and how the work of decolonization begins with challenging and dismantling the ontological demarcation between self and other. Yamashita's essays—published in books, magazines, and journals in the United States, Japan, and Brazil—merit sustained scholarly attention. Her essays would enrich courses in creative writing, literary and cultural studies, globalization, postcolonial studies, visual media, and interdisciplinary studies. Yamashita's recently published essays include "Literature as Community: The Turtle, Imagination, and the Journey Home,"

"Call Me Ishimaru," "Colono:Scopy," "Borges and I," and "Kiss of Kitty." The selected bibliography in this volume lists additional essays that can be integrated into a wide range of courses and curricula.

"Call Me Ishimaru" was Yamashita's keynote lecture for the Tenth International Melville Conference, held in Tokyo in 2015 and hosted by the Melville Society of Japan. The lecture was published in a special issue of *Leviathan*, with responses from respected Japanese scholars of Melville. In the essay Yamashita suggests that "*Moby-Dick* is also the narrative of the endlessly acquisitive and arrogant plunder of the earth's resources. . . . that the great white whale resides also as symbolic space—often exotic, terrifying, and impenetrable, perhaps as the Congo for Joseph Conrad, the Amazon for Lope de Aguirre, the Sahara for T. E. Lawrence, Japan for Herman Melville, and the Matacão for the three-armed JB Tweep" (65). JB Tweep is the name of the CEO of a multinational corporation in *Through the Arc of the Rain Forest* who is out to plunder the Matacão. Yamashita points out that Melville placed on his whaling ship, the *Pequod*, a multicultural brotherhood consisting of men of all shades, languages, religions, and nations. From among that crew, one man survived to sound the warning of the great white whale: "And from those depths, the great white whale, that leviathan, calls us again, and once again. Ishmael. Ishimaru. Ishi maru" ("Call Me Ishimaru" 75).

Yamashita's "Literature as Community: The Turtle, Imagination, and the Journey Home" was one of two keynote presentations at the inaugural Asian American Arts Festival, held in 2017 and cosponsored by the Asian Pacific American Center of the Smithsonian and the Library of Congress. Yamashita's keynote was subsequently published in the *Massachusetts Review*. Her presentation recounts writers, historical events, and literature that have influenced her artistic development. More important, the essay is also a homage to Asian American poets, playwrights, and prose writers and provides a look into the future of Asian American literature.

Interviews

The section of Yamashita's selected bibliography that includes the interviews Yamashita has been invited to give is a partial list. She has had numerous conversations with radio show hosts; with educators researching Asian American and American literature; with other writers and artists at literary and art festivals, academic conferences, and symposia; and with book reviewers from a wide range of publications. She has often been invited by educators to be a guest lecturer. In part 2 of this volume, Jamie Crosswhite's "The Critical Regionalism of *Tropic of Orange*," in the section "Belonging and Nonbelonging," describes a virtual meeting between Yamashita and the students in Crosswhite's high school literature class. The conversations in which Yamashita takes part reveal a writer who is profoundly engaged with students and teachers, other writers and readers, and artists and activists in diverse communities; the recurring themes in

Yamashita's conversations are part of the vast canvas that constitutes her writing. Educators who are interested in incorporating an interview or part of an interview into their discussions of one of Yamashita's short stories, plays, or books have numerous interviews to choose from. Many interviews are available online as audio or video recordings; other interviews have been published in print in journals and magazines.

Translations

While Yamashita's writing is read, studied, and written about in over a dozen countries, her work has been translated primarily into Portuguese and Japanese. Kenji Kazama's Japanese translation of *Through the Arc of the Rain Forest* was published in 2014 (Yamashita, 熱帯雨林の彼方へ; *Nettai Urin no Kanata e*). Yamashita's essay "A Gentlemen's Agreement" has been translated into Japanese, as have a number of her talks, short stories, and sections of her novels. The selected bibliography of Yamashita's work contains sections on Japanese, Portuguese, and Spanish translations, including translations of her novels and excerpts of her novels as well as translations of her essays and short stories.

Papers

The Yamashita Family Archives consist of letters, photographs, and other family mementos. The online version of the Yamashita Family Archives was designed and is curated and maintained by Lucy Asako Boltz, Yamashita's niece.

The Karen Tei Yamashita Papers are held at the Special Collections and Archives in the McHenry Library at the University of California, Santa Cruz. Most of the material that Yamashita wishes to make available to educators and others interested in her writing and teaching career has been cataloged; an online index of this material is available through the Special Collections and Archives of the University of California, Santa Cruz. The collection contains drafts of short stories, essays, plays, and novels; correspondence with editors, publishers, and curators of art exhibits; correspondence regarding speaking engagements, workshops, and residencies; and newspaper and magazine clippings. The papers offer insights into Yamashita's intellectual, cultural, and literary passions dating back at least four decades. Drafts of early short fiction and essays, some of which are out of print, are also included in the papers.

NOTE

[1] Here Sohn quotes from O'Connor 241.

Selected Bibliography

Ruth Y. Hsu

Books

Sansei and Sensibility. Coffee House Press, 2020.

Letters to Memory. Coffee House Press, 2017.

Anime Wong: Fictions of Performance. Edited and with an afterword by Stephen Hong Sohn, Coffee House Press, 2014.

I Hotel. 2010. Introduced by Jessica Hagedorn, Coffee House Press, 2019.

Circle K Cycles. Coffee House Press, 2001.

Tropic of Orange. 1997. Introduced by Sesshu Foster, Coffee House Press, 2017.

Brazil-Maru. 1992. Introduced by Susan Straight, Coffee House Press, 2017.

Through the Arc of the Rain Forest. 1990. Introduced by Percival Everett, Coffee House Press, 2017.

Short Stories

"Japanese American Gothic." *Literary Hub*, 6 May 2020, lithub.com/japanese-american-gothic/. Accessed 15 Jan. 2021.

"Indian Summer." *Race/d: A Journal for You*, edited by Kat Sayareth, no. 1, Spring 2018, pp. 76–89.

"Mystery Spot—95060." *Viz. Inter-Arts: Interventions: A Trans-Genre Anthology*, edited by Roxanne Power, U of California P, 2016, pp. 256–57.

"I, Kitty." *Ploughshares*, edited by Percival Everett, vol. 40, nos. 2–3, Fall 2014, pp. 183–87.

"Paradise: Mystery Spot: 95065." *XO Orpheus: Fifty New Myths*, edited by Kate Bernheimer, Penguin Books, 2013, pp. 359–63.

"The Last Secretary." *2000andWhat? Stories about the Turn of the Millennium*, edited by David Gilbert and Karl Roeseler, Trip Street Press, 1996, pp. 191–201.

"Madama B." *International Examiner*, vol. 20, no. 9, May 1993, pp. 17–19.

"The Orange." Edited by Linda Mathews. *Los Angeles Times Magazine*, 30 June 1991, pp. 12+.

"The Dentist and the Dental Hygienist." *Asiam*, no. 2, 1987, pp. 66–70.

"Asaka-no-Miya." *Rafu Shimpo*, holiday ed., 20 Dec. 1979, pp. 8+.

"The Bath." *Amerasia Journal*, vol. 3, no. 1, 1975, pp. 137–52.

"Tucano." *Rafu Shimpo*, holiday ed., 20 Dec. 1975, pp. 11+.

Essays

"Introduction." *No-No Boy*, by John Okada, Penguin Classics, 2019, pp. ix–xvii.

"John Okada's *No-No Boy* Is a Test of American Character." *The Atlantic*, 21 May 2019, www.theatlantic.com/entertainment/archive/2019/05/karen-tei-yamashita-john-okadas-no-no-boy/588466/.

"Literature as Community: The Turtle, Imagination, and the Journey Home." *Asian American Literature: Rethinking the Canon*, special issue of *The Massachusetts Review*, edited by Cathy J. Schlund-Vials and Lawrence-Minh Bùi Davis, vol. 59, no. 4, Winter 2018, pp. 597–611.

"Anime Wong: Mobilizing (Techno)Orientalism—Artistic Keynote and Conversation." Coauthored by Yamashita and Lucy Mae San Pablo Burns. *Journal of Contemporary Drama in English*, vol. 5, no. 1, De Gruyter Mouton, Apr. 2017, pp. 173–88, doi.org/10.1515/jcde-2017-0013.

"Borges and I." *Mantissa: A Petit Literary Journal*, vol. 12, no. 1, Spring 2017, pp. 31–32.

"'Colono:Scopy': DSM: Asian American Edition." *Open in Emergency: A Special Issue on Asian American Mental Health*, special issue of *Asian American Literary Review*, vol. 7, no. 2, Fall-Winter 2016, pp. 137–41.

"Call Me Ishimaru." *Leviathan: A Journal of Melville Studies*, vol. 18, no. 1, Mar. 2016, pp. 62–91.

"Kiss of Kitty." *Asian American Literary Review*, vol. 7, no. 1, Spring 2016, pp. 116–22.

"In the Lap of a Prayer." *Amerasia Journal*, vol. 40, no. 3, 2014, pp. 14–17.

"Writing and Memory: Images of the Japanese Diaspora in Brazil." *Orientalism and Identity in Latin America: Fashioning Self and Other from the (Post)Colonial Margin*, edited by Erik Camayd-Freixas, U of Arizona P, 2013, pp. 217–29.

"Borges and I." *The Massachusetts Review*, edited by Jim Hicks, Summer 2012, pp. 209–14.

"Borges and I." *Women and Globalization*, special issue of *International Journal of Okinawan Studies*, edited by Kazuko Takemura, vol. 2, no. 2, Dec. 2011, pp. 95–99.

"Borges and I." *VIII Congresso Internacional de Estudos Japoneses no Brasil, XXI Encontro Nacional de Professores Universitários de Lingua* [*VIII International Congress of Japanese Studies in Brazil, XXI National Meeting of University Language Professors*], Universidade de Brasilia, 2010, pp. 334–37.

"Bread Machine." *XCP: Cross Cultural Poetics*, edited by Mark Nowak, nos. 15–16, 2006, pp. 47–55.

"A Gentlemen's Agreement." *Review 72: Literature and Arts of the Americas*, vol. 39, no. 1, 2006, pp. 112–21.

"Blood Type." *Cafe Creole*, 9 Aug. 2004, www.cafecreole.net/travessia/bloodtype.html. Accessed 14 Jan. 2021.

"Deluxe Bread Machine." *Switch*, vol. 19, no. 8, 2001, pp. 88–91.

Theater and Performance

Jan Ken Pon: A Dance Performance Idea. The C. O. U. P., vol. 1, no. 2, Summer 2016, pp. 35–60, issuu.com/thecoupproject/docs/thecoup-issue1-2. Reprinted from *Anime Wong: Fictions of Performance.*

Tokyo Carmen versus L.A. Carmen. Multicultural Theatre: Scenes and Monologs from New Hispanic, Asian, and African-American Plays, edited by Roger Ellis, Meriwether, 1996, pp. 189–96. Scenes 1 and 2.

"Madama Butterfly: The Sense of Sound." *Premonitions*, edited by Walter Lew, Kaya Productions, 1995, pp. 358–59. Scene from *Hannah Kusoh: An American Butoh.*

Interviews

"Speaking for Everyone, Speaking for No One: The Question of (APIA) Canonicity." Interview of Yamashita and Celeste Ng conducted by Jackson Bliss. *The Ploughshares Blog*, 23 Apr. 2017, blog.pshares.org/index.php/speaking-for-everyone-speaking-for-no-one-the-question-of-apia-canonicity/. Accessed 6 Apr. 2019.

"Karen Tei Yamashita in Conversation with Jonathan Crisman and Jason S. Sexton." *Boom: A Journal of California*, vol. 6, no. 3, Fall 2016, pp. 18–24.

"Possibilities Remain Vibrant within Yamashita's *Anime Wong*." Conducted by Roxanne Ray. *International Examiner*, 1 July 2015, p. 11.

"Interview: Karen Tei Yamashita." Conducted by Karen An-hwei Lee. *Your Impossible Voice*, 2014, www.yourimpossiblevoice.com/interview-karen-tei-yamashita/#more-3382. Accessed 21 Oct. 2020.

"Recuperating History: An Interview with Karen Tei Yamashita." Conducted by Rone Shavers. *Fiction Writers Review*, 14 Aug. 2013, fictionwritersreview.com/interview/recuperating-history-an-interview-with-karen-tei-yamashita/. Accessed 6 Apr. 2019.

"Karen Tei Yamashita: A Reading in Paris (June 8, 2012)." Conducted by Françoise Palleau-Papin. *Transatlantica*, no. 1, 2012, doi.org/10.4000/transatlantica.5796.

"Interview with Author Karen Tei Yamashita by Clint." Conducted by Clint Porte. *Reader's Guide to I-Hotel by Karen Tei Yamashita*, 10 Mar. 2011, ihotelguide.blogspot.co.at/p/interview-with-author-karen-tei.html. Accessed 15 Jan. 2021.

"An Interview with Karen Tei Yamashita." Conducted by Terry Hong. *Bookslut*, July 2010, www.bookslut.com/features/2010_07_016303.php. Accessed 6 Apr. 2019.

"Twenty Years after *Through the Arc of the Rain Forest*: An Interview with Karen Tei Yamashita." Conducted by Noelle Brada-Williams. *Asian American Literature: Discourses and Pedagogies*, vol. 1, 2010, pp. 1–5, scholarworks.sjsu.edu/cgi/viewcontent.cgi?article=1001&context=aaldp.

〈想像·書寫·越界：山下凱倫訪談錄〉 ["Imagination, Writing, and Border-Crossings: An Interview with Karen Tei Yamashita"]. Conducted and translated by Te-hsing Shan. 《與智者為伍: 亞美文學與文化名家訪談錄》 [*Yu Zhizhe Weiwu: Yamei Wenxue yu Wenhua Mingjia Fangtanlu*; *In the Company of the Wise: Conversations with Asian American Writers and Critics*], by Shan, Asian Culture, Aug. 2009, pp. 86–116.

〈想像·書寫·越界：山下凱倫訪談錄〉 ["Imagination, Writing, and Border-Crossings: An Interview with Karen Tei Yamashita"]. Conducted and translated by Te-hsing Shan. 《中外文學》 [*Chung-Wai Wenxue*; *Chung-Wai Literary Monthly*], vol. 35, no. 3, Aug. 2006, pp. 171–92.

"An Interview with Karen Tei Yamashita." Conducted by Te-hsing Shan. *Amerasia Journal*, vol. 32, no. 3, 2006, pp. 123–42.

"An Interview with Karen Tei Yamashita." Conducted by Jean Venua Gier and Carla Alicia Tejeda. *Jouvert: A Journal of Postcolonial Studies*, 1998, legacy.chass.ncsu.edu/jouvert/v2i2/YAMASHI.HTM.

Japanese Translations

わたし, キティ ["Watashi, Kitty"; "I, Kitty"]. Translated by Ikue Kina. 『文学から環境を考える: エコクリティシズムガイドブック』 [*Bungaku kara kankyo wo kangaeru: ekokuritisizumu gaidobukku*; *Thinking about Environment through Literature: A Guidebook to Ecocriticism*], edited by Kazuaki Odani et al., Bensei Shuppan, 2018, pp. 3–11.

わが名はイシマル ["Waga Na ha Ishimaru"; "Call Me Ishimaru"]. Translated by Rie Makino. *Mita Bungaku: The Literary Quarterly*, no. 124, Winter 2016, pp. 140–57.

風呂 ["Furo"; "The Bath"]. Translated by Rie Makino. *Sogo Bunka Kenkyu* [*Comprehensive Cultural Research*], vol. 19, nos. 1–2, Dec. 2013, pp. 77–92.

紳士協定から第三世界の女性へ ["Shinshi kyotei kara daisansekai no josei e"; "From Gentlemen's Agreement to the Third World Women"]. Translated by Ikue Kina. 『文科省特別経費プロジェクト, 沖縄におけるジェンダー学の

理論化と学術的実践：沖縄ジェンダー学の創出, 2012 年事業報告』 [*Monbu kagaku sho tokubetsu keihi purojekuto, Okinawa ni okeru jenda gaku no rironka to gakujututeki jissen: Okinawa jenda gaku no soshutsu 2012nendo hokokusho; Gender Studies in Okinawa FY 2012: An Annual Report of the Research Project Funded by the Ministry of Science and Education in Japan*], edited by Ikue Kina, International Institute for Okinawan Studies, 2013, pp. 256–62.

ぶらじる丸 ["Brazil-Maru"]. Translated by Takao Asano and Ryuta Imafuku. *Brasil Nikkei Bungaku*, no. 35, July 2010, pp. 6–24. Chapter 1 of *Brazil-Maru*.

旅する声 ["Tabi suru Koe"; "Traveling Voices"]. Translated by Ryuta Imafuku and Takuo Ssano. *(Watashi) no Tankyuu* [*An Inquiry into ("I")*], edited by Imafuku, Iwanami Shoten, 2010, pp. 91–110.

紳士協定 ["Shinshi kyotei"; "A Gentlemen's Agreement"]. Translated by Lucio Kubo. 『すばる』 [*Subaru*], edited by Ryuta Imafuku, July 2008, pp. 221–55.

オレンジ ["Orenji"; "The Orange"]. Translated Keijiro Suga. *10+1*, no. 11, 1997, pp. 151–57.

シャム双生児と黄色人種 ["Shamu Soseiji to Oshokujinshu"; "Siamese Twins and Mongoloids: Cultural Appropriation and the Deconstruction of Stereotypes via the Absurdity of Humor"]. Translated by Ryuta Imafuku. *Watashi no Nazo* [*The Enigma of Myself*], edited by Kenji Kazama, Iwanami Shoten, 1997, pp. 143–62.

歯科医と歯科衛生士 ["Shikai to Shikaeiseishi"; "The Dentist and the Dental Hygienist"]. Translated by Kenji Kazama. *Hermes*, no. 55, 1995, pp. 121–37.

Portuguese Translations

"A Ultima Secretária" ["The Last Secretary"]. Translated by Roberto de Sousa Causo. *Scarium*, nos. 42–46, 2004.

Matacão, uma lenda tropical [*Through the Arc of the Rain Forest*]. Translated by Cristina Maria Teixiera Stevens and Carolina Berard, Zipango, 1990.

"Asaka-no-Miya." Translated by Silvia Sasaoka. *Pagina Um, Diario Nippak*, 1980.

"Tucano." Translated by Alberto Cidrães. *Colonia Bungaku*, 1975.

Spanish Translations

"Soñar—América" ["To Dream"]. Translated by Gabriel Bernal Granados. *Los Angeles City*, special issue of *Luvina: Revista literaria de la Universidad de Guadalajara* [*Luvina: Literary Journal of the University of Guadalajara*], no. 57, Winter 2009, pp. 102–10. Chapter 33 of *Tropic of Orange*.

"La naranja" ["The Orange"]. Translated by Montse Watkins. *Encuentro: Colectanea de autores latinos en Japon* [*Encounter: Anthology of Latino Authors in Japan*], edited by Watkins, Luna Books, 1997.

NOTE

Works are listed in reverse chronological order. Japanese translations were compiled with the assistance of Rie Makino.

Contexts

Ruth Y. Hsu and Pamela Thoma

The contexts necessary for understanding Karen Tei Yamashita's works are numerous and complex, as the selected bibliography and other materials in part 1 detail. In what follows we discuss Asian America, Japanese America, Japanese Brazilian history, Japanese Brazilian reverse migration, and Asian American literary studies as discrete contexts, but these categories also overlap and converge in various ways. We recommend that instructors ask students to make connections across contexts while also recognizing specific cultural and historical formations with enough detail to grasp their significance in a given work.

Asian America

Yamashita's writing refashions artistic forms from East Asian traditions (for example, in the dramatic pieces of *Anime Wong*) and Euro-American traditions (jazz, for instance, in *I Hotel*), and is rooted in many contexts: national, familial, cultural, and literary. Her reference in *Letters to Memory* to Walter Benjamin's interpretation of Paul Klee's 1920 painting *Angelus Novus* in Benjamin's "Theses on the Philosophy of History" illustrates one aspect of her approach to historical context: "To live like Walter Benjamin's angel, swept into the future while staring into the past, is pretty horrific" (35). Yet in her memoir, Yamashita also writes that "the family saved these letters. You might say that they were historians, that they knew the value of their stories, this proof of their thoughts and actions in unjust and difficult times. History is proffered to the future" (14). This section discusses in broad strokes the major historical contexts for Asian America that undergird Yamashita's corpus as well as relevant reference works.

Asian American history books generally can be divided into two categories: first, books that provide an overview of Asian migration to the United States, including the beginnings of migration, the responses of specific groups to their treatment after arrival, the conception and emergence of an Asian American panethnic identity, and post-1965 and more recent immigration; and second, histories of specific subgroups, such as Vietnamese Americans, or on specific topics, such as religion, media representation, and Japanese American internment during World War II. In the first category, histories written after 2000 stress the Western imperialistic and colonial underpinnings of Asian migration that began in the mid–nineteenth century. Different Asian groups migrated to the Americas in different waves and under different geopolitical circumstances; the social and cultural expressions of these subgroups after arrival are heterogenous and dynamic. Asian American as a panethnic identity category did not crystallize until the Asian American movement of the 1960s and 1970s, a historical context detailed in Yen Le Espiritu's *Asian American Panethnicity: Bridging Institutions and Identities* and fictionalized in Yamashita's *I Hotel.*

For reference books in Asian American history, *Asian American History and Culture: An Encyclopedia*, edited by Huping Ling and Allan W. Austin, provides comprehensive historical and cultural context. Shelley Sang-Hee Lee's *A New History of Asian America* and Erika Lee's *The Making of Asian America* consider Asian arrival in the Americas beyond the mid–nineteenth century and highlight Western colonialism in Asia as a major factor driving Asian migration from Asia and the Pacific regions. Helen Zia's *Asian American Dreams: The Emergence of an American People* offers crucial historical and cultural contexts, particularly on the 1960s, 1970s, and 1980s. The varied cultural and political experiences of Filipinx Americans, one of the fastest-growing groups after the 1965 reform to immigration law, can be found in Veltisezar B. Bautista's *The Filipino Americans.* The question of which ethnic groups compose Asian America is an ongoing source of debate that points to complex and shifting racialization and Asian American efforts to counter racialization. While South Asian Americans have a long history in the United States, it is only relatively recently that this religiously and culturally diverse group has been recognized as a part of Asian America. *Bengali Harlem and the Lost Histories of South Asian America,* by Vivek Bald, addresses erasure, while Vijay Prashad's *Uncle Swami: South Asians in America Today* considers recent immigration and identity formation as well as the effects of Islamophobia in a post-9/11 context. Among earlier histories of Asian America, Sucheng Chan's *Asian Americans: An Interpretive History* is particularly noteworthy.

Roots: An Asian American Reader, edited by Amy Tachiki and published in 1971, consists of three main sections—"Identity," "History," and "Community"—with over sixty contributions that together offer accounts of the Asian American movement in relation to the Third World movement, community organizing, and tactics for opposing stereotypes of Asian Americans. Karen L. Ishizuka's *Gidra, the Dissident Press and the Asian American Movement: 1969–1974* analyzes the fifty-nine issues of *Gidra,* a monthly magazine founded by radical students at the University of California, Los Angeles, that was devoted entirely to the concerns of the Asian American community in Los Angeles; Ishizuka argues that the Asian American movement was as much a cultural revolution as it was a political one. Canonical histories of the movement include William Wei's *The Asian American Movement*, published in 1993; more recent histories of this political movement include Ishizuka's *Serve the People: Making Asian America in the Long Sixties* and Daryl Maeda's *Rethinking the Asian American Movement.*

Japanese America

Migration to the Americas in unprecedentedly large numbers through the Kingdom of Hawai'i to the West Coast of the United States began in the mid–nineteenth century. Japanese were contracted to work on Hawaiian plantations owned by American and European businessmen. After working off what they owed for their passage and living expenses on the plantations, some of the laborers settled in Hawai'i, but many more left for the United States to work as small shopkeepers or in canneries, forestry, and farming, although they faced significant discrimination. The experiences of the Japanese on plantations in Hawai'i have been vividly described in Milton Murayama's trilogy of novellas, the most famous of which is *All I Asking for Is My Body*. Additionally, Gary Okihiro's histories about the Japanese in Hawai'i are best represented by *Cane Fires: The Anti-Japanese Movement in Hawaii, 1865–1945*. The Japanese who migrated from Japan to the Americas, either directly or through Hawai'i, included students, Christian socialists, and non-firstborn sons. Some migrants believed they were helping Japan project its power overseas; others left in order to escape mandatory conscription, to be able to worship more freely, to own land, or for a combination of reasons. The specific factors leading to migration also depended on the time period, and were affected by Japan's relation to the receiving country—for example, Brazil, Peru, or the United States.

The social and political experiences of the Japanese in the pre–World War II Americas can be characterized as attempts to make a home and a living, and to adjust their mores to achieve those goals. This early period of migration to the United States is vividly fictionalized by Toshio Mori (*Yokohama*; *"Chauvinist"*) and by Hisaye Yamamoto, and later, in Yamashita's *Brazil-Maru* and her essays on the Japanese in Brazil. A crucial anthology about the prewar period is *Before Internment: Essays in Prewar Japanese American History*, edited by Yuji Ichioka and colleagues. The Japanese attack on Pearl Harbor, the declaration of war between the two countries, and the mass evacuation and internment of 120,000 Japanese Americans significantly changed how Japanese Americans viewed their place and identity. John Tateishi's *And Justice for All: An Oral History of the Japanese American Detention Camps* will enrich students' understanding of the everyday experiences of internment compared with the lives of Japanese Americans prior to 1941. Similarly edifying is Valerie Matsumoto's "Japanese American Women in the 1930s" in *Asian Americans: An Encyclopedia of Social, Cultural, Economic, and Political History*, edited by Xiaojian Zhou and Edward J. W. Park.

Japanese Brazilian History

The works that make up Yamashita's Brazilian trilogy—*Through the Arc of the Rain Forest*, *Brazil-Maru*, and *Circle K Cycles*—are either set in Brazil or take it as a primary backdrop. *Brazil-Maru*'s frontispiece and sections of the narrative itself provide information on the earliest Japanese immigration to Brazil; *Circle K Cycles* addresses contemporary conditions for Japanese Brazilian *dekasegi*, workers in Japan of Japanese descent from Brazil and elsewhere. *Through the Arc of the Rain Forest* features a Japanese character who seeks his fortune in the Amazon after winning the lottery, a reference to a history of waves of commodity booms and busts—Brazil's "resource curse"—that were buttressed by a colonial system of slavery and later pulled immigrants to the country (Henry 570). "At once a cautionary tale of deforestation, exploitative labor practices, and abusive extraction of natural resources on the part of an avaricious first-world capitalist machine, *Through the Arc* critiques the historical amnesia that often accompanies progress narratives and what María-Josefina Saldaña-Portillo has called 'fictions of development'" (Bahng, "Extrapolating Transnational Arcs" 124).

Several studies of Yamashita's trilogy provide excellent historical, cultural, and political context, including Kandice Chuh's "Of Hemispheres and Other Spheres," which focuses on Brazilian and Japanese modernities, summarizing the late nineteenth century through the late twentieth century (622–27). John Gamber's "'Dancing with Goblins in Plastic Jungles'" provides a useful short summary of Japanese immigration to Brazil, and Nicholas Birns's "An Incomplete Journey" discusses marginalization within Brazil. Provocative treatment of Brazil's contemporary political economy—including *Through the Arc*'s update of Fordlândia, the early-twentieth-century rubber plantation and neocolonizing mission introduced to the rain forest by Henry Ford—is available in recent scholarship by Aimee Bahng ("Extrapolating Transnational Arcs"; "Imperial Rubber"), Matthew Henry, and Treasa De Loughry.

Japanese migration to Brazil is linked to the relatively late abolition of slavery in 1888 and the country's subsequent sharp turn toward the use of immigrants or free wage labor (Luna and Klein 2–9) for its sugar plantations and gold mining, rubber and coffee plantations, and eventually the Amazon rain forest, which extractive capitalism transformed into "another new commodity . . . frontier" (De Loughry 332). With subsidies from the newly (1889) formed Federal Republic of Brazil (Luna and Klein 10), Brazilian plantation owners recruited European and Asian workers, and the first 793 Japanese immigrants arrived in 1908 to replace European immigrant workers after the latter rejected extremely harsh conditions (Adachi 19–20). Frederik Schulze argues that German-speaking and Japanese-speaking immigrants helped constitute Brazilian national identity. Of course, economic conditions in Japan and increasingly restrictive policies in the United States also affected early immigration to Brazil, which doubled the year following the 1924 Immigration and Exclusion Act in the United States (Gamber 41). Immigration from both Portugal and Japan was "impressive" in the 1920s and continued steadily until the Great Depression (Luna and Klein 126). When Brazilian plantation owners abandoned or liquidated farms beginning in the 1920s, Japanese immigrants saw an opportunity and often formed farming cooperatives, a social history fictionalized in *Brazil-Maru* (Adachi 20; Gamber 43). Japanese immigration to Brazil was strong again for some time after World War II. A detailed source for this context is Jeffrey Lesser's short history of Japanese Brazilians, "Japanese, Brazilians, Nikkei," in his anthology *Searching for Home Abroad: Japanese Brazilians and Transnationalism*. Lesser's *A Discontented Diaspora* is also considered innovative by specialists in this area. A work focusing on the sociology of Japanese settlement in Brazil is Stewart Lone's *The Japanese Community in Brazil, 1908–1940: Between Samurai and Carnival.*

Japanese Brazilian Reverse Migration

Yamashita writes in her prologue to *Circle K Cycles*, subtitled "Purely Japanese," that in 1990 the Japanese government passed a law allowing nisei and sansei (second- and third-generation Japanese Brazilians) from Brazil to reside in Japan as unskilled laborers (11–14). This law also designated other foreign workers as illegal aliens, thereby strictly limiting their means of making a living. The policy was based on the notion that Japanese Brazilians would be able to integrate more smoothly into Japanese society. Keiko Yamanaka provides the most substantial and succinct explanation of the Japanese government policy that enabled the so-called return of Japanese Brazilians to Japan for work. A thorough study of the everyday social and cultural experiences of Japanese Brazilians in Brazil and Japan is Mieko Nishida's *Diaspora and Identity: Japanese Brazilians in Brazil and Japan*. The book is based partially on detailed interviews with Japanese Brazilians ranging in age from nineteen to ninety-five. Nishida also analyzes Japanese Brazilian newspapers and the impact that communications between Japanese Brazilians in Brazil and Japan have on the formation of both groups' sense of their place and role in the two countries. After the 2008 global recession, many unemployed Japanese Brazilians in Japan emigrated to Brazil, often taking their Japanese-born children with them. Lesser's *Searching for Home Abroad* includes an especially insightful excerpt on reverse migration from Yamashita's *Circle K Cycles*; this excerpt provides a tongue-in-cheek contrasting of cultural differences between Japanese Brazilians in Japan and the Japanese (Yamashita, "Interlude"). Angelo Ishi's "Searching for Home, Wealth, Pride, and 'Class': Japanese Brazilians in the 'Land of Yen'" presents an in-depth analysis of the choices, goals, and lifestyles of Japanese Brazilians in Japan. Ishi suggests that a significant number of *dekasegi* belong to the well-educated middle class in Brazil; in Japan, however, they resign themselves to the lack of upward social mobility and respond by associating on the weekends exclusively with others in the Japanese Brazilian community.

Asian American Literary Studies

Yamashita scholarship in Asian American literary studies generally coalesces in four ways: the subject of Asian American literary studies; the formal rethinking of national, ethnic, and immigrant literature; the development of transnational paradigms; and the search for alternative scalar frameworks. The sections that make up part 2 of this volume—"Histories and Interventions," "Belonging and Nonbelonging," "Mapping Alternative Spaces," and "New Transnationalisms and Ecocritical Approaches"—build on and extend these conversations.

Yamashita's first novel, *Through the Arc of the Rain Forest*, is set in Brazil, and the second, *Brazil-Maru*, is about Japanese immigration to Brazil in the 1920s. As discussed in "Novels: Critical Dialogue and Long-Form Fiction," literary scholars initially resisted redefining *Asian American* and *Asian America* to a less US-centric ethnoracial experience of Asian migration. As Jennifer Ho observes, while "Asian American epistemology should be inherently anti-essentialist," the many ways in which Asian Americans have been silenced and marginalized in white supremacist society of the United States create discomfort and tensions (123). The subject of Asian American literature began to change in the 1990s, precipitating discussions that are manifest in the conceptual framing of this volume. The pendulum of critical focus swung decisively toward new analytics, prominently represented in Lisa Lowe's trio of heterogeneity, hybridity, and multiplicity—fully articulated in her 1996 *Immigrant Acts*—as crucial dimensions of Asian American political subjectivity and literature. In *Imagine Otherwise*, Chuh's intervention suggested that Asian American literary studies focus on "the discursive constructedness of subjectivity" in order to create a "subjectless discourse" in which Asian America is a site of critique rather than an object of identification (9).

Around the same time that the subject of Asian American literature was being reframed, national literature, ethnic literature, and the immigrant narrative, all of which had been understood in liberal terms of national belonging (defined as assimilation), also underwent rigorous rethinking. Colleen Lye argued in *America's Asia: Racial Form and American Literature, 1893–1945* that an "Asiatic" racial form—expressed as both model minority and its opposite, yellow peril—had been part of a national discursive tradition that enabled not only industrialization in the United States but also neocolonialism in Asia and the disenfranchisement of Asians in the United States (5–11). As Claire Jean Kim theorizes, the model minority stereotype involves positioning Asian Americans as models in triangular relation to African Americans in the Black-white binary of racial dynamics, one that discredits African American claims to equal rights with the premise that distinctive cultural values on the part of Asians lead to success in the United States (118). The yellow peril stereotype reflects xenophobia and positions Asians as figures that threaten evil or destruction (Huang 140–41, 269–75). With interest in how dynamic racialization may be manifest in literary form, Asian American literary studies and American literary studies more generally entered a period of revitalization with respect to narratology, and Yamashita's formal, narrative innovations served as a site of lively conversation among scholars. Yamashita's experiments in storytelling constitute another set of scholarly concerns underpinning the conceptual framing of this volume.

Contributor Zhou Xiaojing argues in *Form and Transformation in Asian American Literature*, edited by Zhou and Samina Najmi, that "in order to recognize the possibilities of Asian American authors' agency in transforming hegemony, it is necessary to understand that dominant American literary discourses are neither homogenous nor bounded by a discrete culture" (13). Many of the essays in this volume deal with how Yamashita reimagines notions of belonging and nonbelonging, as registered in her formal experiments, although those that devote special attention to these concerns are grouped together in the second section of part 2. Contributors rely, moreover, on a nuanced understanding of writing practices, exploring with their students Yamashita's complex narrative negotiation of "accommodation and resistance," as Viet Thanh Nguyen puts it in *Race and Resistance* (4), or how Yamashita's technique appropriates, reworks, and transforms dominant genres, literary tropes, and subjecthood into vehicles for her novelistic purpose. The publication over a decade ago of *I Hotel*, a fictionalized, experimental narrative of the Asian American movement in the late 1960s and early 1970s, moored Yamashita's corpus to Asian American literature, where it is now considered a crucial part of an expansive tradition.

The development of transnational paradigms is a third major scholarly concern through which this volume's pedagogical discussions are conceptually presented, and several essays in the section titled "Mapping Alternative Spaces" focus on such paradigms. When Yamashita's first published novel landed on the national stage of multicultural American literature, scholars were paying much more attention to Asian America's transnational and transpacific foundations (the Manila Galleon trade route between the Philippines and Mexico, for instance). Increasingly, Asian American artists, poets, playwrights, and novelists would craft their narratives around the many Asian crosscurrents, intersections, and transfusions that are an indelible aspect of what constitutes the United States. Yamashita's books are appreciated as pivotal in this essential reorientation of Asian American studies and American studies, especially those books that triangulate Japan with North and South America: *Brazil-Maru* is the first novel ever published about the initial waves of Japanese settlers to Brazil; *Circle K Cycles*, set in Japan in the late 1990s, is about the *dekasegi*; *Tropic of Orange* depicts Japanese American, Chinese American, Chicanx, and African American characters navigating their sense of belonging in contemporary, multiethnic Los Angeles, the cosmopolitan locus of a North and South capitalist nexus and global migration. In a similar vein, *Through the Arc of the Rain Forest* is set in modern Brazil and vividly addresses the spectacular but devastating realities of global capitalism.

The final major set of scholarly concerns that underpin the conceptual framing of this volume involves the effects of globalization and the corresponding efforts toward alternative scalar thinking beyond national geographic, political, and cultural borders. These inform especially the essays within the section "New Transnationalisms and Ecocritical Approaches." Scholarship on Yamashita may be, and is in several contributor essays, positioned within hemispheric studies, transpacific studies, global studies, planetary studies, Anthropocene studies, new materialism, or posthuman studies, all of which represent ways to frame spatiality or scale that do not attempt to denaturalize the nation so much as they aim to dislodge the nation as a conceptual foundation. Often at the center of debates on globalization in literary studies, ecocriticism reveals new and compelling questions in Yamashita's works. Such dialogue illuminates Yamashita's broad appeal to teachers and foregrounds her work as a source of generative tension within scholarship.

Essential Reference Materials

Ruth Y. Hsu and Pamela Thoma

This section highlights reference materials in scholarly fields that are crucial to an in-depth understanding of Karen Tei Yamashita's vast storytelling canvases; accordingly, reference materials collected in this section are not confined to Asian American literary studies but include broader fields to which Yamashita has contributed as a writer, a public speaker, and an educator. In addition to Asian American literary studies, this section includes information on guides, anthologies, and websites in areas such as transnational literary studies, globalization, ecocriticism, and feminist and queer studies. Together with "Contexts," this section offers educators in a wide range of disciplines many options for adopting Yamashita's work in courses at all levels.

Asian American Literary Studies

A recent upsurge in the publication of reference materials in Asian American literary studies, including guides, companions, and primary source collections, provides up-to-date resources. *The Cambridge Companion to Asian American Literature*, edited by Crystal Parikh and Daniel Y. Kim, opens with a useful "Chronology of Major Works and Events, 1763–2014" (xv–xx); crucial chapters include those on the immigrant narrative (Song, "Asian American Literature"); writing on Japanese American internment (Robinson); Asian American drama (J. Lee, "Asian American Drama"); defining diaspora literature (Park); feminist and queer interventions (Grice and Parikh); and mixed-race, adoptee, and disability subjectivities (Keith; Schlund-Vials and Wu). *The Routledge Companion to Asian American and Pacific Islander Literature*, edited by Rachel Lee, is organized around the following sections: "Keywords" (19–188), "Geographies,

Literary Ethnoscapes, and Historical Periods" (189–376), and "Genre, Form, and the Paraliterary" (376–507). *Keywords for Asian American Studies*, edited by Cathy J. Schlund-Vials, Linda Trinh Vo, and K. Scott Wong, builds on Raymond Williams's concept of keywords and may be used, as stated in "Note on Classroom Use," as a primary text or as supplementary reading (keywords.nyupress.org/asian-american-studies/in-the-classroom/note-on-classroom-use/). Accessible online are ten of the print book's sixty-one essays on Asian American studies keywords in the social sciences, humanities, and cultural studies; the introduction to the volume; and the volume's bibliography. Other reference works include the four-volume series *Asian American Literature in Transition*, edited by Min Hyoung Song and Rajini Srikanth, and *The Oxford Encyclopedia of Asian American Literature and Culture*, edited by Josephine Lee, which is online and part of the extensive digital project of the *Oxford Research Encyclopedia of Literature*. Any study of Japanese American literature that is concerned with the World War II Japanese American internment will find the online and open-access *Densho Encyclopedia* invaluable (encyclopedia.densho.org/). *Densho* is designed and written for a general audience and offers a user-friendly table of contents, the ability to browse an extensive digital archive of photographs and historical documents on the internment, sample multidisciplinary curricula, and resource guides developed with educators in mind.

Recent works join classics such as Elaine H. Kim's *Asian American Literature: An Introduction to the Writings and Their Social Context* and Sau-ling Wong's *Reading Asian American Literature: From Necessity to Extravagance*. Scholarly texts that helped chart new directions for Asian American literary studies for the twenty-first century include *Imagining the Nation: Asian American Literature and Cultural Consent*, by David Leiwei Li, who also edited the four-volume *Asian American Literature*, which collects key scholarly work on Asian American literary history, prose, poetry, drama, and performance; Jinqi Ling's *Narrating Nationalisms: Ideology and Form in Asian American Literature*; Rachel Lee's *The Americas of Asian American Literature: Gendered Fictions of Nation and Transnation*; Viet Thanh Nguyen's *Race and Resistance: Literature and Politics in Asian America*; and the collection *Transnational Asian American Literature: Sites and Transits*, edited by Shirley Geok-lin Lim and colleagues.

The anthology has been an important form for Asian American literary studies in the era of field formation, and these now serve as historical references, particularly *Aiiieeeee! An Anthology of Asian-American Writers*, edited by Frank Chin, Jeffrey Paul Chan, Lawson Fusao Inada, and Shawn Wong, and *The Big Aiiieeeee! An Anthology of Chinese American and Japanese American Literature*, edited by Jeffrey Paul Chan and colleagues. In women's literature, significant anthologies include, among others, Asian Women United of California's *Making Waves: An Anthology of Writings by and about Asian American Women* and *The Forbidden Stitch: An Asian American Women's Anthology*, edited by Lim and colleagues. Continuing the tradition are *Charlie Chan Is Dead: An Anthology of Contemporary Asian American Fiction* and *Charlie Chan Is Dead Two:*

At Home in the World, edited by Jessica Hagedorn. Rajini Srikanth and Esther Yae Iwanaga's *Bold Words: A Century of Asian American Writing* is a useful reference for understanding the history and development of Asian American literature, while Stephen Hong Sohn's blog site *Asian American Literature Fans* tracks and reviews contemporary works.

Feminist and Queer Literary and Cultural Studies

While Lisa Lowe's *Immigrant Acts: On Asian American Cultural Politics* influentially mobilized the concepts of hybridity, heterogeneity, and multiplicity to highlight racialized dimensions of gender and sexuality within Asian American critique at the close of the twentieth century, this subsection of essential reference materials points to selected works of scholarship in Asian American feminist and queer literary and cultural studies in the twenty-first century.

For an excellent reference, instructors can consult Helena Grice and Crystal Parikh's "Feminist and Queer Interventions into Asian America" in Parikh and Kim's *The Cambridge Companion to Asian American Literature*, which includes bibliographies of criticism and theory. Helena Grice's *Negotiating Identities: An Introduction to Asian American Women's Writing* contextualizes ethnic and feminist traditions in the United States in relation to those traditions in the United Kingdom. Patricia Chu's *Assimilating Asians: Gendered Strategies of Authorship in Asian America* recognizes the ways in which gender and genre are closely linked, paying particular attention to racialization. Patti Duncan analyzes the politics of cultural production in *Tell This Silence: Asian American Women Writers and the Politics of Speech*. David L. Eng's *Racial Castration: Managing Masculinity in Asian America* examines cultural production using psychoanalytic theory, and Daniel Kim broke new ground with analyses of masculinity as a relational—gendered and racialized—concept in *Writing Manhood in Black and Yellow: Ralph Ellison, Frank Chin, and the Literary Politics of Identity. Ingratitude: The Debt-Bound Daughter in Asian American Literature*, by erin Khuê Ninh, takes up questions about heteropatriarchal family life and the self-disciplining demands of contemporary forms of power and subjectification. Pamela Thoma's *Asian American Women's Popular Literature: Feminizing Genres and Neoliberal Belonging* considers the ways in which popular genres function within and against neoliberal models of subjecthood and cultural citizenship.

Q and A: Queer in Asian America, edited by David L. Eng and Alice Y. Hom, maps queer identities, queer theory, and queer of color critique at the end of the twentieth century, and as a wide-ranging anthology fits precisely the definition of an indispensable reference. Celine Parreñas Shimizu has similarly initiated new ways of thinking about racialized sexualities in *The Hypersexuality of Race: Performing Asian/American Women on Screen and Scene* and *Straightjacket Sexualities: Unbinding Asian American Manhoods in the Movies*. Both Laura Kang's *Compositional Subjects: Enfiguring Asian/American Women* and Denise Cruz's *Transpacific Femininities: The Making of the Modern Filipina* examine archives stretching across geopolitical boundaries to analyze discursive constructions of femininity, the former in the contemporary period and the latter in the early to middle twentieth century.

Transnational Literary Studies

The coeditors discuss the transnational turn in Asian American literary studies in the section of part 1 titled "Contexts." This subsection highlights key reference materials in transnational studies writ large and transnational American studies to provide additional critical context for Yamashita's works. *Comparative Literature in an Age of Globalization*, edited by Haun Saussy, will be useful for thinking about contemporary cosmopolitanism. With Ursula Heise we recognize that *globalization* became "the central term around which theories of current politics, society, and culture in the humanities and social sciences are organized. In literary and cultural studies it has gradually replaced 'postmodernism' and 'postcolonialism' in contemporary theory" (Heise, *Sense* 3). Similar erasure could be observed with respect to the term *transnationalism*. Understanding the transnational in relation to other categories, such as the global, requires recognition of the limitations, as well as the continuing salience, of the term, particularly in the recent era of resurgent nationalisms and isolationist forces in the United States. Rather than flattening differences, it is crucial to recognize the ways in which transnational literary studies overlaps with comparative literary studies; with world, global, or planetary literary approaches; with hemispheric studies; and with postmodern, postcolonial, and decolonial studies. With this in mind, a reference work that remains foundational, and also informs the materials cited in "Feminist and Queer Literary and Cultural Studies" above, is Gayatri Chakravorty Spivak's *A Critique of Postcolonial Reason: Toward a History of the Vanishing Present*, and her enduringly instructive essay, "Can the Subaltern Speak?" Spivak's *Critique* and *In Other Worlds: Essays in Cultural Politics* serve as model interventions. Paul Jay's *Global Matters: The Transnational Turn in Literary Studies* is also a useful reference.

Shelley Fisher Fishkin's 2004 presidential address to the American Studies Association, "Crossroads of Cultures: The Transnational Turn in American Studies" is a necessary reference, as is Rachel Adams's "The Ends of America, the Ends of Postmodernism." Essential material can also be found in Heise's "Ecocriticism and the Transnational Turn in American Studies." *The Routledge Companion to Transnational American Studies*, edited by Nina Morgan and colleagues and published in 2019, is a newer valuable reference and is available as an e-book. For a resource in feminist cultural studies, see Inderpal Grewal's *Transnational America: Feminisms, Diasporas, Neoliberalisms*. American transnationalism could be critically explored in relation to ideas about "the new American exceptionalism," as elaborated by Donald Pease. Peer-reviewed and online, *The Journal of Transnational American Studies* is another outstanding resource.

Ecocriticism and Environmental Cultural Studies

Begoña Simal's "The Junkyard in the Jungle: Transnational, Transnatural Nature in Karen Tei Yamashita's *Through the Arc of the Rain Forest*" includes a comprehensive synthesis of major approaches to ecocriticism. Simal's analysis of the impact of the global shift in ecocriticism adds depth to Yamashita's transnational writing. A helpful study of ecopolitics and the development of environmental policies in Brazil—including pre-1964 Brazil—is Roberto Pereira Guimarães's *The Ecopolitics of Development in the Third World: Politics and Environment in Brazil*. On the issue of environmental justice in relation to the citrus industry and North-South labor migration within the larger context of global neoliberalism, Ryan Palmer's "Citrus Noir: Strange Fruit in Karen Tei Yamashita's *Tropic of Orange*" is essential.

Rob Nixon's *Slow Violence and the Environmentalism of the Poor* shows how, in the Global South, environmental degradation affects the poor most of all. Nixon's book also argues that the scope of the environmental crisis is transnational, a viewpoint that dovetails with Yamashita's thematic orientation to planetary crises. Similarly, Greta Claire Gaard, building on the ideas encompassed in Val Plumwood's concept of critical ecofeminism, offers essential intellectual frameworks for a range of topics that reoccur in Yamashita's corpus: sexuality, climate change, and the mutually constitutive relationship between humans and the more than human.

Two anthologies that contain a wide range of foundational essays on ecocriticism are *Contemporary Perspectives on Ecofeminism*, edited by Mary Phillips and Nick Rumens, and *Sustainability: Approaches to Environmental Justice and Social Power*, edited by Julie Sze. The former gives a comprehensive overview of traditional and more recent ecofeminist theories and examines how such theories can address emerging sociocultural and technological changes. The latter gathers essays from experts on sustainability, discussing the complex connections among race, gender, class, Indigenous land rights, militarization, and environmental crisis. A profound understanding of these connections is essential in furthering our thinking on sustainability at the local and global levels.

Global Ecologies and the Environmental Humanities: Postcolonial Approaches, edited by Elizabeth DeLoughrey, Jill Didur, and Anthony Carrigan, is at the forefront of scholarship on postcolonial environmental humanities. The anthology includes the work of scholars from many disciplines and regions of the globe writing about world ecologies and environmental justice, the Anthropocene and prospects for the planet. The essays in Stacy Alaimo and Susan Hekman's edited volume *Material Feminisms* connect and advance two dynamic fields in exciting ways. An important online resource is the website of the Harvard University Center for the Environment (environment.harvard.edu/), where research and publications across the disciplines and interdisciplines are available, including "Literature and Environment," by Lawrence Buell and colleagues, which provides a useful overview of the development of ecocriticism. Finally,

ISLE: Interdisciplinary Studies in Literature and the Environment is the premier journal in environmental studies, with many libraries providing online access.

Globalization and Diaspora

An essential history of globalization and diaspora is Tony Fielding's *Asian Migrations: Social and Geographical Mobilities in Southeast, East, and Northeast Asia*. Using interdisciplinary approaches, this book explains the complexity of the conditions spurring migrations within and beyond Asia. Fielding deals with migration types that include student and labor migrations, marriage migration, displacement due to war, and human trafficking. *Servants of Globalization: Women, Migration, and Domestic Work*, by Rhacel Salazar Parreñas, was a watershed when it was first published in 2001 and has recently been updated in a second edition; combining ethnographic methods and analyses of gendered processes such as the international division of paid and unpaid caring labor and partial citizenship, it focuses on Filipina domestic workers' lives in Rome and Los Angeles. Sunil S. Amrith's *Migration and Diaspora in Modern Asia* begins with a time line of Asian mobility, Western incursions into and exploitation of Asian countries, and Asian migration within Asia and beyond (xiii–xv). This history examines the main periods of large-scale Asian migration and the complex geopolitical and domestic conditions that led to migration; causes include famine, war, and foreign invasion. Amrith's history can be read with Shelley Sang-Hee Lee's *A New History of Asian America*, which looks briefly at Asian diaspora to the United States in the mid–eighteenth century and then devotes attention to the constitution of Asian America as a political, panethnic identity group. A comprehensive, foundational text on global studies is *Thinking Globally: A Global Studies Reader*, edited by Mark Juergensmeyer. The essays in this collection explain the history of globalization in each region of the world and cover key issues, such as emerging nationalisms, transnational ideologies, and media.

Latin American Studies

An essential guide is the *Handbook of Latin American Studies*, which is available online and consists of sources selected and annotated by scholars (www.loc.gov/hlas/). The multidisciplinary *Handbook* is edited by the Hispanic Division of the Library of Congress and has been in publication since 1936. *The Companion to Latin American Studies*, edited by Philip Swanson, is foundational and includes discussions of Latino culture in the United States, gender and sexuality, race, and colonial cultures. The book also contextualizes the term *Latin American studies* within a global historical, political, literary, and sociocultural context. Helpful chapters include Luis Fernando Restrepo's "The Cultures of Colonialism" (47–68), Elzbieta Sklowdoska's "Latin American Literatures"

(86–105), Brian Gollnick's "Approaches to Latin American Literature" (107–21), William Luis's "Latino US Literature" (122–53), and Peter Wade's "Race in Latin America" (185–99).

Juan Poblete's *New Approaches to Latin American Studies: Culture and Power* examines Latin American studies from the 1980s to 2018, when the book was published. The contents of the book are organized using the idea of "turn," of a shift or change—for example, the transnational turn and the various turns in feminism, Indigenous studies, and performance studies, among others. Poblete's book examines the degree to which these turns indicate more extensive or profound epistemological changes in Latin American studies. "Why Asia and Latin America?," by Jeffrey Lesser, Evelyn Hu-DeHart, and Ignacio López-Calvo, provides specific dialogic treatment of these shifts. James Petras and Henry Veltmeyer's *Extractive Imperialism in the Americas: Capitalism's New Frontier* examines contemporary efforts by multinational corporations, with the assistance of state apparatuses, to exploit at an unprecedented rate of acceleration the natural resources of Latin America. Petras and Veltmeyer argue that this phase of imperialism is a reaction to the rise of China and the demise of late-stage capitalism in the West.

Invisible Ganesh

Karen Tei Yamashita

In the summer of 1984 and just as the Olympic Games opened in Los Angeles, I immigrated home to the US with my Brazilian family. About the same time, my old friend Jack Belkin called to put me in touch with his college friend Ben Huang, who was also living in LA. Jack informed me that Ben had just finished a writing program in Iowa, and he assumed we would have things (writing) about which to talk.

Not that it's an excuse, but I had been away in Brazil for almost a decade. I queried, "Iowa?"

"Yes, the Iowa Writers' Workshop."

"What's that?"

"I assume Ben learned to write there." Obviously Ben could already write. Jack was being supercilious with dumb me.

"There is such a thing?"

"Yes." Jack probably wanted to add that it was famous and also prestigious, but of course I had no idea. In fact I was flabbergasted. Okay, amused, because I had just spent the last decade, and would then pursue another decade, trying to teach myself to write.

In time, I would meet Ben, who was by then pursuing another graduate degree, and learn that among his Iowa cohort were the writers Gish Jen and

David Wong Louie, and probably also around the same time, Sesshu Foster. And I would also become aware of writers who eventually taught at Iowa: Bharati Mukherjee and Lan Samantha Chang. By the time I got what I considered a "real" job at UC Santa Cruz and knew that an MFA was a terminal degree, I was teaching books by these writers under the rubric Asian American literature, likely a designation considered anathema to these American writers. But with respect, students bought and read their books. And I had to be a little jealous; these writers were really educated writers who came from the very center of American letters. These things I learned slowly over the many years I've been employed to teach creative writing in the literature department at UCSC; how I got this job is a testament to this school's idea of risky experiments.

I learned to teach while on the job. This is probably not what my students want to hear, but I appear to be a kind of natural as teachers go, so it might not have been that obvious. I really do like the exchange and giving away what I know, and over time, I think I'm better at it. I've discovered that no matter how much I want to give away, students don't necessarily really want it or maybe don't know what to do with it. Maybe they are scared, but probably this is because the "it" in writing is inscrutable, and you only come upon it by doing it. At least that's what we tell each other.

One of the things I had to learn about is the workshop. I hung around my colleague Micah Perks, who has an MFA from Cornell, to figure this out. What I remember is that after the first five weeks teaching my first fiction class, a student came into my office and asked, "When are we going to start workshopping?" I'm pretty sure I answered something like, "Whatever for?" then slipped into Micah's office and asked, "What do you do in a workshop?" To be honest, after getting to know Ben, I had become fascinated with reading horror story articles about how students at Iowa were psychologically damaged by the workshop experience. It sounded like a brutal hazing to crush the incompetent. I didn't think I should pass that on to student writers in an undergraduate program. I've since given in to the workshop, because actually hearing criticism from your peers in a controlled environment that supposedly exemplifies a culture of nurturing craft and *we're in the same sinking boat together*, and besides that, *Karen is too old and we actually get the references to pop culture*, is useful. Critics have written about how the workshop shapes writing, and maybe it does, but my being there certainly doesn't.

One of UCSC's claims to fame is that Raymond Carver once taught here and started the journal *Quarry West*. By the time I got to Santa Cruz, Carver's fame was complete with occasional snide passes at working-class minimalist short storytelling; mention of The Watering Hole, the bar Carver frequented on Mission Street; the story that to this day he still owes fifty bucks to his poet friend David Swanger; and talk that his old journal was about to be defunded. When two student alum editors and I went in to ask the Porter College provost to extend the funding for *Quarry West*, the provost asked innocently, "Who is Raymond Carver?"

Knowing who Raymond Carver was, but also teaching creative writing, makes me remember that I met John Gardner when I was in college. John Gardner had been invited to give the convocation that year at Carleton and read from his then new book, *Grendel.* For reasons that were beyond my understanding, my professor Mr. Robert Tisdale invited me to his home to join his family and Gardner for dinner. I'm sure there must have been other students and faculty there, but my insecurity in those years made me feel personally singled out. Mr. Tisdale, who is now Bob and after so many years my friend, won't remember that he met me in that enclosed porch area that all Minnesota houses have and proceeded to describe to me his method of cooking rice perfectly. After getting past the rice recipe and into the house, it turned out that Gardner's children were also there, all running around with the Tisdales in kid chaos.

Gardner himself was at a large table spreading out and showing the architectural plans for his house. My memory of Gardner was that he had a shock of white-blonde hair cut in a Dutch boy. His hair hung and moved about his head like a seductive shampoo commercial, a complementing halo to his position as the center of attention. Gardner turned from his blueprints, and at some point I was caught listening to his recipe for making brown rice. The brown rice recipe had a more complicated narrative because it was associated with a small boxy room that Gardner said he designed with a small door that he had to crawl into. Crawling through a small door was symbolic of something; maybe humility, but then I was the one trying not to feel humiliated. I imagined it to be a tatami room with a low ceiling and a table. He would crawl into the room, shut the small door, and stay there and write for days. Maybe it was also soundproof. Samurai, he explained to me, would make salted rice balls stuffed with pickles as a preservative and wrapped in seaweed, pack them in a satchel, and live on this for several days of traveling. I must have tried to make small talk about how brown rice might not be sticky enough for *onigiri*, but Gardner was into healthy. Even with the swirl of kids that evening, I could not at the time relate to the writer's need for solitude, and only later I wondered if Gardner's room was outfitted with some kind of privy.

I still put John Gardner's books on writing on my syllabi, in particular *The Art of Fiction*. Students might complain about his self-righteous ideas of the craft, but it's more effective if Gardner spouts the truth than if I do. In the early years, students knew John Gardner to have been Raymond Carver's teacher at Chico State, that he deserved their respect, but lately my students are no longer reading realism with the moral guts that Gardner professed. For a while I thought it ironic that Gardner's legacy was built, not on his fiction, but on his teaching and writing about fiction. These days, I'm aware that *The Art of Fiction* remains shut on the shelf.

To be fair to Gardner and his samurai rice ball writing retreat, I must have thought a little Asian wisdom in the art of writing fiction couldn't hurt. I confess that my first syllabus for teaching fiction was structured as a series of kata, or martial art moves. Every week we would concentrate on learning a kata. It could be character, scene, dialogue, or timing. The writer, through training in each kata and perfection of the way, might then attain the literary muscles and focus to write. We could progress from white to black belts in ten weeks. If only it were that easy.

I believe however, that finally, it was the small but very significant gesture of Mr. Tisdale's inviting me to dinner that has forever remained in my memory. To be clear, Mr. Tisdale taught English literature, and there were no creative writing classes in fiction at Carleton in the day. My English education was solidly *Norton Anthology* canonical. That tome was supposed to tumble off my shelf in an earthquake and kill me. Another of my professors, Mr. Owen Jenkins, had said very definitively that everything worth writing had already been written, and it was useless for us to try to write anything new. The point was to remove any frivolous pretentions, but even so, what would it mean to my students to be invited to dinner, perhaps even with a writer holding forth on anything, whether a confined writing space or samurai?

The quandary of inviting folks to dinner in Santa Cruz is that they may be vegetarian or vegan, and the menu must be tweaked accordingly. Knowing food restrictions is absolutely necessary for a successful dinner party. This is where I adopted the idea of workshop groups based on what writers eat. I pass out a signup sheet: carnivore, omnivore, herbivore. Typically someone will argue that there is no such human as a carnivore, but some writers always sign up for this category. The writer who argues that carnivores don't exist is usually an omnivore. This brings me to generalize about what writers eat and consequently what or how they write. For example, omnivore writers are generally given to more precision—carefully drafted manuscripts, fewer typos, better grades, memoir and realism. Carnivores are a mixed bunch but can be ethnic writers of color who would never give up pork, writers of vampires and horror, or writers who just like barbecue. The herbivores aren't necessarily nonviolent writers, but they generally bend toward science fiction and fantasy and, at times, moral correctness. Herbivores are worried about the future and their carbon footprint, even if they often live inside a dream. Carnivores might be more experimental and herbivores more imaginative, omnivores more determined. This is not a sure and fast classification method, but I suspect a synergy among writers and eaters is possible.

One day I met the scholar Ursula Heise, who invited me to Stanford to participate in a seminar hosted by the Center for the Study of the Novel. Heise gave a talk about my novel *Through the Arc of the Rain Forest*, and I think I talked about narrative point of view and voice, reading from my work. The other invited author was Gilbert Sorrentino, who at the last moment decided to leave for New York and never showed up; he must have known this was some kind of trap. Sorrentino's paired scholar prefaced his comments by saying that since the founding of the center by Franco Moretti in 2000, this was the first time they had invited actual writers (novelists), then told the story about Vladimir Nabokov being considered to chair the English department at Harvard, to which the

Slavic linguist Roman Jakobson objected, "What next? Shall we appoint elephants to teach zoology?" Elephants? Think of the mighty Ganesh dipping his tusk into ink, but at that moment I should have been a mouse scurrying away from observation into Gardner's little door, yelling nonsense about rice balls and barbecue.

Hanging out with academics means I've had to find deadpan ways to hang out, learn the lingo, try to read what they read. This has been the second half of my continuing education. They have terminal degrees; mine is interminable. With some research of the history of creative writing in America, I can defend it as an American project that arises out of our revolutionary beginnings and eventually the nineteenth century and the ideas of the likes of Emerson and Thoreau, the point being to create the scholar citizen. At its most ideal, it's a democratic idea about every citizen given the opportunity to, well, creatively write. To wit: the Iowa Writers' Workshop. Visiting places like the Barnes Foundation in Philadelphia, one sees how the idea developed over art. My students take it for granted that creativity, like happiness, is a democratic right. In the years I've been teaching, MFA programs have mushroomed from a few to hundreds, the AWP conference from a few hundred writers to thousands. My personal trainer, Aaron Colton, who is also a doctoral student and studies this stuff, has directed me to further reading that places the rise of creative writing as a postwar construction promoted by the Cold War state, sanctioned by the university, and, for better or worse, the foundation for contemporary American letters.[1] He lets me know this while scrutinizing my precarious position under a barbell, adding, "How about another ten pounds?"

Over the years, I've had to notice the controversies about MFAs versus this or that. I think at some point Tom Wolfe, while promoting new journalism and *The Bonfire of the Vanities*, introduced a polemic about his version of realism against the magical and minimal. Somewhere in there I think he was blaming it on the workshop, but I always like to remember that despite how Wolfe gets the reader to ride the bus cross-country with Ken Kesey and his merry pranksters, Wolfe himself was never on that bus. More recently Junot Díaz argued the case of MFA versus POC, that creative writing programs were oppressive spaces for people of color. I can imagine this. Over the years, I've only had a handful of students of color in my creative writing classes. Not many of us want to buck our immigrant, refugee, colored, underserved families to risk a penniless life out there. Having me for a teacher might not be much of a draw, but Díaz is a MacArthur genius with a Pulitzer.

Notice I've never said anything here about whether writing can be taught. I've just been doing my best to be the invisible elephant in the room. What follows in the appendix is an abbreviated syllabus of a creative writing workshop or seminar that uses Italo Calvino's novel *If on a Winter's Night a Travele*r as the central text. Sometimes I've employed Calvino's novel on its own, but I've usually accompanied it with a reader containing the reprints of the excerpted beginnings of ten books by women and queer authors because students complained of Calvino's first person "I" who is consistently a male character pursuing a female protagonist. It's Calvino's satire, but after the fifth week of the quarter, predictably students would send in a representative to ask me to stop making them read Calvino. It was sort of the same request as "When are we going to workshop?" Though by then, I was a convert, and workshops have always been a part of my classes. What I was interested in conveying and studying is Calvino's ability to reduce a genre to its stylistic, plotted, and syntactical components as a construction of a voice in concert with an ideal reader, and thereby to nudge students to think about the writer as chameleon, the invisible Ganesh who is never really on the bus but who can anyway crawl into a small door and exist on rice balls.

I don't know if writing can be taught. Maybe I am part of a project that's falsely promoted the hegemonic claims of American creative happiness, and it's all been a big bust. Gardner's claim to fame was finally his teaching, but even that fades, becomes irrelevant. I'm still writing to figure this out.

APPENDIX

Advanced Creative Writing: Fiction Workshop or Seminar

Writer and facilitator: Karen Tei Yamashita
Course description: Write. Read. Write.

Week 1: Introduction

Italo Calvino, "If on a Winter's Night a Traveler," chapter 1 (the Pleasure of Reading)

Week 2: Who Am I? / The Language of Mystery

Calvino, "If on a Winter's Night a Traveler" and Angela Carter, *Bloody Chamber* (excerpt)

Calvino, chapter 2 (Books and Readers; You Meet the Other Reader)

Week 3: I Come of Age / Family and National Feuds / Time and Place

Calvino, "Outside the Town of Malbork" and Leslie Marmon Silko, *Ceremony* (excerpt)

Calvino, chapter 3 (Clarifying the Question and the Nonreader)

Week 4: I See the Metaphor / A Great Escape / The Prison's Labyrinth / Unreliable Narrator

Calvino, "Leaning from the Steep Slope" and Julia Alvarez, *Yo!* (excerpt)

Calvino, chapter 4 (the Academy and Dead Language)

Week 5: I Take On the Revolution / Ménage à Trois / Spy / Character

Calvino, "Without Fear of Wind or Vertigo" and Wang Ping, *Foreign Devil* (excerpt)

Calvino, chapter 5 (Publishers, Author, and Translators)

Week 6: My Story in Many Stories / Crime / Stories in Layers and Weaves / Plot

Calvino, "Looks Down in the Gathering Shadow" and Jessica Hagedorn, *Dogeaters* (excerpt)

Calvino, chapter 6 (Seer vs. Bestselling Author in Crisis vs. Insatiable Reader)

Week 7: I Am Paranoid / Psychological / Interior Narrative

Calvino, "In a Network of Lines That Enlace" and Virginia Woolf, *To the Lighthouse* (excerpt)

Calvino, chapter 7 (the Reader's House; the Reader's Body)

Week 8: I Am a Magician / Borgesian / Writer as Minister of Nature / Literary Puzzles

Calvino, "In a Network of Lines That Intersect" and Ama Ata Aidoo, *Our Sister Killjoy* (excerpt)

Calvino, chapter 8 (Diary of an Author; Readers Meet Author)

Week 9: I Am Sensitive / Asiaerotic / Heightened Sensitivity / Voyeurism

Calvino, "On a Carpet of Leaves Illuminated by the Moon" and Lawrence Chua, *Gold by the Inch* (excerpt)

Calvino, chapter 9 (Censorship and Revolution; Reader as Character)

Week 10: The Sins of My Mother and Father / Marquezian / Magical Realism

Calvino, "Around an Empty Grave" and Toni Morrison, *Beloved* (excerpt)

Calvino, chapter 10 (Books and the State; the Fiction of Fiction)

Week 11: I Erase the World / Speculative / Surreal / Ideas / Focus / Editing

Calvino, "What Story Down There Awaits Its End?" and Aimee Bender, *An Invisible Sign of My Own* (excerpt)

Week 12: A Happy Ending

Calvino, chapters 11 and 12 (the Nature of Reading)

Bibliography

Italo Calvino, *If on a Winter's Night a Traveler*

First chapters or stories from:

Ama Ata Aidoo, *Our Sister Killjoy*

Julia Alvarez, *Yo!*

Aimee Bender, *An Invisible Sign of My Own*

Angela Carter, *Bloody Chamber*

Lawrence Chua, *Gold by the Inch*

Jessica Hagedorn, *Dogeaters*

Toni Morrison, *Beloved*

Leslie Marmon Silko, *Ceremony*

Wang Ping, *Foreign Devil*
Virginia Woolf, *To the Lighthouse*

Optional

Rabih Alameddine, *I, the Divine: A Novel in First Chapters*
Margaret Atwood, *Negotiating with the Dead: A Writer on Writing*
Jorge Luis Borges, *Borges on Writing*
Italo Calvino, *Six Memos for the Next Millennium*
Hélène Cixous, *Three Steps on the Ladder of Writing*
Marguerite Duras, *Writing*
Umberto Eco, *Six Walks in the Fictional Woods*
John Gardner, *The Art of Fiction*; *On Becoming a Novelist*
Milan Kundera, *The Art of the Novel*
Anne Lamott, *Bird by Bird*
Mario Vargas Llosa, *Letters to a Young Novelist*
Fernando Pessoa, *Always Astonished*
Jeanette Winterson, *Art Objects: Essays on Ecstasy and Effrontery*

NOTE

[1] The works Colton has referred me to include Eric Bennett's *Workshops of Empire*, Chad Harbach's *MFA vs. NYC*, Mark McGurl's *The Program Era*, and D. G. Myers's *The Elephants Teach*.

Part Two

APPROACHES

Introduction: Pedagogical Opportunities and Challenges

Ruth Y. Hsu and Pamela Thoma

The essays in part 2 underscore the capacious breadth of Yamashita's works by assaying the numerous ways in which her writing is taught in a variety of pedagogical contexts, differently inflected by disciplinary conventions, the role of the course in undergraduate curricula, the student population, the type of school and its learning culture, and the geographic location of the institution. Contributors teach Yamashita's writing in Austria, Brazil, Japan, the People's Republic of China, Spain, Ukraine, and urban and rural locations in the United States. Survey participants are based at many other geographic locations. Pedagogical practices in specific geopolitical contexts may shift in certain or necessary ways for effective application in other contexts. At the same time, we encourage readers to attend to resonances as well as differences among teaching strategies in the many experiences and contexts described in contributor essays. Contributors have taught Yamashita's writing at four-year institutions of various sizes, at two-year colleges, and in high schools. Several contributors discuss teaching Yamashita's work in cross-listed courses, and a few include commentary on courses that simultaneously serve undergraduate and graduate curricula.

Part 2—indeed, the volume as a whole—is organized in a way that encourages pedagogical innovation with an eye to the future. Part 2 does not consolidate Yamashita's oeuvre under a single critical orientation or position it within a single area of literary studies, though the coeditors draw particular attention to the importance and influence of Yamashita's works in Asian American literary studies. Educators can use Yamashita's writing to help students comprehend the essential role in their own lives of the imagination and of writing, of literature and literary studies in the twenty-first century. To this end, as well as for goals outside the literary studies classroom, instructors and students may analyze recurring themes in Yamashita's writing, such as resource poverty and global income inequality; nationalism and neocolonialism; racial solidarity movements and multiethnic collisions; environmental degradation of the Anthropocene and emergent posthuman ecologies; transnational and other border crossings, especially racialized and gendered labor migration; and technoscientific capitalism and postindustrial biopolitics.

Essays are organized into sections by both topic and critical or theoretical approach, rather than by text or genre. This organization foregrounds the complexity of Yamashita's world-making and the breadth and depth of her topical concerns and encourages educators to be innovative in their inclusion of Yamashita's writing in their courses. At the beginning and close of each section, bridging essays provide paths into, out of, and across sections. These essays function as coherent transitions, but certainly other conversations may be discovered among and within sections.

The organization of contributor essays showcases Yamashita's category-resistant storytelling and addresses the challenges faced by instructors teaching her corpus. On the one hand, the complex sociocultural, political, and historical narration of Yamashita's fictional and nonfictional works can be daunting. On the other hand, such challenges contain almost limitless pedagogical potential. When read individually or in relation to other essays in the same section or to essays in different sections, any given essay offers educators valuable yet nonprescriptive direction regarding historical and social background at the local, regional, and global level. Additionally, the organization of part 2 encourages educators to examine Yamashita's aesthetic palette—her use of magical realism, postmodern narrative techniques, experimental performance, and other formal innovations—as arising organically and intelligibly from the particular story that Yamashita wishes to dramatize. Many contributors write about how best to engage students in meaningful discussions of Yamashita's dynamic use of literary techniques and genre, or her use of popular cultural mediums and iconography. Another challenge addressed by the essays in part 2 concerns the transnational circulation of Yamashita's oeuvre: How, for example, might an educator at a European university include *Brazil-Maru* or *Through the Arc of the Rain Forest* in an upper-division literature course? The topical organization across and beyond national and ethnic boundaries extracts thematically meaningful issues that invite educators and students alike to think and imagine in global dimensions. Finally, several essays recognize, either explicitly or implicitly, a pedagogical challenge presented by growing institutional constraints on the humanities—larger class sizes, shrinking numbers of tenure-stream faculty members, fewer majors, pressure to graduate students faster—leading instructors to devise compelling ways of teaching Yamashita's work in general education curricula and in many classrooms outside English and Asian American studies, in which students may not receive training in literary studies or in Asian American studies. The essays foreground the critical thinking, careful analysis, and compassion that a humanities education in general and the study of literature specifically develop; they innovatively introduce to students different methodological frameworks (ecocriticism and migration studies, for example) through which to approach Yamashita's writing.

Section 1 of part 2, titled "Histories and Interventions," focuses on teaching historical movements, historiography, and the narration of histories of marginalized peoples. Several of the essays in this section provide strategies for teaching *I Hotel*, given its sophisticated treatment of a specific historical event in the twentieth century.

Section 2, "Belonging and Nonbelonging," consists of essays on courses that introduce students to alternative ways of understanding social, cultural, and political membership, ways that include critiques of national citizenship and of prevailing definitions of community based on racial or ethnic identity.

Section 3, "Mapping Alternative Spaces," builds on the various meanings of *belonging* discussed in section 2 by discussing the deployment of Yamashita's writing in classrooms that deal with geocritical questions about neoliberal globalization. Essays in this section engage a range of topics—from employing Geographic Information Science software in a literary cartographic approach to teaching Yamashita's revision of the road narrative to using affect theory to explore Yamashita's production of narrative space.

Section 4, "New Transnationalisms and Ecocritical Approaches," addresses scalar facets of contemporary globalization—economic, political, cultural, and environmental. Yet each essay discusses the teaching of contemporary globalization from distinct historical, institutional, and cultural perspectives.

Additional Connections

Readers of this volume will recognize productive relations and tensions among essays both within and across sections. Essays are all individually instructive and thoughtful, and the many dialogues among them will surface according to how each reader engages the volume. While the contextualizing materials of part 1 are crucial, we also invite readers to dwell and mingle, to skip around and circle back, as they uncover the volume's pedagogical possibilities.

The "Histories and Interventions" section of part 2 illustrates the ways that each grouping of essays generates pedagogical issues, relations among methodological and interpretative frameworks, and productive tensions among essays. All the essays in this section direct students to the essential role of history, memory, and historiography in Yamashita's writing, including abiding questions of who gets to write histories, whose history is deemed worthy of being recorded, and the impact of history on the present and the future. These essays may also be read in productive tension with one another. For example, Caroline Kyungah Hong writes about using one of the ten novellas of *I Hotel* to introduce her students at the City University of New York to a crucial phase of Asian American history, the Asian American movement during the civil rights era; her aim is to reanimate the Asian American past for twenty-first-century students. Jolie Sheffer's essay offers a somewhat different perspective, describing the experience of teaching *I Hotel* as an exploration of the pitfalls of viewing history as teleology.

An example of a pair of bridging essays includes the final essay in the "Histories and Interventions" section, Wen Jin's "A Glimpse of the Global Sixties: Teaching *I Hotel* in China." Jin and her students at East China Normal University interrogate history and ethnic identity as notions that are subject to the malleability of memory and affective social affiliations. Jin's essay leads to Caroline Rody's essay "Yamashita's Novels and Contemporary Interethnic American Fiction," the first essay in the next section, "Belonging and Nonbelonging." Rody's course also grapples with change, particularly the rapid social, economic, and cultural changes of globalization. Through close readings of *Through the Arc of the Rain Forest* and *Tropic of Orange*, and in juxtaposition to one of Jin's pedagogical aims, Rody has her students consider ethnic identity and literature as no longer delimited by national discourses of membership. Instead, Rody encourages her students to see Yamashita's fiction as interweaving multiple group narratives on a global stage; these narratives consist of complex ethnic encounters through which characters invent unique blends of "interethnicity."

Reading Ikue Kina's essay in "Histories and Interventions" in relation to Rie Makino's contribution in "Belonging and Nonbelonging" is instructive for the ways in which provocative dialogue threads across sections. Both essays concern themselves with how best to introduce to students historical, literary, and cultural contexts of the United States; each essay also presents specific methodological and interpretative frameworks that help students appreciate Yamashita's stories and their focus on everyday reality. Both educators consider how normalized narratives of racialized nationalism erase their own problematic relation to minorities, in the case of Makino, or to the marginalized status of these minorities in their own homeland, in the case of Kina. In "Encountering Others within Ourselves: *Circle K Cycles* and Ethnic Identity in Okinawa," Kina discusses teaching her mostly Okinawan students the history of Japanese colonization through the methodological framework of postcolonial theory and critical race theory. Interestingly, in "*Brazil-Maru* and Ethnic Identities in the Japanese Classroom," Makino writes about offering her students at Nihon University in Tokyo a deeper understanding of immigrant literature of the United States that is crucial to Yamashita's corpus. She, too, encourages her mostly Japanese students to reflect critically on the hegemonic aspects of national belonging through a deeper analysis of racial and ethnic structuring in the United States.

Numerous interpretive relations exist among other contributor essays. Ana María Manzanas-Calvo's "Hospitality, Borders, and Spatial Politics in *I Hotel*" in section 2 complements Robin E. Field's "Troubling Boundaries and Beginnings with 'The Orange'" in section 3. Field's and Manzanas-Calvo's contributions are also in dialogue with the essay by Claudia Sadowski-Smith and Matthew Henry, "*Tropic of Orange* and the Genre of Climate Fiction," in section 4. These three essays ask students to consider border conditions or dangers. However, they can also be read in contrasting relation to other essays in section 4, such as Min Hyoung Song's "*Through the Arc of the Rain Forest* and Planetary Fiction," which asks students to consider the ethical virtues of crossing or rejecting geopolitical and conceptual borders when defying borders is undertaken from the perspective of planetarity.

While some contributors use Yamashita's works to illustrate specific methodological frameworks, others use her writing to complicate concerns within and between frameworks, but nearly all share a sort of symptomatic reading method. That is, most contributors read Yamashita's works as in some way formally reflective of or metonymically linked to social conditions, as well as epistemologically concerned with contemporary problems. Xiaojing Zhou's "A Material Ecocritical Approach to *Through the Arc of the Rain Forest*" immediately follows and pushes back against Nataliya Krynytska's "*Through the Arc of the Rain Forest*, Environmental Apocalypse, and Post-Soviet Allegory." While both are included in "New Transnationalisms and Ecocritical Approaches" and both use an ecocritical framework to interpret Yamashita's *Through the Arc of the Rain Forest*, Krynytska's pedagogy guides students toward a reading of the novel as environmental apocalypse that underscores the need for balance, harmony, diversity, caring, equality, and self-control. In this post-Soviet context, *Through the Arc* is a reinterpretation of biblical cycles of life and death and the Fall of Man as well as an allegory for the plastic pollution that is consigning human life to environmental denigration, or "slow violence" (Nixon). Zhou's material ecocritical approach to teaching the same novel is based on an ecological epistemology and ethics that together dismantle the notion of nature as merely inert material or background for human action or imagination. Zhou's framework undermines notions of agency defined by human intentionality or divine design. Further, there are tensions between Zhou's essay and Aimee Bahng's decolonial feminist approach in "Feminist Anticolonial Science (Fiction) Studies in the Rain Forest," which describes using *Through the Arc* to teach students the methods, theories, and concerns of feminist science and technology studies. These include both the history and the future of imperialist exploitation and neocolonial scientific discourse, including global finance capitalism.

Possible Alternative Reading Sequences

The coeditors recommend that instructors first read part 1, especially "Contexts," even though individual essays can be read out of sequence; for instance, an instructor planning to include *Anime Wong: Fictions of Performance* in a course on contemporary drama in the United States may decide to first read Josephine Lee's essay in part 2.

Readers might also consider those essays on teaching Yamashita's writing in lower-division, general education, or first-year composition courses. The coeditors include in this category Jamie Crosswhite's "The Critical Regionalism of *Tropic of Orange*" and Noelle Brada-Williams's "Teaching Yamashita's Works outside the Ethnic Studies Classroom," both in "Belonging and Nonbelonging." Other essays include those by Field, Anastasia Lin and John Dees, and Song, all in "Mapping Alternative Spaces," as well as T. Christine Jespersen and David Plante's essay in "New Transnationalisms and Ecocritical Approaches."

An alternative sequence is essays that describe a feminist lens for reading, focus on feminist and queer concerns, employ the feminist methodology of intersectionality, or discuss an issue such as gendered and racialized labor migration. In the section "Histories and Interventions," Hong's essay discusses teaching anew the debate between Maxine Hong Kingston and Frank Chin, typically cast as "a gender war," using one of *I Hotel*'s novellas. In the other three sections, essays that address feminist approaches or concerns include those by Lynn Mie Itagaki in "Belonging and Nonbelonging"; Field in "Mapping Alternative Spaces"; and Zhou, Sadowski-Smith and Henry, and Bahng in "New Transnationalisms and Ecocritical Approaches."

Readers might also choose to begin with essays that discuss a specific work, such as *I Hotel*, in terms of various methodological approaches—ecocriticism, transnationalism, or poststructuralism. Several essays that focus on *I Hotel* include those by Silvia Schultermandl and by Sheffer in "Histories and Interventions," and Manzanas-Calvo's essay in "Belonging and Nonbelonging."

Another grouping includes essays on the use of excerpts from Yamashita's novels, her memoir, and her shorter pieces. Essays in this category include Hong's and Kina's essays, as well as Ruth Hsu's "*Letters to Memory* in Hawai'i: Place, History, and National Identity" in "Histories and Interventions" and Delbim's, Field's, and Thoma's essays in "Mapping Alternative Spaces." Essays that discuss Yamashita's writing in juxtaposition to other literary texts and literary archives include Lee's in "Belonging and Nonbelonging"; Mallot's in "Mapping Alternative Spaces"; and Simal-González's and Krynytska's in "New Transnationalisms and Ecocritical Approaches."

Essays on the use of digital technology include Sheffer's "Many Endings, Many Beginnings: Alternative Histories of *I Hotel*" in "Histories and Interventions" and Lin and Dees's "*Tropic of Orange* as Palimpsest: A Literary Cartographic Approach" in "Mapping Alternative Spaces." Other teaching approaches described in this volume—given their topical focus on migration, the road, and toxic pollution—can conceivably incorporate the digital technology described in the essays by Sheffer and by Lin and Dees.

Essays that discuss teaching Yamashita alongside nonprint media, such as film and digitized archives or collections include those by Sheffer in "Histories and Interventions"; the essays by Lee and by Brada-Williams, who discusses her pedagogical approach to the course World Film and Literature in "Belonging and Nonbelonging"; Mallot in "Mapping Alternative Spaces"; and Zhou, Jespersen and Plante, and Bahng in "New Transnationalisms and Ecocritical Approaches."

HISTORIES AND INTERVENTIONS

"1971: Aiiieeeee! Hotel" and Asian American Literary History

Caroline Kyungah Hong

Karen Tei Yamashita's *I Hotel* brings to life a crucial decade in the Asian American movement (1968–77) with incredible breadth and depth. Centered around the I-Hotel in San Francisco and the struggle to save its tenants from eviction, Yamashita's historical fiction travels far and wide to reconstruct the movement's "complex architecture" (Yamashita, *I Hotel* 610). This essay focuses on teaching a vital part of this architecture—Asian American literary history—as reimagined in "1971: Aiiieeeee! Hotel," one of *I Hotel*'s ten novellas. Having taught *I Hotel* as Asian American literature, both in its entirety in graduate seminars geared toward English master's students and excerpted in upper-division undergraduate courses designed for English majors, I've found this novella effective for teaching a range of themes and issues—the relation of literature and culture to politics, questions of genre and the inextricability of form and content, the contested natures of histories and genealogies, intersectional analysis, and so on. Specifically, I discuss here how the novella represents a significant flash point in Asian American literary history that is especially instructive for students of Asian American and ethnic studies, as well as for students of literary and cultural studies more broadly.

The title of "1971: Aiiieeeee! Hotel" alludes to *Aiiieeeee! An Anthology of Asian-American Writers* (1974), edited by Frank Chin, Jeffery Paul Chan, Lawson Fusao Inada, and Shawn Hsu Wong. Among the first to try to define Asian American literature, the editors claimed "Aiiieeeee!" as a rallying cry of self-determination and righteous anger (Chin et al. vii). Unfortunately, they were quite rigid and narrow in defining this literature, excluding many ethnic groups, especially more recent immigrant communities and writers who differed from them politically, ideologically, and aesthetically. Not long after *Aiiieeeee!*'s publication, the mainstream success of Maxine Hong Kingston's *The Woman Warrior* (1976) was met by scathing attacks from the editors, especially Frank Chin, for allegedly "faking" Chinese culture and history,[1] catering to white audiences, and portraying Asian and Asian American men as sexist and emasculated. This marked the beginning of one of the formative controversies of Asian American studies. What began as an argument about the racial and gender politics of Asian American representation was reduced over time to a battle—dubbed the Chin-Kingston debate for short—between its two key figures and to a gender war.[2]

On one side were the *Aiiieeeee!* editors, purveyors of a heteromasculinist, cultural nationalist discourse, promoting an Asian American literature rooted in Chinese and Japanese heroic traditions. On the other side were feminist writers and critics who spoke out against the editors' violent, misogynistic, and homophobic rhetoric and exposed the limits of their literary project. When I teach the Chin-Kingston debate, I screen an eight-minute clip from Curtis Choy's documentary film *What's Wrong with Frank Chin?*, from the section titled "The Chinatown Cowboy Suffers the Woman Warrior," which includes dramatic readings of Chin's and Kingston's letters to each other, in order to convey the vitriol of this debate. We also do close readings of quotations from the *Aiiieeeee!* editors, such as passages from Chin and Chan's essay "Racist Love," to analyze both their trenchant critiques and their deeply problematic rhetoric.

After students have been introduced to this debate in Asian American literary history, we examine its representation in "1971: Aiiieeeee! Hotel," typically over the course of two class sessions. Through guided discussion, I focus primarily on how Yamashita remixes the Chin-Kingston debate in ways that are playful and parodic, that complicate the divisive controversy by simultaneously paying homage to and poking fun at both Chin and Kingston. I introduce students to this playful complexity by directing their attention to the cube net—a two-dimensional figure that can be folded into a three-dimensional cube—that opens each novella and outlines that particular "hotel." The cube nets encourage students to think in ways that are spatial, embodied, inhabited, and multi-angled—in other words, to think three-dimensionally. To that end, a useful exercise involves photocopying and cutting out the cube nets and having students assemble them in class, which allows students to see and touch the cube nets' three-dimensionality as we discuss them.

The cube nets frame the novellas by naming the settings, main characters, and major topics or themes of each novella. The cube net for "1971: Aiiieeeee! Hotel" locates the novella in 1971, during the "Tiao Yu Tai protest," in "Chinatown" and "Asian America"; the cube net also identifies the focus of this novella as "culture," specifically "arts" and "drag pastiche" (Yamashita, "1971" 223). Rather than take this information for granted, I push students to question each aspect of the cube net. For example, though the cube net names the 1971 Tiao

Yu Tai protest, the protest is not mentioned in this novella. It is, however, brought up in other novellas, such as "1968: Eye Hotel," and I ask students to consider what this might signify. Similarly, though the setting given is Chinatown, we note that the novella traverses different spaces, from San Francisco's Chinatown and Japantown to various towns up and down California's Central Valley. We talk about how we are both placed and displaced as readers, grounded in local spaces like the coffeehouse Il Piccolo and the nightclub Jigoku, yet still searching for the imagined spaces of "Asian America (where's that?)" (230, 232, 234). This discussion helps students recognize that the boundaries of each hotel are porous, that time and space are fluid and palimpsestic, and that these different histories are interconnected, even if the connections aren't obvious.

We also spend some time unpacking the term *drag pastiche*. I provide a definition and examples of drag and bring in a few quotations from Judith Butler's *Gender Trouble* to sketch her theory of performativity. I also define *pastiche* and ask students to brainstorm where in the novella we see drag or pastiche being practiced. Collectively we come up with a tentative definition for *drag pastiche*, connecting gender and racial performativity and artistic mimicry, and stressing how the term troubles notions of origins and authenticity. We talk about the eclectic forms that culture takes in the novella—from storytelling, drama, music, and dance to martial arts, silk-screening, and gardening—and how the novella itself enacts drag pastiche in its genre-bending and formal experimentation.

As I then shift our focus from the cube net to specific chapters, I organize our discussion around Yamashita's reworking of three facets of the Chin-Kingston debate—her depiction of Chin and Kingston as literary figures, her engagement with Asian heroic traditions, and her emphasis on doubles and duality. I first note that, despite being a pioneer of Asian American theater and early Asian American literary criticism, Frank Chin has been a contentious figure in Asian American literary circles for reasons we've already covered. We look at how Yamashita recuperates and honors Chin by making his origin story the inspiration for chapter 3, "Liang Shan Po, California," while also invoking Kingston by referring to Chin as "Tripmaster Monkey" (243), an allusion to Kingston's novel *Tripmaster Monkey* and its Chin-esque protagonist. We then discuss how Yamashita brings Chin and Kingston together explicitly in chapter 4, aptly titled "War and Peace." In undergraduate classes, when I'm pressed for time, I often excerpt and assign just this brief chapter, alongside materials relevant to the Chin-Kingston debate. Consisting of multiple pairs of illustrations of Chin and Kingston with pithy captions, this graphic chapter encourages considerations of form and content, and we spend a lot of time engaged in close readings of the drawings and captions as a class or in small groups. We analyze details like the writers' varied facial expressions and body language. We unpack the pairs of words that caption the images and discuss the significance of their order and progression. We talk about how the illustrations of Chin and Kingston are not placed consistently in the same order and how, even though these images are separated by blank space, the backgrounds for most of the paired portraits line up to suggest a continuous background. While Yamashita acknowledges their separation, calling attention to their gendered differences and politics, Chin and Kingston are drawn together and reconciled on the page, linked to each other as kin and to readers as literary ancestors. Though the pairings may suggest oppositional thinking, I underscore for students how the subtle details we've discussed challenge the binary logic that pits these two figures against each other. In that vein, I also point out to students that the novella, ostensibly set in 1971, actually predates *Aiiieeeee!* and the Chin-Kingston debate. This chapter is thus anachronistic, again blurring the boundaries of history and time, and offering the possibility of alternative Asian American literary histories.

We also consider how Yamashita further reframes the Chin-Kingston debate by playing with one of the *Aiiieeeee!* editors' major preoccupations—Asian heroic tradition as a source for "real" Asian American writing (Chan et al. xv). We discuss chapter 1, titled "Outlaws," which tells the story of Iron Ox, one of the legendary 108 outlaws from the fourteenth-century Chinese classical novel *Water Margin* (Yamashita, "1971" 223–28). I provide a brief background on the outlaws, sometimes showing the trailer for the 1972 film adaptation, *The Water Margin*, and mention that this is the same outlaw fictionalized in Chin's novel *Donald Duk*. I then ask students to identify other outlaw figures in the novella. In chapter 2, "Theater of the Double Ax," a short play that dramatizes the *Aiiieeeee!* editors' critiques, the outlaws are undercover as Chinese immigrants who came through Angel Island, and the narrator assures, "baby, I'm by your side, questing the same quest for the Asian outlaw" (229). Chapter 3 tells the story of a Chinese American boy who will "one day . . . become the great outlaw leader" (237). In chapter 8, "Dance," Sandy Hu, one of *I Hotel*'s multiple protagonists, choreographs an embodied performance of myth and history that in part retells the story of outlaw Li K'wei, or Iron Ox (278–84). In chapter 9, "Yellow Peril," the band Yellow Pearl performs a folk song about Li K'wei (285–87).

As we discuss these outlaws, I ask students to contemplate how Yamashita reimagines this martial, masculinist heroic tradition. For example, we discuss how most of the novella is narrated from a queer female perspective. The confident and funny narrator is revealed to be Lady Murasaki, a bisexual Asian American woman writer and performer who was raised by drag queens, and whose name is an allusion to another outlaw figure, Murasaki Shikibu, a Japanese lady-in-waiting during the Heian period (794–1185) and the author of *The Tale of Genji*. I call attention to the fact that Lady Murasaki gets the first and final words of the novella, and it is her talk story that underpins this hotel.[3] When she says, "How I love my outlaws" (223), the possessive determiner indicates her agency and ownership of this tradition. And she too "will always be an outlaw" (223). Here, I typically bring in a couple quotations from bell hooks's *Outlaw Culture* and Kate Bornstein's *Gender Outlaw* to help students think about the outlaw as a transgressive figure and to connect the outlaw trope back to our working definition of *drag pastiche*. We discuss how Yamashita heeds the *Aiiieeeee!* editors' call to respect this heroic tradition and, at the same time, transforms that tradition—for example, by reinserting women and queer characters into these legends and histories.

We also discuss how Yamashita portrays the artists and activists of the Asian American movement as outlaw figures and inheritors of this heroic tradition whose origins and adventures are as mythical and exciting as those of the 108 outlaws. Characters like the poet Jack Sung and the "outlaw literati" (234), the writers and performers Sandy Hu and Lady Murasaki, and the musician Gerald K. Li are not divorced from the era's political struggles, and art and culture are shown to be an integral part of the revolution. This is made especially clear in chapter 5, "Sax and Violence," which cuts back and forth between a nightclub where Gerald plays his two saxophones and an encounter he has with S. I. Hayakawa, the president of San Francisco State College during the 1968–69 student strikes for ethnic studies and against the Vietnam War, the longest college strike in the history of the United States, led by the Third World Liberation Front and the Black Student Union (251–61). In class, I often supplement our discussion of this chapter with videos of local news coverage (see "San Francisco State Strike Collection") or clips from documentaries like *On Strike! (at SF State)*, *"The Turning Point,"* and *On Strike! Ethnic Studies, 1969–1999*. I also bring up recent examples of student strikes, such as the 2016 hunger strikes to fund San Francisco State University's College of Ethnic Studies by students calling themselves the Third World Liberation Front 2016 (see F. Wang). This allows students to see how indebted we are to those student strikes, as well as to think about the university as another critical site of the Asian American movement, connected to both political resistance and cultural production.

Finally, I introduce students to one more critique from the *Aiiieeeee!* editors—their rejection of Asian American duality. In the preface to *Aiiieeeee!* the editors write, "We have been encouraged to believe . . . that we are either Asian (Chinese or Japanese) or American (white), or are measurably both. This myth of being either/or and the equally goofy concept of the dual personality haunted our lobes while our rejection by both Asia and white America proved we were neither one nor the other. Nor were we half and half or more one than the other" (Chin et al. viii). As a class or in small groups, we examine the plethora of doubles and duality in this novella in order to understand how Yamashita addresses this critique. Chapter 2 features *"five sets of Siamese twins"* (229), pairs of pop cultural icons—Charlie Chan and #1 Son, Mao and Confucius, Green Hornet and Kato, Captain Kirk and Mr. Zulu, Fu Manchu and Dragon Lady—who embody the hyphenated Asian American identity that the *Aiiieeeee!* editors disavow (231). In chapter 6, the satirical comic strip titled "Chiquita Banana," there is another set of conjoined twins—Suzie Wong and Anna May Wong, the submissive Lotus Blossom and the femme fatale Dragon Lady, one fictional and one real, who are two sides of the same stereotypical coin (262–64). And Chin and Kingston, of course, are figured as doubles, as foils, in chapter 4. We see the most doubles in the chapters featuring Gerald, with his twin saxophones, especially chapter 7, "Doppelgangsters." Gerald encounters several of his doubles—the white imposter Gerald K. Li (266), the Chinese American who is "the Gerald K. Li of Stockton" (269), and the bartender who is "his actual doppelganger" (271). As the narrator asks in the chapter's opening, "In the case of the doppelganger, who is who? Who is real and who is fake?" (265). I ask students to theorize why Yamashita incorporates so many doubles. We discuss how, once again, Yamashita manages to acknowledge and respect the *Aiiieeeee!* editors' critiques while also moving beyond them, deconstructing their fixations with duality and binary thinking through a proliferation of doubles. In exploding reductive binaries—Asian/American, man/woman, real/fake, and so on—Yamashita exchanges double consciousness for an expansive and inclusive multiplicity of consciousnesses.

Later, usually on the final exam, I require students to reflect in writing on the novella's relation to the Chin-Kingston debate. The prompt asks them, in one or two paragraphs and using concrete examples from a specific chapter, to discuss how Yamashita engages and reimagines the controversy. Students should be able to articulate how this debate that began over forty years ago continues to haunt Asian American literature and culture to this day. Teaching this literary history through Yamashita's *I Hotel* not only provides important contexts for studying the Asian American movement but also helps students think about the stakes and futures of Asian American literary and cultural practices in the twenty-first century.

NOTES

[1] See, for example, Chin's "Come All Ye Asian American Writers of the Real and the Fake."

[2] For more on the Chin-Kingston debate, see, for example, Cheung; Chu, "Authoring Subjects"; Kang; Elaine H. Kim; Robert G. Lee, "*Woman Warrior*"; and Wenxin Li.

[3] *Talk story* is an idiom in Hawai'i that is now widely accepted in the field of Asian American literary studies to mean the storytelling that takes place among friends, family, and close-knit communities.

Palimpsestuous Historiographies of Asian American Activism in *I Hotel*

Silvia Schultermandl

In Karen Tei Yamashita's *I Hotel*, multiple strands of political activism intersect at the physical location of the International Hotel in San Francisco's Manilatown: the Black Panther and Yellow Power movements; the Japan Town Collective; the Third World Liberation Front coming out of the University of California, Berkeley; the Mexican farmworker movement; and the Native American occupation of Alcatraz. Yamashita expounds on these intersections in the novel's afterword:

> I began to create a structure for the project. I found my research was scattered, scattered across political affinities, ethnicities, artistic pursuits—difficult to coalesce into any one storyline or historic chronology. The people I spoke with had definitely been in the movement but oftentimes had no idea what others had been doing. Their ideas and lives often intersected, but their ideologies were cast in diverse directions. Their choices took different trajectories, but everyone was there, really *there*. (610)

This comment reveals the complexity of casting the intersecting trajectories of Asian American history into a linear narrative. It also raises the question of how to depict this multitude of intersecting historical lineages and how to render them aesthetically tangible for readers.

In my teaching of Yamashita's *I Hotel*, I employ Sarah Dillon's idea of the palimpsest to guide students as they think about the processes of historicization and their representation in literature. In her groundbreaking study, *The Palimpsest: Literature, Criticism, Theory*, Dillon defines the palimpsest as "an involuted phenomenon where otherwise unrelated texts are involved and entangled, intricately interwoven, interrupting and inhabiting each other" (4). Yamashita's novel arranges this palimpsestuous history in the form of ten loosely connected novellas. The novel's paratext evokes this history as ten origami boxes, each one of identical dimensions but with different information about the time, place, protagonists, and themes of the individual novellas.

These origami boxes are central to one of two class meetings that I allocate to Yamashita's novel. I use these boxes to highlight the constructed nature of historiography, the transnational patterns of social movements, and the importance of alternatives to prevalent master narratives. I do so in my course Transnational American Literature, a junior seminar in American studies that fulfills the literature requirement for our English and American studies majors. The course is writing intensive and includes short in-class writing assignments, a writing journal, and a fifteen-page research paper in several draft versions. The course is designed to help students gain proficiency in writing about aesthetic-political phenomena. Dillon's idea of palimpsestuous history is crucial to the pedagogy I employ, and I also rely on Shelley Fisher Fishkin's assertion that much of American literature depicts "the inside and outside, domestic and foreign, national and international, as interpenetrating," a claim that challenges the notion of the nation-state as possessing naturally impermeable political borders (21). Selections from *Transnational Asian American Literature: Sites and Transits*, edited by Shirley Geok-lin Lim and colleagues, are especially helpful to students as they tackle the many representations in *I Hotel* of the transnationalism undergirding the formation of Asian American panethnic identity in the 1960s and 1970s.[1]

I encourage students to think about Asian American history as part of global history and to consider the transnational as a heuristic through which to challenge essentialist and nationalist discourses of ethnicity, gender, and class. At the same time, I want students to appreciate Yamashita's aesthetic renderings of this palimpsestuous historiography. In small groups, we discuss the various literary forms she incorporates and the overall effect of Yamashita's avant-garde style. I guide students in thinking about the incorporation within the narrative of plays, poems, and graphic novels. Some chapters offer loosely bound assemblages of historical documentation and fictional narration; I have students locate where fictional narrative and quotations from historical figures are interlaced; I also ask them to reflect on the thematic purpose of transgressions of genre boundaries and the use of intermediality in *I Hotel*.

By the time we attend to questions of aesthetics in Yamashita's novel, students have already studied Fishkin's 2004 Presidential Address to the American Studies Association and have read Henry James's *Daisy Miller*, Jonathan Safran Foer's *Extremely Loud and Incredibly Close*, and Cristina García's *Monkey Hunting*. Students use these texts to examine the ways that narrative perspective can give expression to converging historical events, to global experiences of colonialism and liberalism, and to the slippery nature of the taxonomic category of American identity when filtered through a transnational context. Yamashita's *I Hotel* is the final text they encounter in this course.

Dillon's notion of the palimpsest encourages students to think critically about historiographical projects in general and about their aesthetic representation in literature, film, photography, performance, and conceptual art (see Oishi 132–43). In terms of *I Hotel*, Dillon's concept of the palimpsest invites students to disentangle the semantic and geographic dimensions of America by drawing attention to the rich scholarship on a postnational and deterritorialized field. I ask students to consider the information on the origami boxes presented at the beginning of each novella as a means of apprehending the constructed nature of historiography. Each of the ten cubes represents one of the ten novellas. The six squares that make up each cube feature the dates of the individual chapters, names of the protagonists, dominant themes, and references to place names or fictional settings. The field on time contains references to the years 1968 to 1977 and to a historical event, such as the strike of the Third World Liberation Front in 1968 and 1969 or Bruce Lee's death in 1973. One class assignment asks students to research the various people, events, and concepts featured on these cubes and to elaborate on the thematic, historical, geographic, and ideological connections among them. The completion of this assignment in preparation for our in-class discussion of Yamashita's novel makes students cognizant of the key concepts that shaped Asian American activism of the 1960s and 1970s.

While in their two-dimensional representation in the novel's paratext the origami boxes are assembled in a chronological fashion, their three-dimensional shape begs the question of how to arrange them. When students cut out, assemble, and stack them into the shape of a tower evoking the physical contours of the International Hotel, they quickly realize that there is no one way to configure them. In class, we call these cubes the building blocks of Asian American activism and think of their playful arrangement as a reflection on the constructed nature of historiography. I ask students to experiment with creating alternative narratives by deciding which sides of the cubes touch; this task gets students to ponder which aspects of history are foregrounded and which are not. Like the Möbius strip instructions in the paratext of John Barth's short story collection *Lost in the Funhouse*, this activity of arranging the cubes into various possible orders helps students think about historiography as a constructed narrative, one among various possible others.

This task becomes especially complex since the individual novellas themselves connect various historical moments. These historical cross-references index what Wai Chee Dimock terms "deep time," a concept I introduce by means of Dimock's "The Planetary Dead: Margaret Fuller, Ancient Egypt, Italian Revolution." With the help of Dimock's example, I explain the relation between places and times beyond immediate shared historical moments and how this results in an elongation of any specific time period. Yamashita's novel transgresses the time frame of the years 1968 to 1977 and addresses prior political events. For instance, her novella "1972: Inter-National Hotel" looks back at the Bandung Conference of 1955 and at Malcom X's reference to the conference in his 1963 speech, "Message to the Grass Roots." That these are not only randomly concurring but also interconnected aspects of the history of liberation of people of Asian and African descent becomes clear through the umbrella terms Yamashita uses in the origami box presented as part of the novella's paratext: the theme here is "class, nation & race, aphorism" and the locations are "Manilatown" and the "Third World" as its international counterpart.

I have students report on other aesthetic renderings through which Yamashita calls attention to this palimpsestuous relation among the various aspects of "the movement" (610). The choice to conceptualize the novel as a collection of ten novellas, rather than as a novel consisting of ten chapters, has to do with Yamashita's appreciation of the novella as a narrative form that can capture the "many layers of activities and events that were happening at the same time" (Yamashita, "Interview" [Porte]). The titles of the novellas foreground this intended connection: they include either homophones—such as in "1968: Eye Hotel," "1970: 'I' Hotel," "1971: Aiiieeeee! Hotel," "1976: Ai Hotel," and the eponymous "1977:

I-Hotel"—or variants of I-Hotel—in "1969: I Spy Hotel," "1972: Inter-National Hotel," "1973: Int'l Hotel," "1974: I-Migrant Hotel," and "1975: Internationale Hotel," for example. This seriality, which depends on repetition and variation, presents different versions of the same concept, conceived of and thus spelled in a manner that highlights the concept's different symbolic meaning depending on the political context depicted in the individual novellas. For instance, while "1970: 'I' Hotel" attends to questions of the taxonomic category of Asian American identity, "1971: Aiiieeeee! Hotel" refers to the formation of an Asian American literary tradition. Here, the assignment asks students to interpret the titles and to contextualize them by researching the historical and cultural phenomena these titles imply. In doing so, students familiarize themselves with the political agendas of the various intersecting movements depicted in *I Hotel*.

My course provides students with opportunities to think about the counterhegemonic narratives of American identity, history, and society. For students of English and American studies at the Austrian university where I teach, this poses two challenges: one has to do with canonicity, the other with literary studies methodologies. To be eligible to take my course, students need to pass two consecutive introductory courses that introduce them to genre theories, American literary history, formalist literary analysis, and critique. While they probe the historical and political contexts of the poems, plays, novels, short stories, and autobiographies covered in these courses, they are unlikely to have debated the construction of archival knowledges. Here is precisely where my course intervenes: it calls on students to critically engage with the constructed nature of historiography by asking them to apply their knowledge of literary studies methodologies to depictions of complex historical phenomena. This leads to an understanding that both historiography and American identity are dynamic categories that depend on representational practices. The connections Yamashita unearths between Asian American history and other emancipatory movements both in and beyond the United States prompt students to think in equally connected terms about the place of Asian American literature within American literature and world literature. While we do not fully pursue these links, we theorize the interconnectedness of these various phenomena using Fishkin's idea of the transnational turn in order to account for the broadening of the field and the expansion of the taxonomic category of what counts as American literature.

Moreover, we discuss the role of archival knowledge in the shaping of historiographical narratives. After students' hands-on experiments with the building blocks of Asian American activism, I have students read Michel Foucault's and Diane Taylor's respective critiques of archival practices. Students can appreciate Foucault's insistence that archives are governed by rules and that "since it is from within these rules that we speak," the "modes of appearance," the "forms of existence and coexistence," and the "system of accumulation, historicity, and disappearance" of these rules are always also implicated in the constitution of every archive (130). After Foucault, we discuss Taylor's distinction between the archive and the repertoire, and I ask students to think further about the hidden or largely uncovered palimpsestuous historiographies embedded within written archives that cannot account for performative or dynamic cultural processes. In their analyses of Yamashita's aesthetics, students also benefit from Taylor's definition of the repertoire as that which "enacts embodied memory: performances, gestures, orality, movement, dance, singing—in short, all those acts usually thought of as ephemeral, nonreproducible knowledge" (20).

Departing from the idea that hegemonic power structures form the basis of archival knowledge production (Helton et al.), we link Yamashita's novel to chapter 1 of Lisa Lowe's *The Intimacies of Four Continents* (1–41). Like Yamashita's novel, Lowe's study connects seemingly disparate events by reading across the established categories through which the Great Britain National Archives record the history of late-eighteenth- and early-nineteenth-century British imperialism. Lowe argues that because documents are grouped either geographically (East Asia, Africa, America, the West Indies) or thematically (law, commerce, material objects, people, geography), distinct categories that reproduce prevalent hegemonies have formed. Reading across these categories uncovers the hidden connections among various histories that have been categorized by region or by topics such as commerce. Lowe's first chapter elucidates how the importation of Chinese indentured laborers was intricately linked to the receding control of the slave economy in the Caribbean, on whose remittances the formation of an English middle class depended.

Returning to the experiment with the building blocks of Asian American activism, I ask students to write a two-page journal entry about the function of Yamashita's paratext by linking it to Lowe's project of reading the Great Britain National Archives against the grain. This is, I admit, a complex assignment, one that asks students to establish a link between Yamashita's aesthetic in *I Hotel* and Lowe's critical conceptualization of palimpsestuous historiographies. It is, however, a rich opportunity to reflect on the transnational and its potential to generate new insights in American studies.

NOTE

[1] See, for example, Lim et al., *Translational Asian American Literature* 1–17.

Many Endings, Many Beginnings: Alternative Histories of *I Hotel*

Jolie A. Sheffer

> But she said: I have anticipated the end of the story without first imparting the beginning. Knowing the story's end does not necessarily imply completion or knowledge, for if many endings are possible, so also are many beginnings. History may proceed sequentially or, as they say, must proceed sequentially, but stories may turn and turn again—the knowing end kissing the innocent beginning, the innocent end kissing the knowing beginning.
>
> —Karen Tei Yamashita, *I Hotel*

Karen Tei Yamashita's fictions are innovative and experimental, reimagining familiar literary tropes expected of so-called ethnic or multicultural, or more specifically Asian American, writers. *I Hotel*, Yamashita's magnum opus, features a canvas so large that it literally cannot be contained: the book opens with a two-dimensional diagram illustrating each of its ten interlocking novellas as a three-dimensional cube with its own dramatis personae, central location, key historical event, and literary and cultural form. The work thus builds its story both vertically, as imagined stories of the eponymous building, and horizontally, in the sequential order of conventional history. Yamashita's novel refuses to let any one character speak for an entire ethnic group, gender, social movement, or generation. The result is a Tower of Babel, a chorus or cacophony of different voices. This creates profound challenges for students accustomed to learning about minority history and identity through the exemplary ethnic American novel or memoir—typically a bildungsroman that embodies some aspect of a minority group's history in the arc of a single character's life. Students have trouble orienting themselves to *I Hotel*'s multitudinous narrative structure; they feel overwhelmed by the number of characters, plots, intertextual references, and allusions to Asian American history and literature. After teaching this text several times, I now focus on Yamashita's critical engagement with teleological master narratives of the 1960s and her (re)centering of Asian American communities and contributions. This attention to history and historical narrativization makes clear Yamashita's intervention, formally and thematically, in mainstream narratives of the 1960s.

Reframing the 1960s

I teach *I Hotel* in the context of recent popular texts, television series, and films about the 1960s, such as Robert Zemeckis's Academy Award-winning film *Forrest Gump*, Matthew Weiner's prestigious television show *Mad Men*, and Kathryn Stockett's best-selling novel *The Help* and its popular film adaptation (Taylor). We discuss the ways in which these and other fictionalized representations of the 1960s frequently fall into a cultural memory trap of assuming history is inevitable. Moreover, fictions of the 1960s are particularly likely to reduce the era to a few linear narratives—from youthful idealism about community, cooperation, peace, and interracial solidarity to world-weary cynicism about capitalism, racism, and selfishness. Both fictional and nonfictional accounts of the era tend to reify the master narrative that divides "the good early period from the supposed insanity of the late sixties," when the peaceful tactics of the civil rights movement curdled into the violence of the Black Power movement, multiracial coalitions dissolved into factions, the peace and love of Woodstock degenerated into drug-fueled violence at Altamont, and the collective "we" of the hippie generation transformed into the selfishness of the so-called me generation (Breines 529). But such retrospective readings of the 1960s overwhelmingly come from white male activists with a particular take on, and stake in, the coalitional politics of the era. This familiar, teleological narrative is a kind of mythology that operates around the contributions of white people. As Glenn Omatsu explains, "while white male leaders saw the year as marking the decline of the movement, 1968 for Asian Americans was a year of birth. It marked the beginning of the San Francisco State strike and all that followed" (168). This notion of rebirth is central to rethinking historical narratives of the 1960s, and it is foundational to Yamashita's refusal either to sentimentalize or demonize the past in *I Hotel*. At the level of form and theme, *I Hotel* rejects overly familiar and linear interpretations of history, highlighting the very different shape history might take when focused on Asian American people and their contributions.

By beginning *I Hotel* in 1968 in San Francisco, Yamashita recenters the temporality and geography of the 1960s around Asian American political organizing. Moreover, Yamashita repeatedly highlights how humans impose order and meaning through art, literature, and other narrative forms. As a whole, *I Hotel* demands that its readers recognize the many present tenses of the 1960s. The result is both an imaginative record of—and an alternative version of—history that puts readers in the perpetual now; nothing is inevitable as it is happening—it only appears so in retrospective narratives. This antiteleological approach echoes Michael André Bernstein's description of "sideshadowing" (as opposed to foreshadowing) as a technique for showing "multiple alternatives existing in a potential space and ready to be brought, by the quickening of imagination or desire, out of the shadows and into the light of formal expression" (7).

Rejecting the familiar stereotype of the post-1968 period as defined solely by chaos, destruction, and the devolution of idealism, Yamashita depicts the decade between the Third World Liberation Front strike at San Francisco State University and the demolition of the International Hotel in downtown San Francisco in 1977 as an era of ongoing collaboration and conflict and community, love and loss and reconciliation, birth and death and renewal. The I-Hotel is the locus for demonstrating that social movements are as complicated as humanity itself, and that our versions of this history are far too neat and simplistic to capture the dynamism of the era and its activists. Like the diagram of an unfolded take-out box on its inside cover, *I Hotel* maintains both a two-dimensional sense of history moving forward in time and a three-dimensional sense of expansiveness, a sense of history as open, unfolding, and full of possibilities.

I urge my students to read Olivia Wang's lines in this essay's epigraph as a warning from Yamashita that our ingrained habits of reading retrospectively and prospectively are fictions, not facts. Once a naive and idealistic young activist, Olivia sees the world differently as a wife and mother diagnosed with terminal cancer. But her new sense of time is no more true (or false) than her youthful one was. The novel repeatedly suggests there were myriad paths not taken. For every moment of interethnic solidarity or romantic consummation, Yamashita provides examples of internecine conflict, death, and dissolution. And, conversely, every ending is also a beginning, an opportunity for new social arrangements, alliances, and narratives. Thus, I urge students to think about how Yamashita's deeply researched novel rejects conventional historical narrativization. The following small group, in-class activity (which could, alternatively, be given as an individual assignment prompt for a paper or online discussion board post) gets students to consider the many what-ifs that Yamashita explores. As part of this activity, I provide questions for discussing Yamashita's contribution to reconsiderations of the long 1960s.

Activity

I divide students into groups, and each group is responsible for discussing one of *I Hotel*'s ten novellas. This still requires synthesizing multiple chapters with different characters, points of view, plots, and narrative styles. Given the scope and scale of the novel, instructors could easily assign multiple groups to the same novella and get distinct answers, depending on which characters and events draw each group's attention. After completing this exercise, students are left with a much clearer sense of Yamashita's purpose and of her contributions to narratives of the era and to Asian American literature and history.

I ask each group to respond to the following prompts and questions as these relate to the main characters and events in the novella, and to point out relevant passages for close reading:

Identify key moments of connection between characters or coalition-building among social movements. Who or what is being aligned? What is their common ground?

Discuss how the novella illustrates and complicates the adage that "the personal is political." How do characters connect with each other and with collective action? Is it through romance, friendship, a parent-child relationship, or some other affective tie?

What role does art or literature play in developing these bonds? in shaping narratives about the movement? What is gained and lost in the transformation of experience into art, literature, and narrative?

Identify key moments of separation, when personal or political alliances end. Is this necessarily a failure of the social movement(s)? Why or why not?

How does the novella broaden conventional, teleological understandings of history? Consider characters, point of view, genre, and so on.

What familiar, mainstream narrative(s) of the 1960s is the novella in conversation with? In what ways does Yamashita seem to be directly responding to, rejecting, or reifying the master narrative(s)? How does Yamashita complicate or contradict conventional representations of the period?

Below is an example of some of the issues students might raise in the first novella, "1968: Eye Hotel," based on my own teaching notes. In providing extended answers to the assignment prompt, I hope to give instructors concrete tools for teaching this complex text. Students could also use the material that follows as a sample response to guide them as they complete the exercise for the remaining nine novellas.

Sample Response to the Activity

In "1968: Eye Hotel," Yamashita begins with a conventional ending—the death of Paul's father. Deliberately countering the expected teleology that tells a story from birth to death, "Eye Hotel"—and the novel as a whole—treats death as (just) another story's beginning. Indeed, it is because of this death that Paul comes to better understand and appreciate his recently deceased father and to learn more about his long-gone mother. In addition, Paul grows close to Chen and Edward, in the process learning about Chinese culture, literature, history, tradition, and politics. All three men are connected by reading, writing, and revolution.

The personal and the political are inextricable, as the lessons Paul learns from history, literature, and his parents' own activist and artistic pasts spur him to get involved with the burgeoning Asian American movement and the San Francisco State protests. Edmund and Chen visit China, confronting the new political narratives in their native country. Domestic and international events are constantly in dialogue with one another. Yamashita intercuts intimate moments between these men with important events occurring in other geographies and temporalities, such as the war in Vietnam; the assassination of Martin Luther King, Jr., in Memphis; the detention of Chinese immigrants at Angel Island; and so on.

Yamashita establishes Edmund's death as *the* crucial event in the lives of Chen and Paul: "So maybe there's this moment. It's different for everyone, but it's pivotal. It's the moment . . . everything is changed forever. You can never see life the same way again" (91). But a few pages later, the narration complicates and contradicts this statement, now arguing that "Although the pivotal moment theory might work for some, it might be overblown. As time drags on other events step up to the plate, and one begins to wonder why any fork in the road presented the less traveled option" (95). With regard to Paul and Chen, we learn that "maybe you couldn't exactly compare pivotal moments, but rather a single desire that united the two men: the desire to write" (95). In these lines, Yamashita makes clear that history and literature both require narrative, and that narratives give artificial shape to our lives. Appropriately for a novella about writers and poets, Yamashita echoes Robert Frost's poem "The Road Less Traveled" and its oft-overlooked criticism of memory as a tool for renarrating the past to create a false sense of inevitability. The novella thus cautions its readers against looking for life-changing moments. While Edmund's death is senseless and tragic, it can't be read as a failure of the movement or as the single cause of the fraying of Chen and Paul's friendship. Yamashita insists that history is lived at human scale, which means that coalitions develop or collapse on the intimate plane of relationships. This is not a failure of the movement, but rather a simple reality of human experience. The personal is political, but politics are lived and enacted by individual people, not by abstractions.

The novella expands most versions of history by creating a much larger sense of interrelatedness among generations, social movements, individuals, and geographies. While the narrative moves forward in time, Paul also goes backward in time as he learns more from Chen about his parents' youth. In profound ways, the novella situates Asian American history, traditions, and experience as foundational rather than tangential to the social movements of the 1960s; it doesn't explain everything for readers but presumes or expects a kind of insider knowledge. If you don't get all the references, it's up to you to figure them out. Yamashita doesn't translate these experiences for white or younger audiences.

There are several different master narratives of the 1960s that this novella seems to complicate. "Eye Hotel" rejects the conventional story of the 1960s as defined by the generational divide. Paul's dad, like Chen, isn't a dour individual that Paul must symbolically kill off in order to live his own life. His father was a committed Marxist, which creates a sense of continuity with Paul's growing activism. In addition, Yamashita reminds readers that sexual liberty was not a new phenomenon, as Chen was romantically involved with both men and women long before the present-tense events of the novella. The end of the novella is not the end, but more like a stage in the ceaseless, dialectical struggle for community, creativity, and belonging.

With this activity I aim to help students find patterns within this complex text about a complicated period of history, without reverting to either prospective or retrospective versions of history. By highlighting the misrepresentations of both nostalgia and cynicism, *I Hotel* serves as an important work of historical fiction, cultural memory, and counter-memory. Yamashita's novel shows that the past was not destined to turn out any particular way, nor is the future guaranteed. As such, it is an important text for helping students consider the narratives we choose to tell, and the stakes each narrator has in that story.

Encountering Others within Ourselves: *Circle K Cycles* and Ethnic Identity in Okinawa

Ikue Kina

In the fall semester of 2016, I taught Karen Tei Yamashita's *Circle K Cycles* in a small seminar, Studies in American Literature, at the University of the Ryukyus for juniors and seniors majoring in English. Most of the twelve students in the course assumed that this book by a third-generation Japanese American writer would be about wartime imprisonment. My students were surprised by Yamashita's use of both documentary and fictional styles, such as the journal entries gleaned from her monthly postings on the *Cafe Creole* website and written during her six-month stay in Japan in 1997, her essays, and the short stories based on research into *Nikkei* Brazilian communities in Japan. Though my students understood that *Nikkei*, people of Japanese descent, lived all over the world and spoke languages other than Japanese, *Circle K Cycles*'s multilingual juxtaposition of English, Japanese, and Portuguese confused students; one of them even questioned, "Is this book still a work of American literature?" Similarly, the Japanese language, society, and culture depicted from Yamashita's viewpoint—as both an insider and outsider in relation to Japanese and Japanese Brazilian communities—seemed simultaneously strange and familiar to students. Set in Japan—our country—and written about our society—Japan—in our language—Japanese—*Circle K Cycles* deconstructed students' preconceived image of Japanese American literature in several ways.

My pedagogical goal in teaching *Circle K Cycles* was for students to experience empathy for others by transforming stories that seem unconnected to their lives—their stories—into shared stories, stories of others' lives that students might come to see as connected to their own lives. Before teaching this course, I did not think achieving this goal would be difficult. Like me, most students were Okinawan, a community that had been historically treated as an exotic other in Japanese society and had sent the largest number of emigrants before World War II to such places as Hawai'i, Brazil, Argentina, Bolivia, and Peru. I expected that Yamashita's stories about Japanese Brazilian *dekasegi*, a Japanese word for short-term laborers, would resonate easily with my Okinawan students, due to their historically marginalized status in relation to Japanese society. My assumption did not turn out to be correct as I found that college students were unfamiliar with the historical background of the Okinawan community. Okinawan people of my generation or older would have no difficulty associating the hardship endured by Japanese Brazilian *dekasegi* with that of Okinawan immigrants since they were weaned on stories of how, throughout most of its history as a colonial outpost and later as part of the country of Japan, Okinawa has been plagued with poverty, which eventually led many Okinawans to leave the country. My students, who were born in the late 1990s, had not felt themselves othered by the Japanese; moreover, stories of Okinawan immigrants remained vague, and students thought that stories of the past had nothing to do with them. Therefore, my pedagogical challenge was not only cross-cultural but also cross-generational.

Circle K Cycles contains stories that allow students to understand the hardships and feelings that the Okinawan community—students' ancestors in the case of my students—would have experienced as immigrants in other countries. I assigned each student a ten- to fifteen-minute oral report every week on contexts that were important for understanding the novel, on topics such as Yamashita's biography, Japanese immigrants in Brazil, and Okinawan immigrants abroad. My students were gradually able to perceive themselves as the other—that is, they were able to relate the stories of the *dekasegi* to the stories of their ancestors and to their own stories as Okinawans in Japanese society.

Imagining Others

The course in which I taught *Circle K Cycles* was an upper-level course for English majors, and thus an English as a second language course, focusing on community and communal sensibility and sustainability. The community under consideration was a contemporary ethical, historical, and cultural construct especially valid in the contemporary society of the United States, a community that emphasized collaboration and collectiveness over competition and individualism. Using key terms such as *community*, *place*, *environment*, *race*, *gender*, *class*, and *other*, this course introduced students to a postmodern sense of community while urging them to pay attention to how issues of race, gender, and class help create a specific sense of community in American culture and society.

Sandra Cisneros's *The House on Mango Street*, the text students read prior to *Circle K Cycles*, explores the societal marginalization of Mexican immigrants in the United States. This novel helped students understand that in the United States, a community is constituted in sociohistorical terms by constructs of race, class, culture, and gender. While *The House on Mango Street*'s poignant vignettes enabled students to understand the racially, culturally, and economically marginalized status of the Mexican diaspora in the United States, students did not seem to feel any particular intimacy with the characters, whom they felt had nothing to do with their lives in Japan or in Okinawa. Students perceived *Circle K Cycles*, which depicts the lives of Japanese Brazilians in Japan, as more pertinent to their community. For this reason, *Circle K Cycles* inspired students to tell their stories through others' stories.

Reading assignments encouraged students to confront Yamashita's critique of Japanese society and to look reflexively at the stories of their own lives. Students realized they were both critic and object of critique. For instance, when students read Yamashita's account of the many Japanese Brazilian laborers who were brought to Japan through a Japanese government program that "allow[ed] nisei and sansei to acquire visas to perform unskilled labor" (*Circle K Cycles* 13), students expressed discomfort about the Japanese government's decision to replace "non-Japanese foreign workers with the more familiar faces of Japanese descendants" because they were expected to "integrate more easily into Japanese life and society" (18). To encourage students' awareness that this was a form of racism, I asked questions such as the following: What is the expectation behind the Japanese government's decision to issue work visas exclusively to immigrants of Japanese descent? Is that expectation appropriate? Are Japanese Brazilians really the same as Japanese? Many students didn't feel it was right that race should be the determining factor in obtaining a visa; at the same time, however, some admitted they would feel more comfortable working with people who "look Japanese." The story of Zé Maria Fukuyama in the chapter titled "Thee Marias" especially impressed students as it taught them about the inhumane working environment experienced by the *dekasegi* from the perspectives of the *dekasegi* themselves (33–43). It made students sensitive to questions of social justice; they expressed shock at the economic injustice and social marginalization that Japanese Brazilian immigrant laborers face in Japan. I asked them what they had learned from these stories. One student expressed concern that language barriers might keep these workers from understanding safety instructions, which could lead to injuries. Yamashita's narrative viewpoint, though her narrative maintains an emotional distance from the characters depicted, led students to react against the Japanese government and society. It also increased their understanding of the social injustice endured daily by the *dekasegi*.

The story "What If Miss Nikkei Were God(ess)?" also engaged students intellectually and emotionally (19–28). Yamashita's depiction of Miss Hamamatsu helped students link the condition of Japanese Brazilian immigrant workers to the sense of disabling confinement in Cisneros's portrayal of the Mexican American community in *The House on Mango Street*. Students made the connection that, in both communities, people left home in search of a new home in a new community. The new place, however, did not necessarily welcome them; they had difficulty not only taking part in the existing community but also forming a new community of their own. In *Circle K Cycles*, a young, beautiful Japanese Brazilian girl could end up engaging in illegal work in "her electronic prison" with no promise for the future (28). As a "representative beauty at the local disco" in the Brazilian community in Hamamatsu, Miss Hamamatsu, a mixed-race perfect beauty with a Japanese mother and a Brazilian father, lives in a small room surrounded by video recorders that she uses to produce bootleg copies (19). Her mental life, however, consists of a narrowly constructed type of romantic fantasy that exists only in the world of film and TV drama.

One student expressed a mixture of sympathy for the *dekasegi* and anger at the Japanese government's insensitive treatment of immigrant workers that continue to be seen as others within Japanese society. Many students felt empathy for Miss Hamamatsu, often adopting a feminist perspective in their reading of Jorginho, a fellow *dekasegi* Brazilian, as a representative of the Brazilian men responsible for trying to take advantage of the youth and beauty of Miss Hamamatsu; students also hoped for some resolution to the story in which, for instance, the protagonist might leave the immigrant community for a better future. Yamashita's story, however, betrays readers' sentimentalism and ends with descriptions of Miss Hamamatsu as she awakens from the dream world and hurries "to push all the play/record buttons," while Jorginho never leaves his fantasy "to worship" her as "Miss Nikkei" or "the best of both worlds": the Japanese and Brazilian societies (28).

This sense of confinement with no hope for the future also permeates the stories of the two children José and Iara—whose name onomatopoetically mimics the sound "iya-da," a Japanese word meaning "no," or "I refuse" (Yamashita, Interview)—in the story "Hantai (the Opposite)" (87–98). The reality that children of *dekasegi* are bullied at school by Japanese children is easy for readers to imagine. What readers might not expect, however, is the separation between adults' and children's worlds in the Japanese Brazilian immigrant community. Children's real emotions, which are hidden in other stories that center on adults, and in particular on the mothers' experiences of their daily struggles and affairs as *dekasegi*, are suddenly revealed at the end of "Hantai" when Joji, an adult friend of Iara's family, finally stands up for José and Iara and yells at the Japanese children who bully them:

> Iara was surprised to see Joji so angry. She had never seen him like this. It was really amazing. She wanted to cheer and jump up and down. Finally someone had come to save José and her. As the boys left, ashamed, she ran up to Joji and hugged him fiercely. (97)

The story tells of *dekasegi* who are affected not only by their present life but also by their future—that is, by a concern for their children's education and cultural adaptation. For Iara and José, however, the most pressing issue is their present, everyday life in Japan: Iara's concern is to make sure that José makes it home without getting lost; José is preoccupied by thoughts of figuring out the way home, not in Japan but in Brazil, where he would not have to deal with the everyday bullies at school. The present exists not only for the adults but for their children as well.

Saudade: A Clue to Cross-Cultural Empathy

Toward the end of reading *Circle K Cycles*, we discussed *saudade* as the key Brazilian Portuguese term that describes the life of immigrants and the process of forming a community. *Saudade* means something like "longing, homesickness, nostalgia," but students noted that Yamashita's stories were neither sentimental nor nostalgic, and thus that *Circle K Cycles* redefines conventional understandings of the term (135). In other words, *Circle K Cycles* focuses more on the immigrant family's present than on the past or the future. *Saudade* is the concept that connects the *dekasegi*'s past, present, and future, enabling a process in which present *dekasegi* communities might envision future communities in Japan:

> Saudade, as a collective memory of a premodern past, stands in the way of embracing order and progress and official histories and is perhaps antimodern in its improvisation of a song or intimate poem, an enchanted invocation to stay the inevitable passage of time. Saudade links the past to the present and lives in the magical reality of daily life. (136)

Saudade, which connects the past and the present and creates a future for the community in a new location, does exist in the present of the stories of *dekasegi* people. Yamashita's idea of *saudade* could be "dangerous," as it might also be associated with colonialism (Yamashita, Interview)—which resulted in "the blood and guts spilled" in contact with the unknown others in the new place—and with the reconstruction of one's home driven by colonialist desire (*Circle K Cycles* 136). However, to my students, *saudade* enabled a positive understanding of people who were relocated or dislocated: *saudade*, as Yamashita writes, "must be killed to belong, to make a home, to realize desire" (136). Students finally came to understand that their Okinawan immigrant ancestors might have extinguished or sustained *saudade* to make a community in the new place, surviving every moment of the present in struggle and sorrow until these struggles and sorrows became memories, part of the past.

Circle K Cycles teaches my students about American culture, Japanese Americans, Japanese immigrants within and outside Japan, and, interestingly enough, about themselves in their relationship with those in their own community who are seen as others. The stories in *Circle K Cycles* helped students imagine the stories of others who, toward the end of the course, were no longer others in the minds of students. I was not able, at least in the fall semester of 2016, to include in our class discussions Yamashita's expression of *Nikkei* as a transformative Japanese identity that refuses an essentialist idea of authenticity. However, I believe that students discovered aspects of themselves that they had not been aware of before the course and that they will use as they continue to explore what it means to be Okinawan in this age of globalization.

Letters to Memory in Hawai'i: Place, History, and National Identity

Ruth Y. Hsu

Letters to Memory, published in September 2017, is Karen Tei Yamashita's seventh prose narrative. I taught the book in an upper-division undergraduate elective course on Asian American literature offered through the English department in the spring 2018 semester at the University of Hawai'i, Mānoa, the flagship campus of the ten-campus state university system. In this course I asked students to analyze texts on the reading list in terms of place and identity, belonging and nonbelonging. I have also included *Letters to Memory* on the reading list of a graduate course, Asian American Literary and Cultural Studies. I have always designed both the undergraduate and graduate Asian American literature courses with the following considerations in mind: the degree of preparedness of students who enroll in these courses in terms of both knowledge of the field and as readers and students of literature; the diverse demographics and experiential profile of students, which affect profoundly the ways they interpret and evaluate what they read; and the pedagogical aims of an ethnic literature class that must survive in an educational system that adjusts to its corporate demands by consistently devaluing and marginalizing literature and other humanities subjects. In this sense, the University of Hawai'i, the only public university on this island chain in the middle of the Pacific, is aligned with the diminishing role of the humanities in education in the United States of the past three decades.

This essay focuses on teaching *Letters to Memory* in the upper-division undergraduate course. The undergraduate course is an elective that fulfills a literature and culture requirement in the English major; and even though the course is on an annual rotation, it is one of over a couple dozen English courses from which students can choose each semester. Because this course is writing intensive and exposes students to a diversity of Asian American literature, it can also help students satisfy general education or core requirements. Students who enroll in this course—and this was accurate for the spring 2018 offering—uniformly have had little or no prior exposure to Asian American writing, except perhaps to Maxine Hong Kingston's *The Woman Warrior* in high school; their knowledge of Asian American history is similarly sparse. The course attracts students who are curious about noncanonical—that is, non-Western—literature. Occasionally, however, someone enters the class wanting to read Murasaki Shikibu's *The Tale of Genji*; I point out on the first day of instruction the differences between Asian and Asian American literatures.

Because Hawai'i is home to large concentrations of United States military, military personnel or their spouses are in my classes, and students come not only from Hawai'i but also from the mainland United States. The students whom I teach are Asian American (both local students born and raised in Hawaiʻi and those from the mainland United States), white, mixed race, and, infrequently, Pacific Islander. However, such categories fail to account for the diversity of backgrounds and perspectives of the individuals who enroll in this course. Students read and interpret the literature differently, according to their worldview, their educational history, and their perspectives, which are cumulative yet constantly evolving consequences of their racial, ethnic, sexual, gendered, and national subjectivities.

I devoted four to five class sessions to *Letters to Memory*. Prior to the first session, I asked students to read the *Encyclopedia Britannica* entry on Japanese American internment ("Japanese American Internment"). An alternative to the *Encyclopedia Britannica* is *Densho* (densho.org/), a digital archive that chronicles the World War II incarceration of Japanese Americans. In previous iterations of this course, I have assigned Joy Kogawa's *Obasan* or Seiichi Higashide's *Adios to Tears: The Memoirs of a Japanese-Peruvian Internee in U.S. Concentration Camps*. Students typically express surprise or shock at how little they learned in high school about the internment camps in the United States and Canada, or about what happened to immigrant Japanese communities in South America. The students in the spring 2018 class were no different. I gave a short presentation on Yamashita's *Brazil-Maru* and talked briefly about the importance of redefining the field of Asian American studies from one that concentrates solely on the continental landmass constituted by the forty-eight states to one that is hemispheric and transpacific, a reorientation represented by Yamashita's corpus.[1]

Besides the *Britannica* entry on internment, I asked the class to explore the *Library of Congress* website featuring photographs by Ansel Adams of Japanese American internment at Manzanar (www.loc.gov/collections/ansel-adams-manzanar). Next time I offer this course, I will instead use Dorothea Lange's photographs, which can be accessed on the *National Archives* website (www.archives.gov/news/articles/japanese-internment-75th-anniversary). When I taught *Letters to Memory* in the spring of 2018, I scheduled five- to ten-minute presentations by two groups of students, with two students in each group, on the *Britannica* entry and on Adams's photography, respectively. After the presentations, I asked students to freewrite for fifteen minutes in class on the following questions: Why do you think you reacted the way you did when you found out about the World War II internment of 120,000 Japanese Americans? What expectations about historical facts gave rise to your reaction? I have students continue to write on these questions after class as part of a homework assignment; they then upload their responses to a forum site. We spend about ten to fifteen minutes of the second class discussing their responses. It was helpful to anchor this discussion of a historical event as distant in time and space as World War II and of the importance of having access to a more complete version of a collective history by connecting to this discussion students' personal experiences of being kept in the dark by their family or close friends. Were there negative consequences that resulted from gaps in their apprehension of past events, gaps in knowledge that they were only able to retrieve retroactively? How did they discover the truth from family or friends? How substantially did the student's truth differ from the truth experienced by their family or friends?

My goal in asking students to reflect on the central story in *Letters to Memory* through their own experiences was to humanize the fictionalized characters in Yamashita's book and to underscore the reach of history into everyday living in the present. I asked students if there had been internment camps in Hawai'i after Pearl Harbor had been attacked. Local students volunteered that their parents had spoken about the camps here, but students had not learned about them in their K–12 schooling. I referred students to numerous resources located at the library of the University of Hawai'i, Mānoa, then played a brief National Public Radio news story from 2015 about the Honouliuli internment camp near Pearl Harbor (Solomon).[2] The discussion that followed considered why more local Japanese Americans had not been targeted and arrested like the Japanese Americans on the mainland had been. One student remarked that all Japanese Americans had been uprooted; deported, in a sense; and told that they were not really American and that they did not belong in the place where they had lived for many decades. I noted that a group of people had been defined by their racial identity, and that those with power decided whether that group was American. The topic of how historically distant events affect the present returned when, later in the course, we read Viet Thanh Nguyen's *The Sympathizer* and Serith Peou's *Corpse Watching*; as with *Letters to Memory*, I assigned historical material to provide students with information on the American War in Indochina as well as material on the current circumstances of Vietnamese Americans and Cambodian Americans.

In the third and fourth sessions, we undertook close readings of sections of *Letters to Memory*. I had one group of students give a presentation on Yamashita's depictions of the family's preparations to depart for camp, and another group of students presented on the experiences of Yamashita's father, John, while the family was incarcerated. During the fourth session, another group of students led a discussion of John Yamashita's attempts to reintegrate after his release and the efforts of his church on his behalf. I steered the discussions in sessions three and four in two directions: one direction asked students to attend to the narrator's tone; the other direction had them reframe Japanese American internment through the lens of Toni Morrison's *The Origin of Others*. From Morrison's book I assigned the chapters "Romancing Slavery" (1–17), "Narrating the Other" (75–91), and "The Foreigner's Home" (93–111). I anchored class discussions particularly in the last paragraph of "Narrating the Other": Morrison writes, "Narrating fiction provides a controlled wilderness, an opportunity to be and to become the Other. The stranger. With sympathy, clarity, and the risk of self-examination. In this iteration, for me the author, Beloved, the girl, the haunter, is the ultimate Other, clamoring, forever clamoring for a kiss" (91). These chapters and other passages from *The Origin of Others* connected our discussions of assigned readings and topics, including R. Zamora Linmark's *Leche*, Hanya Yanagihara's *The People in the Trees*, Maya Lin and the controversy over the Vietnam Veterans Memorial, Gene Luen Yang's *American Born Chinese*, and a selection from Yang's *Boxers and Saints*. The story of Maya Lin was an opportunity for the class to delve into the history of United States policy toward and military interventions in Indochina. Information on this history is available on the *Maya Lin Studio* website (www.mayalin.com/).

The Origin of Others gave students a lexicon with which they could apprehend and describe the targeting of Japanese Americans at the outset of World War II. In a forum post assignment on *Letters to Memory* and *The Origin of Others*, students wrote that Japanese Americans, as a group, were made out to be the other, the perpetual stranger and alien, and that it was the physical characteristics of this group—in fact, of Asians as a whole—that led to this perception. Students noted, moreover, that the basis of this perception was different from that of other immigrant groups. During the third session, I had students write about their own family backgrounds or the family background of a close friend if they were not comfortable divulging personal information. A few students recounted family lore about their grandparents or great grandparents coming from Europe. These students had been told that their immigrant forebears endured harsh circumstances and that their family's situation in the United States took decades to gradually improve. Because this section of the course was on a memoir about Japanese American internment during WWII—and not on narratives of European immigrants to the United States and the difficulties they faced—I referred students to examples of Euro-American literature on immigration. Then I brought class discussion to the idea of the model minority and how in the case of the Japanese Americans in *Letters to Memory*, their ordinary (read: respectable) lives failed to prevent their othering by the majority discourse. One student who was a member of the armed forces said that it was important to learn not to stand out in any way in the military, but that it was difficult to blend in as a racial minority. Another student pointed out that if one is the perpetual alien, one never believes that one can belong, even if one's family has been in the United States for many generations. There was general agreement that this meant that the popular belief that Asian Americans are a model and assimilated minority may be a stereotype. It was important for me to point out to students that othering is a paradigmatic operation of classification and not a consequence of group or individual behavior or action in the arenas of politics, cultural production, or economic relations.

In the fourth session, students responding to the group presentation on John Yamashita's post-camp life pointed out that although he carried on, he did not seem to belong at his church. One student offered her opinion that John could not forget that he had been imprisoned. I asked students where they felt they most belonged. The army member said that he was an army brat and that his happiest memories were in the Philippines even though his family hailed from Arizona. But other students spoke in terms that indicated that their sense of belonging was tied to physical places, and not always to feeling happy and secure in those places. I asked students if it was fair to say that our sense of belonging is often strongly associated with the place or places that we recall being happy places for us. A sense of belonging, then, has much to do with our memories of places. The students who were born and grew up in Hawai'i seemed to find this articulation of belonging to be true. In Hawai'i, the belief in place-based identity and belonging is deeply held by many.

In the fourth session, I also steered discussion toward Yamashita's diverse tonal palette, which is one of the distinctive traits of her oeuvre. I asked students to identify instances of irony, sarcasm, bemusement, skepticism, matter-of-factness, and so on. The topic of tone pushed students to pay close attention to word choice—that is, to the artifice of writing. More important, students began to consider the metanarrative-like quality of this memoir—that is, the ways in which the narrative calls attention to its own storytelling. The topic of tone in Yamashita's work led to a discussion of her use of interlocutors such as Ishi, Homer, Vyasa, Ananda, and Qohelet; letters; government documents; a family tree; a bibliography; photographs; lists of titles of sermons; newspaper clippings; a sermon; and the exasperated narrator's one-sided debate with Ruth Benedict over her Orientalizing study of the Japanese character.[3] Students had been assigned to read Terry Hong's review of *Letters to Memory* to help them make sense of Yamashita's use of interlocutors and multigenre storytelling. Additionally, we discussed William Zinsser's introduction to *Inventing the Truth: The Art and Craft of Memoir* and Nancy K. Miller's "The Entangled Self: Genre Bondage in the Age of the Memoir." Students initially took *Letters to Memory* to be wholly factual and unalloyed truth, but after reading Zinsser's introduction and Miller's essay, and after our discussion of the various tones adopted throughout Yamashita's book, some students began to entertain the idea that *Letters to Memory* contained not the truth but rather multiple perspectives about the internment and its legacy. Some of Yamashita's family members resisted expressing in a forthright manner their views about their internment. Yamashita's memoir, then, I point out, consists of the conscious performance of gaps in knowing. Could Yamashita's use of various tones and prose genres, I ask, be a wry commentary on the project of memorializing—its necessity as well as its impossibility? Even more fundamental, how is memory depicted in *Letters to Memory*?[4]

For the final class on *Letters to Memory*, I had five groups research and prepare brief remarks on the narrative function of the "epistolary muses" (167): Homer, Ishi, Vyasa, Ananda, and Qohelet. Due to the packed class schedule, we were able to spend time discussing only the first two: Homer, the name of the itinerant bard of the *Iliad* and the *Odyssey* as well as a historian and philosopher colleague of Yamashita's at the University of California, Santa Cruz; and Ishi, who in 1911 emerged from hiding as the last member of the Yahi tribe in Sacramento Valley, and whose name is the Japanese word for *stone*. The other three "epistolary muses" frame the remaining sections of Yamashita's *Letters*—the "Letters to Love" (Vyasa), the "Letters to Death" (Ananda), and the "Letters to Laughter" (Qohelet)—and are as consequential to the storytelling as Homer is to the "Letters to Poverty" and Ishi to the "Letters to Modernity." As the narrator of *Letters to Memory*, Yamashita interrogates—through her interlocutors—the story of Japanese American internment and the part played by the rest of America in bringing about that internment.

NOTES

[1] In a graduate class, a brief discussion of *Circle K Cycles* would be helpful in extending the discussion of Yamashita's writing as crucial in broadening the scope of Asian American literature to include literature set beyond the political and geographic borders of the United States.

[2] Seventeen sites throughout the islands were used to incarcerate approximately four thousand Japanese nationals and Japanese Americans.

[3] Ruth Benedict (1887–1947) was an American anthropologist whose research focused primarily on Native American myths. She studied under Franz Boas and was a colleague of Margret Mead. Benedict believed that "it is the 'personality,' the particular complex of traits and attitudes, of a culture that defines the individuals within it as successes, misfits, or outcasts" ("Ruth Benedict"). This position foregrounded cultural traits and attitudes rather than race or genetics in explaining patterns of national behavior. Benedict wrote *The Chrysanthemum and the Sword* (1946) using newspaper clippings and films about Japan and with the help of Japanese literature. Her most well-known formulation on Japan was that it was a culture of shame. With the rise of postcolonial studies after World War II, *The Chrysanthemum and the Sword* has been criticized for its essentializing and totalizing representations of Japanese culture and people.

[4] The issue of tone resurfaced later in relation to the construction of the narrator and protagonist in Nguyen's *The Sympathizer*. In a graduate class, selections from Marc Augé's *Oblivion* could be assigned as a way to theorize the construction of memory.

A Glimpse of the Global Sixties: Teaching *I Hotel* in China

Wen Jin

Teaching Karen Tei Yamashita's *I Hotel* was an inspiring experience, though at first it seemed implausible that it could be taught at a university in China since the novel is packed with historical references and written in a style informed by African American Vernacular English. The freewheeling style initially deterred some of my students, but ultimately, *I Hotel* proved to be a timely work that spoke intimately to the present cultural and political concerns of many Chinese students. In many ways, the novel challenged what my Chinese students know about the United States of the 1960s. They are easily exposed to such commercialized icons as Bob Dylan, touted by the media as symbols of the enduring impact of a revolutionary era, but they have little idea about youth gangs and radical organizations in Chinatowns in the United States during the same era. As the narrator of Carlos Fuentes's quintessentially sixties novel *Diana: The Goddess Who Hunts Alone* puts it, the authorities of liberal regimes are adept at harnessing revolutionary energy by creating "an enemy they can count on" (198). This statement is as true today as it was in the 1960s. As we experience a global turn toward conservatism (in the sense of a renunciation of the radical idea of egalitarianism), various false gods of rebellion are manufactured to claim public attention. It is increasingly important to read a novel like Yamashita's *I Hotel* now, not because we can see images of a real revolution in its pages, but to push our students and ourselves to think hard about how to enable forces of opposition to evade the ruses of power.

This is all to say that to teach an obviously political novel like *I Hotel* presents a rewarding challenge in today's China. The book illustrates the revolutionary energy that burst forth in Asian American communities in the decade between 1968 and 1978. It portrays, among many other characters, a young Chinese American, Paul Lin, who—in "1968: Eye Hotel," the first of the ten novellas that make up *I Hotel*—is orphaned when his poet father passes away. Paul Lin can be seen as a Chinese American version of Oedipa, the female protagonist of Thomas Pynchon's famed *The Crying of Lot 49*. Like Paul Lin, Oedipa is in search of an inheritable cultural legacy and spectral flickers of a mysterious underground network. The difference is that the network in which Lin finds himself consists of flesh and blood figures who invariably pay a heavy cost for being part of it. While Pynchon avoids providing a direct account of WASTE, a force of opposition with a purposeful vagueness to it, Yamashita takes up the difficult task of giving bodies and faces to the idea of the underground, without turning away from the vices, foibles, and flawed humanity of those who inhabit it. It is useful to situate the novel in the context of postmodern American writings that portray the political tensions of the 1960s in allegorical terms, not just Pynchon's

Lot 49 but also Donald Barthelme's "Indian Uprising," where the narrator suddenly finds himself at the end of the story a war criminal standing trial, and Philip K. Dick's *The Man in the High Castle*, which depicts an alternative United States. The 1960s was indeed shot through with war fought on multiple fronts.

I was extremely pleased to have had opportunities in recent years to teach a course on the global sixties at universities in Shanghai. I designed it as a special topics course that could be tailored to both undergraduate and graduate levels. I taught it once in fall 2015 at Fudan University (Special Topics in American Literature: The Sixties), and then again as a graduate seminar in fall 2016 at my current institution, East China Normal University (Special Topics in World Literature: The 1960s and Postmodernism). I plan to teach the global sixties course more often at the undergraduate level. Undergraduates in China tend to be quite literate in English, so they can be expected to digest one or two of the ten novellas of *I Hotel*. The novellas on 1968, 1969, and 1970 proved to be a suitable portion. "1968: Eye Hotel" worked well as a hook, as it introduces Paul Lin, a Chinatown kid in his senior year of high school faced with the sudden death of his father, a loss compared to being attacked by land mines on the battlefields of the Vietnam War. The novella also contains a fascinating account of Chinese American returnees landing in the midst of the Cultural Revolution and a harrowing section on the death of a promising young Chinese American writer in a gang conflict.

"1969: I Spy Hotel" adopts the form of a documentary script in narrating the student strikes at San Francisco State University and the University of California, Berkeley. Individual initiatives on the part of minority faculty members to recognize and correct inequality turned out to be ineffectual and vulnerable, so protests by various racial minority organizations insisting on reform of the college curriculum became a necessary response. It was useful to point out to students how leaving out the real names of the racial minority movements sets the novel apart from a documentary. This omission also allowed me to point out that Yamashita may have wanted to imply that there is a continued criminal stigma associated with radical activities.

"1970: 'I' Hotel" captures the frenetic events that took place beyond college campuses. The novella traces the emergence of Chinatown Maoist organizations, especially the Red Guard Party, in 1969, on the back of long, deep-seated connections between Asian and black youth groups. As the novella puts it, the "black-yellow connections" are "deeper than" the Mao influences (201). Whole groups of girls from the Chinatown youth gang Legitimate Way (Leway) dated Black Panther men and the two groups regularly hung out on Jackson Street in the Chinatown pool hall. The Red Guard Party, formed in San Francisco's Chinatown, was one of a host of burgeoning radical Asian American organizations, including Wei Min She and I Wor Kuen out of New York's Chinatown, which then merged with the Red Guard Party and other organizations like the Union of Democratic Filipinos and the Japan Town Collective. These groups were in turn embedded in a loose, chaotic network of global and local countercultures. *I Hotel* shows that youth or hippie culture affected Asian Americans just as much—they were "saved by Janis Joplin as much as by Mao" (194). The members of these radical Asian American organizations actively pursued ways of reconnecting with the Red East and the Third World. Ministers of the Black Panthers and the Red Guard Party visited Moscow and China as part of the US Peoples' Anti-Imperialist Delegation to the Red East. Richard Aoki, a radical Asian American activist and a member of the Black Panthers, remained in the United States, giving rousing speeches about liberating domestic prisoners. In class, we discuss images and documents related to the Red Guard Party and I Wor Kuen from a range of print and digitized materials, including an essay from *Giant Robot* magazine on the Yellow Power movement (Nakamura and Wong). My students either showed remarkable interest or scoffed silently at this history, their perceptions colored by their jaundiced feelings about how the Cultural Revolution panned out. It became important to help students see that a historical novel like *I Hotel* should not be saddled with the task of offering an official evaluation of radical social movements of the 1960s. All it reasonably may be expected to do is populate a broadly sketched historical context with credible, convincing individuals, endowing abstract history with embodied voices. The legacy of a political movement is not determined by its ideological thrust, but by how its texture—the detailed events and specific individuals involved in it—is reconstructed and conveyed to the reader.

That said, I must hasten to add that my students are not necessarily ignorant of the history of 1960s social movements. They have traveled extensively. One of them recalled his experiences while visiting the University at Albany, State University of New York, as an exchange student. He met an elderly woman at a Sino-American friendship party who was introduced to him as having been a famous Maoist activist in the 1960s. The student impersonated the proud demeanor of the activist, as I in turn recalled my own similar encounters in Revolution Books in New York City, dedicated to the ideals of the Revolutionary Communist Party of the United States. For a moment, the radical 1960s seemed to come alive for us.

In teaching "1969: I Spy Hotel" and "1970" 'I' Hotel," I emphasized the pervasive tensions between radical activism on college campuses and community activism. A quirky, short video, available for free on *Vimeo*, helps summarize these tensions in a nutshell. "Betty, a Red Guard" features a conversation between Betty, clad in imitation Maoist apparel, and her friend, obviously an academic. Betty's friend urges her to go to a symposium advocating the founding of an ethnic studies program, but Betty dismisses this notion, making it clear that she has no use for Band-Aid solutions like curriculum reform or panethnic alliance. She believes in protests and engages academics only for the sake of solidarity. The tussle between these two visions of change, as presented in the video, remain at a deadlock, leaving no room for a real alternative.

I Hotel does, however, provide viable alternatives. In the novel, radical politics is not about choosing between words and actions, but about searching for possible ways of effecting an integration of the two. Reading and engaging a novel like *I Hotel* seriously promises just such an integration. Everyday practices, embodied practices, and structures of feeling are provinces of literary representations, and they might well be the areas that need to be changed if we are to imagine more sinuous approaches to radical politics. When students are guided through the process of reading a novel such as *I Hotel*, this process can initiate change that knowledge or protest alone would not accomplish. What does *I Hotel* tell us about the ways in which narrative changes our minds and feelings? How does narrative instigate action? How does narrative, in other words, wield its power over the reader? Proceeding from these questions, I helped students see that the novel can actually serve as a commentary on how reading or talking about radical social movements can be a life-changing event that gestures toward political change by bringing about intimate, personal transformation.

On the one hand, the novel presents its own narrative as a linguistic embodiment of the panethnic alliance that emerged in the 1960s and 1970s. By bringing together loosely connected minority groups and individuals of different ethnicities—the Chinese communists and nationalists, the Manongs (first-generation Filipino Americans) and younger Pinoy (second-generation Filipino American) students, the Native Americans occupying Alcatraz, an America-born Japanese American painter and communist troublemaker and his white wife—who share the cause of fighting the eviction of the hotel's Manong residents, the novel imitates the tactic of the Third World Liberation Front.

On the other hand, Yamashita clearly suggests that the heavy-handed use of narrative as a tactic of mobilization is flawed. The novel is presented not as a well-wrought world, constructed once and for all, but as a continuous unfolding that infects readers at a deep visceral level, bringing before us "the great gathering of bodies" fortified by "passion and stubborn hope" (605). The novel lays bare its own drive toward evoking secret, embodied memories. This revelation comes toward the end of the text:

> But as we tumble into the gravesite left by its [the I-Hotel's] demolition, perhaps our memory may flutter skyward, the City exploding and swirling away from our center—Manilatown, Chinatown, Japantown—spinning away with phallic impressions of Pyramid and Coit, spanning bridges of Wharf, Bay, and Golden Gate, dotted islands of Alcatraz and Angel, Victorians in soft undulating pastels, the rich green of Park and the endless blue of away and away and away. (605)

I encouraged students to discuss the imagery of dispersal and diffusion that fills this passage. "Secret memory" rises up from the debris of the I-Hotel, embarks on uncertain journeys, and waits to crystalize somewhere else (605). These memories fly over the landscape of LA, and here the syntax gets murky: it's unclear whether it is the "exploding" city or the "secret memory" that span bridges and islands (605). The two now become mutually constitutive. Bits of the exploding "center" of the city (Manilatown, Chinatown, Japantown, etc.) are carried by the private memories that keep moving out and away from San Francisco (605). Just like these memories that will rebuild the missing center of the city in some uncertain form, the reader is left to imagine what this scenario entails, gaining a moment of autonomy from the narrative, which now becomes something that the reader doesn't just consume but helps complete.

A literary narrative like *I Hotel*, while it provides a linguistic parallel to the real historical event, remains self-referential. It refers to the arduous, uncertain process of constructing a grand narrative that nevertheless preserves individual experiences at an almost granular level. The novel directs the reader ideologically, but also incites visceral, affective responses that allow the reader to reconstruct concrete historical experiences. At the very end of the novel, Yamashita reinterprets the sign of the International Hotel to clarify what it means to remember meaningfully. The hotel now becomes a symbol of "a larger memory," "a great layered and labyrinthine, now imagined, international hotel of many rooms" (605). The reimagined hotel will have to make room for private memories and imaginings of different shapes.

This, I believe, is what *I Hotel* has to offer a course on the global sixties taught in contemporary China. If the 1960s is an era constituted by "[t]he repercussions of this microcosm of cumulation, convergence, and series of reinforcing contingencies" (Marwick 43), novels from or set in this era, like *I Hotel*, are shaped just like those contingent microcosms. The novel does not give us definitions of a real revolution, but an opportunity for us all to offer a deeply felt and inventive response. It is up to all of us to dream as we read along, and to wait with cunning for a new constellation of miracles.

BELONGING AND NONBELONGING

Yamashita's Novels and Contemporary Interethnic American Fiction

Caroline Rody

When I first began teaching the novels of Karen Tei Yamashita at the University of Virginia, I tended to place them at the end of an Asian American fiction survey, an upper-level English course open to all students. Given that the University of Virginia has a minor but no major in Asian American studies and no ethnic studies program, this kind of course has been important in introducing and legitimizing ethnic literatures in the curriculum. On the syllabi of such courses, Yamashita's early, major novels *Through the Arc of the Rain Forest* and *Tropic of Orange* nicely served to close the term by blowing open in several ways the paradigm of the Asian American text that the course had delivered: these novels offer narrative modes that break from conventional realism into an eccentric magical realism, settings that are dramatically transnational rather than mostly based in the United States, language and discourse that mixes English with other languages and conventional narrative prose with poetry and the lingo of mass cultural media, a genre that is not tragic or comic but both, and a political vision that is progressive, even prophetic, while also persistently, mordantly ironic about human social possibility.

In this essay, I will focus on a further departure from convention, an especially teachable aspect of Yamashita's dazzling, unruly texts: their interethnic characterization. Yamashita's deep investment in multi- as opposed to monoethnic scenarios overturns the most conventional notion of an Asian American text—that is, a text centered on conflict between immigrant parents and their American-born children. Yamashita's fictions instead send multiple protagonists out of the house, so to speak, and into complex, unanticipated matrices of multiethnic encounter.

Indeed, Yamashita's work was crucial for me as I developed the paradigm of interethnicity for my 2009 book, *The Interethnic Imagination: Roots and Passages in Contemporary Asian American Fiction*. I argued there that in the wake of all that is changing in local and global cultures, in patterns of world migration, settlement, and communications, what we have long thought of as ethnic literature is becoming interethnic literature. Still rooted in narratives of tradition and memory, ethnic literatures share an urge toward encounter amid a hybrid collective. The interethnic impulse now shapes the ethnic novel's deepest psychic structures as well as aspects of its form, from its plot and characters to its use of language(s) and patterns of literary influence. No facile celebration, this literature registers an ironic consciousness of a hybridized world laced with conflict, violence, and inequality.

I still teach single-ethnicity courses but working on *The Interethnic Imagination* led me to develop new course models: a course titled Interethnic American Fiction and an interethnic unit in the course Multiethnic American Fiction, both of which are upper-level courses that count toward English department and humanities area requirements. In both courses, I choose texts that stage encounters, conflicts, romances, and varying enmeshments across cultures, languages, and communities. A typical syllabus has included African American slavery novels featuring intricate Black-white relations (such as Sherley Anne Williams's *Dessa Rose*); Native American novels that experiment, against the backdrop of white colonization, with hybridization or dialogue (Leslie Marmon Silko's *Ceremony*); Asian American texts about migrants in transformation, colliding with others on the world stage (Gish Jen's *Mona in the Promised Land*, Chang-rae Lee's *Native Speaker*, and Bharati Mukherjee's The Middleman *and Other Stories*); and Jewish American novels about intimate Black-Jewish relations in the United States (Lore Segal's *Her First American*) and intergroup dialogue across the world (Jonathan Safran Foer's *Everything Is Illuminated*).

In these courses, Asian American texts have had a starring role. Why Asian American literature should be especially interethnic is a question outside the scope of this essay.[1] But Yamashita's novels, her readers will agree, exemplify an interethnic literary vision. Her gigantic canvasses and striking designs, as they accommodate a transnational scope and histories of global migration, become arenas for the dramatic interaction of people of multiple histories, languages, memories, and tastes in food and music who tend to morph into crowds of distinct classes or ethnicities, which then converge in spectacular crowd-meets-crowd scenes.

My focus here is on Yamashita's most frequently taught novel, *Tropic of Orange*. I begin the first of four classes spent on the novel by asking students to define the novel's spatial focus. After a few stabs at answers by those who raise hands, the class grasps that this book is set in a space that traverses the United States–Mexico border. I ask students to consider the implications of that unconventional spatial focus for the novel's content, its vision. Students eventually find their way to saying that it is a border novel, all about passage, crossing lines, the mixing of histories and peoples. Indeed, its primary border traversal seems to spur other expansions of vision. For example, Manzanar Murakami, a mad or magically gifted character conducting the music of the traffic from an LA freeway overpass, can see downward through multiple layers of manmade Los Angeles engineering to prehistoric layers beneath the earth, and can also see around "the great Pacific stretching along its great rim. . . . from the southernmost tip of Chile" to Alaska, then southward along the coast of Asia all the way to New Zealand (171). I then put students in groups to discuss two questions and briefly report answers to the class. First, how does this expansive vision shape the plot? The plot action is equally gigantic: the entire Southern Hemisphere—people, commodities, holy sites, even the landscape itself—crosses the border north into the United States, converging in LA with the lives of immigrants from various parts of Asia and with a crowd of homeless people who take over the abandoned vehicles of the wealthy after a major freeway accident. Second, how does Yamashita's novelistic discourse itself expand across borders? Students can list the multiple literary, popular cultural, and media forms that enter Yamashita's mix: Latin American magical realism and folktales, postmodern fiction, commercial radio, TV, film noir, Los Angeles disaster film, Latino performance poetry, Asian and other ethnic American fiction, and so on.

Having discussed the big picture, we consider Yamashita's multiethnic characters. Each group examines one character: the character's history, the discourse of the chapters in which that character appears (diction, style, forms of realism, tone, reverence, mythification, irony, humor, prominent media and arts). After this discussion, we ask what Yamashita actually does with this motley set of characters amid her vast, chaotic cinemascope. What meanings are produced when she stages extraordinary scenes of encounter among these diverse, distinctively characterized individuals? What happens to traditional characterization and plot; to ideas of identity, family, gender, ethnicity, race, class, and nation; to notions of power, property, and love?

We begin to look for answers to these questions using Yamashita's "HyperContexts" chart, an unconventional supplement to the table of contents, which usefully lists characters' names on the vertical axis and ranges their chapters across the horizontal axis of the novel's seven-day span. What, I ask, is this chart good for? Does it make things clearer or more complicated for the reader? I tell students that Yamashita has identified this chart as the earliest matrix of the novel. It developed when, at a dull secretarial job, she started playing around with a spreadsheet program.[2] Remarkably, the sight of a chart made of columns immediately gave Yamashita the idea of writing a novel on it, running time across one axis and a certain ethnic spectrum down the other. A matrix born of a new moment for both technology and human interaction, the chart is a machine for generating new dramas of interethnic possibility; it offers a compelling visual paradigm for a course on fictions of interethnic encounter. I refer here to a paradigm developed by Susan Stanford Friedman, a "narrative poetics of intercultural encounter," in which narratives move not only through time, driven by desire (as in psychoanalytic theories), but also through space, propelled by an urge toward cultural otherness (*Mappings* 141). Examining Yamashita's "HyperContexts" chart, the class can see the ways she remakes the plot impetus—the "then, and then, and then" of events—by multiplying the axis of time by the axis of human differences, generating a drive toward human encounter across space.

Though this chart makes it look as though the members of certain ethnic groups—Mexican, Chinese, Japanese, and African American—are neatly contained in their narrative enclosures, students notice that over the novel's course Yamashita actually sends characters across the lines, into others' plots and into a swelling interethnic collective. In this way, her characters become not identitarian ethnic representatives but components of a hybrid metropolis, exceeding our expectations for their racial, ethnic, or national identifications.

In this context the class will think of Bobby Ngu, a "Chinese from Singapore with a Vietnam name speaking like a Mexican living in Koreatown" who lunches on Chinese burritos and is married to the Chicana Rafaela Cortes (Yamashita, *Tropic* 15). Students consider what it means that this couple's marriage, made possible by global migration, frames the novel, a novel that begins with their painful separation on either side of a national border and closes with their reunion amid a massive, transnational crowd. Students enjoy talking about the Japanese American Emi, who is so "distant from the Asian female stereotype" that "it was questionable if she even had an identity" (19), and who disdains identity politics, telling her mother, "Maybe I'm not Japanese American. Maybe I got switched in the hospital" (21). Yamashita's complex treatment of interethnic cultural politics emerges when the anti-essentialist Emi fumes over the appropriation of her culture: a white woman at a sushi restaurant wearing chopsticks in her hair. Holding up two forks, Emi counterattacks: "'Would you consider using these in your hair? Or would you consider that,' Emi paused, 'unsanitary?'" (129). A key encounter occurs late in the book when, amid a military assault, Emi dies in the arms of Buzzworm, a "[b]ig black seven-foot dude, Vietnam vet" who walks his African American neighborhood as a professional "*Angel of Mercy*" (26–27), offering social services to all while listening to Spanish radio so as to "get behind another man's perspectives. Hear life in another sound zone. Walk to some other rhythms" and "be ready with the dialogue" (102–03). Emi's death scene nearly produces a beautiful fusion when she looks into his eyes and—both genuinely and parodically—echoes the famous words of LA police beating victim Rodney King: "If *we* can jus' get along, maybe all our problems will go away" (253). But Buzzworm replies, dubious, "Gonna take more than holdin' hands to start that revolution," whereupon irony prevails, and Emi lightly blows off utopian hopes before dying (253). Such examples help the class appreciate the way that, when Yamashita's seven characters escape their "HyperContexts" boxes to intersect with and parallel one another's lives, their plots generate sadly failed connections as well as surprising reunions, even while these characters are all tumbled together with the growing crowds into collective experiences of yearning, fear, celebration, hideous violence, and citywide grief.

In most texts students will have read by the end of my course on interethnic American fiction (or by the end of a course unit on that topic), two characters from different groups collide in love or hostilities or espionage, or sometimes the singular protagonist—often readable as a representative national or ethnic subject—moves through the complicated world to become the living nexus of an expanding interethnicity. Over the next few classes, students observe the way that Yamashita's novel begins instead with the premise of expanding interethnicity and follows the winding paths of novelistic lives into this charged collectivity. What, I ask students at the end of our unit on *Tropic of Orange*, does Yamashita show us about the nature of our era's increasing human convergence? While an opening address to the "Gentle reader" sees in LA a "collective mindlessness that propels our fascination forward," a later poetic vision casts a mass of aspiring migrants from the South as at once both "*the Third World War*" and "*the gliding wings of a dream*" (202). On the negative side, students find in the novel battles that are both intimate and colossal: broken relationships as well as violent public contests between North and South, rich and poor, criminals and innocents, the entitled and the undocumented, the state and the homeless. On the positive side, students are able to trace an impulse of spirit that spreads irresistibly across the novel's breadth: characters hearing others' music in their heads; interethnic lovers reuniting; the multiplication of music conductors holding carrots sticks and toothbrushes on overpasses across the city; the stunning moment when, "like white poppies in sudden bloom . . . [a]ll the airbags in L.A. ruptured forth, unfurled their white powdered wings against the barrage of bullets, and stunned the war to a dead stop" (258); and the satiric, joyous chaos of chapter 35, titled "Jam." "Merge, Merge, Merge. They all converged everywhere all at once," Yamashita writes—quintessential Yamashita lines—at the climax of "the greatest jam session the world had ever known," a traffic crisis musically improvised by "all seven million residents of Greater L.A. out on the town" at once (207). For students finishing a semester of fiction about interethnic human encounter, these extraordinary scenes generate rich, creative questions—about the contradictions and illuminations generated by Yamashita's tragicomic, politically critical, playfully postmodern sensibility, and about reasons for despair and hope in our changing world.

And so, even in an interethnic literature course, I still put Yamashita's fiction at the end of the syllabus, a strategy that lets me build the term toward the largest, most mysterious human visions of both communal disaster and possibility, and which leaves students gripped by a rich sense of the potential of imaginative art to render our dynamic moment. What can Yamashita bring to a classroom grappling with the global population changes now shaping our lives? I like to teach her as a writer who—moved by the interethnic impulse that other writers work out in more modest, contained narratives—instead interweaves the lives and histories and discourses of many people on a huge loom, the gargantuan cinema of what Yamashita has called the "wild . . . crass . . . cheesy" contemporary popular imagination (*Tropic*). I teach her as an artist of the interethnic sublime.

NOTES

[1] On this question, see Rody, *Interethnic Imagination*.
[2] See a note to a lecture by Yamashita in Rody, *Interethnic Imagination* 172.

Intersectionality, Comparative Racialization, and the Racial Pyramid in *Tropic of Orange*

Lynn Mie Itagaki

Karen Tei Yamashita's *Tropic of Orange* provides an opportunity to teach innovative concepts of race and interracial relations in literature. This novel has inspired the construction of my courses and class modules around the topic of comparative racialization. I have taught the novel in upper-division lectures and graduate English seminars, primarily at universities with predominantly White student populations in the Midwest and Rocky Mountain West. Yamashita's ensemble casts, multiple protagonists, and intersecting story lines are particularly effective in courses on literature by writers of color or by women of color and in courses on contemporary fiction. *Tropic of Orange* would also work well in courses that include topics and methods such as comparative racialization and intersectional feminism. Although Yamashita's entire oeuvre can be characterized by its prominent depictions of boundary crossing, genre blending, and race mixing, *Tropic of Orange* appeals to advanced undergraduate and graduate students because of its complex narrative structure and depiction of social stratification. Because the novel is 280 pages long, instructors of introductory literature or writing-intensive courses may choose to excerpt one or two individual chapters that can function as short stories and ground selective discussions of Yamashita's comparative frameworks.

I teach *Tropic of Orange* in courses that study major developments in interracial cultural and literary history by and about writers of color and examine how academics, artists, filmmakers, and writers respond to the material conditions of gendered and racialized inequalities. Thus, intersectionality generally and comparative racialization specifically are important methodologies for achieving these pedagogical goals. The relationships between and among Yamashita's characters crucially illustrate foundational concepts in understanding both methodologies: for example, Gloria Anzaldúa's "*mestiza* consciousness" (25), Claire Jean Kim's "racial triangulation," Leslie McCall's "complexity of intersectionality," and Patricia Hill Collins's "matrix of domination" (227–51). Classroom exercises and discussion prompts introduce these aspects of intersectionality, and then students can engage with these concepts of racial identity and interracial formations. Below, I describe some of the activities and exercises that support students' efforts to connect Yamashita's innovative narrative elements to interracial formations and in order to explain social multiplicity in terms of racial hierarchies and what I call elsewhere "racial pyramidization" (Itagaki, *Civil Racism* 8–9). Students respond to some of these discussion topics online before each class so that I have a sense of their level of knowledge and interpretations of the text and can modify my minilectures as needed.

Comparative racialization identifies the tools, methods, and concepts used to compare the experiences of different racial groups. Describing the differential management of racial groups' competing claims on the state, comparative racialization delineates the racial hierarchies of what Neil Gotanda has called "racial stratification" as well as the history of and potential for creating and maintaining cross-racial alliances and coalitions. Through its multiple protagonists and various narrative forms, *Tropic of Orange* encourages its readers to self-reflexively engage in dismantling and reconstructing interracial identities. The novel's dynamic interactions between characters and narrative structure parallel those between interracial individuals and the institutions that shape the lived experiences of those individuals.

I discuss concepts of comparative racialization by beginning with the term *interracial*, thereby introducing various intersectional strategies. Students usually think of the word *interracial* in terms of conflicts between or among differently racialized individuals or groups, or in terms of bonds between these individuals or groups. I encourage students to take into account how presumably monoracial identities depend on relationalities with other racial groups. To this end, I deploy McCall's intracategorical "complexity of intersectionality," a concept that scrutinizes an ostensibly stable category of identity, thereby showing its internal incoherence. Taking Whiteness as an example, I ask students which identities are included in this category. Since students usually name European nationalities immediately, I query them further about religious identities—Jewish and Muslim, for instance—and Middle Eastern, Latinx, and multiracial identities. Students are typically surprised that Arab and Latinx individuals are legally considered White. We evaluate Karen Brodkin's analysis of Jews in the post-1945 racial hierarchy of the United States as one of a "racial middleness": "of an experience of marginality vis-à-vis whiteness and an experience of whiteness and belonging vis-à-vis blackness" (2). I talk about ongoing census debates and project a slide containing past and current census questions about race that have officially subsumed Middle Eastern, Latinx, and multiracial categories under single racial categories. I explain how Latinx soldiers were assigned to White or "colored" units based on their skin color before the military was desegregated. I also tell them the story of my Japanese American grandfather from Hawai'i, who in a Texas boot camp during WWII was confused by which segregated bathroom to use. If he used the one designated for Whites only with impunity, did that mean he was White? No, but it did mean that he was afforded a racial privilege and protection African Americans and Afro-Latinxs did not have.

Next, I ask students to reflect on what is meant by interracial identity and subjectivity. Students have usually responded first by noting multiracial or mixed-race individuals. I push them to consider an interracial identity and subjectivity for someone who claims only one race. Here, Anzaldúa's "*mestiza* consciousness" and Maria Lugones's "'world'-traveling" are useful concepts to discuss in terms of their inclusion of multiple and conflicting identities and perspectives within an individual subjectivity. Because students might latch onto the positives of these concepts, I point out that both Anzaldúa and Lugones incorporate possibilities of not only interracial harmony and reconciliation but also racist violence that makes it difficult or impossible for people to practice and achieve "*mestiza* consciousness" or "'world'-traveling." To uncover these tensions, I explain W. E. B. Du Bois's concept of "double consciousness" and how this interracial perspective was one of survival during the violence of Jim Crow segregation and anti-Black racial terror (8–10).

I bring this discussion of comparative racialization back to *Tropic of Orange* with in-class analyses of the protagonists. In an opening exercise, I ask students how Yamashita portrays each of the seven protagonists and challenge them to identify any symbolic or allegorical possibilities in the characters' traits and actions. In undergraduate courses, I then assign students to groups. Each group is assigned one protagonist and tasked with these questions and later reports their findings to the entire class. Protagonist names refer to Abrahamic archangels (Rafaela and Gabriel), Spanish invaders (Cortés and Balboa), and a World War II Japanese American concentration camp (Manzanar). The novel thus features Asian, Black, and Latinx protagonists and draws attention to the characters Rafaela, Bobby, and Arcangel, who are documented and undocumented immigrants. These entangled histories of imperialism, genocide, enslavement, exploitation, and oppression across the Americas importantly contextualize our discussions about how racial identities are formed.

This exercise usefully segues into conversations about intersectionality and comparative racialization. Students readily offer memorable character idiosyncrasies: Arcangel, more than five centuries old, remembers Columbus's first voyage to the Caribbean; Buzzworm listens to channels in any language on his portable radio twenty-four hours a day; and Manzanar conducts random city noises from a downtown LA freeway overpass. In their groups, students exhaustively list different categories of identity based on these idiosyncrasies. Since the novel is primarily set in Los Angeles, students need prompting to discuss Rafaela's remigration to Mexico, Bobby's crossing of the United States–Mexico border to bring his undocumented cousin back to the United States, and Arcangel's northward journey across the Americas.

In a minilecture, I discuss Arcangel in terms of immigration from Latin America since his mysterious life immediately stands out to students. They note the awkwardness, yet also the appropriateness, of interpreting Arcangel as a modern-day undocumented immigrant in the context of his Indigenous identity, his five-hundred-year life span, and his superhuman abilities. Students specify which documents are needed for official immigration status and how this requirement has changed over time or is different based on one's country of origin. As Mae Ngai points out, it is difficult to be historically precise while using the less pejorative term *undocumented*—rather than *illegal*—because documents were not always required for legal immigration throughout the history of the United States (xix). Just as Arcangel has earlier pulled an entire bus out of the mud through flaps on his back, so too he pulls Central and South America, their lands and people, into Southern California. This altering of physical topography and geography provokes the question of how geopolitical instruments such as the 1848 Treaty of Guadalupe Hidalgo, the 1942 Bracero Program, and the 1994 North American Free Trade Agreement (NAFTA) have historically moved borders, people, and money north and south of the current division between the United States and Mexico. In relation to Anzaldúa's notion of the border as "*una herida abierta*" ("an open wound"; 24) and Ngai's history of immigration to the United States, I encourage students to consider the axis of nationality in the figurative and literal lines we draw cartographically that then shape identities and limit their possible expressions. For example, why do North Americans think of the Americas as two separate continents whereas residents in other countries identify the Americas as one continent? Who or what belief systems are served by such an arbitrary separation? These questions provide a different framing for questions of citizenship. As detailed in Ngai's historiography, the US House of Representatives immigration committee noted in 1930 that if national border enforcement can occur miles inland and anywhere in the interior, then that would make the whole country into a border (56). After mentioning this anecdote, I ask students to think of all the airports that are designated as international, no matter how small—for example, the eight-gate airport I used often in Missoula, Montana. With international arrivals, these airports must have Department of Homeland Security infrastructure in place to process foreign goods and noncitizens, and each and every one of these airports represents a national border to be crossed.

My literature courses are grounded in the idea that race itself is an interracial formation. Race makes visible histories and relations of domination and subjugation and is thus not a neutral descriptor, as students in predominantly White classrooms often believe, although they may not articulate these beliefs. Since these histories of oppression and violence are not foremost in students' minds, I remind students of a definition of ideological racism (Feagin and Feagin 6–8) and the different manifestations of race in political, economic, legal, social, and affective terms. Students who focus on literary studies often have limited awareness of race and racism—their complexities, the wide range of research available, and how other axes of identity might affect their manifestations. I provide a brief overview of research on microaggressions (see Sue) and implicit bias (see Harvard University's *Project Implicit* [implicit.harvard.edu/implicit/]) so that students are able to identify the more subtle and covert forms of discrimination that characters such as Emi and Gabriel face, as they do in chapter 20, "Disaster Movie Week–Hiro's Sushi."

Although intersectionality is mentioned in many diversity statements on campuses across the nation, many students do not have more than a hazy notion of multiple categories of identity, much less how these axes interact and how interracial conflicts and coalitions are formed. I take the first two weeks of any undergraduate literature course to discuss basic definitions of race and gender, including those found in Joe R. Feagin and Clairece Booher Feagin's introduction to *Racial and Ethnic Relations*, Derald Wing Sue's article on racial microaggressions, and Peggy McIntosh's "White Privilege and Male Privilege." By the time we address *Tropic of Orange*, the class will have read these texts and discussed intersectionality and racial triangulation, concepts that are crucial for understanding depictions of race and interracial relations in literature. I remind students of Collins's concept of the "matrix of domination," defined as "the overall organization of hierarchical power relations for any society" (299). Collins writes, moreover, that "[a]ny specific matrix of domination has (1) a particular arrangement of intersecting systems of oppression, e.g., race, social class, gender, sexuality, citizenship status, ethnicity and age; and (2) a particular organization of its domains of power, e.g., structural, disciplinary, hegemonic, and interpersonal" (299). I discuss Claire Jean Kim's expression of this matrix through her notion of "racial triangulation," which describes how some non-White racial groups are deemed superior or inferior to others in order to maintain White hegemony: Kim specifically explains how mainstream media and politics characterize Blacks as lacking good cultural values when compared to Asians (a form of relative valorization); at the same time, Asians are seen as foreign when compared to Blacks (a type of civic ostracism). Building on this notion, I posit a model of racial pyramidization in which the hypervisibility of the intersecting axes of identity also obscures the invisibility of the vertex always hidden from view but crucial to the pyramidal structure itself. After this progression of concepts, I ask students which identities in the novel are obvious and which remain hidden. This exercise is especially provocative in the final discussion of the novel. For example, Bobby and Rafaela's nuclear family is cosmically brought together at the end, a reunion that seems to promote interracial heterosexuality through their marriage and the idea of a multiracial future through their biracial son, Sol. However, students discuss whether Bobby—as a means of pursuing his upwardly mobile, middle-class aspirations—will continue to exploit his wife as his employee and commodify his son even after the family's separation and supernatural reconnection. Students also tend to overlook Arcangel's Indigenous *and* Latinx identities, instead remarking on his unbelievably long life and physical strength. Moreover, students often neglect to mention the violence against women: Emi's death and Rafaela's rape and possible death. I suggest the ways in which imperialist violence and exploitation are experienced differently depending on a subject's gender and sexuality.

That these relations of domination are naturalized and hidden in plain sight owes itself in part to the conspicuous nature of interracial formations and multiracial identities, to the fact that these personal histories and private relationships are often seen as spectacular and out of the ordinary despite their continual albeit unacknowledged presence. Interracial formations are also complex: while some might inspire solidarity among those who experience racial oppression, they can also lead to conflicts, unequal treatment, and discrepant outcomes for different racial groups. Deeply rooted de facto and de jure segregation—

among other geographic, physical, legal, and customary separations—have usually enforced these racial divisions through bodily violence and terror. However, this focus on interracial formations and comparative racialization reminds students that we have always already been interracial in thought and action.

Tropic of Orange emphasizes characters' interactions as crucial to understanding the larger significance of racial identities and interracial relations. Students appreciate untangling the novel's complexities and structure in this way. Yamashita's distinctive ensemble of characters and multiple story lines demand a discussion of comparative racialization in the contexts of critical ethnic studies and women of color feminism, especially in terms of intersectional analyses, in order to delineate and more fully appreciate her visionary and ethical conceptions of race and interracial formations.

Through the Arc of the Theater: Yamashita Does Asian American Drama

Josephine Lee

During the spring 2017 semester, I taught Karen Tei Yamashita's short theater piece *Jan Ken Pon: A Dance Performance Idea* in an upper-division course on American drama by writers of color. Students responded to this parody of an academic lecture on evolutionary science, race, and social dominance with a mixture of confusion and delight. After our discussion of Yamashita's blend of PowerPoint slides, narration, *YouTube* videos, and dance, even those students who initially dismissed the play as bizarre concluded that it was worthwhile reading. Its experimental aesthetics made students conceptualize racial difference in ways that were vastly different from the more realistic dramas on our reading list (Lorraine Hansberry's *Raisin in the Sun*, August Wilson's *Ma Rainey's Black Bottom*, and Ayad Akhtar's *Disgraced*, among others). Students appreciated how Yamashita juxtaposes scientific conclusions about the evolutionary biology of lizards (for instance, a clip of a radio interview in which certain male lizards are characterized as "sneaky yellow bastards" [351]) with references to Claire Jean Kim's essay on Asian American "racial triangulation" and the rock-paper-scissors-lizard-Spock game popularized by the television show *The Big Bang Theory*. Despite the playful style of delivery, students clearly understood Yamashita's serious commentary on the typecasting of Asian Americans and the continuing racial fear of Asian domination, highlighted by one of her final slides that contained a recent news reference to China's growing economic power with the caption, "What will we do when those sneaky yellow bastards change the game plan?" (351).

I was first introduced to Yamashita's plays in 1996 at a reading of her energetic satire on Japanese American masculinity, *Noh Bozos: A Circus Performance in Ten Amazing Acts* (1993), at the Playwrights' Center in Minneapolis. Though I have been a fan of her theater work ever since, I did not have much opportunity to use it in the classroom until the 2014 publication of *Anime Wong: Fictions of Performance*. As Stephen Sohn comments in his excellent afterword to the volume, Yamashita's plays are not as well-known as her fiction. They have not been produced widely, and their experimental and multimedia format makes them challenging to envision fully through reading the script alone. That being said, the plays in *Anime Wong* urge students to address foundational questions in Asian American drama and performance about the reappropriation of racial stereotypes, the legacies of Orientalism, and the continued relevance of Asian American histories.

This volume has inspired me to create new curriculum modules for two other upper-division courses that I offer regularly: an Asian American literature course and a course on Asian American drama. Like the spring 2017 course, both courses are cross-listed under English and Asian American studies; they also count as electives for English majors and minors and as core courses for Asian American studies minors. These courses also attract other students who want to fulfill liberal education requirements on diversity and social justice in the United States, or who are simply interested in the topic. Each semester I include several works by a single author so that students can see how a body of writing develops over time. Featured playwrights have included David Henry Hwang, Philip Kan Gotanda, Ping Chong, Young Jean Lee, and Julia Cho. *Anime Wong*, which includes plays from *Kusei: Endangered Species* (1986) to *Jan Ken Pon: A Dance Performance Idea* (2012), now makes it easy to incorporate Yamashita's theater work into future classes as well.

Yamashita's plays can be described as a type of devised theater in which the playwright's script represents only part of the larger collective work of artists, performers, and designers. *Anime Wong* makes this clear by including not only playscripts but also production photographs, excerpts from musical scores, and theater programs and posters that highlight the collaborative and community-based nature of Yamashita's plays. These highly interactive plays are perfectly suited to my hands-on approach to teaching theater and my emphasis on racial diversity and social justice issues not just as abstract knowledge but also as inspiration for art and action. I regularly assign student presentations on casting, design, and concept choices, and make students perform group readings of scenes. I also give them the opportunity to write original dramatic scenes based on moments in Asian American history, and I make service-learning internships with local arts organizations part of their coursework.

Yamashita's plays help students connect familiar racial stereotypes to the history of the legal and social exclusion of Asians and Asian Americans. They also prompt students to recognize the violence of these images and encourage students to imagine creative approaches to dismantling them. For instance, in preparation for our discussion of how Asian countries and immigrants are typecast as the hostile and invasive "yellow peril" in *Jan Ken Pon*, I showed students late-nineteenth-century anti-Chinese political cartoons and the opening scene of Henry Grimm's 1879 farce *The Chinese Must Go.*[1] Another Yamashita play, *Hannah Kusoh: An American Butoh* (1988), pairs well with Hwang's play *M. Butterfly* since both deconstruct Giacomo Puccini's well-known 1904 operatic fantasy centered on the submissive and self-sacrificing character of Cio-Cio-San. Yamashita's unorthodox staging includes a wild scene entitled "Madame Butterfly: The Sense of Sound" that begins with a dance in which women emerge in kimonos made from "*Styrofoam balls/popcorn, nori, mini-blinds, shimmering transparent plastic, crazy eyes, and so on*" (*Hannah Kusoh* 41). While one dancer sings Puccini karaoke-style, the others eat noodles and brandish chopsticks "*in a sort of a breast-beating, bizarre, ritualistic fashion, threatening suicide*" (41).

Unlike Hwang's play, *Hannah Kusoh* not only lampoons *Madame Butterfly* but also makes clear how its typecasting affects the real lives of Asian and Asian American women. One scene opens with the "Chinese Dance" from Pyotr

Tchaikovsky's *The Nutcracker*, then segues into a monologue in which a sansei (a third-generation Japanese American) woman tells a story about her blind date with a white man who fetishizes Japanese culture. Later, the same story is retold from the critical perspective of a Japanese immigrant woman waitressing at the restaurant where the couple go for dinner on their blind date. By contrasting these more realistic monologues with the surreal exaggeration of Oriental stereotypes, *Hannah Kusoh* emphasizes for students how plays can illustrate different perspectives on the same event. This examination could be effectively supplemented with a discussion of Akira Kurosawa's film *Rashomon*, in which the use of multiple narrators also questions the representation of a single truth; pairing the play with film clips would also allow students to compare how cinematic perspective and stage monologues differ in their effect (a lesson that could be continued by also comparing stage and film versions of Hwang's *M. Butterfly*).

Since an adaptation of *Rashomon* was the first production by East West Players in Los Angeles (the first Asian American theater company, established in 1965), pairing *Hannah Kusoh* with *Rashomon* also encourages reflection on the complicated history of intercultural theater practice. Yamashita actively employs traditional and contemporary Japanese performance and visual art forms such as Noh, Kabuki, *Butoh*, manga, and anime, often using them to parody the long tradition of Orientalism in Euro-American culture. Selected scenes from *Noh Bozos* or her equally boisterous comedy *Siamese Twins and Mongoloids* (2012) can serve to highlight how both late-nineteenth- and early-twentieth-century works such as *Madame Butterfly* or Gilbert and Sullivan's *The Mikado* and contemporary intercultural theater works often reproduce Orientalist spectacle under the guise of art.

Teaching students about the politics of theatrical interculturalism can also lead them to reflect more deeply on *Asian American* as a term that not only describes the social positioning of American subjects but also refers to patterns of cultural and economic exchange between Asia and the United States. The references made by Yamashita's drama to Japanese performance forms or culture are far from superficial, decorative, or convenient. Rather, they affirm that Asian American racialization also manifests the dynamics of transnational and global exchange. For instance, the program notes for the premiere of *Hannah Kusoh*, which are included in *Anime Wong*, comment on how a renewed interest in Asian commodities is part of what is imagined as a modern multicultural American identity; "things Japanese, once enjoyed or acquired only within the boundaries of the Japanese American community, have suddenly been absorbed by an all-inclusive and ever-evolving American culture" (47). However, the program observes wryly that the popularity of sushi, though undoubtedly "a major achievement," does not necessarily mean the end of anti-Asian racism (47). Yamashita's plays consistently link domestic experiences of immigration, assimilation, and racial exclusion to changing relations between Asia and the United States.

This connection becomes particularly important in Yamashita's *Anime Wong: A CyberAsian Odyssey* (2008), a play that demonstrates the popularity of techno-Orientalism, a cultural fantasy associating Asian nations and people with advanced technology and futuristic scenarios. Students raised in this era of digital enhancement and special effects will respond readily to Yamashita's video sequences, which rely on familiar images that include notable Asian and Asian American actors and characterizations from science fiction, martial arts, and action films:

> *On screen: manga with various representations of Pat Morita morphing into Key Luke morphing into Toshiro Mifune morphing into Bruce Lee morphing into Yoda morphing into Chow Yun Fat morphing into Master Splinter morphing into Jet Li morphing into Jackie Chan morphing into Batou morphing into John Cho morphing into Federation viceroys from Star Wars, and so on. You get the morphing picture.* (314)

Students could easily collate their own related set of images inspired by Yamashita's sequence, which highlights how historic stereotypes of despotic emperors, invading hordes, and nameless, faceless servants and laborers might be echoed in more contemporary racial figures such as aliens and robots. Other possible classroom exercises for this play might include building a composite sketch of the central character, Anime Wong, who is described as "*some kind of androgynous Asian Barbie with Anna May Wong makeup and hair and maybe a version of a* Thief of Baghdad *costume, the apron flap being the image of a Warhol Mao covering her hot pants*," or constructing Yamashita's "*mishmash of urban scenes (a là* Blade Runner) *of Tokyo, Hong Kong, Taipei, Singapore, Seoul, Beijing, L.A., the global Chinatown*" (295). Yamashita's futuristic amalgamation of cultural images and references—including a tribute to "[o]ur global Chinatown" as "Confusing. Multilingual, Transnational. Sub(di)versity on every corner. . . . One hundred blooming flowers! One hundred million miracles!" (295)—not only makes for vivid theatrical spectacle but also urges students to think about new imaginings of Asian Americans as diligent, uncomplaining, and upwardly mobile model minorities (as signaled by the allusion to Rodgers and Hammerstein's *Flower Drum Song*) who are distinctively linked to global capitalism, speed, and technology.

With plays that look both backward and forward in time, Yamashita explores the ever-changing nature of Japanese American identity and Asian American racial formation. Her *GiLArex (or Godzilla Comes to Little Tokyo)* (1992) makes a distinctive contribution to a unit on Japanese American incarceration. In the past, I have largely worked with plays that emphasize oral histories and realistic representation, such as Hiroshi Kashiwagi's dark comedy *Laughter and False Teeth* (1954), Chay Yew's dramatizations of oral history in *Question 27, Question 28* (2004), or Jeanne Sakata's one-actor show based on the trial of Gordon

Hirabayashi, *Hold These Truths* (2007). Yamashita's irreverent musical takes a radically different approach; the monstrosities of anti-Japanese racism emerge as a modern-day version of Los Angeles is threatened by GiLArex, a giant lizard who emerges from under the site of the Manzanar concentration camp. One character, Sally Ogata, sings "Mutant Gila Monsters" about "Years of infamy / years of shame":

> It was a wartime necessity.
> No yellow face could be trusted.
> It was for our own protection,
> This phony military game.
> (114)

Ogata is a former internee and a community activist who ultimately meets her fate in the devastation wreaked by GiLArex. However, it is the disenfranchised teenager Emi who is really at the center of the play's action. Emi, who has no awareness of camp history and no apparent ties to Japanese heritage, undergoes a process of self-discovery through bonding with Manzanar Murakami, a homeless Japanese American man who claims to be the first sansei born in the camps.[2] Their relationship provides an opportunity for students to reflect on the gaps between older and younger generations and on the importance of telling stories. Emi's father is an archeologist who has become disconnected from his Japanese American heritage, and Emi is even more resistant to identify herself as Japanese American. As Manzanar tries to figure out which generation she is, she snarkily comments, "But what's the big deal? It just sounds like the same bunch of people getting married to the same bunch of people six times is all" (145). Manzanar responds, "But in your case, maybe it's not the marrying that's important; it's the stories. After six generations, you oughta have some stories" (145). In this interaction, Yamashita affirms the importance not only of knowing facts about the past but also of connecting younger generations to this knowledge in newly imaginative ways.

Plays in the volume *Anime Wong* are grounded in a strong sense of local Japanese American community and place. For instance, one of Yamashita's earliest plays, *Kusei: Endangered Species* (1986), jokes about Japanese American communities in Southern California and their anxieties about the preservation of ethnic heritage. The play shows alien scientists, charged with preserving Japanese American identity from extinction, who revive a cryogenically frozen Japanese American beauty pageant winner to mate her with the clone of a Japanese American man. Japanese Americans, the audience learns, were relocated during "the Ford-Mitsubishi Wars" to "the planet Topanzanar" and are now called "Topanzanees" (15). The aliens use *taiko* drums to signal "the beginning of the mating ritual" and offer the couple a Toyota convertible to stimulate their libido (11).

While my students at the University of Minnesota can easily enter into a discussion of the issues of cultural assimilation and inter- and intraracial dating that are depicted in this enjoyably silly comedy, the 1980s references and Los Angeles setting can be far afield from their experiences. Many of them are Southeast Asian American or transnational Asian adoptees; few have ever lived in or even visited Southern California. But perhaps this is the best reason for examining this early work in addition to Yamashita's later plays: in doing so, students come to understand how Yamashita's drama moves from the concerns of particular communities toward other ways of understanding what *Asian American* means. Whenever I teach Asian American drama and literature, I ask my students to question the homogeneity implied by racial categories. The plays collected in *Anime Wong* can help students reconsider the term *Asian American* both as it fails to describe a multitude of different experiences and cultures and as it serves as a potentially unifying social rubric. Yamashita's complex and engaging work for the theater can also inspire students to move past their own comfort zones and explore more creative approaches to the performance of race and identity.

NOTES

[1] For an example of a late-nineteenth-century anti-Chinese political cartoon, see Keller, "'Coming Man.'"

[2] Yamashita develops similar characterizations in *Tropic of Orange*—with Manzanar, who also imagines a symphony in the chaotic sounds of Los Angeles, and with an older version of Emi. Other plays such as *Siamese Twins and Mongoloids* also resonate with Yamashita's essays and fiction.

Teaching Yamashita's Works outside the Ethnic Studies Classroom

Noelle Brada-Williams

In a large, comprehensive state university, required classes are more likely to attract enough students to meet minimum enrollment requirements than are specialized courses in ethnic studies. In general education courses at both the lower- and upper-division level, the attainment of content knowledge and the development of reading and writing skills must compete for the same limited class time. Even in advanced classes where more specialization can be expected, courses may still need to meet specific demands, and students often require a great deal of supplemental knowledge to understand the cultural and aesthetic contexts of ethnic American texts. Although institutional forces have dictated many of the parameters for the courses I have taught, in some ways these forces have been a blessing in disguise because they have enabled me to introduce ethnic literature texts to a variety of student populations who might never have chosen to enter an ethnic studies or ethnic literature classroom and yet have much to gain from interaction with these texts. This essay describes the effectiveness of teaching three of Yamashita's novels in classrooms with different learning objectives.

Reader's Theater and I Hotel

Yamashita's work is ideal for introducing students at any level to cultural and political moments they may not be aware of as well as for broadening students' understanding of literary form and technique. The complexity and richly allusive nature of Yamashita's works make them exemplary teaching texts, since much of the cultural context needed to understand them is contained within them. *I Hotel* is perhaps the ultimate example as it is a history of the first ten years in the development of the social and political collective identity that the term *Asian American* now represents. Soon after the book came out, I assigned it in an upper-level American literature class.[1] Due to *I Hotel*'s length and complexity, I had been nervous about assigning it. Ironically, it was a collective reading of the text's most complex passage that ended up engaging the class most thoroughly.

Chapter 8 of "1971: Aiiieeeee! Hotel," *I Hotel*'s fourth novella, focuses on the politics of artistic production and engages a range of different modes of representation including illustration and various combinations of text and visuals. But this chapter, titled "Dance," takes its experimentation with the possibilities of literary representation to the next level when the character Sandy Hu choreographs a dance "based on the story of the outlaw Li K'wei reuniting with his blind mother. Sandy has this idea to combine Peking Opera with what Gerald is calling avant-garde jazz, as long as he throws in a little tango, her nod to Borges, of course" (278). Yamashita then provides a six-page written representation of this aural and visual performance in which as many as seven different narratives or actions take place at the same time. A mixture of music, folklore, and personal and collective history are printed as parallel columns running vertically down the page as a means of representing rather than merely describing this performance.[2] The ability to conceive of art across different modes of expression and production is at the heart of Yamashita's own process, as she once explained in an interview with Lai Ying Yu: she tried to conceive of her novel as architectural blueprints that use a two-dimensional space to imagine a three-dimensional work (Yu 75). My original motivation for having seven of my students read aloud this passage in its entirety was my personal desire to better grasp the polyphony of voices, sounds, and movements that are represented by words on paper. However, the process brought our class back to the fundamental goal of our discipline: how to read and interpret language.[3]

Instructors might ask for a wide range of performance in this exercise, from the rough read-through I initially required to a more long-term project that would include detailed analyses of how different forms of staging and sounds could be utilized and how they would influence the interpretation of the text.[4] Students and instructors can decide to include in these performances anything from recorded music to actual live instruments, and can enact anything from seated readings to fully choreographed presentations, depending on what talents and resources they have access to.[5]

Through the Arc of the Rain Forest *in a World Film and Literature Course*

The upper-division World Literature and Film course I have now taught for many years was originally conceived to meet a general education requirement in global culture. Initially, I chose a book and film from five different continents. *Through the Arc of the Rain Forest* was one of my first choices.[6] One problem of sampling works from across the globe is the difficulty in creating productive and useful comparative topics for midterm and final exam essays that do not overgeneralize or obscure the specificity of each text's local context. I began with large topics such as colonialism and gender as a means of comparison, but I slowly began to focus more closely on establishing thematic linkages. Eventually, I subtitled the course "The Politics of Viewing." *Through the Arc of the Rain Forest* dialogues with other texts and films that thematize both surveillance, which uses viewing as a means of controlling its object, and the power of media or other spectacles such as mass protest movements to shape viewers' beliefs.[7] Daniel Alarcon's *Lost City Radio*, for instance, focuses not only on how people live in a world of constant surveillance and on the impact of spectacle, but also on the role of another kind of media, the titular radio, which connects to the role of radio and television in Yamashita's novel.

The film most closely linked to Yamashita's novel is Anselmo Duarte's *O Pagador de Promessas* (*Payer of Promises*). This film follows the character Zé and his wife Rosa as they make a pilgrimage not unlike Chico Paco's pilgrimage to the Matacão in *Through the Arc*. Representatives of various parts of Brazilian society—of the church, the press, the police, business, and a variety of spiritual beliefs—respond to Zé as an antagonist, a hero, or, more frequently, someone to be exploited. Thus, Zé is a helpful character to compare to both Chico Paco and, to a lesser extent, the naive central character, Kazumasa. The film explores the uses of spectacle for a variety of purposes. It also helps provide a visual representation of the various pilgrimages depicted in Yamashita's novel, from Chico Paco's original trek to all whom he inspires through Radio Chico.

Another useful film pairing with *Through the Arc* is *Bye Bye Brazil*, which thematizes the power of film and other forms of entertainment to inspire, enchant, and even mislead us.[8] It also draws attention to environmental devastation in the Amazon basin, which allows students to delve more deeply into these themes as they arise in Yamashita's novel. One of the numerous documentaries on the work of the Brazilian environmentalist Chico Mendes or on environmental issues in general could also be useful to students and instructors. Introducing the class to examples of ecocriticism has also proven helpful to students seeking models and new perspectives for their own analyses. Working with this novel has taught me never to be afraid to bring in complex and even seemingly esoteric topics, as students with a variety of skill levels will rise to the occasion if instructors can make the relevance of these topics clear.

Introducing Freshman Composition Students to Research Using Tropic of Orange

Yamashita's works not only encourage students to resist easy essentialisms but also challenge them to grasp the historical realities that underpin her artistic representations. I was reminded how important this aspect of her work is when my multiethnic literature course was cancelled and I was asked to teach a second-semester freshman composition course with a week's notice. The main learning objective of this class is to prepare students for the writing and research they will be responsible for in a variety of disciplines. Thus, teaching more than one long work of literature is discouraged. I didn't have any textbooks preordered for the composition course, and so I assigned *Tropic of Orange*, which I knew was already in the bookstore from my literature course order, along with *Rereading America*, a popular composition anthology by Gary Columbo, Robert Cullen, and Bonnie Lisle.

To introduce students to research and to engage them in the complexity of *Tropic of Orange*, I came up with a list of topics that each student could pick from and do a brief presentation on at the beginning of each class session during which we read and discussed the novel.[9] The topics I assigned are ordered roughly in terms of when they become relevant to the section of the book we are reading.[10] The section in which Arcangel seemingly remembers all of Latin American history (145–48) and the scene in which Rafaela battles the jaguar (220–21) are particularly productive in supplying names and events with which students are likely to be unfamiliar. Such sections provide good topics for research projects, but there are a number of other topics that could be used, such as the twentieth-century popular culture or technology references made by Emi and Gabriel.

This project satisfied a requirement that students do an oral presentation during the course of the semester; it gave them a small topic on which to test out their research skills before advancing to larger projects and helped them learn about our library and its databases. Most important, it helped us replicate the communal nature of research because students were able to see how each contribution added to our collective knowledge.[11] The very structure of *Tropic of Orange*, which joins disparate narratives into a collective whole, emphasizes communal knowledge.

An especially memorable moment in the freshman composition course occurred when a young Latinx student who had lived all twenty years of his life in San Jose (which is very similar to the multiethnic Los Angeles Yamashita depicts) stated that until he read Yamashita's work, he had not realized how much Asian and Latinx immigrants had in common. Working with Yamashita's texts at every level of college teaching continually reminds me of the very practical real-world skills that literary study can engender, skills that are valuable not only for academic work but also for how students understand and respond to the world around them.

NOTES

[1]The course was called Race, Ethnicity, and Historiography in American Literature and included John Steinbeck's *East of Eden* (1952), E. L. Doctorow's *The Book of Daniel* (1971) and *Ragtime* (1975), Luis Valdez's *Zoot Suit* (1979), Maxine Hong Kingston's *China Men* (1980), Toni Morrison's *Beloved* (1987), and Louise Erdrich's *Tracks* (1988).

[2]The possibility of using one form of art to represent another is itself thematized in the text when the narrative opines, "They say architecture is frozen music" (Yamashita, *I Hotel* 278).

[3]One unexpected benefit of this activity was that it brought out a level of honesty about what students were able to comprehend and when they needed more help. Some admitted that they had initially skipped over this section, viewing it as "unreadable" instead of asking for help. Rather than making them feel less capable, this activity made many of my students say they felt more confident in tackling a difficult text, and it appeared to make them more likely to ask for help or clarification during the rest of the semester.

[4] Analyzing this section in detail allows students to explore how personal and collective stories intertwine; the impact of art forms such as music, dance, and folklore on our understanding of the personal; the role of the body in both individual identity and collective experience; and the contrast between the experience and the representation of gender in the various narratives expressed in the chapter and the novel as a whole.

[5] Other resources that will prove useful to teachers and students of *I Hotel* are Grace Talusan's "Teaching with Collaborative Writing Projects" and Lai Ying Yu's "'Capturing the Spirit'," which is especially helpful with "1971: Aiiieeeee! Hotel" and which includes Yamashita's own description of how she originally conceived of "Chapter 8: Dance." In the first book-length study of Yamashita's work, Jinqi Ling focuses on this chapter to discuss the novel's depiction and use of "performative activism" (*Across Meridians* 182–89). Teachers and students in need of additional historical context should read Estella Habal's *San Francisco's International Hotel* or watch Curtis Choy's *The Fall of the I-Hotel*. Pairing the novel, or even sections of the novel, with additional literary works, such as Lysley Tenorio's "Save the I-Hotel," may also be useful.

[6] When I was a graduate student in the early 1990s, Karen Tei Yamashita's name circulated through word of mouth, and her texts went from hand to hand. We all agreed that we loved her work but complained about not knowing how to teach *Brazil-Maru* and *Through the Arc of the Rain Forest*, both set in Brazil, in the Asian American or ethnic American literature classes we fantasized about teaching, since courses on such literatures were at the time structured largely around narratives of national identity set in the United States.

[7] Book and film pairings that work well with *Through the Arc* include Manuel Puig's novel *Kiss of the Spider Woman* and the films *Cat People* or *The Enchanted Cottage*, Salman Rushdie's novel *Shalimar the Clown* and the film *Mughal-E-Azam*, and Jessica Hagedorn's novel *Dogeaters* and Douglas Sirk's film *All That Heaven Allows*. These novels all have plots that involve surveillance; they also examine the impact of media on their characters, media that includes the specific films each novel has been paired with.

[8] Yamashita herself was kind enough to suggest this film. She once came to visit my class and gave a reading complete with a soundtrack of Brazilian music, yet another form of media that might be incorporated into a class focused on her novel.

[9] My original list of twenty-five topics for twenty-five student presentations included the following: a biography of Yamashita; García Márquez's short story "A Very Old Man with Enormous Wings"; Guillermo Gomez-Peña (a biography or a report on his *The New World Border*); film noir; homelessness in Los Angeles; the geography of Los Angeles (especially the freeway structure and the location of various communities such as South Central Los Angeles); the Justice for Janitors movement; the Mexican general Pancho Villa; the Tropic of Cancer; Latinx immigration in Los Angeles; Asian immigration in Los Angeles; Mike Davis's *City of Quartz* (individual chapters or smaller sections can be divided up among many students); the Mexican American journalist and civil rights activist Ruben Salazar; Chico Mendes; the Uruguayan writer Eduardo Galeano (a biography or an overview of his work); a biography of Emiliano Zapata; the performance artists John Malpede and Luis Alfaro; Manzanar Japanese American internment camp; Scott-Heron's "Revolution"; the women of Cochabamba and the 1812 Bolivian battle against Spanish forces; Las Madres de La Plaza de Mayo (Mothers of the Plaza de Mayo); Coatlalopeuh, Coatlicue, and other female Mesoamerican mythological figures; the 1946 film *The Big Sleep*; the North American Free Trade Agreement; and *lucha libre* wrestling.

[10] I had five students present each day for five days, but instructors may want to prolong discussion of the novel to seven meetings in order to replicate the seven-day organization of the book and to allow time for focused discussion and in-class writing projects.

[11] This communal dynamic helped us keep in mind the role of the researcher across the disciplines, which allowed students to engage with topics they might otherwise have seen as boring or irrelevant, such as proper citation format. "Good works cited are road maps for those who build on our work" and "accuracy and clarity are what we owe to our audience, those who come after us" became a couple of our classroom mantras.

The Critical Regionalism of *Tropic of Orange*

Jamie Crosswhite

On an academic whim a few years back, I handwrote Karen Tei Yamashita a letter, thanking her for a signed copy of *Tropic of Orange*. In a postscript I nervously asked if she would be willing to attend a Skype session with one of the literature classes I would be teaching the following academic year. I hoped our virtual seminar would be the culmination of a unit on critical regionalism, a place-based study examining my students' own dwelling place and those regions outside their familiarity. This virtual conference, uniting both spatial regions and speakers within those places, would occur after the class had spent weeks unpacking *Tropic of Orange*. Yamashita graciously accepted the invitation. What started as an agreement for one virtual discussion led to a three-year collaboration. I am eternally grateful for not only the gift of Yamashita's writing talents but also the sacrifice of her time and her willingness to work with a group of rural students from the Texas Panhandle.

At the time, I was teaching advanced placement (AP) high school seniors who were enrolled in an AP English Literature and Composition course. Class sizes ranged from twelve to twenty students, depending on the time slot(s) in which the course was offered and the number of students interested in taking an advanced literature course. Because we were a comparatively small school, some years allowed for two sections of AP Literature and Composition, while other years only one section was offered. The high school offered a few AP courses but was not a preparatory school. We were located in a small rural Texas town, right in the middle of the Bible Belt. Most of my students had grown up together in this conservative place, some had never crossed Texas borders, and most harbored a deep sense of Texas pride. While my students felt connected to and proud of their shared landscape, they had little understanding of the metropolitan complexity and diversity found in cities such as Los Angeles, and Yamashita's *Tropic of Orange* explored these features in ways students could comprehend. Reading her work through a critical regionalist lens allowed students to analyze the place where they lived as compared to Los Angeles—the busiest city in California—and the borderlands of California and Mexico. After reading *Tropic of Orange*, students felt as though they had visited LA, a place and community vastly different from their own "homeplace" (hooks, *Belonging* 2). Before entering a four-year university, the workforce, or the military, whether students would travel (literally) down the street to West Texas A&M University or across the country, it was essential they understood and questioned the place(s) that had shaped and the new places that would continue to shape their lives, both spatially and metaphorically. Most students who left my program would attend colleges in Texas or Oklahoma, one or two ventured to faraway state universities, a handful would select service in the United States military, and two or three would go on to work on their family farms or follow family trades. Though some students chose to stay close to home, other students saw themselves on the threshold of change, transitioning from the comforts and monotony of a place, people, and identity they had grown out of and were familiar with, to spaces and communities that were at the time unknown.

Before I outline the experiences and lessons of my course, it is necessary to clarify my conventionalization of critical regionalism. Like the scholar of Western studies Alex Hunt, I understand critical regionalism to be a "fusion of local culture with universal culture" founded in the theories of the architect Kenneth Frampton in which "local influences and materials (environment, landscape, history, narrative, folk-culture)" are used "to build works of art that are responsive to the local/regional environment while also speaking to cosmopolitan aesthetic and political issues" (Hunt 184). Building on this critical regionalist theory, I initiated our place-based studies in my own advanced literature course with the following questions: What is place, and how do you define it? What makes the place we currently share different from any other? These were journaling questions used to open the first class session, and they led to lengthy discussions regarding terms such as *globalization*, *placelessness*, and *sense of place*. As mostly Texas natives, students struggled to see their own place critically. Those who have engaged with the Texas education system are aware of the often exaggerated place-based history, culture, and lore woven throughout curriculum. Students began their studies of identity and place quite confident they were living in "the greatest state" and were overwhelmingly loyal to the myths of their upbringing. However, when I asked them what made Texas so "great," they were silent, proffering only a few explanations. From day one, students confronted the realization that they had fallen for romanticized versions of a place they thought they knew and were proud to be a part of.

As students read *Tropic of Orange* outside class, we worked in class to define and unpack terms relating to place and threads of regional rhetoric. Students defined, found examples of, and taught their peers about the following concepts, among others: sense and spirit of place, placelessness and nonplaces, borders and boundaries, betweenness of place, roots, dwelling, uprooting, the ecology of place, art and place, nostalgia, sacred places, territory, place marketing, gender and place, locale, topology and topistics, global sense of place, time and place, ghosts of place, thrown-togetherness, displacement, place branding, place names, the production and destruction of place, architecture and built place, and finally, virtual place and cyberplaces. The opportunity to define and explicate these terms gave students a foundation to begin a critical regional analysis of the novel and their own community.

We moved from basic terminology to an examination of Yamashita's literary techniques—for instance, her use of the braided narrative, differing narrative voices, elements of magical realism, characteristics of traditional regionalism, and meticulously crafted, culturally rich, and varied characters—in order to understand how stylistic choices contribute to regional rhetoric in literature.

In comparison to the primarily white patriarchal community of West Texas—the place which we were not only looking out from but also examining simultaneously—students found Yamashita's work offered a perspective of resistance and a new way of seeing. We explored how Yamashita's use of the braided narrative in lieu of a singular linear account speaks to the multiple voices that always exist within a shared space; it is not one story that resides in a given place, but the overlapping stories of many. Students enjoyed engaging with the distinct voices in *Tropic of Orange*, and they examined how each voice reflects a particular character's view of the shared region. For example, Manzanar is homeless by choice and spends his days recycling the sounds of the city, conducting a symphony of synthesized urban noise that most do not acknowledge as music. Sections written from Manzanar's perspective are fluid, layered, and constructed in lengthy sentences, mirroring his choice to see the often overlooked layers of the city as he composed a music that only a few could hear or imagine. This distinct voice and melodious fluidity are found in each of Manzanar's chapters, as they are in the following passage:

> On the surface, the complexity of layers should drown an ordinary person, but ordinary persons never bother to notice, never bother to notice the prehistoric grid of plant and fauna and human behavior, nor the historic grid of land usage and property, the great overlays of transport—sidewalks, bicycle paths, roads, freeways, systems of transit both ground and air, a thousand natural and man-made divisions, variations both dynamic and stagnant, patterns and connections by every conceivable definition from the distribution of wealth to race, from patterns of climate to the curious blueprint of the skies. (Yamashita, *Tropic* 57)

The cadence of Manzanar's chapters and the rhythmic syntax used to exhibit his view of the city fit with his artful approach to understanding his place, embracing each layer as a detail within the whole constructed symphony, his Los Angeles. Conversely, Bobby, a hardworking husband, father, and brother figure who is constantly hurrying through daily activities and juggling a chaotic work schedule to provide for his family, speaks in short, fragmented sentences and maintains this staccato style throughout; his chapters are fast-paced and always on the move, giving a feeling of quickness, change, and the constant hustle of survival within this urban space: "Happier he is, harder he works. Can't stop. Gotta make money. Provide for his family. Gotta buy his wife nice clothes. Gotta buy his kid the best. Bobby's kid's gonna know the good life. That's how Bobby sees it" (17). Like his view of Los Angeles, his voice is swift, his diction repetitive, his syntax direct, and his narrative style is to rapidly move forward with no opportunity to appreciate the layers of life that exist apart from pragmatic considerations. Each of the seven protagonists sees their shared region differently but also similarly in some respects; Yamashita's writing style in *Tropic of Orange* mirrors the layered reality of Los Angeles, an interconnected city of modernity and history, a tangling of cultures and ethnicity. Her characters walk the same streets, travel the same highways, and watch the same news channels as they shape and are shaped by this place and those inhabiting it.

As students tried to see and understand the uniqueness of Los Angeles through literary analysis, we simultaneously read texts that helped us demystify our shared space in Texas. I assigned shorter reading selections such as "Texas on Everything" and "Is Texas America?," by Molly Ivins, as well as selections from Sandra Cisneros (*House* and "*Woman Hollering Creek*"), Naomi Shihab Nye, and the regionally rooted John Graves. We discussed how the Texas Panhandle and West Texas are both part of and different from some of the more popular portrayals of Texas in history and mythology. We played with the idea of what it means to be a westerner today and in stories of the past. Though my students clung to the idea of being Texan, few embraced the label of "westerner." This idea of being a westerner became the point of intersection between the Texas students lived in and the California borderland depicted in *Tropic of Orange*. As we surveyed these convergences, students began to accept the idea that place can be constructed through media and myth and not always in relation to a lived reality. They found that images that glamorized Los Angeles and Hollywood looked nothing like the real layers of these places that Yamashita illuminates in her multiethnic portrayal of place, just as westernized portrayals of Texas, both historically and today, exaggerate the realities of the environments and communities within actual Texas topographies. Both California and Texas are in the West, and yet neither is truly western.

By examining ideas about a given place in relation to the reality of that place, students had the opportunity to explore how self-identification as a raced and gendered subject is both defined by and resistant to regional and outsider rhetoric, such as that found in literature, film, and the media in general. This led students to question and scrutinize their own sense of self within the classroom, within the local community, as Texans, and even as citizens or residents of the United States. Likely for the first time, students understood that what is referred to as Texas pride is often Texas arrogance, and they sought to diagnose how their residence within a particular place had a hand in constructing their identity, just as they too shaped the place in which they lived. Many students were from agricultural families; they understood irrigation, ranching, and what it meant to be stewards of the land, to literally create from the ground up. They had often seen themselves in positions of power, reigning over the landscape, but had rarely appraised the power asserted over them by the very forces they imagined themselves to be in control of.

From the time we began studying *Tropic of Orange*, I included students in planning our virtual meeting with Yamashita. While reading *Tropic*, students were required to compose three questions for Yamashita: one linked to a specific passage in the novel, one related to our critical regional approach to the novel, and one general, place-based question, which could be anything from a question connected to Yamashita's expertise or personal experiences to a thematic place-based question related to the novel to a question about *Tropic of Orange* as it might apply to other regions, art forms, or everyday life experiences. Students brought drafts of questions to class, where we conducted a roundtable discussion to help each student select one question they would pose and refine it for diction and syntactical clarity. Among the questions that made the cut were the following: Why is it important that the novel be set around the Los Angeles region, and could it be set in different regions such as southern Texas or the Miami area? What did you learn about the city while writing your book and what initially inspired you to compose it? Who was your intended audience? Did you write the novel for a specific region or group of people? After deciding on questions and editing them, students mapped out the order in which questions should be posited in order to facilitate a fluid and pragmatic discussion. They were both excited and nervous about the virtual conference, and even gave thought to the dress and speech appropriate for such an engagement. They joked about wearing cowboy hats and other cliché place identifiers and laughed as they practiced their questions in thick Texas accents. The day of our meeting, they came as they were, no hats and no artificial dialects, just small-town Texas students interested in place.

There was a bit of irony in unpacking gradations of place in this seemingly placeless virtual world, but all parties involved embraced the opportunity. Yamashita was candid and comical, and she responded thoughtfully to each question. She engaged students as if she were in the room, making them laugh and getting them to speak; her carefully considered answers to students' questions made students feel validated and helped them see themselves as a real part of the conversation and learning. Some of the critical regional commentary offered by Yamashita included her response to a question that asked about her intended audience: "I was writing to Los Angeles as a city and as a character itself," she said, "and I wanted to write to people who knew Los Angeles so I wanted to get that right. I was also writing to people who live in cosmopolitan cities and knew what that life was like." She also discussed some of her initial inspirations for composing such a piece:

> My Japanese community was a little pocket that lived within an African American neighborhood, Buzzworm's neighborhood in the novel. I had grown up in a city that was really African American and white with Hollywood on one side, and then I left for Brazil. In the 1980s the city had turned what they said was Hispanic or Latin American and my family who is Brazilian suddenly fit into this picture. But, when I started to read literature about Los Angeles what I discovered was there was very little about migration or these Latin American people. Part of the reason I wrote the book was to put these voices into the literature to create a book that I recognized was Los Angeles.

Students relished hearing that place was a part of Yamashita's purpose and process as she composed; they appreciated that truths they found in art were in fact truths that existed outside of it. They took comfort in recognizing that they were not misguided in a critical regionalist analysis of *Tropic of Orange*, knowing Yamashita had toiled to formulate a work she "recognized was Los Angeles" for the people who inhabit that space and who could appreciate the phoniness of Hollywood when compared to the authenticity of their lived experiences in that region.

We concluded our place-based lessons with the very questions we began with: What is place, and how do you define it? What makes the place we currently share different from any other? Responding to these questions again after our place-based examination of Yamashita's work, students wrote reflective responses with much more clarity and depth of thought. While many still adhered to their initial claim that Texas was a unique and worthy place of pride, they now had details to support and defend such a bold claim. A few students relinquished their previous worldviews, admitting the possibility of livable beauty outside the Lone Star State. Collectively, students left my course with the knowledge that place is a powerful force, one that can both alter and be altered, and that they too were a part of this phenomenon.

While I found *Tropic of Orange* suited to critical regionalist analysis at my students' academic level of understanding and an appropriate work with which to explore our similar yet different western landscape, many of Yamashita's texts speak to notions of place and could thus function fruitfully under a critical regionalist lens. In *Tropic of Orange*, however, Yamashita's representation of Los Angeles makes for an apt pairing in terms of similarity or difference, depending on the locale scholars and students are working from. Yamashita's depiction of the City of Angels is an influential rendering of place. And the opportunity to work directly with Yamashita significantly affected how my students conceptualized not only place but also the role writers and literature play in constructing and challenging lived landscapes.

Brazil-Maru and Ethnic Identities in the Japanese Classroom

Rie Makino

For students majoring in American literature in Japanese universities, questions about what it means to be Japanese in North and South America, rather than generally exploring what America is, is a good starting point for learning about American literature. In other words, studying American literature in Japan requires imagining our multiple racial and immigrant subject positions in the age of globalization. In this learning environment, the Japanese American writer Karen Tei Yamashita's second historical novel, *Brazil-Maru*, provides an excellent tool for Japanese students to reimagine the experiences of Japanese immigrants in Brazil and the United States.

Students in Japan are customarily not familiar with the history of Japanese Americans in the United States because Asian American literature is still a relatively minor subject area in the English departments of Japanese universities. Japanese American exchange students at Japanese universities are rare. In addition, textbooks about American ethnic or immigrant literature generally tell a history of Japanese immigrants that emphasizes their victimization in the United States—for instance, through plantation labor and the internment during WWII. Japanese students therefore tend to read Japanese American literature through the lens of narratives of victimization. Such narratives create two discourses, one of resistance and one of accommodation, as the Vietnamese American writer and professor Viet Thanh Nguyen points out. Nguyen posits the existence of a racial dichotomy between a resistant subjectivity—"the bad subject"—and an assimilated, capitalist one—"the model minority"; he criticizes Asian American academics who choose "the bad subject" as their strategic discourse to challenge capitalistic exploitation in the United States yet eventually present this form of resistance as a commodity (*Race* 143–57). After four years as a teaching assistant in the United States and later more than ten years in Japan as a tenure-track professor, I started to notice that we can use neither the concept of "the bad subject" nor that of "the model minority" in our approach to teaching American ethnic literature in Japan. In fact, Japanese students are even more willing than Japanese American students in the United States are to position themselves as a model minority since Japanese students have been acculturated to align themselves with representations of Japan—a nation of hard workers—in the United States during the period of strong economic growth from the 1970s to the 1990s. Such automatic identification with the model minority discourse makes it more difficult to learn about other aspects of the identity of Japanese immigrants. *Brazil-Maru* tells a completely different story of the Japanese immigrants in South America. In this text, the Japanese are portrayed as expatriates rather than immigrants, colonists rather than subalterns, and socialist Christians rather than an ethnic minority subscribing to a capitalist social model. The text consequently disrupts commonly held perceptions of the Japanese immigrant experience in North and in South America.

How can we, as Japanese professors of American literature, teach the representation of Japanese in the Americas from a critical viewpoint, one that does not reproduce mainstream and reductive stereotypes of Japanese as merely a version of the Japanese American model minority? Yamashita's portrayal of Japanese immigrants in *Brazil-Maru* is a good place to start for students whose understanding of Asian American literature frequently falls prey to the dichotomy pointed out by Nguyen.

Pedagogical Goals

I had two pedagogical goals in introducing students to *Brazil-Maru*: the first was to disrupt students' stereotypical understanding of Japanese Americans in the United States, which is based on a discourse of victimization; the second was to unsettle their negative perceptions of Japanese Brazilians, which were largely constructed by the Japanese media.

Students in Japan who study American literature tend to be more familiar with African American literature than with Asian American literature. Late-twentieth- and early-twenty-first-century American ethnic literature focuses more on the civil rights movement and less on the Yellow Power movement of the 1970s. As a result, they may assume that Japanese American literature is similar to African American literature. Viewing Japanese Americans as an ethnic group that has been victimized and stigmatized by the nation-state of the United States, students express a sense of guilt for what this group experienced, especially the internment as a result of Pearl Harbor. Even though Yamashita is a Japanese American writer who was born after WWII and who did not experience the internment, Japanese students still attempt to understand her life and work as part of this discourse of victimization.

While students do not have much if any contact with Japanese Americans, they do have opportunities to interact with Japanese Brazilians. This is because Oizumi-cho, a city in Gunma Prefecture, and Hamamatsu, a city in Shizuoka Prefecture, are home to two major communities of Japanese Brazilians who work at automobile companies and a famous lunch box company, Origin Bento. Some Japanese have unfavorable images of Japanese Brazilians simply because their customs are not Japanese.[1] *Brazil-Maru*, the story of relatively wealthy Japanese immigrants who are Christian socialists and intellectuals, presents an opportunity to challenge students' stereotypical preconceptions of Japanese Brazilians.

Teaching Strategies and Student Reactions to **Brazil-Maru**

I began the class session on *Brazil-Maru* by providing a historical background on the immigrant group depicted in the novel. I also created an atmosphere in which students could ask any kind of question. My students therefore freely articulated their ideas since this was their first introduction to Japanese immigrants in Brazil and also to a Japanese American writer. On the first day of class, I asked students how they would categorize this text. Most students maintained that *Brazil-Maru* was a "colonial text" and even found it similar to nineteenth-century American literature by American Renaissance authors. One student commented, "I am interested in this text, but I do not know how to categorize this type of literature. Does this belong to the subcategory of American literature or is this part of Brazilian literature? Or it could be part of Japanese immigrant and colonial literature. Which one is appropriate?" Such questioning provided a basis for discussing how to define American literature.

In class I usually provide students with basic information on the authors and their works before delving into the texts. After learning about the authors' lives, students begin to focus on the topics they will write essays on. In the case of *Brazil-Maru*, the disparity between the work and the author's background led to a discussion of how to categorize this type of novel in the field of American literature. Yamashita was born in the United States but spent more than ten years in Brazil. If we focus on Yamashita's background as an American writer born in the United States, we might say that *Brazil-Maru* is part of American literature. However, the text is about a group of Japanese immigrants with a socialist Christian background living in São Paulo, Brazil. In class, I described *Brazil-Maru* as literature written in English in the age of globalization, and I consider this the most appropriate category for the novel.

Due to its transnational setting, the novel deviates from the victimization narrative Japanese students tend to associate with American ethnic literature set in the United States. The novel details the rise and fall of a Japanese immigrant, Kantaro Uno, who establishes a community called Esperança in São Paulo in the 1920s. Yamashita's portrait of Kantaro's character is neither ultranational (i.e., subsumed under the influence of Japanese imperialism) nor assimilated under the influence of the United States. Kantaro is unique in that his characterization transcends nation-state politics—that is, he belongs neither to imperial Japan nor to Brazil.

The uniqueness of Kantaro Uno's character divided the class. To promote further discussion, I asked students the following questions: What is your impression of this protagonist? Do you notice any similarities to the patriarchal figures in other books you have read? If so, which ones? Some students did not have a positive impression of Kantaro, a sentiment that was reflected in their comments: "I do not like him because he is very patriarchal"; "I expected more unique representations of Japanese immigrant masculinity in this novel, but seemingly it is a simple transplantation of Japanese patriarchy on the other side of the earth"; "I really do not think he is Japanese." Their criticisms were largely based on parts 3 and 4 of the book: Kantaro's and his nephew Genji's narratives (115–83, 185–241). I also received a few unique, positive pieces of feedback: one student said, "I am sort of interested in him even though I do not like his violent and megalomaniacal nature in his later years. I am just interested in his transformation. It could be ugly but very humane." A graduate student said the following of Kantaro: "This character reminds me of Thomas Sutpen in William Faulkner's *Absalom, Absalom!*" Indeed, one of Yamashita's reviewers discusses the similarity between *Brazil-Maru* and *Absalom, Absalom!*[2] While the character elicited several negative reactions, Kantaro's characteristics were also attractive to some students.

As a result of these comments, I started to think about how to avoid stereotypical depictions of Japanese immigrant masculinity, such as Kantaro's patriarchal or hypermasculine characteristics, when teaching this text. I tried instead to emphasize the positive aspects of Brazilian society and its national character. When compared to the racial tensions experienced by Japanese immigrants in the United States, it is significant that Japanese immigrants in Brazil were welcomed as citizens in the 1920s as a means of expanding Brazilian national power.[3] The period of the 1920s, when Kantaro is actively engaged in his business in Brazil, also coincided with an artistic movement called Brazilian modernism, a cultural renaissance grounded in cultural cannibalism, the willing digestion of foreign cultures.[4] During the 1920s, immigrant groups in the United States were not allowed to own land and were severely restricted by the country's immigrant laws because of racial biases that deemed them unassimilable. While Japanese immigrants were prevented from assimilating into the society of the United States during the early twentieth century, the story for Japanese immigrants in Brazil was different, which challenges the general notion that immigration policies of all nation-states are restrictive. I also focused on the idea that Kantaro is only one product of Brazil's cultural heterogeneity.

Yamashita's portrayal of Kantaro avoids any suggestion of possible imperialist impulses. History suggests that the 1920s witnessed the peak of Japanese imperialism. However, when we pay close attention to Kantaro's motivation for leaving Japan, it is related neither to Japanese imperialism nor to ultranationalism. Rather, Kantaro's immigration is motivated by a natural disaster, namely the Great Kanto earthquake of 1923 (*Brazil-Maru* 6). In addition, Kantaro is described as a person who does not have any attachment to his native country, Japan. This also helps dispel preconceptions of the Japanese immigrant experience and the essentialist nature of Japanese national loyalty.

Although *Brazil-Maru* contains an informative discussion of many issues, we cannot ignore the controversy this book raises. The novel is a product of Yamashita's interviews with the people of the Japanese immigrant communities in São Paulo, communities that were established by the upper-class Japanese immigrants who came to Brazil in the 1920s.[5] As a professor who introduced this novel to students in Japan, I emphasized that this is not history but is rather one way of representing Japanese immigrants in Brazil. The novel provides an opportunity for students to discuss the differences between history and an author's artistic representations of specific histories.

Teaching *Brazil-Maru* in Japanese universities challenges students' preconceptions of the status and experiences of Japanese immigrants and offers perspectives different from those encountered in much of the canonical American literature customarily taught in the Japanese education system. Against the backdrop of globalization, Yamashita's *Brazil-Maru* is a good starting point for transcending national boundaries and values we have learned in past educational environments.

NOTES

[1]Tsuda reports on the discrimination experienced by Japanese Brazilians: "A number of Japanese I spoke with had negative images of Brazil not only as backward and underdeveloped (*okureteiru kuni*) but also as a country with a 'low culture' (*hikui bunka*) and directly associated the nikkeijin with such images by virtue of their Brazilian origins" (119). Lesser also asserts, "In Japan dekasegi are considered to be 'Brazilians' whose role is to provide temporary labor and little more, which leads many Nikkei to feel uncontestedly Brazilian for the first time in their life" ("Japanese" 13).

[2]Comparing *Brazil-Maru* with *Absalom, Absalom!*, Dephtereos asserts, "Yamashita is less than successful in her manipulation of the point of view of the commune's patriarch, the Colonel Sutpen-like megalomaniac Kantaro Uno" (512).

[3]This generosity is in stark contrast to the United States immigrant policy that utilized Asian labor to prop up the economy of the United States without allowing Asian workers to apply for citizenship (Lowe, *Immigrant Acts* 154–73).

[4]The concept of cultural cannibalism was advocated by the Brazilian modernist poet Oswald de Andrade in his "Manifesto Anthropofago" ("Cannibalist Manifesto"), originally published in the *Revisita de Anthropofagia*. For a translation of Oswald's "Manifesto," see Bary. For Japanese-language resources on cultural cannibalism in Brazil, see Motohashi 55–56; Imafuku 121–22.

[5]See the acknowledgments in *Brazil-Maru*. Yamashita expresses her gratitude to the people she interviewed in the communities in São Paulo during her stay from 1975 to 1977.

Hospitality, Borders, and Spatial Politics in *I Hotel*

Ana María Manzanas-Calvo

Western literature in general and classical literature in particular offer memorable acts of hospitality. In Homer's *Odyssey*, for example, we find nameless guests who nonetheless are welcome, abusive guests who behave like parasites while the lord is absent, and examples of cannibalistic hospitality where the guest is devoured by the host. The practice of hospitality (*xenia* in Greek, *hospitium* in Latin) was one of the most cherished virtues in ancient Greece and Rome. *Hospitium* initially signified the simple but sacred duty to welcome and protect any stranger. There was *hospitium privatum* ("private hospitality") established between individuals and *hospitum publicum* ("public hospitality") established between two states. This doubleness alerts us to the complexity of the term, for hospitality may be understood not only as a disposition pertaining to the individual (and hence to ethics) but also as an institutional prescription belonging to politics (Schérer 15). The welcoming of a guest was of special interest to the supreme god, Zeus, and the gods punished more severely the crimes committed against strangers than the crimes committed against citizens (16).

Comparing this vision of hospitality to its current usage in political campaigns and speeches offers ample opportunities to discuss the evolution of this ancient virtue. Furthermore, hospitality can be used as a lens to evaluate how the United States has dealt with its others, from the European colonization of the American continent and the transformation of Native Americans into unwanted guests to the enslavement of African Americans; from the Chinese Exclusion Act of 1882 to present-day exclusionary policies. Hospitality cuts across the courses I teach at the University of Salamanca, Spain, from the compulsory undergraduate course A Cultural History of the United States to the undergraduate elective courses Multiculturalism in American Literature and Autobiographical Narratives in American Literature to the master's course Trans-Nations in American Literature.

Public Hospitality: A Hotel

In *I Hotel* we find the public and conditional sort of hospitality that a country extends to its immigrants. Yamashita exemplifies this public hospitality through the history of the International Hotel (I-Hotel) in San Francisco. What is the meaning of situating a hotel (and hence, commercial hospitality) at the center of the novel? Most have stayed temporarily at a hotel, but what does it mean to live in a hotel? (cf. F. Ng, *Bone* 2). A hotel is initially not a home. But what is a home? Who has traditionally felt at home in the United States? Students should be familiar with the relocation of Japanese and Japanese Americans during World

War II, with the history of the civil rights movement in general, and with the Asian American movement in particular. Theoretical conceptualizations such as the concept of home as expressed by Gaston Bachelard in *The Poetics of Space* are useful. Bachelard claims that "the house shelters daydreaming, the house protects the dreamer, the house allows one to dream in peace" (6). Without it, he claims, we would be just "dispersed beings" (7). At the same time, and to supplement Bachelard's remarks, students consider the ways in which a home can be envisioned as a mechanism that may not only welcome but also reject whoever is on the outside, as Rosemary Marangoly George remarks: "Homes are not about inclusions and wide open arms as much as they are about places carved out of closed doors, closed borders and screening apparatuses" (18). In contrast, a hotel is nobody's home. It is not a final destination, nor does it shelter any dreams. A hotel cannot be defined as "relational, or historical, or concerned with identity," and hence it would qualify, at least provisionally, as a non-place, according to Marc Augé's distinction (*Non-Places* 77–78). Excerpts from these critics' works should ideally be assigned prior to the discussion of *I Hotel*.

Another opportunity for student discussion is the spatial politics in the novel. Located in a segregated part of San Francisco, the I-Hotel was surrounded by solid, if invisible, boundaries. There are, George Lipsitz argues, "'pure' and homogeneous spaces" from which "'impure' populations have to be removed" (*How Racism Takes Place* 29). Given these inner borders and enclosures it is important to realize that inclusion does not imply belonging (Mezzadra and Neilson 62). As the narrative voice claims, the tenants were aware that they were already "displaced people in the city's plan to impose a particular meaning of *home* and a particular meaning of *nation*" (Yamashita, *I Hotel* 590). In *I Hotel* inclusion implies a kind of commercial hospitality that paradoxically includes as it excludes. This oxymoronic sentence adds to the instability of hospitality, always mediated by its own parasitic other—hostility—and always limited and conditional. Jacques Derrida has coined the term *hostipitality* to refer to this kind of impossible hospitality.

Specially favored by students, the term proves helpful in understanding Yamashita's text as well as the forces of inclusion and exclusion represented by the novel's titular hotel. To have a more focused discussion I assign the section titled "We" from "1968: Eye Hotel," sections of "1975: Internationale Hotel," and two complete novellas, "1973: Int'l Hotel" and "1977: I-Hotel." "We," "1973: Int'l Hotel," and "1977: I-Hotel" detail the arrival of immigrants to the United States, offer examples of the different forms of hospitality they encounter, and describe their occupation of and eviction from the I-Hotel.

A Hotel Country

Once the concept of the hotel has been situated between hospitality and hostility, I introduce Mireille Rosello's *Postcolonial Hospitality*. Rosello bases her thesis on the premise that countries have traditionally portrayed immigrants as guests. For Rosello, this is not an accurate metaphor to describe immigrants. If we talk about immigrants as guests, we forget the reason why they are in the host country: immigrant workers cannot be regarded as guests because they have been hired (Rosello 9). Given this proposition there is no reason to identify the nation-state as a house. The "so-called hospitality of nations," Rosello argues, "may more closely resemble commercial hospitality" (34). Thus, it is more accurate to imagine the state as a hotel rather than as a private house (34). Discussing Rosello's conclusions in class is illuminating, since replacing the concept of the house with that of the hotel changes the nature of the guest, who automatically becomes a paying guest instead of a burden to or a parasite on the country (35). The implications of parasitism, however, are not as clear-cut as they may seem, and it is useful to refer students to Michel Serres's *The Parasite* for further reading.

Once this correlation between a country and a hotel has been established, the question is how it may be applied to *I Hotel*. Initially, the trope of the country as a hotel that includes and excludes its migrants seems straightforward. However, it is important to emphasize in class that nothing stays put in the ten novellas that make up the novel, and neither does the concept of the hotel, which turns into the opposite of its initial meaning: through their resistance to eviction in the years 1968–77, the tenants manage to fashion a hotel-nation that provides a new sense of "we-ness," a home, and a new form of political belonging. As an elderly Filipino tenant puts it, "Have here a good neighborhood, and good and very kind countrymen, old and new friends. . . . I have stayed here so long that I called this Hotel my HOME" (Yamashita, *I Hotel* 45). How is this transformation possible? How do we get from the nation-state as hotel to the hotel as nation-state? The answer is that *I Hotel* evokes the workings of an alternative nation-state that can offer a sense of shared memory and space as well as new modalities of membership and inclusion. This transformation through occupation is not new in Yamashita's novels. In *Tropic of Orange*, a group of homeless individuals occupy empty vehicles during a massive traffic jam in LA and transform them into homes. The stalled vehicles became a community, a border town, a Babel that subverts conventional spatial hierarchies. Similarly, a former surgeon, Manzanar Murakami, occupies a specific space on the freeway, the overpass, thus making a home out of the non-place.

Hostile Hospitalities and the Repossession of Place

The discussion of different examples of inhospitable places in *I Hotel*—from Angel Island to Alcatraz to internment camps in the desert to the persistence of the camps in the characters' everyday lives—figures prominently in my course on multiculturalism in American literature. As described in the novel, hostility started as the migrants disembarked on Angel Island. The island barracks offer talking walls, the inscriptions of those who saw the hostility of a country that kept them captive for months, even years. The barracks also stand as a reminder of the exclusionary practices that collide with the celebration of the United States as a hospitable country (Behdad, *Forgetful Nation* 9–20).

As a place of detention, Angel Island parallels other places of imprisonment that punctuate the novel, such as the camps where Japanese and Japanese Americans were detained during World War II. Yamashita previously introduced the Manzanar concentration camp in *Tropic*, where readers learn that the character Manzanar Murakami has taken his name from his alleged birthplace, Manzanar. The Manzanar camp stands as an oblique—if ghostly—presence, for it comes back every time the name is mentioned in the novel (Crawford 86). The camps resurface in "1975: Internationale Hotel" when a group of activists drive to the Tule Lake relocation camp, where those individuals were sent who were deemed disloyal or who gave unsatisfactory answers to questions 27 and 28 on the "Application for Leave Clearance" questionnaire. Both questions tried to determine loyalty and allegiance to the United States as well as the internees' willingness to fight. The novella zooms in on Mo Akagi, who was interned at age five and paroled at age nine. A similar experience of incarceration reverberates in the life of Takabayashi, who was interned with his family in Tule Lake when he was sixteen. He later becomes a professor in the School of Criminology at the University of California, Berkeley, but eventually loses his position. For him, as for Akagi, the camps did not belong to the past, nor were they solely situated in the desert. When the university chancellor announces his decision to close down the Berkeley School of Criminology (Yamashita, *I Hotel* 126), Takabayashi is banned to a cold office on an empty campus. As he comments to his son, Wayne, he has been exiled to his Walden (401). Like Herman Melville's Bartleby—the paradigmatic, static hero of American literature—Takabayashi stages his resistance by staying in. Like Bartleby and the tenants of the I-Hotel, Takabayashi prefers "to be stationary" (Melville 148).

Being stationary is a form of resistance that also undergirds the act of a group of Asian and Native Americans that departs the mainland on a boat called the *Turtle* and comes to occupy another prison island, Alcatraz. If the nation-state has immobilized and corralled these contingents into spaces that are deemed impure, one may wonder what the boat offers instead. What kind of "we-ness" or "imagined community," to use Benedict Anderson's term, emerges on the boat and on the occupied territory of Alcatraz? How does this sense of community relate to other experiments of political belonging and occupation? Like the I-Hotel, the boat is a nation in motion, a new form of belonging for those who were never welcome in the hotel-country. The place where Native Americans were incarcerated for resisting government policies now welcomes the occupiers as the land of the free, "home of the brave" (Yamashita, *I Hotel* 380). The occupation resonates with other acts of resistance in the novel, such as Takabayashi's occupation of the premises of criminology and the I-Hotel tenants resisting eviction notices for decades.

"Mi casa es su casa / Mi tierra es su tierra / Mi mundo es su mundo" ("My home is your home / My land is your land / My world is your world"; Yamashita, *Tropic*

182; my trans.). The simplicity of this poem, which Arcangel writes for Rafaela's son, captures the meaning of hospitality: an opening of the self and the space of the self toward the other. There is no border dividing what I call my territory from what I call yours, just the equalizing power of "is." The current reception of the other, whether in the United States or in Europe, is a far cry from the poem, however. A useful in-class exercise is for students to rewrite the poem according to their assessment of hospitality today. One possible rewriting is the following: "Mi casa no es su casa / Mi tierra no es su tierra / Mi mundo no es su mundo" ("My home is not your home / My land is not your land / My world is not your world"). It is possible to claim that *I Hotel* is located somewhere between these two poems, between hospitality and hostility. The novel responds to the latter version by creating a palimpsest of occupations and acts of resistance. Simon Critchley argues that resistance "begins by occupying and controlling the terrain upon which one stands, where one lives, works, acts and thinks" (114). In *I Hotel*, inhospitable locations are the genesis of a narrative of occupation and repossession for those whom the state has dispossessed, excluded, and been hostile toward. Tenants and occupiers fashion modes of belonging based on what the narrative voice calls a "connective wave that carries you to the same infinite space, and you feel more alive than you have ever felt" (Yamashita, *I Hotel* 380). This is the connectivity that reverberates throughout *I Hotel*. A variety of meaningful writing exercises—including research papers on current government policies designed to manage inclusions, exclusions, and in-between conditions—are possible in relation to the novel's engagement with hospitality. Borders, spaces, and hospitality create a theoretical framework that enables new ways to interpret and teach *I Hotel*. Perhaps more important, this framework can help us relate what we read to a globalized world torn between the mandates of hospitality and the exercise of hostility.

Tropic of Orange as Palimpsest: A Literary Cartographic Approach

Anastasia Lin and John Dees

Karen Tei Yamashita's sprawling novel *Tropic of Orange* can prove challenging to teach given its seven overlapping character narratives, historical references, mix of literary styles, and commentary on American sociopolitical issues. Yet more confusing to many students is the substantial geography covered in the novel; though ostensibly set in Los Angeles, the first chapter opens with the subtitle "Not Too Far from Mazatlán" while the final section of the novel is titled "Sunday: Pacific Rim." As Yamashita explains in an interview with Ryuta Imafuku, *Tropic of Orange* layers her own understanding of a multiethnic Los Angeles—one fraught with socioeconomic disparities exacerbated by governmental ordinances—onto a geographic map of the city itself (Yamashita, "Latitude"). In so doing, Yamashita's novel mirrors the aims of cultural geographers such as David Harvey in *Social Justice and the City* and Edward Soja, whose work reveals "the way dominant narratives conceal the constructedness of space and its effects" (Blair 545). Yamashita's approach, which Elisabeth Mermann-Jozwiak terms "spatial archaeology" (1), allows *Tropic of Orange* to present a critique of globalization, liberal multiculturalism, and the erasure of immigrant histories in the official narrative of Los Angeles. To effectively teach Yamashita's themes of dislocation and globalism, a pedagogy influenced by the spatial turn is warranted.[1]

In 2013 I (Lin) collaborated with coauthor John Dees (then an undergraduate researcher trained in geographic information system, or GIS, technology) to create a series of maps for Yamashita's *Tropic of Orange*.[2] The maps help students visualize and reimagine Los Angeles, revealing both its history of immigration and the ways in which governmental regulations, construction, and zoning processes often further constrain the mobility and socioeconomic realities of immigrants, minorities, and the homeless. I teach Yamashita's work primarily in a sophomore-level survey course that fulfills a core requirement for graduation at a predominantly white, undergraduate institution in the rural Southeast. In 2016 I collaborated with two professors well-versed in GIS to create a cross-disciplinary project where students in a senior-level English seminar worked with a cartography class to create their own maps of the novel.

In both the sophomore survey and senior seminar, I begin by introducing students to the concept of literary cartography and invite them to both map out the action of the novel and catalogue places visited as they read. In the sophomore survey course, the list of destinations students compile figures into their final projects. Like Barbara Piatti and her colleagues, I define literary cartography as an interdisciplinary field that draws on geography, critical literary analysis, and technology to offer additional contexts and new ways of analyzing literature (Piatti et al. 2–5). The maps prove especially helpful for those nonliterature majors enrolled in the sophomore survey class who might struggle with literary analysis because the maps allow students to visualize the novel's themes. At the senior level, working with maps offers a broader frame of critical inquiry, which subsequently encourages new ways of seeing and understanding the text.

One of the goals of *Tropic of Orange* is to question the feasibility of a Los Angeles devoid of immigrant labor and a transnational economy. In class I present a map of Arcangel's and Rafaela's roots and routes to promote discussion of both transnationalism and globalism (fig. 1).[3] The map asks students to reimagine Los Angeles as Arcangel does—"The Village of the Queen of the Angels of Porciuncula, the second largest city of México, also known as Los Angeles"—emphasizing both the colonial past of Los Angeles as well as the interconnectedness of Los Angeles and the Global South in terms of immigration and economic trade (Yamashita, *Tropic* 211). Throughout the novel, Yamashita draws attention to the flow of immigrants and goods over the border, foregrounding the relative ease with which goods cross as opposed to people. Bobby sums this up succinctly as he reflects, "Cuz is staring at her new Nikes. Made in China. Nikes get in. But not the bro" (230). The map helps students visualize Yamashita's interrogation of both the delimiting nature of borders for those without economic means as well as the porousness of these borders when it comes to transporting goods (and less often laborers) valued in the United States.

Once the broad expanse of Arcangel's geography is presented in map form, students can then begin to explore the subtle connections Yamashita draws between current socioeconomic and racial realities and their precolonial histories. Arcangel's narration of the fifty-two-year cycles of doom present an index of North and South American conquest, while his march northward, pulling with him "the very hemline of the Tropic of Cancer and the great skirts of its relentless geography," imagines the reterritorialization of Los Angeles by those whose

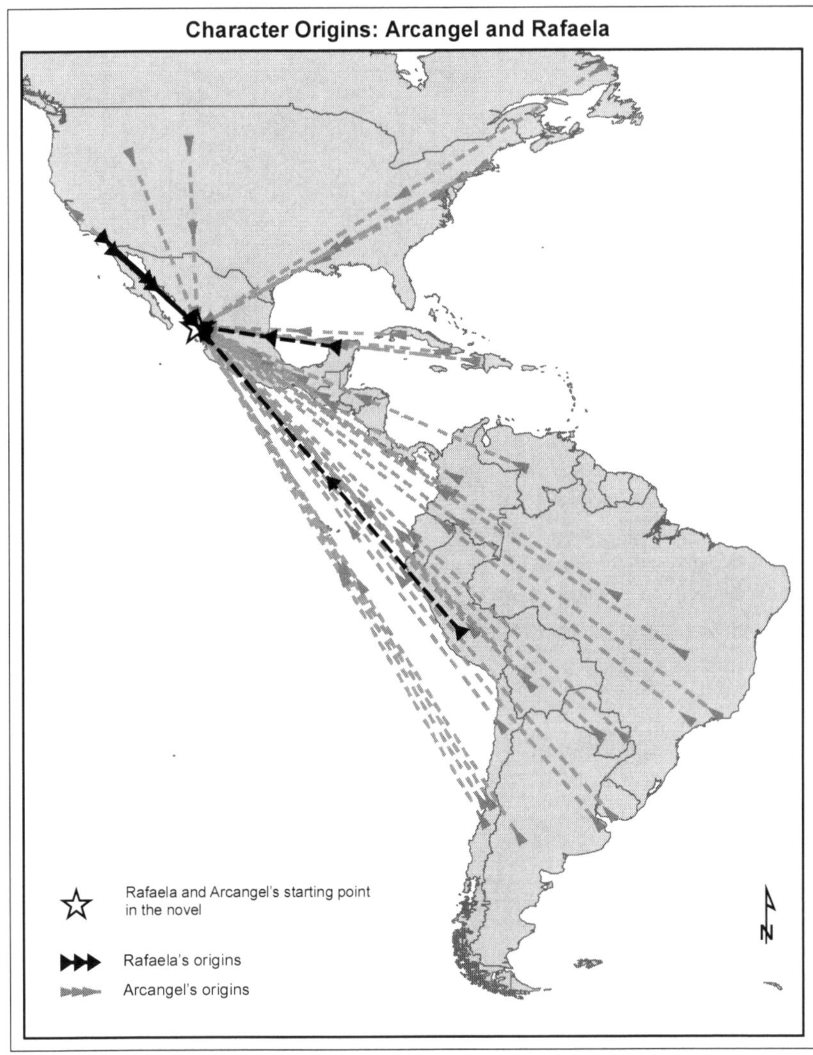

Figure 1. Map by John Dees in ArcGIS 9.3.

labor supports it (197). To augment this reading, I present another map that drills down into the specific history of each location Arcangel mentions.[4] The map reveals the majority of these sites as points of contact (Christopher Columbus's alleged discovery of the New World [49], Juan Rodríguez Cabrillo's arrival in San Diego [50]), colonization (Hernán Cortés's slaughter of the Aztecs and Francisco Pizzaro's execution of Atahualpa [200]), or geopolitical upheaval (the California gold rush [133], Ruben Salazar's murder [39])—quite literally every time the map changes due to a discovery or major event. Discussing the current locus of economic power against the backdrop of the map invites students to question how capitalism and globalization extend the displacement and disenfranchisement of imperialism, echoing Arcangel's questions: "Is it a crime to be poor? Can it be illegal to be a human being?" (211).

Yamashita is equally interested in the ways official histories and maps can obscure a location's sociocultural realities. To reflect on this theme and to clarify the plot of the novel, we created palimpsestic maps that charted the locations of specific characters against the social, cultural, and economic geographies of those locations. For example, students are often discomfited by the characterization of Bobby Ngu as "Chinese from Singapore with a Vietnam name speaking like a Mexican living in Koreatown" (15). Many students initially write this line off as Yamashita making full use of artistic license to prove a point. Yamashita describes Bobby's arrival in the United States as a result of the Chinese diaspora, American capitalism, and the Vietnam War, a clear reflection of her critique of capitalism and United States international policy. Yet the second half of Bobby's characterization—"speaking like a Mexican living in Koreatown"—requires further research. Most students assume that Los Angeles's Koreatown is an impermeable ethnic enclave of Korean Americans. However, showing students a map of the location of Bobby's home against census data collected in 1990 and 2000 demonstrates that Yamashita's characterization of Bobby is based in fact (fig. 2). Bobby's house is indicated by the star. Comparing the census data from 1990 and 2000 reflects the changing economic status of many Korean Americans in Los Angeles and its effect on the Koreatown area; when many of the established inhabitants of K-Town moved to the suburbs, they left behind cheap housing and menial jobs in the still predominantly Korean-owned businesses and restaurants. New immigrants from Central and South America took advantage of both. Thus, despite the number of Korean storefronts and signs, most current residents of Koreatown are Latino; as of 2000, Latinos made up 60% of the population (Lee and Park 246). These maps help students see Yamashita's representation of Bobby in terms of place and race as a further extension of her overall project of questioning static identities given our transnational reality.

By superimposing locations visited by the characters on the average median income of Los Angeles, the last map I introduce synthesizes Yamashita's focus on borders, socioeconomic status, and geography in order to highlight mobility

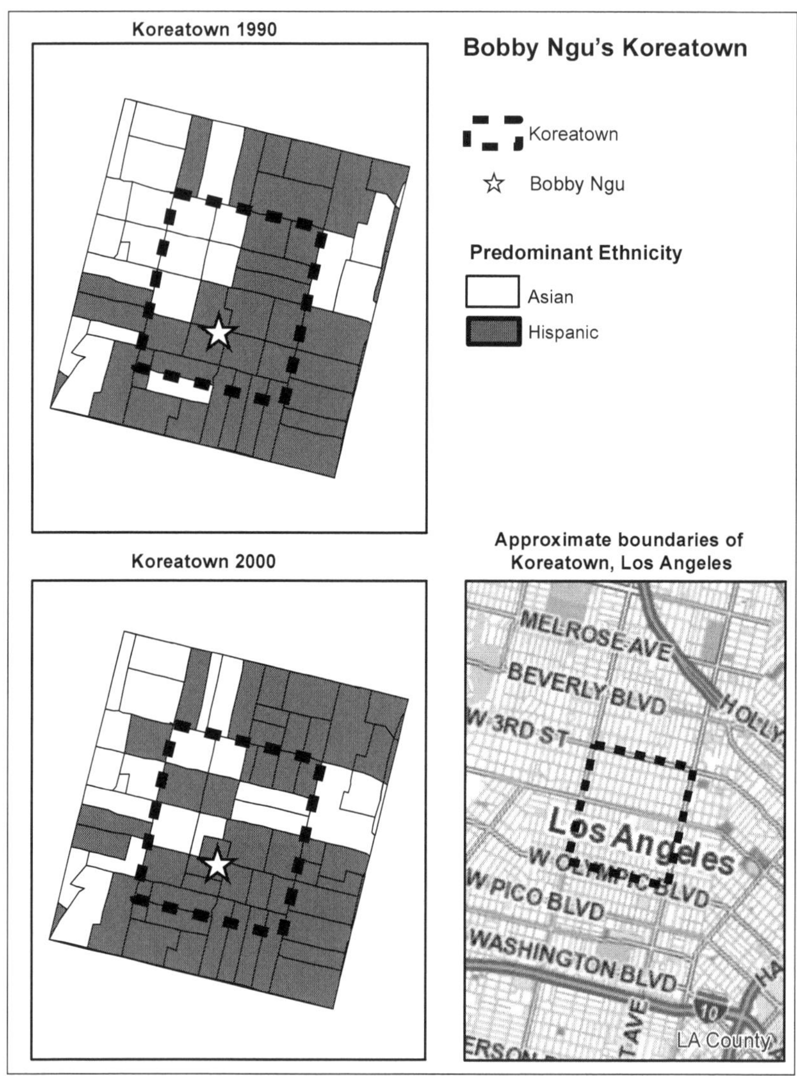

Figure 2. Map by John Dees in ArcGIS 9.3. Sources: Steven Manson et al., "Table: NP10. Hispanic Origin by Race, 1990 U.S. Census STF1 [CSV file]." *IPUMS National Historical Geographic Information System: Version 14.0*, 2019, doi.org/10.18128/D050.V14.0; Steven Mason et al., "Table: NP008A. Population by Hispanic or Latino and Not Hispanic or Latino by Race, 2000 U.S. Census SF1b [CSV file]." *IPUMS National Historical Geographic Information System: Version 14.0*, 2019, doi.org/10.18128/D050.V14.0.

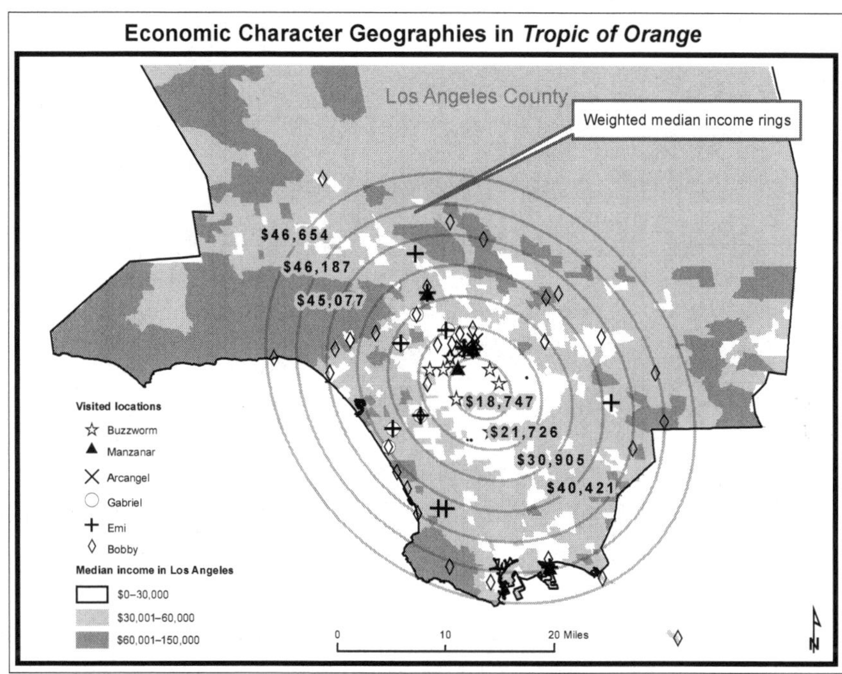

Figure 3. Map by John Dees in ArcGIS 9.3. Source: Steven Manson et al., "Table: NP80A. Median Household Income in 1989, 1990 U.S. Census STF3 [CSV file]." *IPUMS National Historical Geographic Information System: Version 14.0*, 2019, doi.org/10.18128/D050.V14.0.

(fig. 3). Students note the relative immobility of the poor and homeless compared to the free range afforded to the middle-class characters who have access to cars. During class discussions, students are often surprised by Bobby's expansive mobility; given his profession as a janitor and his home in Koreatown, they often expect his movements to be limited. Yet Bobby's profession is what allows for his mobility—he cleans the offices of wealthy individuals. This prompts students to reflect on both the very real immobility of people with lower socioeconomic status as well as the invisibility of the poor within affluent neighborhoods. Finally, the map serves to further discussions of the impact of LA freeways; designed to ensure easy access to affluent areas of LA as well as the efficient transport of goods and people, the construction of these freeways disconnected older communities in the poorer sections of town from the rest of Los Angeles.[5] In class, we focus on Buzzworm's recounting of the history of his neighborhood. Buzzworm, an African American Vietnam veteran and longtime member of the community, acts as "walking social services," doling out information on local clinics and soup kitchens (26). He describes where the widening of the freeway shuttered stores by dividing the community in two: "Break down the overpass crossing the freeway. Make it impossible for people to pass" (83). Mapping mobility prompts students to reimagine the ways space and geography construct and reflect social and economic realities.

In the classroom, these maps assist students struggling to understand the novel's geographic details by offering a data-backed graphical rendering that clearly visualizes the novel's themes. The maps have proven especially helpful in classrooms resistant to critical multiculturalism; they also encourage students to research issues relating to transnationalism, capitalism, and hybridity. At the sophomore level, I require further research in a final assignment that invites students to focus on a single character. The assignment asks students to create a study guide for this character. The study guide consists of seven sections:

- a self-designed cover image representing the character students choose;
- an introduction to and outline of the novel as a whole with special attention to the character's place in it;
- a summary of each chapter the character narrates;
- a character study describing the character, replete with quotations from the text;
- a list of six to fifteen places visited or referred to by the character;
- an annotated bibliography of scholarly sources relating to *Tropic of Orange* and other issues raised by the character; and
- a final synthesis that draws on the external research to mount a brief argument about how the character furthers Yamashita's themes.

Like the maps, this assignment allows students to refocus their analysis by examining the themes represented by an individual character. Place and space are again privileged, as the section on places focuses on establishing Yamashita's impetus for connecting her characters to certain locations in the text. The assignment is approachable for sophomore-level nonmajors who may struggle to construct a solid essay given the expansiveness of the novel. Yet the sum of the assignment demands that the student do the groundwork required of a full-fledged literary argument without the stress of a sustained and polished essay. The study guide could be used as a prewriting assignment; students could easily write a longer research essay using the synthesis from their study guide as the base argument and the summary and annotated bibliographies as a means of bolstering their argument.

Last year I collaborated with two colleagues trained in GIS to partner students in my upper-level English seminar with student teams in a cartography class.[6] The project asked English majors to look at the text spatially and suggest ideas they would like to see become maps; the cartography students then independently created these maps. While some of these projects further investigated the impact of changing highway structures in Los Angeles, another concentrated on the smuggling of illegal goods that threads through the narrative. The English majors then wrote conference-length essays utilizing the maps. Half of these essays were later presented at state or national conferences. Including students in the process of mapping allows them to create meaning and to develop their own critical approaches to literature.

As Buzzworm expounds, "If someone could put down all the layers of the real map, maybe he could get the real picture" (81). Utilizing and creating maps in the classroom allows students of all levels to read Yamashita's novel spatially, which leads to a clearer understanding of her focus on border crossing, immigration, socioeconomic disparities, colonialism, and multiculturalism. Approaching the text geographically encourages students to appreciate the text both aesthetically and as a reflection of current national and spatial realities.

NOTES

[1] For a more detailed explanation of the spatial turn in the humanities, see Warf and Arias.

[2] See Lin for in-depth information on the creation of these maps as well as a more thorough treatment of the body of criticism surrounding literary cartography and the spatial turn.

[3] The three maps presented in this essay are also available on the companion website to this volume (readteachyamashita.mla.hcommons.org).

[4] Since this map is too large to be replicated here, an alternate approach might ask students to research the history of individual places referred to by Arcangel and to then explain why Yamashita includes them.

[5] Both Wald and Mermann-Jozwiak offer excellent discussions of this theme in their articles on *Tropic of Orange.*

[6] Special thanks to Jamie Mitchem and Zac Miller at the University of North Georgia for collaborating on the learning community.

Tropic of Orange in a Literary Theory Course

Jessica Lewis Luck

When I took my first literary theory class as an undergraduate English major in the mid-1990s, the experience was transformative. Reading and thinking about literature had always been meaningful to me, but this class offered me a giant toolbox for understanding and explaining how literature works and how and why it matters. In the class, we applied the theories and critical approaches we were learning to two literary texts—Herman Melville's *Billy Budd* and Joseph Conrad's *Heart of Darkness*. Now an English professor teaching literary theory myself, I hope to provide that same transformative experience to my students. But I wanted to choose a different kind of text, a noncanonical work that would help students realize that theory is deeply relevant to contemporary literature and culture and all our diverse identities. Karen Tei Yamashita's novel *Tropic of Orange* is an excellent choice for a literary theory course. It is a fun read, which is important to me in a class where most of our theoretical readings are quite dense; indeed, my extraordinarily diverse student population at California State University, San Bernardino, finds the characters and their world very "relatable," in students' own words. Moreover, in terms of the larger learning objectives for a literary theory course, *Tropic* allows us to apply multiple theoretical approaches, while at the same time offering helpful implicit critiques of certain theories and extensions of those theories into new contexts. This essay outlines and analyzes some of the activities and assignments I created for teaching Yamashita's novel in a theory course.[1]

One of my main objectives in this course is for students to understand that careful analysis of the literary text and its details is still an essential part of theoretical approaches to literature. For this reason, we begin our study of *Tropic of Orange* by making some of those more familiar moves of close reading using the elements of fiction. With its cast of seven main characters set in motion in specific sites across Los Angeles and western Mexico, the novel invites an initial discussion of characterization and setting. I break students into seven groups, assigning each a particular character to analyze by considering where that character is located and what images, themes, or ideas the character is associated with. Yamashita includes a helpful chart at the beginning of the novel that maps out the chapters focused on each character, and students use it to find and discuss a particularly rich passage related to their character that would be fruitful for analysis. Each group then reports its findings. In this way we begin to discern some key themes and patterns—frontiers and borders; mapping; the city as a body, the freeway as organic; shifting notions of space and time; hybridity of language, race, and culture; work and labor; consumer capitalism; the (un)reality of television specifically and media more generally; and the role of the artist in all this. I also plot each character's specific location using *Google Maps*: Rafaela and

Arcangel are near the Tropic of Cancer in Mazatlán, Mexico, and the other characters are scattered across the sprawling cultural patchwork of LA—Bobby in Koreatown, Emi on the Westside, Buzzworm in South Central, Manzanar on the Harbor Freeway, and the journalist Gabriel downtown. This activity allows students to see how the novel's plot leverages and thematizes space in powerful ways.

With the basic structural and thematic landscapes of the novel established, we are ready to start applying theory on the second day of discussion. The act of using a specific theoretical lens to interpret a text is one of the most important analytical moves that we practice in the course and likely the least familiar to fledgling English majors. Borrowing a technique from David Rosenwasser and Jill Stephen's *Writing Analytically*, I ask students to try the "Yes, but . . ." method (60–61). That is, students think about the way that the literary text aligns with the theory ("yes") while also taking the crucial step of explaining how the text might offer an implicit critique or complication of that theory, question its assumptions, or extend its implications in a new context ("but").

We then try out this method on *Tropic of Orange*, applying theories of the alienation of labor under capitalism from Karl Marx and Friedrich Engels that we read earlier in the quarter. After students review their notes and remind the class of the basic tenets of the theory, we turn to the novel. I assign small groups a key passage from the book that seems to speak to the questions that Marx and Engels raise.[2] I ask students the following questions: In what ways do Marxist theories seem to apply to your section? How does your section complicate Marxist theory? What new ideas might it add? As groups report back, they discover, among other things, that the novel extends, and presents an implicit critique of, the Marxist theories we read in that it considers how individual creative and critical subjects might push back against the alienating effects of capitalism. I conclude by having students write down the ideas they came up with using the "Yes, but . . ." method in a potential paragraph for a critical essay. Afterward I show them as an example what I have written:

> *Tropic of Orange* offers an alternative model of work and labor through the character of Rodriguez, a mason building a wall in Mazatlán with the help of Arcangel. Rodriguez criticizes the factories, or *maquiladoras*, emerging in northern Mexico as a result of the North American Free Trade Agreement: "'A lot of big words about programs and production, but who does the work? They always forget the people who sweat for their bread.' . . . 'This,' he pointed at his wall, 'is work you can see'" (Yamashita, *Tropic* 143). Rodriguez is aware that in these factories driven by capitalism, as Marx and Engels assert, workers are dehumanized and sink to the level of mere commodities (653). While "the worker is related to the *product of his labor* as to an *alien object*" under a capitalist system (653), Rodriguez is deeply invested in and proud of the products of his labor: "'Everyone knows my work around here. "If you want a straight wall, call Rodriguez,"

> they all say'" (Yamashita, *Tropic* 142). Still, these are two old men talking about a model of work associated with the past. Rodriguez's son does not admire his father's focus on labor: "'My son thinks I am working all these years only to die. . . . We eat and drink all our earnings because anyway we will die'" (143). Though the novel acknowledges Rodriguez's belief in an artisan's "noble work" with his hands as a positive alternative to capitalism's dehumanizing labor (143), it also suggests that this past model is not a viable answer to the alienating effects of capitalism.

Another important objective in the class is for students to understand that theory is best used as a tool to ask questions, rather than as something that provides set answers. The theory should not be wielded as a static device for dissecting a literary text etherized like a patient on a table. Instead, we understand the literature as a co-theorizer of sorts, exploring its own answers to the questions raised by the theory. The questions asked by theory help us shape the initial questions we ask about literature, and those questions launch us into a process of negotiation and analysis that leads to complex thinking and interpretation.

To put this idea into practice, the next theory we apply to *Tropic of Orange* is Jean Baudrillard's idea of the hyperreal from *The Precession of Simulacra* (1557). Baudrillard's analysis of Disneyland in relation to Los Angeles could have been an epigraph to *Tropic of Orange*: "Los Angeles is encircled by these 'imaginary stations' which feed reality, reality-energy, to a town whose mystery is precisely that it is nothing more than a network of endless, unreal circulation—a town of fabulous proportions, but without space or dimensions" (1565). Baudrillard, of course, sees Los Angeles as a kind of hopeless illustration of his notion of the hyperreal, where signs and images have come to stand for the real and to take the place of reality itself, but Yamashita's novel offers some possible avenues for hope. Examples of the hyperreal abound in *Tropic of Orange*, especially surrounding Emi and the mediating role of the news in spectacles of violence. I have students again get into small groups to explore some of these examples, investigating how the novel theorizes the role and effects of hyperreality in Los Angeles differently than Baudrillard does. I ask what sources, if any, the novel offers as possibilities for resistance. The homeless takeover of the media, for example, or Arcangel's performance as the *lucha libre* wrestler El Gran Mojado (colloquially translated as "The Great Wetback").[3] At several key moments, I point out, the novel seems to make an important distinction between the magically real and the virtually real, as when Arcangel's magical feats of superhuman strength are diminished by their virtual appearance on television (Yamashita, *Tropic* 197). How does this fit with questions of the hyperreal? Starting with a good question may lead to a complex answer that can be used as the basis for a strong thesis statement, and that's how we end class that day. After one discussion, for example, we came up with the following provisional thesis: "While at first glance *Tropic of Orange* seems to offer magic as an alternative and a source of resistance to a hyperreal consumer and media culture, the novel ultimately suggests that this is a binary that should be deconstructed: we must embrace and wield the hyperreal nature of our culture to effect change."

The final essay for the course asks students to take a particular critical approach or apply a literary theory as a lens to generate their own unique interpretation of *Tropic of Orange*. They can take a Marxist, psychoanalytic, feminist, or critical race studies approach; apply Baudrillard's or Fredric Jameson's theories of postmodernism; or use Michel Foucault's ideas about discourse and power. Several students used the scaffolding of our in-class discussions to build their own interpretations utilizing new evidence from *Tropic of Orange*. Ruby S., for example, was moved by Manzanar's ability to connect the disparate communities of LA at the end of the novel as they all begin to conduct and make music with him (238). She writes in her Marxist analysis, "Manzanar leaves readers wondering if an artistic revolution, instead of a political revolution, could perhaps be an answer to many problems in the world—if it can inspire change. If anything, he certainly proves that establishing human connection is a way to push back on a capitalist society that causes alienation and disconnection."

Some students combined critical race theory with Baudrillard's notion of the hyperreal to create a compelling hybrid approach to the novel. Jen S., for example, examined how Gabriel's idealized vision of Mexico functions as a kind of simulacrum in the novel. She writes, "Gabriel has probably been too absorbed by the precession of simulacra in LA to now allow Mexico to resemble anything close to reality. . . . It becomes hard for him to tell what is authentic and what is a simulation." Kristine K. even coined a new term, *hyperculturalism*, to describe the hyperreal forms of cultural diversity that the novel seems critical of: "[B]y using this hyperculturalism, Yamashita is demonstrating how white America uses these cultures to make themselves feel more diverse without really having to think about what each of these different cultures means or where they came from."

Many students made some strong efforts with the "Yes, but . . ." method, though the essays also demonstrated some potential problems with that device. The use of *but* seems to signal to students that the novel has to offer a strong counterargument and challenge the theory in some way. One student, for example, argued that *Tropic of Orange* poses some problems for contemporary critical race theories, specifically bell hooks's theory of "postmodern blackness" and Gloria Anzaldúa's theory of "the new mestiza," because characters such as Rafaela and Buzzworm are not focused solely on empowering African American or Chicanx people (hooks, "Postmodern Blackness"; Anzaldúa, "From Borderlands"). As teachers, we often learn more about our pedagogy from the problems in students' writing than we do from their most polished work. In the future, I plan to put more emphasis on how the literature might extend the theory—perhaps a "Yes, and . . ." method. What the student above seems to uncover in her analysis, as I pointed out in my comments to her, is that the novel's characters see class as another important factor for empowerment and resistance, which is something that hooks and Anzaldúa don't address as much in their work.

One of the more fascinating examples of the challenge faced by students who employed the "Yes, but . . ." method appeared in several essays that engaged with Marx and Engels. Many of my students at Cal State San Bernardino are from working-class backgrounds and their responses to Marxist theory are always very thoughtful and illuminating. They often appreciate its critique of capitalism and the deleterious effects and affects of labor within a capitalist system. At the same time, they are deeply invested in the promises of class mobility offered by the American dream. One essay offers a complicated example of the "Yes, but . . ." conundrum:

> Whereas Marx believed that the working class has no upward mobility, Bobby proves that with hard work and dedication upward mobility is indeed possible, even in light of unjust labor laws. This would seem to show that anybody who is hardworking enough can eventually get a well-paying job and be able to provide for their family.

This essay and several others like it work to resist the notion of economic determinism at the heart of Marxist theory, so much so that they have to overlook the novel's fairly clear critique of Bobby and his interpellation within a capitalist system. In my comments on these essays, and in future classes in which I teach the novel, I hope to help students uncover that the novel's implicit critique of Marx is not necessarily that capitalism doesn't have the effects he says it does, but that his vision of the worker is rather abstract and disconnected from the lives of actual workers in the pieces we read in class. As a co-theorizer of labor under capitalism, *Tropic of Orange* helpfully puts a face on those workers and their plight and explores what individual agency they might have to resist seemingly deterministic forces.

Ultimately, what impresses me most about adopting Yamashita's novel as opposed to a more classic canonical text is the way it seems to enable and empower students to see themselves as co-theorizers of labor, race, identity, postmodern culture, and so on. One student was so inspired by critical race theory and our analysis of *Tropic of Orange* that she went on to do an honors research project focused on the inclusion—or, more precisely, the lack—of writers of color in current K–12 curricula and the Common Core standards. While the literary theory I learned in the 1990s gave me a useful toolbox for analyzing literature, I hope for my students that it becomes a powerful mechanism for reflecting critically on and transforming their worlds.

NOTES

[1] For their insights into the novel and for permission to quote from their essays, I would like to thank the students in my Literary Theory and Criticism courses at Califor-

nia State University, San Bernardino, who read Yamashita with me in fall 2015 and winter 2016.

[2] I assign individual groups labor-related passages from chapter 23, "To Labor"; chapter 33, "To Dream"; chapter 34, "Visa Card"; and chapter 42, "Drive-By."

[3] *Lucha libre* is Mexican freestyle professional wrestling, characterized particularly by its colorful masks.

Rerouting the Road Narrative in *Tropic of Orange*

J. Edward Mallot

Manzanar Murakami, one of seven principal characters in Karen Tei Yamashita's novel *Tropic of Orange*, witnesses the collaborative potential of drivers, vehicles, and freeways every day as he stands at an overpass of the I-110 freeway and conducts the ebbs and flows of traffic below:

> [T]hey would all head toward their cars, their buses, their motorcycles and limousines . . . all slam their doors, all buckle their belts, all gun their motors, all simultaneously. . . . And then, the syncopated REAR VIEW CHECK IT OUT and a one and a two, and AC UP TO MAX and a three and a four, and CREEP ON OUT and a five and a six, and MERGE, MERGE, MERGE. They all converged everywhere at once. . . . And Manzanar, loathe to lose any moment, writhed with exhilaration and christened it all: the greatest jazz session the world had ever known. (207)

"To envision the automobile as an orchestral device with musical potential was an idea lost upon the motorist within," Yamashita's narrator notes (208). But for Manzanar, the freeway is "nothing less than the greatest orchestra on Earth" (37). He imagines the complexity of lives that are vastly distinct in their non-transit lives, brought for a stretch of time into close proximity—if not, in more potent ways, together—by a shared roadway space; he considers the helpful homogeneity of freeway travel alongside the hopelessly heterogeneous populations of passengers. And in so doing, until the conclusion of *Tropic of Orange* takes a tonal detour near its own destination, Manzanar hears music that sounds beautiful nevertheless.

This is why Yamashita's *Tropic of Orange* seems to me such a useful complement to a course on American road narratives, a genre commonly, and perhaps mistakenly, assumed to be dominated by stories focused on white males. For Ronald Primeau, "American road narratives are fiction and nonfiction books by Americans who travel by car throughout the country either on a quest or simply to get away" (1). Given such a limited definition of the genre, perhaps unsurprisingly Primeau also finds that "the automobile journey became the province of the white male—generally middle class, established, and free to embark on the kind of journeys around which road conventions would be shaped" (107), until writers of color and women writers began to loosen the stranglehold around the 1970s. To be fair, others have since employed a wider lens, highlighting texts written by authors who are representative of a cross section of the society of the United States. Still, the typical road narratives course will feature white male authors and protagonists (novels such as Jack Kerouac's *On the Road* and Vladimir Nabokov's *Lolita*) along with now familiar additions (such as Ridley Scott's film *Thelma and Louise*). Thematically, texts traditionally taught in such courses often adhere to Primeau's script: the primary motivations for travel are adventure or escape.

For me, then, the first task in designing a course typically intended for upper-division literature majors is to consider other ways to understand what constitutes a road narrative. I initially describe Yamashita's novel to my classes as "the road narrative of an orange." Indeed, the eponymous piece of fruit—carried by another main character, Arcangel—does make its way from Mexico to the United States, bringing the entire tropic with it. Many commentators have seen in this plotline intriguing explorations of new ways in which goods and people are trafficked, and various and nefarious networks that came to define millennial America. But my reasons for including the novel lie elsewhere, as I want students to consider not only why characters go on the road or what happens along the way but also broader questions raised by the fact that road narratives are possible in the first place. Why are roads built, and for whom? Are roads genuinely public, genuinely egalitarian spaces? Why is American society obsessed with automobile travel, and how do vehicles signify individual and collective identities? What else is trafficked on roads, other than human passengers? What happens when roads exist, but travel is somehow not possible?

To some extent, Yamashita's novel engages with all these questions, using a stretch of the I-110 freeway as its central stage. Often breathtakingly, the text adopts this specific section of the highway not so much as motor stretch but as Möbius strip, flipping and reversing thematic and rhetorical positions about race, class, gender, and generation. Teaching in Arizona—at an institution where a large number of out-of-state residents hail from Southern California—I have met several students who have themselves experienced Los Angeles's infamous traffic jams (or others, including Phoenix's own), which never seem to mirror the sociospatial transformations Manzanar, Buzzworm, and other Yamashita characters witness. Because many present-day undergraduates will not have been alive at the time of the novel's publication, instructors may want to outline ways in which automobile travel and local history—particularly, LA's racial history—intersected during the 1990s. If time permits the exploration of outside resources, students might consult scholars such as George Lipsitz and his notion of space as an elastic and often racially biased social construct, self-cyclically perpetuating punitive practices affecting living conditions for already disadvantaged populations, including the design and deployment of freeway networks (*Possessive Investment* 26–37).

Within the context of a class on road narratives, my goal is for students to discover how a road—a construction designed for transport, for movement, for allegedly egalitarian motion—can become something quite different, calling into question whom such spaces are, theoretically and pragmatically, designed to benefit. Yamashita's novel exposes how various passengers occupy shared geographic spaces, and what happens if and when such co-occupied spaces ultimately expose instead familiar fault lines of socioeconomic striation. Shortly after a highway incident involving a Porsche that founders as its driver consumes drug-laced orange slices, subsequently causing a petrol truck to overturn, the drivers of now useless motors flee on foot, inspiring an entirely different population to create a makeshift neighborhood from the abandoned vehicles. But these new residents have different agendas than one might expect; luxury cars, for example, are largely ignored in favor of more spacious models that suit other purposes. As Buzzworm explains, this stretch of the I-110 has become its own unique kind of environment, mimicking and morphing familiar notions of urban space, "creating a community out of a traffic jam. There's already names to the lanes, like streets! . . . There's a truck could be a Seven Eleven. Got everything—beers, Cokes, even nuke you a burrito. Only thing's missing is the lottery tickets" (Yamashita, *Tropic* 157).

But while the traffic jam helps generate and foster a wholly different kind of community, it will not last long. Octavia E. Butler's dystopic novel *Parable of the Sower* notes that "[i]t's against the law in California to walk on the freeways, but the law is archaic. Everyone who walks walks on the freeways sooner or later. . . . [T]he freeway crowd is a heterogenous mass—black and white, Asian and Latin, whole families are on the move" (176–77). Echoing Butler in *Parable*, Yamashita writes in *Tropic of Orange*, "People get killed on highways all the time" (xv), and for the characters of *Tropic*, the I-110 is not allowed to remain a place of traffic stasis and demographic dynamism simultaneously. Something must be done, it would seem, to return the city and its congestive systems to normal, inherently inegalitarian functioning, and as authorities close in to eradicate the new neighborhood, characters such as the news reporter Emi, who earlier famously remarked that "[c]ultural diversity is bullshit," die in the crossfire (128). Readers are left with questions about the rights of the road: Who can use public transportation space, and for what purposes? Do pedestrians have the right to access the space? Who can claim the spaces of overpasses, medians, or shoulders? These questions provide fertile possibilities for small group discussions, or for short written assignments after students have read the novel.

Yamashita's focus extends to how civic space is imagined, represented, and ultimately appropriated. In this vein, *Tropic of Orange* challenges traditional notions about the alleged impartiality of maps before the novel even begins, in an alternative table of contents that offers another chart by which to navigate the subsequent storyscape. As Elisabeth Mermann-Jozwiak argues, Yamashita's text offers a "palimpsestic urban space," providing a "historical excavation of the city's neighbourhoods. This excavation reveals various layers—of past and present inhabitants of the city, of regulations that restricted access to certain areas, and of the distribution of resources and development of infrastructures in those neighborhoods" (2). To be certain, maps reflect and distort spatial reality, and have done so for centuries; J. B. Harley and others provide an initial, influential understanding of how cartography has not only reflected the world as humans have seen it but also helped re-create that world, for the practice of depicting space has always been intricately connected to the control and maintenance of cities, countries, and continents. To assume that maps are somehow unbiased arbitrators of reality is to fundamentally misunderstand what maps do, and why they are drawn. As Manzanar knows full well,

> [*t*]*here are maps and there are maps and there are maps.* The uncanny thing was that he could see them all at once, filter some, pick them out like transparent windows and place them even delicately and consecutively in a complex grid of pattern, spatial discernment, body politic. Although one might have thought this capacity to see was different from a musical one, it was really one and the same. For each of the maps was a layer of music, a clef, an instrument, a musical interaction, a change of measure, a coda. (Yamashita, *Tropic* 56–57)

Yamashita's highway conductor sees LA's layers, which encompass geology and geopolitics, history and demography, music and time. This ability to understand how each map is both partial and part of an overall story proves crucial to recognizing spatial dynamics at play in the metropolis; indeed, Buzzworm begins to realize that because any given map is almost necessarily obsolete as soon as it is finished, recovering and retaining the countless geography-based histories of LA's inhabitants becomes increasingly necessary: "If someone could put down all the layers of the real map, maybe he could get the real picture" (81).

For some undergraduates, the rhetorical possibilities inherent in cartography is a relatively new idea. To initiate a discussion of maps in Yamashita's work, a teacher might have students bring to class or even create their own alternative maps of LA not focused on streets and highways. Because I typically devote two weeks to the novel, I tend to opt instead to use cartography as a springboard for classroom conversation, projecting various maps of LA as conversation progresses. Thus, I begin one session by asking students what a typical map of LA would likely feature, and for what purposes; the initial responses will likely include place names, thoroughfares and so forth. But if I ask what other ways LA could be mapped outside the typical methods of freeway representation, municipality designation and the like, other possibilities slowly emerge, such as maps designed for tourists, maps illustrating bus routes, maps indicating voter registration districts. When I then ask what kind of alternative map a family new to the area might want to have, the conversation takes an even more productive turn. As students mention a family's likely curiosity about school districts, median incomes, and often masked and uncomfortable questions about racial demography, the implications of how mapping can intersect with other systems of power and prejudice begin to become clear. Students will inevitably note that the realities behind these maps can and do change over time, and often very quickly; an instructor might want to bring Mike Davis's *City of Quartz* into conversation here, particularly his discussion of gang-related maps and the unstable porousness of territorial boundaries (298–301), for this is precisely where

Buzzworm—who is looking at a 1972 map torn from Davis's book—begins to think through the problematic nature of mapping both places and populations (Yamashita, *Tropic* 80).

Because Yamashita creates radically different appropriations of spaces in *Tropic of Orange*, and because those reconfigurations force readers to reconsider, for example, what freeways signify, what cars represent, and our ongoing obsession with road space and who belongs there, *Tropic of Orange* should fit effortlessly into a road narratives course, precisely because of what the novel doesn't do and refuses to pretend. Characters are not simply free to wander wherever they please. And my focus in teaching the novel does not principally concern the journey itself, but the methods and mechanisms by which travel remains circumscribed and controlled. Yamashita's book reveals how maps and motorways can both liberate and limit movement, challenging students to rethink the opportunistic exuberance of traditional American road narratives.

Troubling Boundaries and Beginnings with "The Orange"

Robin E. Field

Karen Tei Yamashita's short story "The Orange" was published in the *Los Angeles Times* and the *Chicago Review* (Yamashita, "Orange" [*Los Angeles Times*] and "Orange" [*Chicago Review*]). In the *Los Angeles Times*, Yamashita calls the story "a children's fable . . . a seed for a work that I hope may become an adult novel." Clearly, *Tropic of Orange* is the realization of this hope; yet while *Tropic of Orange* has been widely studied and taught, "The Orange" has not received such recognition. However, at five pages and easily accessible on the *Los Angeles Times* website, "The Orange" is an ideal text for introducing the crossing of cultural, socioeconomic, political, geographic, and environmental boundaries, as well as for challenging conventions of genre and form. To these ends, I have used this story in courses from Introduction to Literature, part of my college's core curriculum, to a seminar for English majors titled Multicultural Women Writers.

The plot of "The Orange" differs slightly from that of *Tropic of Orange*. The story's unnamed first-person narrator details the myriad upheavals that occur as the Tropic of Cancer, entangled in an orange, moves northward from Mexico to Los Angeles. Yamashita turns the intangible—a line of latitude—into a tangible entity to detail the effects of invisible boundaries on everyday lives. Initially, the changes are received positively, as people suddenly speak multiple languages and restaurants serve unfamiliar but tasty new cuisines. But when people's jobs begin to change daily and the civil war in El Salvador moves northward, the narrator frantically works to send the orange—and the Tropic of Cancer itself—back to its place of origin. In this way, Yamashita's story questions to what extent boundaries should be traversed and whether the maintenance of certain boundaries is in fact desirable. The end of the story offers a return to normal, signaled by the decomposition of the orange under its parent tree, which troubles the joyous cultural mixing seen previously and complicates any easy moral for this "children's fable."

From the first, "The Orange" tests students' assumptions about the world, as Yamashita's use of magical realism underscores the significance of the physical environment depicted in the text. After we read the story aloud, I ask students to examine the first three paragraphs to determine the setting and major characters. Typically, we discuss these ideas as a class, but these initial questions also work well as prompts for think-pair-share exercises, which help some students first collect their thoughts on paper before discussing them with others. In my experience, students quickly identify the time and place and the two most prominent characters: the narrator and Gabriel, the narrator's cousin in Mexico. But by the second and third paragraphs, students notice how the lines between setting and character become blurred as the orange tree on Gabriel's farm reacts to the weather with humanlike characteristics: the tree "believed" it was time to issue buds; the first bud develops because of "curiosity" ("The Orange" [*Chicago Review*] 12). The titular orange thus is identified as a character in the story just as the narrator and Gabriel are. This personification of plant life demonstrates the artificiality of the boundary between nature and people; and Yamashita goes one step further in the third paragraph when she introduces the Tropic of Cancer as a character. This imaginary line of latitude becomes tangible—"as supple and potent as a continuum of light through optic fiber"—as it becomes enmeshed in the orange (12). The line exhibits decidedly human characteristics when it "shudder[s] with delight" as a bee lands on the orange blossom (12). The movement of the line entangled in the orange drives the story, affecting the lives of people throughout the Americas—and presumably the rest of the world. Yet Yamashita does not simply make the intangible tangible; she repeatedly calls the line "invisible" and "imaginary" (12). Hence, students are forced to consider the existence of this line, which is at once both real and imaginary, and which thereby challenges ideas about what does and does not exist and what influences how the world functions. The orange proves to be the most important character, even more so than the narrator, as its movements affect the lives of countless humans. This startling revelation allows for a more flexible understanding of constructed hierarchies that prioritize human beings over the natural world, and it encourages students to approach future texts with an eye toward environmental considerations. In Introduction to Literature, for example, students write a short paper connecting "The Orange" to T. C. Boyle's *The Tortilla Curtain*, another Los Angeles–based novel that complicates the hierarchies between animals and humans.

For those students beginning their study of literature, Yamashita's text productively complicates boundaries with respect to genre and form. "The Orange" is a short story, but Yamashita also calls it "a children's fable," which allows students to explore why different labels lead to different interpretations of the text. Describing the characteristics of magical realism to students leads them to question boundaries. For instance, while the narrator's ability to spontaneously speak in Mandarin to a bus driver certainly is fantastical, should speaking a language other than English really be unusual? It would be a geographic impossibility to see the countries of Latin America sliding up into Los Angeles behind an exhausted Latinx migrant worker who is inadvertently dragging the Tropic of Cancer northward by carrying an orange, but Latin American farmers have been coming to work in the United States for over a century. While Yamashita is not attempting to collapse all boundaries between genres, her text reminds students that the magical and the real are more similar than we may realize.

Formal elements are also complicated in "The Orange." This can already be seen in the first paragraphs, where the boundaries between setting and character collapse. For the more conventionally depicted human characters, Yamashita creates other complications. The story's first-person narrator, for instance, is unnamed and genderless. Once students have used gender pronouns to speak about this character, I ask them why they chose one gender over others. Given the lively discussion that customarily follows, this topic could also work as an in-class writing exercise that asks students to explain or find textual evidence for the various gender possibilities of the unnamed narrator. Some students point to the narrator's interaction with two male peers—Gabriel and Ben, for whom Yamashita uses male pronouns—as evidence of the narrator's male gender identification. Other students point to Yamashita's gender identity as their reason for assigning a female gender to the narrator, linking the first-person "I" of the narrator to the author of the text. Generally, both beginning and advanced students are not conscious of the fact that they are assigning a gender to the narrator, and probing their rationales allows them to see how they construct gender by prioritizing certain beliefs. Just because the narrator interacts with two young men, rides a bicycle, or watches professional basketball on television does not mean that that character's gender identity is male. Similarly, those students who connect the gender of the narrator to Yamashita herself realize that the author's biography should not dictate the fictional world of the text. The indeterminacy of the narrator's gender proves to have little impact on our understanding of this story, but it does further underscore the constructed nature of identity thematized in Yamashita's text. This discussion of gender easily leads to a discussion of gendered language and gender pronouns; because the narrator is Latinx, we also discuss how language has evolved to address the problematic nature of rigid binary categories of identity. The *YouTube* video "What's with the X in Latinx?" offers a concise and humorous overview of the term *Latinx* and the reasons for its implementation and evolution; if time permits, this three-minute video nicely supplements in-class discussion and underscores how a critical feminist approach may be applied not only to literature but also to language.

The complexities of genre and form that become evident throughout the text may also be related to other culturally constructed notions of identity. Yamashita's text initially seems to demonstrate how differences in language, culture, and economic status may prevent meaningful personal connections and intercultural experiences. The Tropic of Cancer first moves southward as a man tosses the orange into his cart and walks to a market. The narrator notices the consequences of the line's movement for life in Los Angeles. People suddenly speak different languages: "My Chinese-American friend Ben was fluent in [Spanish], too, but stranger yet, so was his grandma who had survived the Cultural Revolution" (14). Cuisines shift in households and restaurants: "One night, my mother, for no apparent reason, stir-fried vegetables in the big iron pot she usually makes beans in. . . . The Korean market was selling homemade tamales and the Mexican place had Afro bean pie" (13). Significantly, these changes are portrayed positively: "Everything was a great jumble. People were laughing in the streets. People who had never talked to each other before were cracking jokes together" (14). Students examine the positivity surrounding such linguistic and culinary melding, discussing whether people may better understand each other—literally and figuratively—once they relinquish their everyday habits. I temper the oversimplification of this celebratory melding by pointing to this line: "After all, there are teriyaki tacos, and even McDonald's has Chinese chicken salad" (13). Here students discuss cultural appropriation and the pitfalls of capitalism by asking whether a fast-food behemoth is promoting cultural understanding or homogenizing cultural difference for profit; later they analyze cultural appropriation more deeply in an essay or exam question by connecting "The Orange" to other texts that probe this issue, such as Gish Jen's *Mona in the Promised Land.*

This cautioning against the celebratory impulse that accompanies cultural melding helps explain the darker turn the story takes in its second half. The orange is purchased by the migrant worker, who boards a bus heading north. Hence, the Tropic of Cancer moves beyond its usual location and shifts northward: "[T]hen things really started to change and change fast. It was as if the geographical rug were being pulled out from under everything and everyone. It was not just the languages and the food that were getting jumbled up; people who used to have one job suddenly had another" (14). The rich become homeless, and the homeless wear suits and carry briefcases in the downtown highrises. More Spanish and Indigenous dialects are being spoken, and "the weather was heating up; the Equator was moving [Gabriel's] way" into Mexico (15). Even the violent civil war in El Salvador threatens to envelope Gabriel's farm. The economic and political consequences then give way to planetary concerns: "'What about the Earth's orbit?' I yelled" (15). The upheavals in life circumstances that these changes denote are posed as untenable, and the narrator then bikes through Los Angeles, seeking the migrant worker carrying the orange in order to send the Tropic of Cancer back to its proper place in the world. Here I have students examine the northward movement of the Tropic of Cancer—and Latin America—into the United States. They notice how the cultural changes are portrayed positively when the United States is pulled southward; this geographic adjustment may be linked to the imperialism of American culture worldwide. Conversely, students observe that the movement of Latin America into the United States is depicted ambivalently at best or threateningly at worst: "If [the man with the orange] had looked back a few blocks south of Olympic, he could have seen it all himself—Gabriel's little farm and Mexico and then the rest of Central America, the coffee and banana plantations, the civil war, the crowded cities, the poor and the rich people, the rain forests and all those tropical plants and animals" (15–16). Here students see that the northward movement of Latin America results in Americans losing control of their life circumstances, as people's jobs and economic statuses are suddenly in flux and even the ability to communicate with others is not guaranteed. Such a negative depiction of the Global South and its relation to the United States allows students to ponder the national and cultural hierarchies that have been constructed in American society and to assess the merit of these hierarchies. The end of the story certainly appears to affirm the existing order: the narrator stops the migrant worker just as he is about to cut the orange and therefore reify these new borders and life circumstances by permanently lodging the Tropic of Cancer in Los Angeles. Once the orange is taken back to Gabriel's farm, the Tropic of Cancer returns to its seemingly proper place and the world is restored to its previous condition. The traversing of these boundaries—linguistic, cultural, economic, political, and geographic—ultimately is posed as problematic, undesirable, and perhaps also impossible.

This conclusion troubles students. If "The Orange" is read as a fable, students often interpret the moral to be a caution against change, particularly regarding cultural melding. Yet the tone of the story is so buoyant and energetic that it is virtually impossible to interpret the story simply as a cautionary tale. Yamashita has said in an interview with Elizabeth Glixman that her longer work, *Tropic of Orange*, is "about migration and border crossing and the consequences for those who cross and for those who find themselves in the mix" (Yamashita, "Interview" [Glixman]). I conclude the discussion of "The Orange" by reminding students that a fundamental aspect of studying literature is to imagine oneself in new circumstances and to grapple with complex ethical questions. Reading and analyzing this story enables students to understand and appreciate the myriad consequences of deconstructing or maintaining the boundaries that shape their lives. Whether students are the ones doing the border crossing or are those people thrust into new cultural circumstances, they are certain to find themselves in the magical world of "The Orange."

Through the Arc of the Rain Forest, *Brazil-Maru*, and Other Short Stories in a Brazilian Context

Gloria Karam Delbim

The decision to teach Karen Tei Yamashita's texts at a Brazilian university was a daring one I made back in 2000 when I began to offer a course titled North American Literature at Universidade Presbiteriana Mackenzie (Mackenzie Presbyterian University) in São Paulo. It was the first course of its kind in the bachelor of letters degree at the university, one designed for the study of works by African American, Asian, Hispanic, and Native American writers of the United States. I created a pedagogy intended to foster students' professional growth as educators as well as their personal growth in modern Brazil, a country with complex historical and contemporary global connections.

In this essay I first describe the pedagogical motivations for developing a course on ethnic literature for English majors who are preparing for careers in teaching. Then I discuss the connections between Yamashita's fiction and the experiences of Brazilian students. Photographs and other archival documents introduce students to the Brazilian cultural and historical context of Yamashita's work; assignments include student interviews with immigrants and their descendants. The course aims to develop students' understanding of identity, gender, citizenship, tolerance, and interculturality, a goal that builds on, in the words of Laura Izarra, a professor at the University of São Paulo, "[t]he role of the English Literature teacher as a 'cultural educator' within the Brazilian context" (73).

North American Literature was a semester-long course designed to give future educators an understanding of ethnic writers in North America. I also hoped the histories and experiences of these writers might converge with students' own histories and experiences. Many students were descended from immigrants and, through their critical engagement with Yamashita's fiction, they were able to (re) create their own histories and those of their families, thereby enriching their sense of belonging within a larger world. I organized the course by topic and selected texts from Yamashita's corpus to use in each unit, the concerns of which also organize this essay.

Humans versus Computers

Yamashita's "The Last Secretary" was the crux of this unit on humans versus computers; the story focuses on the replacement of workers by technology and how this affects their lives socially, economically, morally, and physically. It also touches on the question of stereotypes, in this case the stereotype of the Asian woman as a docile and robotic worker, a figure that has increasingly been recognized as part of techno-Orientalism, or "the phenomenon of imagining Asia and Asians in hypo- or hypertechnological terms in cultural productions and political discourse" (Roh et al. 2). After seeing most of her coworkers gradually fired, the Asian American secretary is one of the few who continues to work in the same place until her death. In the meantime, she must cope with diseases caused by the repetitive work; yet she never complains and instead endures her job with discretion and patience. Nobody seems to care that she works well past the typical age of employment as long as she does what is asked of her. As a human being, she is quite invisible to her boss and the other employees.

Across the seven semesters that I taught the course, students were quite engaged during class discussions of "The Secretary" because they knew someone with a similar profile who either retired or was let go because of an occupational disability and then replaced by automation or another form of technology. Students understand the frustration of ending a career with little or no recognition after having proven oneself a reliable, faithful, and dedicated employee.

Typically, students tried to find solutions to cases like that of Yamashita's secretary, such as suing the company for working conditions that are stressful both physically and morally, requiring extra pay, hiring another employee to help, asking for better working conditions and changing jobs or professions. The topic of humans versus computers was one of students' favorites, and they seemed to become aware of the harm that technology can cause if not used properly. To complement this theme, I also assigned Isaac Asimov's "True Love"—both Asimov's and Yamashita's stories show how a machine can affect a person's livelihood when society considers technology more important than human life.

Immigration

Besides short stories, excerpts from Yamashita's novels were of special interest in this course. Because Brazil has the second-largest population of Japanese descendants outside Japan and is indeed a cosmopolitan country of immigrants, Yamashita's writing appealed to students for the ways it invites readers to delve into the issue of immigration.

In the unit on immigration, students read the first chapter of *Brazil-Maru*, which details the early-twentieth-century arrival of a group of Japanese in Brazil and their reasons for settling in a country so different from Japan. Students researched the historical period represented in the first chapter within the context of American, Brazilian, and Japanese politics; specifically, students had to interview Japanese immigrants or their descendants about their reasons for coming to Brazil. In-class discussion compared the results of students' research with the assigned chapter of *Brazil-Maru*. Students were also required to examine archival photographs and to read theoretical texts on immigration to Brazil.[1]

Students additionally conducted research on Japanese immigration and their own individual ancestries at São Paulo's Museu de Imigração (Immigration Museum). The museum archives information on all ships and passengers that disembarked in Santos, the most important port in Brazil, located in the state of

São Paulo. In the past, the museum was the place where immigrants were quarantined before they were allowed to travel to different parts of the country.

In their archival research, students typically learned quite a bit about their own backgrounds and those of Japanese immigrants. Students were surprised about the facts collected and would share them with their families and, in the process, learn more about their ancestors. Such surprises included, for example, the long and arduous journey taken by immigrants, the type of clothes worn during the journey, the tools and furniture they brought along, the diseases they contracted, the food they shared with other immigrants, and some aspects of the hardships they had to face in search of a new land and hope for a better life. Students interviewed immigrants, doing primary research in the form of oral history; those whom they interviewed did not necessarily have Japanese ancestors, but still students learned about the reasons these individuals came to Brazil as well as about their expectations, dreams, frustrations, homesickness, sense of inclusion and exclusion, and so on. A story told to one student by a seventy-five-year-old nisei, a second-generation Japanese Brazilian woman, presents an interesting example. This woman related that her paternal grandfather, who was a samurai, and his Catholic wife, both from Nagasaki, came to Brazil with their six children to work on a farm. As the youngest child, the interviewee's father was the only one who had a chance to work in the city and study, and he became a baseball coach. She added that her three sisters and two brothers also went to college and that she was the first to marry someone of European descent, which meant breaking strict family rules. Despite her mother's refusal to accept or even attend her wedding, she had the blessing of her father, who was more open-minded.

We discussed in class how people who leave their native countries hold on to their memories with a sense of nostalgia while also attempting to embrace a new home—that is, they create myths, and when they confront a new culture and reality, tensions emerge between the myth of their native country and the reality of the new country. According to R. Radhakrishnan, this is when immigrants question their own identity between being and belonging, because "the home country is not 'real' in its own terms and yet it is real enough to impede Americanization, and the 'present home' is materially real and yet not real enough to feel authentic" (123).

Although Radhakrishnan refers here to the United States, these words can also be applied to other places, including Brazil. According to Radhakrishnan, "when people move, identities, perspectives, and definitions change" (123). This is reflected in the identity construction of the immigrant who lives between two cultures, two value systems. Interculturality is a natural part of the process of successfully adapting to a new culture and society.

Students were asked to write short essays of two to four pages on the topic of immigration and assimilation and to share their results in oral presentations of ten to fifteen minutes. They then compared their research with Yamashita's narrative and discussed any similarities and differences they observed. This assignment enriched their own personal stories by allowing them to realize that immigration to Brazil was a part of their own history.

Stereotypes

The class also focused on *Tropic of Orange*, a novel in which Yamashita sidelines the presence of white Americans and focuses instead on ethnic groups such as Asians, Latinos, and African Americans; the novel situates the multicultural city of Los Angeles as the center of the narrative. A good example of how ethnic groups are stereotyped by the dominant culture appears in a passage about Bobby Ngu in chapter 2, "Benefits—Koreatown." This passage describes how Bobby is racially and linguistically othered. At the same time, however, Bobby's character also undercuts physical and linguistic stereotyping in the United States:

> That's Bobby. If you know your Asians, you look at Bobby. You say, that's Vietnamese. That's what you say. Color's pallid. Kinda blue just beneath the skin. Little underweight. Korean's got rounder face. Chinese's taller. Japanese's dressed better. If you know your Asians. Turns out you'll be wrong. And you gonna be confused. Dude speaks Spanish. Comprende? So you figure it's one of those Japanese from Peru. Or maybe Korean from Brazil. Or Chinamex. Turns out Bobby's from Singapore. You say, okay, Indonesian. Malaysian. Wrong again. You say, look at his name. That's gotta be Vietnam. Ngu. Bobby Ngu. They all got Ngu names. Hey, it's not his real name. Real name's Li Kwan Yu. But don't tell nobody. Go figure. Bobby's Chinese. Chinese from Singapore with a Vietnam name speaking like a Mexican living in Koreatown. That's it. (Yamashita, *Tropic* 14–15)

What is unique and interesting about this novel is its distinctive voices and characters, despite the fact that all characters speak English. Recognizing that the pressure to assimilate does not automatically translate into sameness in the proverbial melting pot, each character speaks and behaves in ways that feel authentic to the reader.

This excerpt is pertinent to the Brazilian context because there are those who also tend to stereotype Brazilians from the nine states in the Northeast, as if Brazilian-ness is or is supposed to be homogenous. Located in the Southeast and considered the richest state in the country, São Paulo attracts the most migrants from different parts of Brazil due to job opportunities. The Northeasterners who come to live and work in the state suffer prejudice because of the way they speak. Their regional accents are not easily recognized by people from São Paulo. For this reason, they are grouped together as if they come from a single place, and their diverse backgrounds and regional characteristics are often not considered, which can lead to cultural conflict in some instances. This was an important point for students to discuss, and Yamashita's text opened up a space for them to do just that. We worked with the passage about Bobby as a way for students—future teachers—to understand the challenges they will most likely face when teaching their own classes; recognizing these challenges prepares educators to work as a bridge between individuals of different backgrounds in order to avoid clashes and promote better acceptance and respect for diversity and pluralism. After all, the ability to accept and respect differences is crucial for successfully navigating a globalized world.

Ecology

Yamashita's first novel, *Through the Arc of the Rain Forest*, has a special connection to Brazil since it explores issues of ecology and economic globalization and is based on Yamashita's keen observations about Brazilian nature, culture, and society. In the words of Gregory Rabassa, the American translator of Gabriel García Márquez's *One Hundred Years of Solitude*, in his comment on the back cover of *Through the Arc*, "Yamashita has given us a mingling of aspects, faces, and points of view that in concert reveal the complex pith of Brazilian culture. *Through the Arc* is a "fine, satirical piece of writing."

Despite living in Brazil, students are not always aware of the extent of the ecological disasters we face every day, much like other students of their generation who live elsewhere. Students were given the task of researching the current state of Brazil's ecology. They learned a great deal about the greed of those who negotiate to destroy the forests, the minerals, and the plants that are part of our country, and how these are smuggled across our borders just for the sake of some people's financial benefit, an idea exemplified in "Chapter 16: The Matacão."

Meeting the Author

When Yamashita twice came to lecture at the university, students wrote about the most relevant aspects of her talks. The first talk in 2007 focused on "July: Circle K Rules" in her book *Circle K Cycles* (107–14), and the second in 2010 was on *I Hotel*.

Yamashita's presentation on *Circle K Cycles* exposed students to a set of social rules showing how Americans, Brazilians, and Japanese react differently to similar situations involving physical touch, dress code, social interaction, and so on. It was amazing to see how much students enjoyed Yamashita's talk, in particular her comparison of these three groups, which highlighted her keen insight into the behavioral patterns of specific nationalities.

Yamashita's lecture on *I Hotel* was a history class for students who knew little about the real history of Filipinos in the United States or what this group had been subjected to. Prior to the lecture, students had read the short story "Immigration Blues," by Bienvenido N. Santos, in a unit on ethnic writing and representation, and had been introduced to the history of Filipino immigration to the

United States. "Immigration Blues" and *I Hotel* both show in different contexts the adversities this group of immigrants was exposed to.

After these lectures, students were asked to write an essay of two to four pages in which they reflected on the most important points in Yamashita's talk. The next step was an in-class discussion in which students had to justify their choices. This generated a lot of information and students profited from hearing others' points of view. The opportunity to listen to Yamashita's lecture and to have a conversation with her was invaluable to students.

Given the rich variety and intriguing complexity of Yamashita's oeuvre, there are many other ways to explore her texts and to use them in conjunction with works by other writers, in addition to newspaper, magazine, and internet articles and even oral histories. Instructors can adapt the teaching of Yamashita's work to their own context and take the opportunity to expand on topics such as patriarchy, feminism, history, identity, diaspora, and so forth.

As instructors we help professionals to be attentive educators. In the words of Izarra, it is important to reflect "not on HOW to teach but on asking WHY and WHAT is important for the students to know, HOW it is to be known and HOW this production of knowledge turns [students] into agents in the construction of social identities" (80). Although Izarra's focus is on teaching literature, her words can be extended to other fields as well.

Whether an instructor chooses to teach Yamashita's texts alone or in relation to works by other writers, instructors and students alike can always enjoy and profit greatly from a writer like Yamashita, who is deeply aware of what is happening in the world with respect to ecology, technology, migration, diversity, and interculturality, among other concerns, and who consistently calls our attention to questions that can only be answered by those who seek respect, tolerance, and harmony among people and nature. By emphasizing the diversity that characterizes our world and that is highlighted in Yamashita's work, we can prioritize what is ultimately most important: the formation of future educators.

NOTE

[1] For example, Meade's "Constructing a Nation" and Safran's "Diasporas."

Brazil-Maru and the Narrative Space of Impersonal Feelings

Pamela Thoma

This essay is based on my experience teaching "Part I: Emile" of Karen Tei Yamashita's novel *Brazil-Maru* in Late-Twentieth- and Early-Twenty-First-Century American Literature, a special topics elective course for the Department of Languages and Cultures at the University of the Ryukyus in Okinawa, Japan. Part of a 2016–17 Fulbright American Scholar Award for a project titled "Gender and Citizenship in Asian American Literature and Culture," the course was designed to survey contemporary literary culture of the United States, but the more specific intention was to explore newer ideas about what is considered American literature, which is connected to the relentless question of who is considered American.[1] Yamashita's writing inspired a pedagogy that I hoped would encourage students to embrace an expanding rather than a shrinking role for literature in discourses of belonging and conceptions of citizenship.

I do not claim that my approach was carefully orchestrated toward a specific goal that was supremely realized. Instead, I offer this account of how Yamashita's writing sparked provocative conversations around some broad but key ideas about contemporary American literature, with the hope that it will aid the development of other approaches to teaching Yamashita's works. Tailored to students for whom English is a second language, this pedagogical approach may prove useful to others in parallel situations, given the especially broad variety of geographic and cultural contexts in which Yamashita's works are taught; its concerns and goals could easily be applied to largely anglophone contexts and at both the undergraduate and graduate levels, with adjustments in the amount of reading and writing depending on level.

The sixteen-week course met once a week for one and a half hours, as is typical in Japanese higher education, where students take as many as ten classes in a single term. Students in this discussion-based course were juniors or seniors and possessed advanced English proficiency in reading and writing, and a wider range of proficiency in speaking. The course was conducted primarily in English, though I was able to interject with my very basic Japanese and more or less follow along when students occasionally switched into Japanese to clarify for other students particularly difficult topics or ideas, a practice I encouraged given the conceptual ground I had hoped to cover. A few students had previously studied in the United States while others had polished their English conversation skills hanging out with American friends in Okinawa or working in businesses that cater to international tourists or the many United States military personnel and contractors on the Ryukyu Islands.

Three units—"Transnational Literature in the Global Era," "Graphic Narrative; or, Visualizing Gender, Race, and Sexuality," and "Popular Feminized

Genres and Adaptations"—organized the course into sections of roughly equal length, with two weeks at the beginning and end for introduction and reflection, respectively. During the second class meeting we discussed a 2015 article from *The Guardian* about a BBC poll that asked critics from the United States what the greatest novels of the twenty-first century were, at only fifteen years in (Flood). Junot Díaz's *The Brief Wondrous Life of Oscar Wao* topped mainstream critics' lists most often. Although we had not yet read any of the novels mentioned in the article, I invited students to focus on Rigoberto Gonzalez's rationale that Díaz's novel "re-energised" the questions of "Who is American?" and "What is the American experience?" (qtd. in Flood). I extended these questions to two others about literary culture: What are the traditional elements of American literature? What makes a novel "great" in our current era?

Initial discussions, explicitly bracketed as provisional, predictably included the American self-made man, a concept we recognized as ableist and masculinist since it emphasizes the independent, strong, and productive individual; the bootstrap narrative and the immigrant narrative surfaced as exemplary of the American experience; as for features of American literature, students proposed that there is often a long and potentially complicated journey, which they related to the size of the United States and its history as an immigrant nation. During these discussions, I observed that students in the United States are often taught that American literature traditionally emphasizes the notion of American exceptionalism or the supposedly unique status of the United States and American character. Students were hesitant to identify what makes a novel great in our time. Therefore, we generated a list together about what seems to appeal to contemporary readers, acknowledging that commercial success is only one limited measurement of greatness or value. Our general list included action, violence, or a strong plot; romance; the fight between good and evil; and horror, or a focus on fears.

I urged students to keep these questions in mind. After each of the three course units, students wrote a one-page response to a prompt that brought us back to the framing questions in some way, and at the close of the semester they were assigned a two- to three-page paper in which they were asked to synthesize what they had learned throughout the semester. In the first four-week unit on transnational literature, students read Yamashita's "The Orange," chapter 1 of Díaz's *The Brief Wondrous Life of Oscar Wao*, and "Part I: Emile," the three-chapter section of *Brazil-Maru* devoted to Ichiro, a character compared to the principal figure of Jean-Jacques Rousseau's *Émile, ou De l'éducation* (1762; *Emile; or, On Education*). At the end of the unit, we watched and discussed Paul Haggis's *Crash*. Each class meeting was devoted to one of the texts, though there was overlap across weekly meetings for coherence and to help students make connections.

To prepare for discussion of the first assigned reading, I asked students to write a one- to two-sentence response to the following question for homework: How is "The Orange," a short story published in 1991, relevant to issues and concerns of the present? When we met, and intending to introduce the concept of magical realism, I opened by asking why "The Orange" is briefly introduced and described by Yamashita as a "children's fable" in its publication in the *Los Angeles Times*. Students observed that fables usually end with a moral or lesson and often include magic. I pointed out that magical realism is a mode of fiction more closely associated with Latin American literature than with literature of the United States. We then identified other connections in the story to points south of or outside the United States. Finally, students shared their homework responses, relating Yamashita's story to the fear of global warming, inequality among social classes, immigration, diversity, and unclear borders, which one student commented changed and mixed up everything, including distance. Another student observed that "The Orange" is about chaos and people not having control, which the student believed distinguished the story from what most would call traditional literature. We discussed possibilities for a moral, and how, in terms of its style or form and with respect to its content, the story is an example of "interethnic literature" (Rody, *Interethnic Imagination*), a term we compared to "border fiction" and would continue to think about in relation to other readings (Sadowski-Smith, "U.S.-Mexico Borderlands" 91–94). This brief sequence of writing and discussion helped students begin to consider how Yamashita's storytelling opens up narrative space to imagine worlds beyond the narrow parameters of closed cultural categories and bounded political communities. Although set largely in Los Angeles, "The Orange" dramatizes modern-day conditions in a global city or place, where flows of capital, culture, and politics converge, and often, as Yamashita demonstrates, where they collide in ways that seem spectacular or outside normative concepts of space and time.

For our second meeting devoted to transnational literature, I prefaced our reading of chapter 1 of *Oscar Wao* with a basic summary of the plot. In the following class, students brainstormed questions about Oscar de Leon in a short writing exercise: individually they composed "why" or "how" questions that contained keywords and concepts from the book that I projected on a screen one at a time, including, for example, "Amor de Pendejo" (*Brief Wonderous Life* 36), roughly translated as "Crazy Love"; "X-Men" (2); "Shazam" (14); and "masculine" (15). Using these questions—for example, Why does Oscar love superheroes like X-Men and Shazam?—as the basis for a free-flowing discussion, we then created a profile of Oscar and what makes him a compelling protagonist, which included his development as a writer and a "nerd" who likes superheroes and comics, his code-switching and other linguistic practices, his ethnic background, and his anxieties and questions surrounding masculinity and sexuality. In various ways, students observed what Gregg Barrios refers to as Diaz's "mash-up of Dominican history, comics, sci-fi, magic realism and footnotes," and that this formal "mash-up" was reminiscent of Yamashita's story (qtd. in Flood). In Diaz's text, however, there is sustained focus on a single character's imagination and feelings. This was a challenging reading, given its cascade of cultural references, footnotes, and the scale of its neo- and postcolonial political landscape, and I assured students that most readers find it difficult, pointing to the many guides and commentaries that exist as testimony.[2] I asked if this sort of writing might fit the concept of hemispheric literature, introducing some ideas elaborated by Claudia Sadowski-Smith and Claire Fox and by Kandice Chuh ("Of Hemispheres"). We then considered how the novel opens narrative space for reimagining who is American and which features might characterize American literature through its recognition, on various levels, of the ways in which cultural forms and media as well as national and geopolitical entities are becoming increasingly connected and interdependent within our current globalized world.[3]

As we turned to *Brazil-Maru*, I summarized historical information about Japanese migration in the early part of the twentieth century, when Ichiro and other characters in the novel go to Brazil and settle Esperança. We reviewed facts referred to in the front matter of the novel, which acknowledges that the story sprang from Yamashita's interviews with Japanese Brazilians and observes that the largest community of people of Japanese descent outside Japan (often Okinawan, more specifically) lives in Brazil. The front matter also points out that, for Japanese immigrants to Brazil, "immigration . . . has followed patterns of their exclusion from the United States." Specifically, we discussed the 1908 gentleman's agreement between the United States and Japan as well as the 1924 Immigration Act (otherwise known as the Johnson-Reed Act), since both paratextual and textual elements in the novel underscore this historical context. However, rather than a portrayal of victims of exclusion or displacement, *Brazil-Maru* complicates this history. I pointed both to the frontispiece that refers to travel in search of home and to a passage in the novel students had read, a quotation from Kantaro Uno in which the founder of the fictional Christian and socialist community rationalizes leisure activities, specifically baseball, with the reminder that "[w]e in Esperança came here to settle and to create. We are unlike others who have come here to make money and return with monetary wealth to Japan" (41). In class, we then considered how this character's portrayal of his own immigrant community (within Yamashita's complex portrayal of immigrants in the novel) might connect to and redefine the idea of American exceptionalism.

Our review of the historical context of the novel included some of the most impassioned and difficult conversation of the semester, eliciting various opinions about immigration, reflections on the history of Okinawan migration and diaspora specifically, and thoughts about anti-immigration sentiment and policy in the contemporary United States. The 2016 presidential election was just weeks away and incendiary comments in the news media about building a wall and making Mexico pay for it were accompanied by equally controversial comments about making Japan (in effect, Okinawa) pay for United States military protection—or, as many living in Okinawa understood it, militarization. Our lively discussions seemed to confirm that Yamashita's writing moves students because "they recognize its form and themes . . . as belonging to their own contemporary moment" (Adams 249). As Rachel Adams observes, Yamashita is part of a group of contemporary writers, many of whom are immigrants or children of immigrants, whose works respond to the upheavals associated with globalization, even when stories are set in the past or the future; "their fiction reacts against the [cool] aesthetic sensibilities of high postmodernism while providing American literature with a new set of genealogical, geographical, and temporal referents" (251). Importantly, *Brazil-Maru*'s epilogue adds "the histories of displaced indigeneity" to this book's new set of referents, for it indicates "awareness of the infinite other stories existing beyond the bounds of this novel and beyond the trope of immigration, which are as yet unrepresented and perhaps unrepresentable within the economy of visibility marked by national, transnational, or global" frameworks (Chuh, "Of Hemispheres" 628). *Brazil-Maru* thus serves as a temporally and spatially complex example of transnational literature writ large and specifically of American literary globalism, defined as a style of writing in the United States that comes after postmodernism and responds to an intensification of global processes that began during the Cold War: such processes include an integration of the world's markets, technologies, and systems of governance; surprising and innovative new forms of cultural fusion; and the mobilization of political coalitions across race, class, nation, and other affiliations and categories (Adams 250–51).

At this point, I asked students to think about their responses to the characters in *Brazil-Maru* and to Ichiro in particular—whether the strong feelings and views voiced in our discussion about immigration were connected to personal feelings about or identification with this fictional character. One student remarked that they did not feel any specific connection to the characters because they had never experienced moving to another country, though they did recognize that these characters were able to pursue their dreams in Brazil at a time when the United States would not allow them entry, and the possibility that people might soon face exclusion again from the United States was frightening. I circled back to our earlier discussion of the greatness or value of literature to engage what Rachel Greenwald Smith terms "the affective hypothesis," or the dominant view today that literature's primary value and most important contribution is its ability to help readers feel intimacy or relate to people who are unlike them—all with the goal of helping readers develop or "invest" in their personal feelings (1–2). In other words, literature is considered valuable to the extent that it provides an affectively profitable experience for readers. I explained Smith's argument that this view of literature is connected to the specific virtues espoused in neoliberal capitalism—a form of capitalism in which individuals are defined by their marketplace aspirations and feelings, particularly their enthusiasm for work—but that some literature, such as *Tropic of Orange*, challenges this view by creating disturbing and unsettling feelings, or what Smith refers to as "impersonal feelings" (2).[4]

To be sure, part of what I wanted us to explore in the course was whether *Brazil-Maru* may also be concerned with impersonal feelings—that is, whether this novel expands or opens narrative space affectively, traversing the emotional logics and economies of a neoliberal structure of feeling. To this end, the writing prompt for the unit on transnational literature asked students to take a stance and respond to one of the following two questions about a text we had read as part of the unit: How does this text help readers feel emotionally connected to other human beings? How does this text make readers feel emotionally distant? One student who wrote about *Brazil-Maru* observed that if readers dream of being independent, then the story of a group of Japanese immigrants trying to create a self-sustaining commune may be appealing, and in this way readers may easily identify with or feel connected to these characters. The same student also observed, however, that "Part I: Emile" of *Brazil-Maru* contains limited detail of Ichiro's inner emotions, which might make it difficult for readers to feel a close emotional connection to him. We then discussed the fact that each of the novel's four parts is devoted to a different character, which means there is less of an opportunity for intimate familiarity with a single character, and we discussed why an author might choose this structure. Another student insightfully shared that one problem with the affective hypothesis is that readers have many different emotional experiences and capacities, and the expectation that all readers feel, or learn to feel, a particular way in relation to a character or novel might exclude some emotional responses as inappropriate or even compel a reader to deny their feelings. We then discussed how Haggis's film *Crash* seems entirely devoted to dramatizing various kinds of emotional connections among people while it also suggests that many or even most of these connections are accidental collisions rather than emotionally cultivated and sustained relationships.

In the United States, the academy has long been contending with an erosion in public support for higher education and a declining belief in the value of the humanities and the study of literature in particular.[5] This has been the case for several decades, especially since the global recession of 2008, and it seems unlikely to change soon, given the recent global health crisis of COVID-19 and its financial effects. A frequent response has been to point out that literature helps readers consider others' suffering, pain, grief, and loss; teaches them how to respond with compassion when they encounter the hardship of others; and perhaps helps them understand how not to contribute to this hardship. In short, literature aids in the creation of good character through the development of emotional capacity.

This is no small feat, and few would deny that the United States and the world are in need of this type of capacity. Because this defense of literature is most often presented in terms of how reading or study will benefit the individual, however, it is actually a contraction in the understanding of the value of literature, at worst a whittling down to schooling individuals in what is now frequently referred to as emotional intelligence, or the ability to manage and monetize one's own as well as others' emotions, a necessary skill for success in the contemporary workplace. Such a view aligns with the neoliberal values of responsibilization and self-care, as well as with the new spirit of affective capitalism (Boltanski and Chiapello). In teaching *Brazil-Maru*, and by connecting Adams's ideas about American literary globalism to Smith's ideas about impersonal feelings, I sought to emphasize that literature has the potential to push back—against the romanticization or naturalization of the current form of global capitalism, given the obvious devastation global capitalism has led to; against the notion of feelings as something to be accumulated for personal or individual profit; and against the entrepreneurial subjecthood that now forms the bedrock of neoliberal belonging in the United States. Yamashita's storytelling certainly urges readers to think and feel in relation to how the world is changing under late capitalism. Her work characteristically stages the reconfiguration and increasingly chaotic blowup of cultural, political, technological, and affective horizons. These dramatic renderings open space for narratives that upset the comforting celebration of individual self-improvement and other neoliberal virtues that restrict rather than expand understanding of feelings, connection, and belonging, thereby demonstrating the valuable role literature may play in the creation of a more socially just future and a better world.

NOTES

[1] Relations among cultural form, gender, and belonging in contemporary neoliberal times are primary interests of mine and are also the focus of my book, *Asian American Women's Popular Literature: Feminizing Genres and Neoliberal Belonging*.

[2] See, for example, *The Annotated Oscar Wao* (www.annotated-oscar-wao.com/).

[3] Our discussion of the convergence of literary and popular culture paved the way for the later units where Asian American literature would continue to appear as an innovative player through works such as Lynda Barry's *One! Hundred! Demons!*, Adriane Tomine's *Shortcomings*, MariNaomi's *Turning Japanese*, and Jhumpa Lahiri's *The Namesake*.

[4] Smith observes that experimental narratives such as *Tropic of Orange* are atypical both for the ways in which the form of their storytelling produces emotional responses in readers and for the disturbing or unsettling feelings they aim to create.

[5] In 2015 the Japanese Ministry of Education proposed to radically slash funding for humanities education at the country's eighty-six national universities (of which the University of the Ryukyus is one); while the proposal has since been dialed back a bit, institutions have been restructuring, humanities programs have been shrinking, and *rikei* (science, engineering, and agriculture) departments have been growing; see Kakuchi.

Through the Arc of the Rain Forest and Planetary Fiction

Min Hyoung Song

In 2000 Gayatri Chakravorty Spivak gave the Wellek Library Lectures in Critical Theory at the University of California, Irvine, on comparative literature and the challenges facing this discipline. These were later published in 2003 in a slim volume entitled *Death of a Discipline.* Spivak's lectures are where most discussions about the distinction between the global and the planetary originate. The former refers to space that is defined by financial speculation, far-flung corporate enterprises, and an imperial way of seeing the world. The latter suggests something less hierarchical and more mobile, a contingency of relatedness that perhaps might lead people to develop relationships to each other and to the natural environments they share that are different than those that capitalism usually allows. As Spivak puts it, "The globe is on our computers. No one lives there. It allows us to think we can aim to control it. The planet is in the species of alterity, belonging to another system; and yet we inhabit it, on loan" (*Death* 72). The idea of what in academic circles has come to be known as *planetarity* has become the subject of increasing critical discussion in the past decade or so: important works include those by Paul Gilroy, Susan Stanford Friedman ("Planetarity"), Elizabeth DeLoughrey, Ursula Heise (*Sense*), and a volume of essays edited by Amy Elias and Christian Moraru.

How does Karen Tei Yamashita's much respected novel *Through the Arc of the Rain Forest* help us think about the difference between the global and the planetary, or globalization and planetarity? How does our understanding of the novel change when we pay closer attention to the kinds of social and ecological relatedness that thinking of the world we occupy as a planet entails? This essay addresses these questions by considering how to explain to undergraduates the growing scholarship on the idea of planetarity and the implications of this idea. It also explores how the novel itself can speak to our present in exciting and new ways. The essay builds on my experience teaching *Through the Arc of the Rain Forest* to first- and second-year students in a required course for English majors.

What I discovered in teaching Yamashita's novel in this course is that it disrupted students' ideas about what a narrative work should look like, given its play with genre and its unusual narrator. Yamashita herself understands the ways in which her novel upends conventions and emphasizes alterity, often at great expense to her career. When I interviewed her for a book project, she told me that the novel "wasn't Asian American feminist literature; it wasn't magic realism; it wasn't science fiction. . . . That was and still is my problem. I think a lot of Asian American authors or authors of color find merchandising their work difficult because bookstores and publishers and publicists are looking for niches for these books" (qtd. in Song, *Children* 182). A focus on planetarity, then, helps foreground the ways in which this novel, like many by authors of color, is difficult to categorize and may even be valuable precisely because it does not easily dovetail with preconceived ideas about what literature is. Thus, much of my approach to teaching this novel is organized around the need to prompt students to talk about their different narrative expectations, and to question what they hope to get out of reading the novel.

What follows is an outline of a four-day unit on *Through the Arc of the Rain Forest*. This is based on my own past experiences as well as a consideration of what worked and what didn't.

Day 1

Prior to the first day of discussion, I ask students to read through the end of chapter 13 of *Through the Arc*. Much happens during these pages, including an introduction to the novel's many major characters. Because students will thus already know who the characters are, what kind of narrative arc each is on, and how they are connected to one another, I begin class by asking students to name all the characters. As they do, I write the names on a blackboard, making sure to space them in a way that helps illuminate their relationships to one another. This is what I call a character map. It helps students remember the names of the novel's characters, reminds students of what they've read, and considers in an analytic way how these characters are connected to one another. This is a useful exercise for discussion of a novel with multiple characters and plot threads. Once we have finished this exercise, I ask students why the novel contains so many characters. This question should then lead to a discussion about globalization.

Here I launch into a minilecture on the origins of the term *global*, how the term has been used, and how the novel can be read as a global novel. I then introduce the term *planetarity*. I haven't prepared a slideshow for this minilecture in the past, but instructors might find it useful to create a few slides with relevant quotations that students can later consult online.

I explain in this minilecture where the term *planetarity* comes from and how it has evolved in critical discussions. I emphasize how it has increasingly been given an ecological meaning, so that more attention is directed to the Earth as a planet as opposed to a globe in its physical and biological entanglements. In a planetary model, humans are so much a part of their surroundings that the distinction between humans and their environments is no longer quite as relevant. If time permits, I might at this point also introduce terms like *Anthropocene*, *deep time*, and *vibrant materialism*. We end the class by talking about the advantages and disadvantages of thinking about Yamashita's novel through the lens of each of these two terms, and in the process I ask students to ponder why globalization may or may not seem such an obvious framework.

Day 2

Prior to our second day of discussion, I ask students to read chapters 14 through 20. I like to have students read more in the first week and to slow the pace down in the second, leaving more time for discussion as we reach the end of the novel. At the start of this class session, my goal is to call attention to the ways in which the first half of the novel is full of exuberant discovery. To this end, I ask students to read out loud some of the dreamlike descriptions of a depot of abandoned "aircraft and vehicles of every sort of description" (Yamashita, *Through the Arc* 99). This is a long passage, and it is interesting for students to consider why the novel lingers over the details of the fantastic creatures that have evolved in this depot. I tell students that critics have written extensively about this passage, and I ask them why this description would attract such scrutiny. Are we seeing here a different sense of time that we might call planetary? Are things and animals given more agency than we usually grant them? What would it mean, in the context of this description, to talk about being in a geological age dominated by human activity?

To contrast the sense of discovery that fills these early sections, one that seems to culminate in the description of the abandoned depot, I turn to the ways in which the day's assigned reading adumbrates a growing dissatisfaction with the developments, especially the economic developments, that have taken place. Characters are disappointed by the kinds of successes they are finding. Relationships become frayed. More and more, people who used to be close find themselves living farther away from each other and being in touch less often.

Day 3

The reading assignment for the third day is chapters 21 through 26. Building on where class discussion ended on day two, this class begins by turning attention to the increasing discontent felt by many of the novel's characters. This idea is emphasized in the last chapter of part 4, which focuses on the development of a communication system built on homing pigeons, an enterprise that grows and becomes global. It's interesting to speculate with students whether this communication system is meant to anticipate the rise of the Internet and other forms of advanced telecommunications that have been instrumental in shaping our contemporary sense of the global. To consider this possibility, we begin by reading about the growth of the pigeon message system (137), which makes the Aparecida family wealthy but ends up geographically separating Tania, who is the financial mastermind of this enterprise, and Batista, who, as the expert on pigeons, must travel to set up this system. I invite students to consider why this chapter ends with a section entitled "Loss of Innocence." What is "innocence"? I write their responses on the board and try to achieve a consensus definition. At this point, we start to discuss the limits of our definition of innocence as it applies to the story of Tania and Batista, and in particular how innocence can be a cover for what we may not want to know.

To help track the changing affective state of the characters, I redraw the character map from the first day. (I like to draw this before the start of class so it's there when we are ready to move on to this discussion.) The focus in this discussion should not be on who these characters are or what kinds of relationships they have to one another; rather, it should focus on what has happened to them. In other words, I want students to think about plot. What is the role of plot in a discussion of a novel? What can we say about plot that is more than a summary of what happens? Does the movement of these plots in similar directions, toward dissatisfaction and disappointment, suggest a weakening of human agency, and perhaps also the need for greater humility when it comes to the limits of this agency?

Day 4

Students should have finished reading the novel at this point, although I also find that many students have already read ahead. I begin class by asking students to consider what happens to both the feathers, which were granted enormous curative powers, and the Matacão plastic, the substance that had been found underneath the Amazon. Why does the former cause mass typhus and the latter get eaten by bacteria? Here it is useful to have students read certain passages out loud, especially the sections about how the disease cannot be confined to the poor and about the logic the state uses to kill all the birds in the area (182–84, 198–201). How might these passages be understood in a planetary sense? I then ask students to consider who the narrator is—a spinning ball made of Matacão plastic. We read the passage where it too dissolves (205–06). Can we read the ball as a metaphor for a global perspective or a planetary one?

My experiences teaching this novel have shown me that it is important to give students a sense of the rich body of scholarship that informs what we are discussing in class. This is especially true for the idea of planetarity. By concentrating on this idea in our reading of Yamashita's *Through the Arc of the Rain Forest*, we can think about the ways an idea like globalization affects our approach to reading a story that crosses borders and focuses on far-flung commercial enterprises. This approach encourages students to think more self-consciously using different ecological frames. An expansion of the framework used to discuss this novel, afforded by an attention to planetarity, can provide students with tools for thinking about ecological and racial issues together. This kind of retooling, I believe, is vital as environmental issues are taking on an increasing urgency. The point is not to suggest that an ecological approach provides a better lens through which to interpret this novel than the one provided by Asian American studies (as exemplified by Rachel Lee in "Asian American Cultural Production") or hemispheric studies (Chuh, "Of Hemispheres"), but rather to consider how essential it is to think ecology and race together.

NEW TRANSNATIONALISMS AND ECOCRITICAL APPROACHES

The Voice of the Globe: Narrating Globalization in *Through the Arc of the Rain Forest*

Begoña Simal-González

In 1990, just as the buzzword *globalization* was becoming audible, Karen Tei Yamashita published *Through the Arc of the Rain Forest*. Within the specific academic context of Asian American studies, Yamashita's novel is one of the first examples of the process of "denationalization" that Sau-ling Wong would later discuss in her landmark 1995 essay, "Denationalization Reconsidered." On a larger scale that can be tentatively called world literature—still a contested label according to Franco Moretti (44–46)—Yamashita's novel certainly invites a consideration of the new global era. It is this theoretical framework that has shaped my teaching practice over the last few years. In this essay I will focus on the teaching strategies I have employed in three courses offered at the Universidade da Coruña (University of A Coruña) in Spain in recent years: Postcolonial Literature (for English majors), English Literary Texts (for Spanish majors), and A Trans-cultural Approach to Literatures Written in English (part of the master's degree program in advanced English studies). I have consciously chosen three courses that differ substantially with respect both to the type of students and to class size in an attempt to show the different strategies teachers may employ when exploring the same text.[1]

Preparing the Syllabus

Prior to the intensified forms of globalization witnessed in the current era, literature, like other arts, had been approached and envisioned within the national paradigm (Scholte 225; Moretti 61). In most Western countries, including Spain, this translated in practical terms into educational curricula that contained subjects like French literature, Spanish literature, or English literature, which originally focused on the literary traditions of France, Spain, and Great Britain, respectively. However, the postcolonial impetus, first from so-called settler colonies like Canada and Australia and later from the rest of the world, contributed to an expansion of the meaning of the term *English* in *English literature* to include any literature written in English. By the end of the twentieth century, most universities in Spain and in other European countries had either added these (purportedly) new national literatures as separate subjects or covered them under the general heading of literatures in English. It was no longer nationality or territory that determined the scope of these subject areas; language now provided the nexus for diverse literary traditions. In recent years, the broadening and rethinking of disciplines like English literature have coincided with a deepened realization that the culture we are living in is becoming increasingly global. That is why, when approaching literature in and outside the classroom today, the transnational paradigm needs to complement, if not supersede, the traditional national framework. This is what I have tried to do in my literature classes in the last few years, by moving from an understanding of American literature tout court to one of transnational American literature, or by incorporating intriguingly resonant novels, like Yamashita's *Through the Arc of the Rain Forest*, in different courses on contemporary literature. Before plunging into the specific strategies applied to the teaching of the novel, I explain the academic context in which I teach, emphasizing in particular the process of constructing a syllabus.

English Literary Texts is an optional course offered to undergraduate students majoring in Spanish who have just read several canonical texts from the fifteenth to the nineteenth centuries, such as Shakespeare's *Hamlet* or Mary Shelley's *Frankenstein*, in previous English literature courses. When in 2014 I had a chance to create the syllabus for this course, I turned it into a survey course of recent literature in English and structured it around four themes. The first unit, "Literature, (Neo)Colonialism, and Globalization," included works by Merlinda Bobis, Wole Soyinka, and Helena Viramontes. The following unit, "Literature and Diversity," emphasized class, gender, and ethnicity; this unit focused on texts by Aravind Adiga, Maxine Hong Kingston (*Woman Warrior*; *China Men*), Gish Jen ("Who's Irish?"), and Toni Morrison ("Recitatif"). The third unit, "Literature and Cinema," considered works by Don DeLillo, David Henry Hwang, and Alice Munro ("Bear"). The final unit of the course was titled "Other Challenges for the New Millennium." This unit, which focused on the environment and on information and communications technology, considered works by Margaret Atwood (*Oryx*) and Yamashita (*Through the Arc*).

In the last unit, I focused on two novels that use literary modes that go beyond conventional realism: Atwood's *Oryx and Crake*, which can be characterized as speculative fiction, and Yamashita's *Through the Arc*, which employs magical realism. In our interactive sessions we performed an ecocritical reading of *Through the Arc*. In undergraduate classes like this one, I often select chapters for close reading, preferably excerpts that can be understood even when students have not read the whole novel. An apt example is the junkyard episode in *Through the Arc* (99–101).[2]

In the courses offered to graduate students or to undergraduates majoring in English, I complemented an ecocritical approach by asking students to read Yamashita's work in relation to larger debates about globalization. When I created the syllabus for Postcolonial Literature, a mandatory course for third-year English majors, I decided to include Yamashita's novel in the fourth and final unit. I divided this unit, which was devoted to the transnational paradigm, into five sections. The first section examined key concepts in transnational and diaspora studies, with an emphasis on globalization, neocolonialism, and cosmopolitanism. The second section focused on cultural globalization—on new diasporas, transnational identities, and discrepant cosmopolitanism. The next section considered the idea of economic globalization with respect to migration, neocolonialism, and exploitation. In its consideration of political globalization, the fourth section asked students to consider the future of the nation-state. The fifth and final section of the unit attended to the idea of a global environment and the related concept of a planetary consciousness.

To tease out the different strands of globalization and consider how literature reflects or presents a critique of the phenomena associated with contemporary globalization, we read *Through the Arc* alongside Yamashita's *Tropic of Orange* and the narratives of authors from different parts of the world who have recently addressed the new global dynamics. In the case of Postcolonial Literature, the other texts analyzed in unit 4 were four short stories published at the turn of this century: Bobis's "The Long Siesta as a Language Primer," Anita Desai's "Winterscape," Chitra B. Divakaruni's "Doors," and Viramontes's "The Cariboo Café."

In A Trans-cultural Approach to Literatures Written in English—the course offered to graduate students, whose command of English allowed them to engage with non-Spanish literature in more sophisticated ways—I chose longer texts for the analysis and discussion of globalization. I paired Yamashita's *Through the Arc* with Adiga's novel *The White Tiger*, which won the Booker Prize in 2008.

Classroom Strategies

Yamashita's *Through the Arc of the Rain Forest* has often served my pedagogical goal of encouraging students to engage with the various interconnected facets of present-day globalization—economic, political, cultural, and environmental.[3]

Although I have devised different strategies when teaching Yamashita's novel, they all derive from the same premise: the fact that *Through the Arc* was one of the first English-language novels to reflect critically on modern-day globalization. I provide students with a basic introduction to the main debates surrounding globalization since the 1990s, with the help of schematic presentations, handouts and, in the case of advanced groups, scholarly articles. Typically, I open the session with some initial questions (e.g., What is globalization? Is globalization a new phenomenon?), thought-provoking quotations from different scholars of globalization, and audiovisual prompts (cartoons, clips from *The Story of Stuff*, the elephant analogy used by Manfred Steger in the first chapter of his book *Globalization: A Very Short Introduction*, etc.). Background materials are presented either as preliminary reading or as shorter handouts and generally include excerpts from pioneering studies by Arjun Appadurai, Frederic Jameson, Ulrich Beck, or David Harvey (*Condition*) and from more recent introductions written by John McLeod, Jan Aart Scholte, or Steger (*Globalization*). Among the key concepts and polemical issues discussed in class are Harvey's notion of space-time compression as theorized in *The Condition of Postmodernity*; Marshall McLuhan's concept of "global village" versus "global pillage," discussed in Jeremy Brecher and Tim Costello's *Global Village or Global Pillage*; John Tomlinson's concept of deterritorialization; Ursula Heise's "sense of place" versus "sense of planet" (*Sense*); the persistence and end of the nation; Appadurai's new *-scapes* (*ethno-*, *techno-*, *media-*, etc.); and Michael Hardt and Antonio Negri's biopolitical understanding of the new empire. I either devote time to each of the major debates, as I often do in the graduate class, or focus on just one of these subtopics, for instance neocolonialism or the global environmental crisis, as I often do in undergraduate courses.

In smaller classes of fifteen to twenty students, as in graduate courses or electives, I can engage with the entire novel, and I often incorporate full critical essays that facilitate a more thorough analysis of Yamashita's book. When working with large classes, I have devised and used three different strategies: selecting excerpts for close reading and discussion with the whole group, presenting the whole book as optional reading and offering an assignment (for instance, an essay or oral presentation) for extra credit, and designing small-group projects and including follow-up activities for the entire group. In this last approach, the lecture on globalization and its discontents does not precede but follows students' first encounter with *Through the Arc*. In the other two cases I start by introducing the concept of globalization and the debates surrounding this contested term. Once students are familiar with the different aspects of globalization (economic, cultural, environmental, and so on), I ask them to explore how a specific chapter or, if they have read the entire novel, a given character, such as Tweep, or leitmotif, such as the Matacão (the novel's main setting, an intriguing plateau that seems to attract all characters), exemplifies any of the phenomena discussed in class: the expansion of transnational corporations, the global environmental crisis, the neocolonial exploitation of formerly colonized countries, increased human mobility and cross-cultural contacts, the impact of global media and information and communications technologies, and so on. Students have frequently designed illustrative graphic (slide) presentations for this assignment.[4] These are just a few of the ways in which students show that they have learned one of the basic "transferrable skills" of higher education (Showalter 24): the ability to apply complex concepts to the analysis of a particular text, the ability to read that text through this newly acquired theoretical knowledge, which is good practice when trying to read or interpret meaning in the world outside literature.

Teaching a large group can prove challenging, especially when one wants to move beyond the lecture format. This is where the third strategy mentioned above proves useful, for its goal is to encourage students to adopt a more active role in the classroom. In this case, organizing and planning the sessions of this alternative teaching approach proves particularly important, for this strategy revolves around the need to withhold certain information to foster students' creativity and resourcefulness. In this approach, as one might expect, the first class is not a lecture introducing globalization or the novel. Instead, one week prior to the session for which Yamashita's *Through the Arc* is scheduled, I ask students to form small groups, with four to five students in each, and I assign one of the initial chapters to each group. I stress that students should only read their assigned chapter and nothing else. The following week, before introducing the concept of globalization, I ask students to work with their groups to come up with a brief summary of their respective chapters and a description of the main character in that chapter: Kasumasa, the Djapans, Mané, the corporation GGG, Chico Paco, and Tweep. I then ask students to present their chapter to the rest of the class using the notes they have compiled during their group work. I provide ample opportunity for the other groups to pose questions if anything is unclear, since they know they will be asked about these characters later.[5]

I open the second class period by writing on the blackboard or showing a slide with the following questions: What will happen next? How will the lives of these characters become entangled? How will these characters change or develop?[6] The ensuing discussion can take the form of a brainstorming activity with the whole group or, especially in very large classes, it can be organized by giving each small group time to write down their reactions to these questions, discuss them with other members of their group, and then share with the rest of the class what they imagine lies in store for their respective character. Like Jessica Richard, I have found that the modest reflection involved in this in-class exercise can help students "not only to make interesting comments, but also to talk to each other, not just me" (qtd. in Showalter 54). One week later, students will have read a few more chapters or possibly the entire novel, and we can then discuss the ways in which the characters have actually interacted with one another. In this follow-up activity, it is my role to tease out and stress the intriguing ways in which the characters become increasingly linked, thus introducing one of the key elements of contemporary globalization: interconnectivity both in its technical sense and in its broader, planetary sense. This is the time to introduce Anthony

Giddens's famous description of contemporary globalization as "the intensification of worldwide social relations which link distant localities in such a way that local happenings are shaped by events occurring many miles away and vice versa" (64). Once the mystery of the Matacão is resolved, students realize that the ecological dynamics creating the plateau underscore global interrelatedness and complement the planetary consciousness prefigured in the narrator, an omniscient ball orbiting near Kazumasa that can be regarded as the very voice of the globe.

The voice of the globe is not one but many. Among the many voices that make up this global voice are those of students and teachers from the North and the South, the East and the West, the United States and Spain. I hope that other instructors can benefit from these modest insights that have been drawn as much from my experience in the classroom as from the critical reflection prompted by it. "Authentic teaching," Elaine Showalter reminds us, "requires reflective practice" (142). Fortunately, we teachers never stop learning. Each academic year texts are new, even if they are not new. Each year we start a new life, and we try new things. When neither the old teaching methods nor the new strategies work, we can always overcome our shyness and don the "Kazumasa ball," the little planet "secured by [a] transparent headband" and dangling before our eyes (Yamashita, *Through the Arc* 193). This will certainly call students' attention, if not to us then certainly to the globe.

NOTES

The publication of this essay has been made possible by the generous funding that my first research project, "Literature and Globalization," received from the Spanish State Research Agency of the Ministry of Science, Innovation and Universities (ref. FFI2015-66767-P, AEI/FEDER, UE).

[1] Students enrolled in a master's degree program usually have a stronger command of the English language and of critical tools. The size of the class is also important, since only ten to twelve students are able to enroll in graduate courses, in contrast to undergraduate courses, where one can find between fifty and eighty students.

[2] I have used this episode to illustrate the transnational turn in ecocriticism as discussed in Heise, *Sense*; Wallace, "'Bizarre Ecology'"; and Simal, "Junkyard."

[3] Although I have occasionally discussed literary mode (magical realism), narratological issues (the voice of the globe as embodied by the narrator), and the workings of power (biopolitics) in relation to the novel, my recent teaching usually revolves around global matters.

[4] For examples of student work that focused on a particular trope or character, see the companion website to this volume (readteachyamashita.mla.hcommons.org). The first and second examples analyze two characters, Mané de Costa Pena and Michelle Mabelle, respectively. The first student, Sara López-Mariño, starts by explaining the narrative structure into which the character is inserted (slide 1), and then teases out the ways in which Mané both actively and passively engages with globalization in each of the novel's five parts (slides 2–3). The second student, Elena Canido-Muiño, reads the relation-

ship between Mabelle and Tweep as an allegory of neocolonialism (slides 4–5), following models of allegorical interpretation carried out in class, like that of Bobis's "The Long Siesta" (see Simal, "Waste"). Other students explore certain leitmotifs, such as the feather or the Matacão, as in the case of the third student, Anabella Barsaglini-Castro, who applies the lens of neoliberal globalization to the magical Matacão and reads it as a magnet for capitalist ventures. In particular, she focuses on the different "businesses" that crop up around that symbolic site (slide 6) and humorously applies a businesslike pie chart to explain the different interpretations of the Matacão that are given in the novel (slide 7).

[5] This activity was originally designed for a class in which only thirty students attended on a regular basis. I selected excerpts from the six chapters that make up part 1, but the activity would also work with larger classes; instructors could either use more chapters or assign each of the first six chapters to two groups.

[6] These questions could also be posed at the end of the first class period, as food for thought to return to in a later session after students have finished reading the novel.

Through the Arc of the Rain Forest, Environmental Apocalypse, and Post-Soviet Allegory

Nataliya Krynytska

I discovered Karen Tei Yamashita's oeuvre in 2010 during the Institute on Contemporary American Literature, in which I participated as a representative of Ukraine. The institute was a program for scholars sponsored by the United States Department of State and hosted by the University of Louisville. The Study of the United States Institute on Contemporary American Literature surveyed contemporary American writers and writing in a variety of genres and researched how the themes explored in those works reflected main currents within contemporary society and culture of the United States. Participants also traveled to Santa Fe, New Mexico, where Yamashita was one of the guest presenters. She conducted an inspiring seminar on *I Hotel* and participated in the other seminars and discussions. During one of my conversations with her, I mentioned offhandedly that students and teachers in Poltava, Ukraine, had little opportunity to read contemporary American literature in the original. Yamashita remembered my remark, and since 2010, she has been mailing me her books and other books, primarily novels by Asian American authors and works on creative writing, thereby enriching the library of our university. I am no doubt one of many people whom Yamashita helps in her quiet and modest way.

I teach English and English-language literature at Poltava V. G. Korolenko National Pedagogical University to students in bachelor's and master's programs who are pursuing degrees in English and pedagogy. But the situation in Ukraine, as in many other post-Soviet areas, does not allow us to study Yamashita's works in detail: students' limited proficiency in English and a lack of class hours mean that students have to read American literature translated into Russian or Ukrainian and discuss it in English. Unfortunately, Yamashita's works have not yet been translated into Russian or Ukrainian, although Yamashita is an author who would be extremely interesting to readers in the post-Soviet world.

Thus, I aim to promote Yamashita's fiction in my context in Ukraine by making connections between her works and post-Soviet reality and literature. During the optional course for fifth-year students, Contemporary Literature Studies in English-Speaking Countries, we use Peter Barry's *Beginning Theory: An Introduction to Literary and Cultural Theory* as a foundation and works by modern authors who write in English as texts for analysis.

Yamashita's first published novel, *Through the Arc of the Rain Forest*, provides a splendid opportunity for applying various critical approaches. First, using a lecture format I present Yamashita's novel to students, emphasizing the plot, characters, symbols, settings, themes, motifs, and style with recourse to a study guide available online ("*Through the Arc*").

After this, students are invited to analyze and discuss the text in a group, applying the critical approach or approaches of their choosing, including mythopoeia, structuralism, poststructuralism and deconstruction, postmodernist criticism, psychoanalytic criticism, feminist criticism, Marxist criticism, new historicism and cultural materialism, postcolonial criticism, stylistics, narratology, ecological criticism, comparative studies, and so on. Before the seminar, students are given independent work to prepare. The most helpful work for students proved to be their summaries of the basic tenets of structuralist, poststructuralist, Freudian psychoanalytic, and feminist criticism, among others, an exercise suggested in Barry's *Beginning Theory*. Since the seminar is eighty minutes long and class sizes are large (from sixteen to twenty-five students), we do not have time for every seminar participant to give an oral presentation. Because of this, and depending on the level of the group, I opt instead either to conduct a discussion with the entire class or to break students into smaller discussion groups, after which they present their results to the other groups.

If the group is not as proficient in English, I use the first strategy and lead the discussion, asking open-ended and follow-up questions, encouraging everyone to participate, and moving the discussion forward as needed. If the group has more advanced linguistic proficiency, I first ask students to name four approaches that they consider the most applicable to Yamashita's book. Generally, the approaches my students find most engaging are ecological criticism, postmodernism, postcolonial criticism, and comparative studies. I then have students divide into four groups, and each group discusses a particular approach. Students are given twenty minutes for discussion. Next, each group presents a brief summary of their discussion to the other groups and fields questions. After that I take about ten minutes to sum up what we have discussed and to evaluate students' performance using a five-point scale. In both scenarios (discussion as a class or small-group discussion) I assess students' engagement in discussion using five criteria: activity (i.e., the degree of attention, curiosity, interest, and passion), understanding of the text, understanding of the literary theory, originality and critical thinking skills, and speaking skills.

After this class session, students write individual analyses of approximately five hundred to seven hundred words. I usually assign each student a different chapter from *Through the Arc*. I ask them to produce an analysis in which they briefly apply as many approaches of contemporary literary criticism as possible to their reading of Yamashita's novel. In most cases the essays reflect points brought up in the discussion.

Three years of teaching Yamashita's novel have shown me that the most obvious approach to *Through the Arc* for Ukrainian students is ecological criticism, since environmental problems resonate with the everyday lives of the Ukrainian people. The tragic fact of recent Ukrainian history is the catastrophic accident that took place at the Chernobyl nuclear power plant in 1986. Living not far from the radioactive zone and witnessing for years the awful consequences of the disaster for people's health and the environment, students have a poignant and deep understanding of the ecological issues written about in contemporary literature.

To help students develop a more nuanced understanding of ecological criticism, I ask them to read the novel from an ecocentric perspective, with particular attention to the representation of the natural world and to concepts such as growth and energy, balance and imbalance, symbiosis and mutuality, and sustainable and unsustainable uses of energy and resources.

Next, I introduce the tropes of pastoral and environmental apocalypse, and we search for the mythopoeic elements in the novel. Since my students all belong to the European Christian cultural tradition (although only a few of them are religious), they often maintain that Yamashita tells a market economy or capitalist variant of paradise lost, by which they mean that the beautiful Amazonian nature and communities are the victims of market forces and multinational capitalism. Indeed, from this perspective, the plot of *Through the Arc of the Rain Forest* can be considered a fictionalized critique of the decline of the Christian pastoral ideal, the dream of Eden. Students notice that the Matacão, an anomalous black substance discovered on the floor of the Brazilian rain forest, forms a plastic paradise full of wonders for pilgrims and believers. But this false paradise disappears at the end of the novel, ruining lives and hopes. To some degree, *Through the Arc* follows the biblical structure, retelling in a satirical and postmodernist way a story about the Fall of Man and the people's expulsion from the plastic Garden of Eden. Some students discuss how parts of the book have titles that may be understood metaphorically: "The Beginning," "The Developing World," "More Development," "Loss of Innocence," "More Loss," and "Return." These titles reflect biblical motifs from Genesis and Exodus, which students recognize may be parodied in the novel.

The protagonist of the novel is Kazumasa Ishimaru, a caring, sympathetic, and humble person with mysterious abilities provided by a strange ball that orbits his head and serves as the quasi-omniscient narrator of the novel. Kazumasa was a successful railroad engineer in Japan. Later, when new technologies were introduced and his services were no longer needed, he immigrated to Brazil, where he could still be helpful. Kazumasa's fall and loss of consciousness in chapter 1 are connected to the appearance of the ball, his strange alien satellite. Symbolically, this ball is like Kazumasa's halo, and after its death the Matacão disappears as well. Again and again, the loss of holiness leads to the loss of Eden in our world. Again and again, humans strive for paradise, like Kazumasa and Lourdes, Kazumasa's housekeeper and eventual love interest, do at the end of the novel.

We also discuss the environmental values reflected in Yamashita's work, which include the need for balance, harmony, diversity, caring, equality, naturalness, and self-control. Following the traditions of soft science fiction and magical realism, Yamashita defends these values over inanimate manifestations of technological progress. This approach lies within the frame of the first wave of ecocriticism and helps students understand its foundations. In the future, I plan to apply the ecocritical approach of the second and third waves to class discussions of *Through the Arc* (see Slovic for a discussion of the third wave of ecocriticism).

For students in post-Soviet countries, it has been helpful to elucidate intertextual parallels between Yamashita's novel and *Roadside Picnic* (Пикник на обочине; Piknik na obochine; 1971), a famous short science fiction novel by Arkady and Boris Strugatsky whose first American edition, published by Macmillan in 1977, boasts a preface by the science fiction writer Theodore Sturgeon. The novel details the aftermath of an extraterrestrial visit, which leads to the appearance of six "Zones"—dangerous and mysterious places on the surface of our planet (Strugatsky and Strugatsky 2). The Zones, one of which is described in the book, are visited only by "stalkers"—courageous thieves who enter the Zones to steal artifacts for profit (4). Many post-Soviet students are familiar with the 1979 science fiction film *Stalker*, which is loosely based on the novel and directed by Andrei Tarkovsky, with a screenplay written by the Strugatsky brothers. Students also know the video game series *S.T.A.L.K.E.R.*, which is heavily influenced by *Roadside Picnic* and the Chernobyl disaster. Students in the United States who are interested in a post-Soviet ecological context for comparatively reading Yamashita's novel might find the 2017 American TV series pilot of *Roadside Picnic*, directed by Alan Taylor, an interesting gateway into the analogies I customarily emphasize in my classrooms in Ukraine. Students might read Jeff VanderMeer's novel *Annihilation* and watch Alex Garland's film of the same name, which is based on the novel: Area X in these works (a strange, dangerous region of coastline in an undisclosed part of the United States where mysterious phenomena occur) has obvious parallels to *Roadside Picnic* and *Stalker*.

Yamashita's and the Sturgatskys' novels also share certain motifs and images: devastated lands, extraterrestrial mysteries, human mutations, mean people who profit from devastation, children with disabilities (Gilberto in *Through the Arc* and Maria Schuhart, nicknamed Monkey, in *Roadside Picnic*) whose relatives hope to heal them through magic land (the Matacão and the Zone) that is actually a rubbish dump, and alien spheres (Yamashita's ball and the Strugatskys' wish-granting "Golden Ball"). At the end of *Roadside Picnic*, Redrick, the protagonist of the novel and Maria's father, makes his only wish, one the text suggests is achieved through lifelong suffering: "HAPPINESS FOR EVERYBODY, FREE, AND NO ONE WILL GO AWAY UNSATISFIED!" (153). The dream of an idyllic happy world survives in the touching words of an undefeated hero.

Both the Strugatsky brothers and Yamashita proved to be tragically prophetic: the Soviet writers predicted the radiation zone in Ukraine caused by the Chernobyl disaster in 1986, and Yamashita foresaw the catastrophic plastic pollution of present times. Both works can be considered within a postcolonial framework: Brazil in *Through the Arc of the Rain Forest* is a postcolonial locus in relation to the imperialism of the United States in the same way that the Zone refers to the unknown alien civilization that exploited the Earth and polluted it. To some degree, the Zone became an allegory for the future Chernobyl zone in Ukraine, a zone that is also a part of the post-Soviet imperial legacy since the dangerous experiments initiated by the experts from Moscow led to the catastrophe in Ukraine.

The reinterpretation of the environmental apocalypse presented by these authors from different hemispheres teaches us that it is not too late for us to stop harming our natural world. Students see Yamashita as an inspiring and up-to-date author whose experiments with form and genre delight and astound them. In her fiction, Yamashita is able to look to the past with the goal of improving our future. Such a wise and intelligent vision means that our globalized world has a chance for survival.

A Material Ecocritical Approach to *Through the Arc of the Rain Forest*

Xiaojing Zhou

Karen Tei Yamashita's *Through the Arc of the Rain Forest* begins with a ball of plastic mutated from nonbiodegradable garbage as its narrator and ends with "the crumbling remains of once modern high-rises and office buildings" juxtaposed with the rejuvenation of "the old forest" that "will never be the same again" (212). In this way and others, Yamashita's novel undermines anthropocentric discourses that conceive nature as a passive resource to be managed, exploited, and controlled by humans through science and technology. Thus, it is a useful text for my pedagogical aim to foster an ethical planetary citizenship. This essay describes how I seek to provide students with critical tools for investigating the intricate socioecological connections underlying Yamashita's narrative strategies through a material ecocritical approach to teaching *Through the Arc*, set primarily in Brazil. Before it is devoured by bacteria, the narrator is a piece of debris that first hits the protagonist, Kazumasa Ishimaru, on the head and then becomes a tiny ball spinning inches from his forehead, altering his abilities and changing his relation to the environment, a fact that demonstrates the mutability and trans-corporeal agency of matter. Both narrator and protagonist, part of Kazumasa and part mutated plastic, the ball is "brought back by a memory" to tell a story that highlights the centrality and hybrid agency of matter in a story where human beings are not the only actors (3).

Through the Arc is one of the required readings in an upper-division English seminar I teach called Environment and Literature, which is an elective for English and environmental studies majors, an elective for gender studies and ethnic studies minors, and a core general education requirement in the category of "science, technology, and society" for all undergraduates. By the time students discuss this novel in class, they have read a wide range of writings about the environment from the natural sciences, social sciences, and humanities. But they have not read a work of speculative fiction such as *Through the Arc*. To enable students to better understand the significant implications of Yamashita's narrative strategy, I introduce them to some key concepts of material ecocriticism. Since students come from different disciplines and have varied academic backgrounds, most are not familiar with material ecocritical theories. To make these accessible for students, I highlight quotations from various texts, and engage students in discussing the meanings and implications of these brief excerpts as conceptual tools for exploring the layered meanings of Yamashita's speculative fiction. The theories I draw from include Jane Bennett's concept of "vibrant matter," Stacy Alaimo's notion of "trans-corporeality" (2), and Bruno Latour's theory of "actor-network" agency (Latour, *Reassembling the Social*). Bennett explores the impact of material forces on the operations of sociopolitical and economic systems by highlighting "the capacity of things . . . not only to impede or block the will and designs of humans but also to act as quasi agents or forces with trajectories, propensities, or tendencies of their own" (viii). Exploring further the interconnections of the material world and signaling one version of feminist materialism, Alaimo emphasizes "the movement across bodies," noting that "trans-corporeality" opens up a new critical space "that acknowledges the often unpredictable and unwanted actions of human bodies, nonhuman creatures, ecological systems, chemical agents, and other actors" (2). Refuting nature as a passive entity outside the human, Latour calls critical attention to the mutations of apparently "risk-free objects" and their unintended, catalytic, and proliferating effects (*Politics* 22–23). The "actor-network-theory" Latour proposes reveals the hybrid agency of matter, humans, and systems through unexpected associations, assemblages, movements, displacements, and transformations (*Reassembling the Social* 64–65). Part of the ecological ethics and episteme in Yamashita's novel are embedded in the ways in which human beliefs and actions are entangled with the mutations of matter, which result in ecological and economic catastrophes. Latour's "actor-network-theory" helps make clear that the spread of the typhus-causing virus and the devouring bacteria as depicted in the novel are mobilized by the trans-corporeal interactions and hybrid agency of animate and inanimate actors, whose efficacy "always depends on the collaboration, cooperation, or interactive interference of many bodies and forces" (J. Bennett 21).

To engage every student in active participation in applying the theories to their reading of the text, I divide the class into working groups and assign each group specific tasks. Group one is tasked with analyzing the attributes of the protagonist, Kazumasa Ishimaru, and the functions and implications of his relation to the ball. Students in this group also consider Kazumasa's and the ball's connections to the Matacão—a plastic substance formed from industrial waste hidden beneath Brazil's rain forest that becomes hotly sought after by multinational corporations that "turned plastic into gold" (Yamashita, *Through the Arc* 142). At the same time, students are required to examine the implications of the Matacão's connections to two characters in the novel: Jonathan B. Tweep, from the American transnational corporation GGG located in New York City, who is sent on an assignment by the GGG International Research and Funding Division to the Matacão in Brazil's rain forest (75), and Michelle Mabelle, the French ornithologist, who is "the first recipient of the GGG Fellowship for Scientific Studies in Ornithology and the Relationship for the Feather to Human Health" (75). To encourage students to ground their analyses in textual evidence, I also assign group one selected passages related to their assigned characters and ask students to discuss the connections between the passages and the characters, and the implications of these connections for the central concerns of the novel. The following are partial examples of the assigned passages:

> As advanced as the technology behind Matacão plastics was becoming, the means of discovering new sources of the material eluded scientists. Kazumasa and I, alone, were the key to this incredible source of wealth.
>
> In this great task of combing the countryside for Matacão plastic, J.B., with his usual thoroughness, sent Kazumasa and me out with a team of specialists. . . . In this, J.B. was ruthless. . . . [H]undreds of species of plant and animal life bulldozed under. (144–45)

> Then, there was the growing concern over the mining process of Matacão plastic. The chemical runoff from GGG's secret technique had been collected and analyzed and found to cause genetic mutations in rats after five generations. (160–61)

Students are asked to identify major thematic threads embedded in the text, and they must apply at least three theoretical perspectives in their analyses, such as Arturo Escobar's theory about the "war" of "capitalist modernity" on "every ecosystem on the planet" (8), Latour's "politics of nature" (*Politics*), and Jane Bennett's concept of "vibrant matter."

Group two's assignments include investigating the unexpected, uncontrollable trans-corporeal and actor-network agencies through a different cluster of characters—Mané da Costa Pena, "the feather guru" (Yamashita, *Through the Arc* 8); the pigeon couple Batista and Tania Aparecida and their respective connections to the Matacão; the GGG enterprise; and the disease-causing, plastic-eating microorganisms. Students are then able to situate the experience of Mané Pena, an Indigenous inhabitant of the rain forest, in the intertwined ecological, economic, and social catastrophes in Brazil within larger historical contexts, and to link the Amazon rain forest to other parts of the world. While Mané's failed farm demonstrates the agro-economic consequences of destroying the rain forest's ecosystem, Mané's knowledge that "the primeval forest" was no longer "primeval" because the mysterious "underground *matacão* . . . always blocked well-diggers" has far more sinister implications than deforestation does (16, 17). I encourage students to draw out the implications underlying the entanglement of Mané's life with the Matacão, the magical bird feathers, the typhus-causing rickettsia, the bacteria that devour Matacão plastics, and eventually the transformed rain forest. I require students to include specific passages of the novel in their discussions and to apply at least two material ecocritical theories to their analyses, such as Alaimo's theory of "trans-corporeality," Jane Bennett's concept of "vibrant matter," or Latuour's "actor-network-theory." The following are partial examples of the passages students examined through the lenses of critical theories:

> Rickettsia were microorganisms that traveled via a minute species of lice, which in turn traveled via feathers, which, of course, traveled via birds and, of late, humans. . . .

> Banning feathers, however, was not enough, authorities stated. It would be necessary to go to the source. (198–99)

> Batista sat in the dark and wept. He could hear the small biplanes and the camouflaged bombers flown by the Air Force. . . . Hundreds of these planes flew back and forth all day and all night long, dropping their poison bombs and spraying a dense fog over everything. . . . The Matacão was soon covered, knee-deep with the lifeless bodies of poisoned birds. (201–02)

> It was true. Something was eating me, carving out delicate pinhole passages. . . . The Matacão, too, was slowly but definitely corroding, as was everything else made of Matacão plastic. (205)

Through close examination of passages like these, students learn to identify the unexpected convergences and effects of networks of hybrid agencies as portrayed or implied in the text.

The legacy of American (United States) imperialism is also interwoven with the stories of flora and fauna in the rain forest. I provide secondary sources for the third or fourth discussion session, which group three uses to investigate the connections between Henry Ford's failed rubber plantation and "civilizing mission" in Brazil (Grandin 5) and the scene of an abandoned parking lot as depicted in the novel (*Through the Arc* 99–101). Greg Grandin's *Fordlandia: The Rise and Fall of Henry Ford's Forgotten Jungle City* offers detailed information about the ways in which the mesh of ecological and socioeconomic forces brought down Fordlândia, Ford's empire of rubber in the rain forest enterprise (1928–45). Usually, students quickly recognize the colonialist ideology and management of Fordlândia, and some state that it reminds them of George Orwell's *1984*.

Material ecocritical theories also enable students to recognize that the failure of the plantation is in part the result of the rupture in the ecological web of the jungle: a local resident at the time of the plantation's construction observed that to clear the land for the plantation, the Ford company "burned hundreds of hectares of primitive forest," and "the fire lasted for days and days" (qtd. in Grandin 136–37). "Yet the Amazon was a place where 7,882 organisms could be found on any given five square miles," Grandin points out (294). "One tree alone could serve as home to a dazzling variety of insects, along with an array of animals, orchids, epiphytes, and bromeliads" (294). After the land was cleared of native trees and plants, Fordlândia plantation's topsoil was washed away by heavy rains, the rubber tree seedlings became vulnerable to strong winds and the baking sun during the dry season, and diseases and insects attacked the trees (299–300, 316–18). The fog from the Tapajós River "accelerated the spread of the rubber-destroying fungi" to "over two thousand acres of six-feet-tall rubber trees" at Fordlândia (226). While students understand that the manipulated yet unconquerable ecosystems of the rain forest were a major factor in the downfall of Fordlândia, they recognize that Yamashita's novel shows more unsettling effects of the network agency, spotlighting the ways in which apparently inert inanimate objects can become agents of a dynamic mutation in an abandoned parking lot that evokes the Ford rubber plantations:

> What was most interesting about the discovery of the rain forest parking lot was the way in which nature has moved to accommodate and make use of it. The entomologists were shocked to discover that their rare butterfly only nested in the vinyl seats of Fords and Chevrolets. . . .
>
> There was also discovered a new species of mouse, with prehensile tails, that burrowed in the exhaust pipes of all the vehicles.
>
> (Yamashita, *Through the Arc* 100)

In this rain forest junkyard, the so-called wildlife is no longer natural. The flora and fauna have become hybrid, part nature and part industrial products. Moreover, their mutations proliferate, creating new life forms while also killing other living creatures. The ruins of the empire continue to affect human and nonhuman lives even after the colonialists have left. I urge students to explore the connections between environmental transformation and colonial enterprise in the Amazon and beyond. To this end, I ask students to use particular statements or passages from Aimee Bahng's article on Yamashita's novel, "Extrapolating Transnational Arcs." In her article, Bahng explores how Ford's civilizing mission and the racialized labor on the rubber plantation are part of "European imperialist discourses on race and nature" that underlie the socioecological devastation of the Amazon (125).

Through research and close reading informed by material ecocriticism, students are able to link the parking lot scene to environmental degradation by colonial empires, and to the formation and transformation of the Matacão. The dichotomies between natural and artificial and between raw materials and products have collapsed in the novel. The implications and effects of this collapse underlie Latour's argument that substances like asbestos "have no clear boundaries, no well-defined essences, no sharp separation between their own hard kernel and their environment. It is because of this feature that they take on the aspect of tangled beings, forming rhizomes and networks" (*Politics* 23–24).

A material ecocritical approach to *Through the Arc of the Rain Forest* enables students from different disciplines to draw out the novel's ecological episteme and ethics, which dismantle notions of nature as merely inert material or a background for human action or imagination and undermine notions of agency defined by human intentionality or divine design. The result is more than an in-depth understanding of the novel; a material ecocritical approach allows for anti-anthropocentric ways of knowing and being and helps cultivate in students an ethical planetary citizenship. As Jane Bennett asks, "would patterns of consumption of things change if we faced not litter, rubbish, trash, or 'the recycling,' but an accumulating pile of lively and potentially dangerous matter? . . . What difference would it make to the course of energy policy were electricity to be figured not simply as a resource, commodity, or instrumentality but also and more radically as an 'actant'?" (viii). It is questions such as these that Yamashita's novel raises. Material ecocriticism offers an enabling, provocative conceptual framework for reflecting on such questions—and others that are necessary for understanding Yamashita's employment of fictional speculations—in order to nurture ecologically responsible planetary citizenship.

Critical Globalization and Political Economy in *Tropic of Orange*

T. Christine Jespersen and David J. Plante

Karen Tei Yamashita sets *Tropic of Orange* within the context of the 1990s, during the era of high globalization. Calling for the recognition of the deep structures of globalization and attending to the significance of narrative power in resisting neoliberal globalization, the novel represents globalization as an interconnection between cultural and economic forces. Whereas literature students may be accustomed to interpreting culture, most are not well-versed in political economy. To understand the cultural significance of the novel, it is useful to step into the political economy debates of the 1990s. In this essay we focus on two aspects of political economy that inform the novel: the debates around neoliberalism and the significance of class in relation to the economic concept of crises.

We teach at a small, moderately selective, rural state university. As professors of economics (Plante) and English (Jespersen), we began writing together after recognizing the crucial role political economy plays in Yamashita's novels. Since then, Jespersen has incorporated material on political economy into her Junior Seminar on Literatures of Globalization, a requirement for all English majors. She has used the more accessible material in Borders and Crossings, a general education course taken by English majors and first- and second-year students fulfilling area requirements.

Because many students know little about neoliberalism, we begin by providing background material. Manfred Steger's *Globalization: A Very Short Introduction* provides an easily digestible introduction to neoliberalism and the institutions that construct it: the Washington Consensus, the World Bank, the International Monetary Fund, and the World Trade Organization (37–59). David Harvey's *A Brief History of Neoliberalism* offers an excellent introduction for instructors, and chapters 1–3 may be assigned to upper-division students. To summarize, Harvey argues that neoliberalism combines a theoretical market fundamentalism—that is, the subordination of democratic and political processes to market decision-making—combined with state minimalism—the classical liberal idea of a constrained state. Pragmatically, however, since the 1980s, the state has become increasingly activist, particularly in the financial sphere as guarantor of economic stability and profitability. The pragmatic version of the neoliberal state has underwritten financialization through deregulation, stabilization, and periodic bailouts, working together to restore profits to elites.

Prior to assigning *Tropic of Orange*, we show *Life and Debt*, a film that portrays neoliberal globalization's impact on Jamaica. Based on Jamaica Kincaid's *A Small Place*, the film works well for students accustomed to interpreting literary narratives and offers opportunities to discuss the interrelations of narratives of globalization and their structures. Close shots of national agreements interspersed with the director's dialogue between the former Jamaican prime minister Michael Manley and the former International Monetary Fund chief economist Stanley Fisher allow students to see the effects of international agreements between organizations and countries on local farmers and businesses. We invite students to interpret the film's narratives and then to elaborate on their analyses using Harvey's and Steger's texts. Connecting the readings to the film helps students solidify the concepts, attach abstract ideas to concrete instances, and see how stories and economic structures intertwine in complex ways.

We discuss the narrative strategies used in *Life and Debt*, then assign two-page essays in which students employ Harvey's and Steger's texts as interpretative lenses to a small portion of the film. In the following class session, we use these texts as a basis for discussion. Through this work, students gain some understanding of the global context of *Life and Debt* and begin to understand the power of international agencies. They also begin to see the power of narrative in representing neoliberalism. This becomes significant in teaching *Tropic of Orange* because in the 1990s the triumph of neoliberal globalization hinged on narratives that represented it as a natural form. Like *Life and Debt*, however, Yamashita's novel tells the story of neoliberal globalization from the viewpoint of the underclasses and powerfully suggests that this type of globalization is one choice among many.

Because the current context of globalization differs from that of the 1990s, it is beneficial to review the disparities. In particular, the election of Donald Trump in 2016 and the Brexit referendum in the same year highlighted a discontent with globalization. We invite our classes to discuss the significance of Trump's election with regard to globalization. How has globalization been reconfigured, if at all? Students might brainstorm on paper or share news clips about issues relating to globalization such as trade, immigration, unemployment, child separation at borders, and returns to nationalism. Students might raise ideas relating to Trump's anti-immigrant stance, the wall, and his rejection of trade agreements. If there are political science or economics majors in the class, they may delve into how Trump has altered the role of the state. We also ask, Why did people vote for Brexit? How do young people view the referendum and why?

While there was also resistance to globalization in the 1990s, most of the economic and popular press of the era represented globalization in glowing terms as a natural and unstoppable force that would benefit all, unlike the ideology that emerged during the 2016 election. We assign short excerpts from the work of the journalist Thomas Friedman, who compared globalization to the dawn (xvii), and Howard Wiarda from the Center for Strategic and International Studies, who argued that "[e]conomists are in virtually unanimous agreement that NAFTA will be mutually advantageous" (144)—both of which offer rich opportunities for close reading. These texts provide invaluable background for students as they wade into *Tropic of Orange*. SUPERNAFTA, the *lucha libre* villain and an embodiment of NAFTA, echoes the elation and promises of universal benefits surrounding neoliberal globalization, while the characters Arcangel, Buzzworm, and Rafaela sound concerns about those left behind.

As our classes read *Tropic of Orange*, we analyze moments when the novel comments on neoliberal globalization. We also introduce the idea of unevenness (i.e., the concept that not everyone is affected by globalization in the same way). How are characters differently affected by neoliberal globalization? Where do they see its benefits and pitfalls? How do neoliberal policies animate characters' actions? Why must Buzzworm become an angel of mercy? Why do Bobby and Rafaela differ in their attitudes toward the Justice for Janitors movement? Why must Bobby smuggle his cousin across the border? How do we read the recurring metaphors of the unnatural beyond allusions to climate change?

Literature students, particularly those who are versed in poststructuralism, may have difficulty understanding why people saw globalization as anything but constructed, while general education students may require help seeing how it was constructed. Steger's distinction between globalization and globalism is instructive for talking about the ideology of neoliberal globalization. Steger defines globalism as "an Anglo-American free-market doctrine that endows . . . globalization with neoliberal norms, values, and meanings" (*Globalisms* x). Students can then identify how characters such as Arcangel, Rafaela, and Buzzworm expose globalism's ideological nature. They can also debate Yamashita's complex representation of the connections between ideology and the structural components of globalization. We ask students to interpret Arcangel's poems recounting the history of Latin America as well as Manzanar's descriptions of the historical layers that make up Los Angeles.

Because the novel centers its discussion of globalism on the North American Free Trade Agreement (NAFTA) debate, students should know that NAFTA was a trade agreement established in the 1990s that was supposed to join Mexico, Canada, and the United States as part of a common trading area. "Free trade" was a misnomer, however, because trade would be governed by complicated regulations. While the actual agreement is a complex, two-thousand-page tome that covers investment, trucking, legal rules, and trade, public debate portrayed NAFTA in simplistic terms, which led to a so-called fast-track trade agreement. This meant that the legislature was given the power to approve or deny the whole agreement rather than its various components. The debate subsequently narrowed to classifying NAFTA in polar terms instead of creating meaningful exchange about what the agreement should incorporate (Plante 213–48). In the novel, NAFTA becomes a metaphor for simplistic for-or-against conceptions of globalization. Chapter 6 of Kim Moody's *Workers in a Lean World*, which views NAFTA as a corporate project meant to reorient the social economy toward corporate interests, offers helpful background reading.

After providing information on NAFTA and on *lucha libre*—a Mexican form of wrestling featuring fixed fights, aerial acrobatics, and masked heroes and antiheroes—we invite students to analyze the match between SUPERNAFTA and El Gran Mojado, "The Great Wetback" (256–63). How does each wrestler characterize his opponent and the benefits of or problems with NAFTA? What is each character's evidence? How are the theatrics of *lucha libre* symbolic of debates about NAFTA? What are the effects of theatrical rather than reasoned debate? How does the crowd react? How does the fight end and how can one interpret the ending? Students' analyses can be enhanced by assigning Ross Perot's "The Giant Sucking Sound."

From a political economy perspective, it is essential that a series of crises, particularly in Latin America, form the novel's backdrop. For political economists, crises are breakdowns in the economic structure that lead to a possible failure in the reproduction of the existing social order—for instance, the Mexican peso crisis, the subprime mortgage crisis of 2008, and the Great Depression of the 1930s. Political economists do not employ the adjective *economic* when referring to such crises, because the term is so pervasive. Since literature students use the term differently, we point out the different meaning of the term in literature and economics and discuss translation as a challenge in interdisciplinary work.

Time permitting, upper-division students read Harvey's chapter, "The Disruption," in *The Enigma of Capital* (1–39). For Harvey, crises are the norm in capitalism, not the exception: "Crises are, in effect, not only inevitable but also necessary, since this is the only way in which balance can be restored and the internal contradictions of capital accumulation can be at least temporarily resolved. Crises are, as it were, the irrational rationalizers of an always unstable capitalism" (*Enigma* 71). *Accumulation* refers to the continuous increase in capital. For Harvey, capital is a process with multiple forms—money, industrial production, and commodities (*Seventeen Contradictions* 70–71). Crises occur when the flow among these forms becomes blocked.

Post-1989, with the fall of the Soviet Union, market triumphalism dominated. The supremacy and stability of market capitalism was largely unquestioned in popular consciousness. Almost prescient, however, Yamashita alludes to long-term and acute crises in Latin America and Asia. The novel foreshadows impending domestic crises, highlighting a sense of imminent instability for the most economically vulnerable characters. In the years preceding the novel, Mexico implemented a series of neoliberal reforms that culminated in crises and insurrection. To give students context, we assign ten- to fifteen-minute PowerPoint presentations on the Mexican debt crisis of 1994, the Mexican peso crisis, and the Zapatista uprising in Chiapas, Mexico. Junior Seminar students working on developing research skills find and synthesize three scholarly sources, while general education students employ encyclopedia sources, which we augment. We then guide our students through one of the novel's chief representations of crisis: the massive car crash that closes down the main arteries of the city and the ensuing movement by the homeless to take control. The crash represents historical crises—it, too, is tied to trade and trucking since it is a "monstrous semi" that causes the crash (Yamashita, *Tropic* 55). The episode also focuses on homelessness and the attempt to find a solution to it, thereby foreshadowing the impending housing crisis in the United States.

Most students will have read F. Scott Fitzgerald's *The Great Gatsby*, which, like *Tropic of Orange*, represents the logical endpoint of uneven accumulation and wealth concentration as a literal crash. We note that both novels perceptively mark historical conditions that lead to crises. This is a good time to review characteristics of neoliberalism and point out that the euphoria that characterized the Roaring Twenties is not so far removed from that of the 1990s. In both cases the economy and banking industries were deregulated, the financial sector expanded, a euphoric sense of a new era where economic rules no longer applied was pervasive, and the wealth gap grew.

After discussing each crash, we remind students about the unevenness of globalization and ask them to interpret two chapters from *Tropic of Orange*, namely "Rideshare—Downtown Interchange" and "Jam—Greater L.A." (55–57, 204–07). We explain that NAFTA resulted in expanded trucking from Latin America through Mexico into the United States amid debates about the safety of Mexican trucks and concerns about increased drug trafficking. We then ask, How does Manzanar represent the trucks? How do the freeways function as metaphors? Who are the victims of "the metallic crash and crunch of the unfortunate who shared the same lanes, the snap of delicate necks, the squish of flesh and blood" (55)?

A key to understanding crises is the complex phenomenon of financialization—the layering of debt and deregulation of global financial relations. During the era of neoliberalism, globalization and securitization (the pooling and repackaging of financial assets) led to a massive expansion of both the size and role of the financial sector. At the same time, debt relations further entangled the economies of the Global North and Global South. To maintain expenditures as wages stagnated, many Americans fell further into debt. During the years leading up to the global financial crisis, household savings diminished, net wealth decreased, and indebtedness increased, leaving many households in a precarious and illiquid state (Tymoigne 92). L. Randall Wray's "Minsky and the Global Financial Crisis" presents an excellent analysis that is legible to undergraduates.

Because financialization is multifaceted, instructors may wish to focus more narrowly on one component of it, namely debt. Since the 1980s, debt has been increasing domestically and between the North and the South. Additionally, debt's role in maintaining expenditures and livelihoods in the developed and developing worlds has been expanding. Our students readily converse about student loans and credit card debt and some students report the impact of debt on their families during the 2008 crisis. A conversation about personal debt leads easily to an analysis of Bobby and Buzzworm and the American dream. What does Bobby do to achieve and maintain the American dream? What does a close reading of the chapters from his point of view reveal?[1] Why is he in an impossible situation? Why is it so remarkable that Buzzworm's house is paid for? After discussing domestic debt, we turn to Arcangel's chapter, "To Labor—East and West Forever" (141–48). What is the effect of locating this chapter in the section titled "The Eternal Buzz" (137–71)? What does Arcangel chant on page 147? How does the novel understand the connections among debt, labor, idealism, revolution, and drug trafficking?

In 1997, when *Tropic of Orange* was published, most elites failed to foresee the 2001 dot-com crash or the 2008 financial crisis. In the 1990s, however, progressive economists such as Robert Pollin questioned the unevenness of the form of neoliberalism promoted under the administration of Bill Clinton, which though it provided economic growth was highly skewed toward the financial sector and the wealthy elites.[2] Between 1976 and 1997, the share of household wealth accruing to the top 1% of households rose from 19.9% to 40.1%, a level not seen since just before the 1929 stock market crash (Phillips 122–23). Furthermore, globalization meant that crises were interlocking. While it directly alludes to the global crises that were happening at the time when it was written, Yamashita's novel also signals the coming crises in the United States.

Early on, we ask students to characterize the central characters of Yamashita's novel. We assign each small group a character and invite students to explain what the character represents more generally and what happens as that character navigates neoliberal globalization. Our students argue, for instance, that Bobby is a stereotypical hardworking immigrant who believes in the American dream. Some students contend that this belief helps him get ahead, while others claim that his ideological steadfastness destroys his relationship with his family and makes it impossible for him to see the underlying neoliberal structures that hold him back.

Most classes notice that the characters in *Tropic of Orange* are multiethnic, but few observe that none of them are from the upper 1 percent.[3] At this juncture, we discuss intersectionality and introduce the concept of "globalization from below" (Brecher and Costello 7). We examine the significance of telling the story of globalism from the perspectives of the underclasses and ask students what each character notices and fails to notice. What indications of coming crises do the characters see? How is what political economists call *crisis* linked to a broader sense of it? What connects the novel's characters? As we conclude, we return to the idea of "globalization from below." Although a global resistance to neoliberalism never materializes in the novel, where do students see resistance? How effective is it?

Tropic of Orange is a challenging novel with many possible points of entry. One lost on many literature students is the novel's contextualization of certain crises and of debates over neoliberalism in the 1990s. Through interdisciplinary analysis, students gain a better understanding of intersectionality and the possibilities for resistance portrayed in the novel. They see how class becomes a critical element that unites the characters in their own interpretations of globalization. Such analysis also illuminates a powerful role for the humanities in reading narrative often taken by the public and specialists as natural and transparent.

Framed within the debates of 1990s and with literary, economic, and social crises on the horizon, Yamashita's novel opens up possibilities for reconfiguring globalization in a more humane way.

NOTES

[1] See Yamashita, *Tropic* 14–18, 76–80, 97–102, 158–62, 201–04, 228–34, 226–68.

[2] Pollin's chapters "Clintonomics: The Hollow Boom" and "The Downside of Fabulous" in *The Contours of Descent* work well for undergraduates (21–47, 49–75).

[3] DeLillo's *Cosmopolis*, whose central protagonist is a multibillionaire, makes a good counterpoint for discussion.

Tropic of Orange and the Genre of Climate Fiction

Claudia Sadowski-Smith and Matthew S. Henry

Karen Tei Yamashita's *Tropic of Orange* is often taught as a novel that deals with migration and the United States–Mexico border. While our undergraduate students at Arizona State University generally enjoy *Tropic*'s mass media references and its setting in nearby Los Angeles, some find it difficult to connect to the novel's magical realist trope of Mexico—and its people—being pulled north by an undocumented performance artist named El Gran Mojado ("The Great Wetback") who represents cross-border migration between the United States and Mexico.

In our courses on contemporary literature of the United States and on environmental humanities, we emphasize how *Tropic* maps intersections of human movement; environmental, economic, and social justice concerns; and a rapidly changing climate, especially as these intersections relate to the implementation of the North American Free Trade Agreement (NAFTA) in 1994.[1] The novel shows how the carbon-fueled economic policies manifested in NAFTA perpetuate the long history of colonialism in the Americas and affect cross-border migration patterns that include an increase in climate refugees.

We teach *Tropic* as a work of climate fiction avant la lettre, and as a novel that adds to this genre a concern with cross-border migration. While cultural representations have long dealt with climate issues, the term *cli-fi*, short for *climate fiction*, was coined approximately a decade after *Tropic*'s publication, popularized by Margaret Atwood in a 2012 tweet, and gained traction in discussions of this growing contemporary literature (Ullrich). Cli-fi's focus on pollution, rising sea levels, the decimation of natural resources, and climate change indicates a heightened awareness that we live in a new geological epoch, the Anthropocene, in which collective human geophysical agency has altered Earth's biophysical processes (Ullrich; Pérez-Peña; Trexler 24–26).[2] While Adam Trexler has proposed other labels, such as "Anthropocene fiction," to discuss this literature, we feel that the designation *climate fiction* is more accessible to students who are accustomed to public discourses surrounding climate change. Like Stephanie LeMenager, we believe that the most crucial goal of teaching climate change in the humanities is to enable a form of "scenario-imagining" of adaptation and survival (qtd. in Pérez-Peña).

Our courses are upper-level undergraduate classes offered through the English department, and the environmental humanities course serves as the centerpiece of the department's Environmental Humanities Certificate. The course on contemporary literature of the United States emphasizes how post-1980s fiction experiments with form in order to link issues of social and economic justice to the longer histories of settler colonialism in and migration to the United States. In discussions of *Tropic*, the course highlights how Yamashita employs magical realism to connect modern-day border crossings from Mexico and China to the settler colonial and migratory histories of the Americas. In the most recent iteration of the course, students studied the novel as an example of cli-fi whose emphasis on migration is overlaid with a focus on climate change as symbolized in the northward movement of the Tropic of Cancer. By the time we get to *Tropic*, students will have read texts about the United States–Mexico border by the writer-theorist Gloria Anzaldúa and by the performance artist Guillermo Gómez-Peña; Saskia Sassen's work on migration and urban spaces, which explores the centrality of the foreign economic and military involvement of the United States for migration; and the work of the Colombian writer Gabriel Gárcia Márquez, whose story "A Very Old Man with Enormous Wings" inspired Yamashita's portrayal of Arcangel in *Tropic* (as did Gómez-Peña's work). We discuss how *Tropic* represents the increasing importance of climate change as a contributing factor to migration in addition to economic and political considerations.

The environmental humanities course explores how literature, art, and film engage with environmental issues. The class studies literary fiction, film, photography, art, and other cultural representations to explore the intersections of nature and culture, climate change, environmental justice, and ecofeminism. Discussions of *Tropic* emphasize how the novel links human migration to freak weather events and fluctuating climate patterns; how it explores the disproportionate effects of environmental disaster on the poor, on ethnic minorities, on migrants, and on Indigenous peoples; and how it depicts environmental and cultural flux over multiple timescales. Prior to encountering *Tropic*, students will have read Julie Sze's work on environmental justice literature, "From Environmental Justice Literature to the Literature of Environmental Justice," and Rob Nixon's scholarship on the "slow violence" of ecological disaster and climate change in the Global South. *Tropic* serves as a useful bridge into a concluding unit on speculative cli-fi and climate justice.

In both courses, we also provide students with scholarship by Ignacio Sánchez Cohen and colleagues on the cultural and ecological effects of trade relations between the United States and Mexico and the impact of these relations on cross-border migration. The ratification of NAFTA in 1994 prompted the import of heavily subsidized, low-priced agricultural products that led the Mexican government to abandon its agricultural policies, including water management. The implementation of NAFTA dovetailed with the effects of climate change, in particular drought and desertification, resulting in a sharp increase in disenfranchised laborers migrating northward to Mexican cities and mostly undocumented workers into the United States (Cohen et al. 57). In 2010 researchers estimated that climate change alone would prompt between 1.6 and 6.7 million adult Mexican citizens to emigrate by 2080 (Feng et al. 14257).

To illustrate *Tropic*'s dual focus on human border crossings and climate change, two issues that have been affected by neoliberal trade agreements like NAFTA, we place students in small groups and ask them to examine Rafaela and Arcangel, two of the novel's protagonists; *Tropic*'s central magical realist metaphor of a border-crossing orange; and the novel's many extraordinary events, such as drastic changes in weather patterns, shortening geographic distances between the United States and Mexico, and the sudden overlapping of languages and cultures. In the novel's opening scene, Rafaela, who returned from living in the United States to her native Mexico, tends to the Chicano reporter Gabriel's vacation home, which is located in Mazatlán in the state of Sinaloa and directly along the Tropic of Cancer, twelve hundred miles south of Los Angeles. Each morning, Rafaela sweeps out crabs that typically live on Mexico's coast but have strangely migrated inland. One day she also notices an "aberrant orange" that has sprouted out of season on one of Gabriel's many citrus trees, which he imported from the United States, and explicitly links the fruit to climate change: "Rafaela knew it was an orange that should not have been. It was much too early. Everyone said the weather was changing. The rains came sooner this year. 'What do they call it?' mused Doña Maria. 'Global warming. Yes, that's it'" (Yamashita, *Tropic* 11).

Through discussion, students come to understand that, like other magical realist works that employ literalized metaphors to allude to societal upheavals, the novel's central image of a border-crossing fruit literalizes the links between migration and climate in the context of neoliberal economic policies. The orange is connected to a "wisp of thread" that represents the Tropic of Cancer, the northernmost latitude dividing the temperate and subtropical climate zones (151). In one of his performance acts, Arcangel drags a bus with the orange on board across the United States–Mexico border. Because the orange is attached to the wispy thread representing the Tropic of Cancer, its northward movement influences climate and migration patterns. In addition to being a performance artist, Arcangel is a mythological figure purportedly born in 1492 who symbolizes links between the sociopolitical and ecological history of the five-hundred-year period spanning the precolonial and settler colonial eras to the post-NAFTA era in the Americas. Arcangel's sporadic poetic asides allude not only to pilgrimages north by pre-Columbian Indigenous peoples, (undocumented) laborers, and Latin American revolutionaries and poets like Che Guevara, Pancho Villa, and Pablo Neruda but also to the irregular seasonal flux associated with climate change and the effects of this flux on nature and wildlife: "*Then came the rain forests, El Niño, African bees, panthers, sloths, llamas, monkeys, and pythons*" (201).

To assist students in visualizing the novel's shifting geographies, we study maps of migration and historical climate patterns. This assignment helps students better grasp the movement of the orange—and with it, the Tropic of Cancer. This movement alters time, creates new cultural mixings, and brings to the temperate zone that lies north of the Tropic of Cancer the climatic patterns of Mexico's

Mazatlán, a seasonally wet-dry subtropical environment that is subject to considerably more precipitation (approximately twenty-six inches annually) than arid Los Angeles typically receives (approximately fifteen inches annually). The weather in LA becomes volatile, alternating between heavy and sudden monsoon rains and seemingly endless intense sunshine. These climatic shifts emerge as the Anthropocene's catastrophic temporal analogue of chaotic and unpredictable weather. The out-of-season orange corresponds to what Nixon has called the slow violence of environmental attrition, particularly in unpredictable and therefore unreliable agricultural yields. At the same time, the monsoon-induced flooding and sudden, endless sunshine emerge as media-ready spectacle, amplified by *Tropic*'s hyper-referential news-media subtext, which is often associated with popular representations of climate change.

After discussing *Tropic*'s protagonists and the novel's central metaphor of the border-crossing orange, we ask students to focus on the novel's ending when Arcangel transforms into El Gran Mojado to confront SUPERNAFTA in a Mexican-style *lucha libre* wrestling match, which leads to the two fighters' mutual destruction. Since it is described in magical realist language, which allows for simultaneous magical and realist interpretations, the battle alludes to the possibility that Arcangel may return in yet another incarnation to continue his five-hundred-year life cycle tied to colonialism (Sadowski-Smith, *Border Fictions* 67), while SUPERNAFTA's fiery implosion also points to the effects of a warming climate (Ammons 154).

This cataclysmic clash between the two characters parallels another world-ending apocalypse in the novel to which we direct students' attention, one in which state and federal authorities raid a community established by LA's homeless and immigrant populations among abandoned vehicles along a mile-long stretch of gridlocked freeway. We ask students to consider how this event may provide alternative perspectives. Students often realize that the novel shows how marginalized people "repossess the manufactured and natural world" in order to create a sustainable, equitable, repurposed community meant to circumvent "the flow of energies leading to social inequality, a greater carbon footprint, and dependency on fossil fuels" (Ammons 153; Rozelle 27). In a concluding writing assignment, we ask students to imagine similar scenarios in which social, economic, environmental, or climate justice interests are prioritized and put into practice. Subsequent class discussions highlight that the novel's concern with decentering the human and elevating the agency of a nonhuman entity is a common theme in Yamashita's work, which places *Tropic* alongside more recent fiction that contemplates the Anthropocene "by locating forms of sentience within the material stratum under production" (Marshall 533–34).[3] Even though *Tropic* ends with an apocalypse, it is one that offers the tenuous possibility of Arcangel's rebirth and thus provides a somewhat more optimistic view than do many cli-fi novels that draw heavily on dystopic and apocalyptic themes. By contextualizing *Tropic* within scholarship on migration and environmental justice, we help students discern a productive politics of climate change in the novel, which can serve as a blueprint for their entry into this complex issue and its connection to other important developments in the twenty-first century.

NOTES

[1] There is a significant body of scholarship on *Tropic*'s themes of environmental justice. Julie Sze argues that the contemporary struggles depicted in *Tropic* "are linked to the historical exploitation of nature and people of color" ("From Environmental Justice Literature" 164). Chiyo Crawford has emphasized connections between the novel's focus on Japanese internment and the transgenerational implications of environmental injustice; Ryan Palmer has focused on the novel's critique of NAFTA; and Jessica Maucione has examined *Tropic*'s vision of a "postcapitalist urban collective that connects human healing to environmental recovery" (90). Elizabeth Ammons has most directly discussed how *Tropic* links environmental justice to climate change (151–52).

[2] In 2000 the atmospheric chemist Paul Crutzen and the biologist Eugene Stoermer proposed the term *Anthropocene* to denote a new geological epoch (Crutzen and Stoermer). Texts that are often discussed as cli-fi or Anthropocene fiction include J. G. Ballard's novels *The Drowned World* (1962) and *The Wind from Nowhere* (1961), Ian McEwan's *Solar* (2010), Nathaniel Rich's *Odds against Tomorrow* (2013), Paolo Bacigalupi's *The Windup Girl* (2009) and *The Water Knife* (2015), Barbara Kingsolver's *Flight Behavior* (2012), Kim Stanley Robinson's *New York 2140* (2017), Maja Lunde's *The History of Bees* (2017), and David Walton's *The Genius Plague* (2017).

[3] Yamashita's novel *Through the Arc of the Rain Forest* is narrated by a molten sphere made of rock and plastic, which recounts the ferocious Freudian-like return of repressed nature in the Brazilian Amazon after a long period of resource exploitation and environmental degradation. The novel advocates for the political potential of human-nonhuman coalitions that view nonhuman entities as rights-bearing subjects (Henry 577–80).

Feminist Anticolonial Science (Fiction) Studies in the Rain Forest

Aimee Bahng

Karen Tei Yamashita's 1974 Thomas J. Watson Fellowship would open onto a nine-year residency in Brazil—an experience that would undoubtedly form the basis of not only *Through the Arc of the Rain Forest* but also *Brazil-Maru* and *Circle K Cycles*. While this piece of Yamashita's biography has certainly grounded avenues of inquiry in Asian American literary studies that focalize the author's attention to a more hemispheric set of Asian/American migrations,[1] it is also important to consider the methodological and epistemological questions the Watson Fellowship may have occasioned for Yamashita. The Watson Fellowship presents itself on its website as a competitive, postbaccalaureate study abroad program and a prestigious fund for budding ethnographers. When the Watson Foundation says it "is investing in you as a leader, an investment that provides a lifetime of compounded interest in the form of perspective, confidence and insight," what kind of outcomes does it imagine ("Frequently Asked Questions")? When Thomas J. Watson was the chairman and CEO of International Business Machines (IBM) from 1914 to 1956, he adopted for his company the slogan "World Peace through World Trade" (Schlombs 14). Did Yamashita understand her Watson Fellowship as an uncomfortable participation in the grooming of a transnational elite through travel abroad? Could the conditions of her movements among Japan, Brazil, and the United States have honed her keen understanding of the connections between technology and global capitalism and the uneven "distribution of wealth and life chances" (Spade 6)?

In what follows I make a case for teaching Yamashita's work as part of an explicitly anticolonial feminist science and technology studies framework. Where the broader fields of science and technology studies (STS), queer and feminist theory, and anticolonial thought intersect lies a group of scholars whose research links capitalist expansionism and resource extraction to the epistemic violence of colonial scientific expeditions and ethnographies (Subramaniam, *Ghost Stories*; Foster; TallBear; Rusert; Asher; Roy; Atanasoski and Vora; Subramaniam et al.). Meanwhile, a number of scholars of feminist science fiction studies have argued for science fiction writers such as Octavia E. Butler and Leslie Marmon Silko to be considered contributors to the production of scientific thought (Bahng, "Plasmodial Improprieties"; Streeby; Schalk). This essay adds Yamashita's *speculative fiction*, a more capacious term than *science fiction*, to the list of literary works written by women of color whose critiques of scientific and technological progress myths are inherently anticolonial as well.[2] Among Yamashita's most significant contributions is her willingness to push beyond conventional generic forms. Though English departments across the United States have begun to integrate science fiction and Asian American literature into their curricular offerings, these courses are often electives rather than part of the core learning requirements for majors. Asking students to consider how canon formation works to consolidate understandings of national belonging by means of inclusion within or exclusion from established and esteemed literary forms becomes a first step toward investigating how Yamashita's *Through the Arc* defies the racialized, classed, and gendered hierarchies often exercised through syllabus and curriculum formation and proliferation (D. Eng, "Queer/Asian American/ Canons"). For the purposes of this essay, I share how students read *Through the Arc*'s interventions using feminist STS frameworks to interrogate the imbricated histories of science and empire, and I posit how such an interrogation usefully opens onto a demonstration of feminist speculation as a praxis of excavating histories and situating knowledges more broadly.

Through the Arc was a regular part of an upper-division, undergraduate seminar I taught at Dartmouth College. The course, called Science, Fiction, and Empire, served as a capstone experience for English majors and gender studies students alike. It asked students to read science fiction alongside queer theories of futurity, feminist histories of science, and Indigenous and critical ethnic studies critiques of settler colonial and neocolonial logics. Perhaps because the word *science* appears in the title, the course also piqued the interest of several senior computer science and life sciences majors who needed to fulfill a literature requirement for graduation. Many of these students had encountered science fiction as part of their leisure-time reading, though they had read work primarily by writers such as Isaac Asimov, Philip K. Dick, or maybe Margaret Atwood. Introducing science fiction readers to feminist decolonial science studies as a theoretical framework foregrounds ideological and epistemological questions about what counts as science or technology, and how such categories become established. Yamashita's *Through the Arc* takes aim at the knowledge-making institutions that form around such categories, and it points to how racialized and gendered notions of Western modernity, progress, and a liberal Enlightenment subject continue to inform assumptions in Euro-American understandings of science and technology.[3] Indeed, the course title gestures not only to science fiction but also to fictions about science (i.e., the cultural production of science) as its focal subject. When read alongside other texts on the syllabus, *Through the Arc* provides an example of what one might call a minor fabulation, along the lines of how Tavia Nyong'o formulates the crafting of "a vantage point from which to peer into," in this case, the production of science fiction and scientific fictions without simply taking those generic conventions for granted (*Afro-Fabulations* 34–35).[4]

To orient students toward a feminist STS set of questions, I ask them to complete a homework assignment titled "Tracing Science Fictions" alongside their first forays into the novel. The assignment directs students to take note of moments when the novel challenges conventional distinctions between science and fantasy, technology and mythology, native and alien, or new and old. Almost immediately, and over the course of reading the first half of the book (part 1, "The

Beginning"; part 2, "The Developing World"; and part 3, "More Development"), students encounter the fantastic elements of the story: the narrator, a sentient ball of seemingly extraterrestrial origin orbiting around the protagonist Kazumasa Ishimaru's head; another character's magical feather, which, "[l]ike the remote control and the buttons on [a] new TV . . . made things happen" (Yamashita, *Through the Arc* 18); and the third arm of the corporate wonk J. B. Tweep, which he "accepted . . . as another might accept ESP, an addition of 128k to their random access or the invention of the wheel" (30). The details that yoke the fantastic with the technological—feather to remote, extra appendage to added RAM—accumulate quickly over the course of the novel. As these examples accrete, they form one of the novel's central interrogations into what does or doesn't count as technology and "for whom, and when, and how much it costs to produce [technology] at a particular moment in history for a particular group of people" (Haraway, "Donna Haraway" 2:10–2:30).[5] When students arrive in class, I call on a few to share one example from their assignment. The conversation gains momentum quickly: other students, already prepared with their own examples, begin to chime in and extrapolate from their data to make a guess as to what Yamashita might be up to in blurring the distinctions between the hallowed halls of empirical science and the ostensibly unscientific belief systems of superstition, mythology, or religion. The point sinks in that as much as science may strive for empiricism, it remains tethered to belief systems and authorizing mechanisms that have served as rationalizations for conquest and imperial expansion. Given the politicization of climate change and the contestations around teaching evolution in schools, it is crucial to differentiate between this practice of critical inquiry and denying scientific research outright.

To focus the conversation on science's interactions with empire, I gesture ahead on the syllabus to Nalo Hopkinson's speculative fiction *Midnight Robber* and share with students a snippet of an interview in which the writer addresses the intertwined logics of empire, technology, and development that take for granted a Eurocentric account of civilization:

> The current metaphors for technology and social behaviors and systems are largely from Greco-Roman mythology. We call our spaceships Apollo and our complexes Oedipus. We talk about cyberspace. So I wondered what metaphors we (Caribbean people) would create for technologies that we had made, how we would think about those technologies.
>
> (Hopkinson, "Interview" 149)

This quotation goes up on a slide at the front of the classroom, and I explain a bit more about *cyberspace*, a term attributed to William Gibson, a fairly specific touchstone for mainstream science fiction associated with a white male readership and fan base. After taking a minute to mull over how the term *cyberspace* affects the way one might imagine what the Internet is and how it works, I ask students in small, informal groups to generate some other metaphors they see circulating around digital, online experiences. I can rely on at least one group to come up with the Web as a metaphor, and some students run with how *web* and *net* seem to emphasize lateral connectivity more so than *cyberspace* does. As more than one student has pointed out, many mainstream narratives around cyberspace use a discourse of exploration and conquest that, for example, *Star Trek* fans might recognize in the show's opening incitement to "boldly go where no man has gone before." These students echo what feminist and Indigenous scholars have at this point clearly demonstrated: constructions of space as a final frontier often coalesce around gendered concepts and settler epistemologies of virgin land and of discovery as penetration.

In contrast, *Through the Arc* seems to take more interest in cyclical or unraveling structures of space-time. Without fail, class discussions of Yamashita's work eventually arrive at the novel's structure, which disrupts conventional progress-over-time teleology. Beginning with the arc invoked in its title, the novel sustains its curving and bending of developmental narratives throughout the many twists and turns of several interwoven plotlines. One prompt that pulls in even the least prepared student is to reflect on the titles of parts 1 through 6, which move readers through development and "more development" to "loss" and "more loss." The novel may begin with "beginning," but it ends with "return," as if Yamashita has anticipated the cyclical structures she would continue to think through in *Brazil-Maru* and *Circle K Cycles*. These formal literary decisions not only signal the triangular migrations of Asians to, from, and between the Americas that Yamashita's work excels in helping Asian Americanists formulate but also undermine a development narrative that subjects the Global South to the capitalist vicissitudes of the World Bank and the International Monetary Fund. *Through the Arc*'s divestment from capitalist futurity manifests in the spectacular failure of Chicolandia—an overwrought amusement park constructed in a frenzy of speculative investment. Made completely out of the seemingly miraculous substance of Matacão plastic, Chicolandia eventually disintegrates, along with everything else made of the rubbery material, which had been heralded as having the tensile strength of steel but then becomes susceptible to avian-borne bacteria that consume the substance just as quickly as it was consumed by global capitalist entrepreneurialism.

This contrast between colonial and decolonial metaphors, between *Star Trek* and *Through the Arc*, forms a good starting point, but when comparative moves such as these come up in conversation, the challenge can often be to get students to push their inquiry beyond the formal, structural differences to interrogate what makes a frontier an imperialist metaphor, what decolonial politics might manifest structures of unraveling, or what feminist decolonial insights might inform cyclical patterning. To connect formal analysis to political significance, the conversation necessitates some historical and geopolitical grounding. After students have practiced tuning into those moments when science or technology comes up in Yamashita's novel, I send them into the second half of *Through the Arc* (part 4, "Loss of Innocence"; part 5, "More Loss"; and part 6, "Return"), asking them to look in particular for allusions to the entangled histories of empire and science. On day two of class discussion, I introduce students to Henry Ford's neocolonial development in the Brazilian Amazon (see Bahng, "Extrapolating Transnational Arcs"). I take ten to fifteen minutes to narrate the utter failure of Fordlândia, the Fordist rubber plantation and neocolonial development in question, supplementing the overview with some of the arresting archival images of the plantation, which are available online.[6] Fordlândia provides a convincing real-world analogue to *Through the Arc*'s Chicolandia—a connection strengthened by, as students tend to note, the buried, rusting Model Ts that the reader stumbles upon earlier in Yamashita's rain forest (*Through the Arc* 100). To transition back to discussion, I close my minilecture by highlighting some of the archival research on Fordlândia that points to the frustration about the rain forest and its denizens that was expressed by the plantation managers in their reports back to Ford headquarters in Detroit.[7] I share with students excerpts from these archival materials that document how managers complained of the purported laziness of Indigenous workers and of the plantation clinic's ineffectiveness at stemming the influx of tropical diseases. After pointing to the racialized discourse at work in Fordlândia, I then ask students to locate similar dynamics at work in Yamashita's novel. Students immediately cite the global entrepreneur J. B. Tweep and his constant petty complaints that the conditions of the rain forest "kept jamming and chewing up the tape" of his small tape recorder: "'It's the humidity,' Mr. Tweep fumbled in exasperation. 'Nothing seems to work in this country!'" (74). Tweep may be a comic character, but when students hear how Ford tried to enforce North American labor practices such as the nine-to-five workday, which was maladjusted to the conditions of the tropical rain forest, they begin to see the tragicomic recalcitrance of an actual neocolonial enterprise that mobilized notions of modernity and technological advancement as the premise for global capitalist incursion.

For the second day of discussion, my primary goal is for students to realize how science can produce fictions that help sustain imperialist rationales and epistemologies. Nancy Leys Stepan's essay "Race and Gender: The Role of Analogy in Science" helpfully opens with a discussion of the extent to which metaphors, analogies, and other forms of linguistic modeling participate in scientific reasoning and knowledge production. "Metaphor," Stepan begins, "occupies a central place in literary theory, but the role of metaphors, and of the analogies they mediate, in scientific theory is still debated" (261). A historian of science, Stepan interrogates the crucial role of figurative language in materials designed to share scientific knowledge, inquiring more specifically after the "normative consequences" of scientific metaphors that attempt to render scientific data recognizable to human experience (262). Her primary examples draw on analogies that link race to gender in late-nineteenth- and early-twentieth-century scientific theories about human variation and evolutionary biology. The essay, which I assign alongside the second half of Yamashita's novel, also historically contextualizes how progress narratives, imperial conquest, and racialized and gendered social hierarchies converged under the ideological and economic aegis of empire. In class, I break students into small groups of three or four, first asking each member to share one specific example Stepan's essay provided of analogic thinking in nineteenth-century evolutionary biology. One popular example among students is that of phrenological scientists who argued that white women "shared with Negroes a narrow, childlike, and delicate skull, so different from the more robust and rounded heads characteristic of males of 'superior' races" (263). Students are quick to recognize the racism and misogyny of such examples, but they are often too quick to write the examples off as pseudoscientific quackery from over a century ago. To press them on this point, I ask them to consider the moments in Yamashita's novel when characters seem dismissive of one another's scientific beliefs and practices. When we reconvene after group work, students revisit their earlier cataloging of technologies in the novel but this time focus on how Yamashita characterizes the range of technologies—from rubbing feathers on one's ears for luck to divining underground caches of Matacão rubber using Kazumasa's ball to using pigeons as a courier service. Students quickly realize that Yamashita plays with the reader's hierarchical assumptions about which technology is ultimately better, especially considering the ecological devastation brought on by Ford's rubber plantation disaster. The class session concludes with individual reflection pieces that prompt students to synthesize in writing Stepan's history of racial science, the questions she raises about the power of analogy, and Yamashita's own fictionalization of the scientific enterprises at work at the Matacão. By the end of the session, students come away with a sense of how narrative and science may not be such wholly discrete disciplinary endeavors as the fiction/nonfiction binary would have us believe.

These encounters with the socially constructed aspects of technological advancement and with examples of science used in the service of white supremacy, imperialist expansion, or heteropatriarchy can sometimes problematically lead students to an outright vilification of technoscience as an always-already colonizing force. The lessons of feminist STS, though, can focus students' critique on the authorizing mechanisms that work *through* technoscience. In her analysis of such authorizing mechanisms, Donna Haraway identifies the "god-trick" of disembodied, scientific rhetoric produced from the "unmarked positions of Man and White" ("Situated Knowledges" 581). In her formulation of feminist objectivity, Haraway posits "situated knowledges" as feminist scientific praxis, and by experimenting with the locus of narration in *Through the Arc* and across the rest of her oeuvre, Yamashita demonstrates precisely how different knowledges emerge from differently situated narrators. Because reading Haraway can be daunting, I recommend covering this ground in a minilecture and making this article suggested rather than required reading. In the case of this class, though, students grappled with Haraway's "Situated Knowledges" earlier in the term on its own, and it became a touchstone for many students as they made their way through several of the other speculative fictions on the syllabus.

Feminist STS has long interrogated how cultural narratives shape scientific inquiry. The Amazon rain forest has been repeatedly configured by Euro-American colonial, neocolonial, and late capitalist incursions as an impenetrable jungle in which the natural world must be brought under the ordering regimes of Western modernity. Yamashita's *Through the Arc* provides us with multiple examples of the entanglement of nature and culture—an entanglement often theorized by Haraway, who argues that the "nature or nurture" question sets up a false binary (*Companion Species Manifesto* 3). After introducing this concept using Haraway's work, I give students a moment to locate in the novel instances when nature and culture seem entangled. The examples that emerge often overlap with the passages students gathered for the initial "Tracing Science Fictions" assignment: The ostensibly natural resource found at the Matacão is in fact comprised of First World waste that has made its way back up to the surface of the planet decades later. The butterflies in the rain forest are bright orange because they have been hydrating on the "rusty water from the oxidation of abandoned U.S. military vehicles" (Yamashita, *Through the Arc* 100). The sphere in orbit around Kazumasa Ishimaru's head turns out not to be alien at all but derived from the same material as the Matacão. The process of discerning local from foreign, citizen from alien, might best be understood as part of a performative process of naturalization (Subramaniam, "Aliens").

Reading Yamashita's *Through the Arc* within the framework of feminist decolonial science and technology studies helps students hold the categories of science, fiction, and empire open to one another as inextricably linked sites of knowledge production. At every turn, students discover, the novel signals feminist disruptions of disembodied knowledge production at the intersections of scientific and imperialist exploration. By the end of the unit on Yamashita, students become attuned to the novel's formal and figurative emphases on questions of authority, authorship, and authorizing mechanisms. Some students may also register a peculiar kind of feminist humor that relies less on the comedic energy that derives from punching down the power chain than on a radical kind of fabulation. It is in the process of stumbling through Yamashita's rain forest that students come to realize just how tripped up on certain conceptualizations of modernity and authorial positions they can get.

NOTES

[1] See, for example, Chuh, "Of Hemispheres"; Rachel C. Lee, *Americas*; Jinqi Ling, *Across Meridians*; Rody, "Transnational Imagination." In his book *Asian/American*, David Palumbo-Liu fully theorizes the use of the solidus in the term *Asian/American* to signify simultaneous division and conjuncture in the relation between the terms *Asian* and *American*. Here I deploy *Asian/American* to decenter the United States in the varied histories of migration to, from, and between Asia and the Americas more broadly. While I use *Asian American* to refer to the study of the literature or culture of Asians in

the United States, I use *Asian/American* to accentuate the specific migrations Yamashita is interested in.

[2] For a more thorough explanation of how I parse the terms *speculative fiction* and *science fiction*, see Bahng, *Migrant Futures* 9–17.

[3] Ruth Hsu makes a similar point about Yamashita's third novel, *Tropic of Orange*, which, Hsu argues, "critiques and subverts the ideological meanings and values undergirding the epistemology of cartography and the related 'scientific' fields of trigonometry, geography, meteorology, mathematics, and so on" ("Cartography" 84).

[4] For more on queering utopianism, minor fabulation, and alternate futurities, see Bahng, *Migrant Futures*; Haraway, "Manifesto"; Muñoz; Nyong'o; and Rifkin. In *Migrant Futures*, I argue that speculative writing such as Yamashita's can be a resource for crafting alternative futures oriented not toward financial profit (i.e., speculative futures markets) but toward nonhierarchical exchanges of knowledge and integrated circuits of social organization (17–21).

[5] This quotation from the 1987 video "Donna Haraway Reads 'The National Geographic' On Primates" emerged around the time Haraway published her groundbreaking feminist science studies works, "Manifesto for Cyborgs" and "Situated Knowledges."

[6] A search for "Fordlandia" in the Digital Collections of the Henry Ford Archive of American Innovation will produce a wide selection of photos: www.thehenryford.org/collections-and-research/digital-collections.

[7] Companhia Brasil—Newspaper Articles, Pictures, Booklets, etc. Benson Ford Research Center, The Henry Ford, Accession 74, Box 6.

NOTES ON CONTRIBUTORS

Aimee Bahng is associate professor in the Gender and Women's Studies Program at Pomona College. She is the author of *Migrant Futures: Decolonizing Speculation in Financial Times* and has published articles on techno-Orientalism and on speculative fiction by people of color. Her research sits at the intersections of queer-feminist science studies, comparative ethnic studies, and disability and environmental justice. Her monograph-in-progress is provisionally titled "Transpacific Ecologies: Settler Environmentalism and the Gentrification of the Sea."

Noelle Brada-Williams, chair of the Department of English and Comparative Literature at San Jose State University, is the founder of *Asian American Literature: Discourses and Pedagogies*, an online, open-access, peer-reviewed journal focused on the teaching of Asian American literature. She has published articles on Gish Jen, Maxine Hong Kingston, Jhumpa Lahiri, Chang-rae Lee, Miné Okubo, and Salman Rushdie. She is a coeditor of *Crossing Oceans: Reconfiguring American Literary Studies in the Pacific Rim*.

Jamie Crosswhite is a recent PhD graduate and teaching assistant in the English department at the University of Texas, San Antonio. She has published articles on Annie Proulx and Cormac McCarthy and served as a short-term fellow for the New York Public Library. Her dissertation examines how regional narratives foster generative relationships within local landscapes and conceptualize new ways of troubling local-global networks and coded perceptions of gender, racial difference, sexuality, and environmental agency.

John Dees is a PhD student in the Energy and Resources Group at the University of California, Berkeley. His research centers around energy system transitions for climate change mitigation. He specializes in life-cycle assessment of energy technologies, spatial analysis, and resource economics. In addition to his academic specialty, he nurtures his passion for learning in a broad range of intellectual and creative pursuits.

Gloria Karam Delbim is a retired English professor. Her MA thesis is entitled "A Interculturalidade no Romance *Brazil-Maru* de Karen Tei Yamashita" ("Interculturality in the Novel *Brazil-Maru* by Karen Tei Yamashita"); she cotranslated the chapter "Zero Zero Hum . . . aravilha" in *Circle K Cycles*, by Karen Tei Yamashita, and the Constitution of the State of São Paulo. Her research interests include diaspora, memory, postcolonial literature, American literature, history, civilization, and culture.

Robin E. Field is professor of English and director of the Center for Excellence in Learning and Teaching at King's College. She is a coeditor of *Transforming Diaspora: Communities beyond National Boundaries* and has published essays on Sandra Cisneros, Alice Walker, Jhumpa Lahiri, Lynne Sharon Schwartz, and Ayad Akhtar. She is the author of *Writing the Survivor: The Rape Novel in Late Twentieth-Century American Fiction* (2020).

Matthew S. Henry is scholar in residence with the Haub School of Environment and Natural Resources at the University of Wyoming. He has published work in *Environmental Humanities*, *ISLE: Interdisciplinary Studies in Literature and the Environment*, *ARIEL: A Review of International English Literature*, and elsewhere. His current book project, entitled *Hydronarratives: Water, Environmental Justice, and Imagining a Just Transition*, will be published by the University of Nebraska Press in 2021.

Caroline Kyungah Hong is associate professor and director of graduate studies in English at Queens College, City University of New York. She is finishing a book on Asian American comedy and has published articles on Asian American comedy and comics. She is currently a board member of the Circle for Asian American Literary Studies, the Association for Asian American Studies, and the *Asian American Literary Review*.

Ruth Y. Hsu is associate professor of English at the University of Hawaiʻi, Mānoa, where she received her appointment as an Asian American specialist. Recent publications include a chapter on Yamashita's *Tropic of Orange* in *Karen Tei Yamashita: Fictions of Magic and Memory* and an interview with Yamashita on her 2017 book, *Letters to Memory*. She has also published on Derek Kirk Kim, *Orange Is the New Black*, and *Sense8*.

Lynn Mie Itagaki is associate professor of English and women's and gender studies at the University of Missouri. She is the author of *Civil Racism: The 1992 Los Angeles Rebellion and the Crisis of Racial Burnout* and has published in *Modern Fiction Studies*, *PhiloSOPHIA: A Journal of Continental Feminism*, and elsewhere. She is writing monographs on the role of the bystander in human rights debates and on representations of race and gender after the Great Recession.

T. Christine Jespersen is professor of English at Western Colorado University. Her recent publications include "Literary Identification as Transformative Feminist Pedagogy" in *Feminist Teacher* and "Unmapping Adventure: Sewing Resistance in Linda Hogan's *Solar Storms*" in *Western American Literature*. Her research interests include literatures of globalization, environmental justice, gender studies, and codisciplinary work in literary theory and economics. She is currently working on a monograph, "Adventure in the Ages of Empire."

Wen Jin is professor of comparative literature at East China Normal University. She is the author of *Pluralist Universalism: An Asian Americanist Critique of U.S. and Chinese Multiculturalisms* and has published in *PMLA*, *American Quarterly*, *Journal of Narrative Theory*, *Chinese Literature and Culture*, *Critique*, *Contemporary Literature*, and collected volumes. Her research interests include American literature, Asian American literature, the long eighteenth century, and Sino-Western comparative literature. She is a recipient of China's Junior Changjiang Scholar award.

Ikue Kina is professor at the University of the Ryukyus. She is the author of 『< 故郷 > のトポロジー』(*Kokyo no Toporoji*; *Topology of Home: Ecocritical Sense of Place and Belongingness*; 2011) and "Subaltern Knowledge and Transnational American Studies: Postwar Japan and Okinawa under US Rule," a book review published in *American Quarterly*. Her research interests include gender and ethnicity in American literature, Indigenous women writers, and ecofeminism.

Nataliya Krynytska is associate professor in the Germanic and romance department at Poltava V. G. Korolenko National Pedagogical University, Ukraine. Her publications include textbooks on the history of English and on contemporary English-language literature and translations of fiction from Ukrainian into English and from English into Ukrainian. Her research interests cover English-language literature, science fiction, dystopia, and fantasy. She is currently working on a monograph on national mythologies in contemporary science fiction and fantasy literature of the United States.

Josephine Lee is professor of English and Asian American studies at the University of Minnesota, Twin Cities, and editor-in-chief of the *Oxford Encyclopedia of Asian American Literature and Culture*. Other books include *Performing Asian America* and *The Japan of Pure Invention: Gilbert and Sullivan's* The Mikado as well as the coedited volumes *Re/Collecting Early Asian America: Essays in Cultural History*, *Asian American Plays for a New Generation*, and *Asian American Literature in Transition, 1850–1930*.

Anastasia Lin is professor of English and assistant vice president of research and engagement at the University of North Georgia. She has published articles on Frances Chung, Marilyn Chin, and Karen Tei Yamashita and coedited a special *MELUS* volume on pedagogy in 2017. She has won multiple teaching and leadership awards and is a past participant in the Asian Studies Development Program at the East-West Center. Lin currently serves as secretary of *MELUS*.

Jessica Lewis Luck is professor of English at California State University, San Bernardino. Her research interests include experimental poetics, poetry and cognition, literary theory, and disability studies. She has published articles on authors including Harryette Mullen, Sylvia Plath, Laura Redden Searing, and Larry Eigner. She is currently working on two monographs, "The Poetics of Cognition: Thinking through Experimental Poems" and "Prosthetic Poetics: Contemporary Poetry of Disability."

Rie Makino is professor of English at Nihon University, College of Humanities and Sciences. Her research interests include Asian American literature and transnational studies. Her publications on Yamashita's writing include "Japanese Santa Claus: Levi-Strauss' Perspective of Non-assimilation and the Spirit of Charity in Karen Tei Yamashita's *Through the Arc of the Rain Forest*" in *The American Review: The Japanese Association for American Studies* (2012). She translated Yamashita's short story "The Bath" and Yamashita's 2015 keynote lecture at the Tenth International Melville Conference.

J. Edward Mallot is associate professor of English at Arizona State University. His publications include *Memory, Nationalism, and Narrative in Contemporary South Asia* and articles on Amitav Ghoshh and Kamila Shamsie, Shauna Singh Baldwin, Karen Tei Yamashita, and Romesh Gunesekera. His research interests include contemporary British literature and postcolonial studies with a focus on South Asia. He is currently researching the nonnormative body in Indian writing.

Ana María Manzanas-Calvo is professor of American literature and culture at the University of Salamanca. Her most recent publications include *Hospitality in American Literature and Culture: Spaces, Bodies, Borders* and *Occupying Space in American Literature and Culture: Social Movements, Occupation, and Empowerment*, both coauthored with Jesús Benito Sánchez. She is currently working on a chapter titled "Urban Border," which will appear in *The City in American Literature and Culture*, edited by Kevin R. McNamara, as part of the Cambridge Themes in American Literature and Culture series.

David J. Plante is professor of economics at Western Colorado University. His research interests include economic history, macroeconomics, money, American political economy, globalization, and social economics. He has published articles in *New Political*

Science, the *Radical History Review*, and the *Journal of Management Education*. His current projects include case studies on macroeconomic history of the United States.

Caroline Rody, professor of English at the University of Virginia, is the author of "Between 'I' and 'We': Viet Thanh Nguyen's Interethnic Multitudes" (*PMLA*, 2018), *The Interethnic Imagination: Roots and Passages in Contemporary Asian American Fiction*, and *The Daughter's Return: African-American and Caribbean Women's Fictions of History*. Her recent work includes a chapter on magical books in Jewish fiction in *The Palgrave Handbook of Magical Realism in the Twenty-First Century* (2020) and an in-progress monograph on the great house trope and the national imaginary across world fiction.

Claudia Sadowski-Smith is professor of English at Arizona State University. She is the author of *The New Immigrant Whiteness: Neoliberalism, Race, and Post-Soviet Migration to the United States*, *Border Fictions: Globalization, Empire, and Writing at the Boundaries of the United States*, and *Globalization on the Line: Culture, Capital, and Citizenship at U.S. Borders*. She has also (co)edited special journal issues on border studies and postsocialist literatures of the United States.

Silvia Schultermandl is associate professor of American studies at the University of Graz. She is the author of *Transnational Matrilineage: Mother-Daughter Conflicts in American Literature* and the editor of several volumes on transnational identity, transnational kinship, and kinship and online media. She is currently working on a monograph on the aesthetics of transnationalism in American literature and is a series editor, along with May Friedman, of the Palgrave Studies in Mediating Kinship, Representation, and Difference.

Jolie A. Sheffer is associate professor of English and American culture studies at Bowling Green State University. Her publications include *Understanding Karen Tei Yamashita* (2020) and *The Romance of Race: Incest, Miscegenation, and Multiculturalism in the United States, 1880–1930* (2013). Her current projects include a special issue of *MELUS* on ethnic historical fiction, coedited with Cathy Schlund-Vials, and a monograph on recent cultural memory and counter-memory of the Long Sixties.

Begoña Simal-González is professor at the Universidade da Coruña, Spain. Her books include *Selves in Dialogue: A Transethnic Approach to American Life Writing* (editor) and *Ecocriticism and Asian American Literature* (2020). Her articles have appeared in the *Journal of Transnational American Studies*, the *Journal of Postcolonial Writing*, *MELUS*, *Concentric*, *Revista de Estudios Norteamericanos*, and essay collections.

Min Hyoung Song is professor of English at Boston College. He is the author of *The Children of 1965: On Writing and Not Writing as an Asian American* and *Strange Future: Pessimism and the 1992 Los Angeles Riots*. He is a coeditor of the *Cambridge History of Asian American Literature*. His research interests include Asian American literature, twentieth- and twenty-first-century American literature, and environmental humanities. His book *Climate Lyricism* will be in print in early 2022.

Pamela Thoma is associate professor of English and director of the Program in Women's, Gender, and Sexuality Studies at Washington State University. She is the author of *Asian American Women's Popular Literature: Feminizing Genres and Neoliberal Belonging* (2014). A chapter, "Contemporary Asian American Women's Popular Literature and Neoliberal Form," will be published in *Asian American Literature in Transition* in 2021. She is currently working on a monograph about twenty-first-century narratives of decline.

Xiaojing Zhou is professor of English at the University of the Pacific. She is the author of *Migrant Ecologies: Zheng Xiaoqiong's* Women Migrant Workers, *Cities of Others: Reimagining Urban Spaces in Asian American Literature*, and *The Ethics and Poetics of Alterity in Asian American Poetry*. Currently she is working on a critical anthology, *Empire and Environment: Confronting Ecological Ruination in the Transpacific*, coedited with Jeffrey Santa Ana, Heidi Hong, and Rina Garcia Chua.

SURVEY RESPONDENTS

Yanoula Athanassakis, *New York University*
Noelle Brada-Williams, *San Jose State University*
Claudio Roberto Vieira Braga, *Universidade de Brasilia*
Christopher Breu, *Illinois State University*
Daniel Burns, *Elon University*
Floyd Cheung, *Smith College*
Sylvia Chong,*University of Virginia*
Jamie Crosswhite, *University of Texas, San Antonio*
Daniel Dale, *University of Cincinnati*
Gloria Karam Delbim, *Universidade Presbiteriana Mackenzie*
Jigna Desai, *University of Minnesota, Twin Cities*
Robin E. Field, *King's College*
Hiroshi Fukurai, *University of California, Santa Cruz*
Johanna X. K. Garvey, *Fairfield University*
Andrew Hageman, *Luther College*
George Hart, *California State University, Long Beach*
Alison Harvey, *University of Nevada, Reno*
Caroline Kyungah Hong, *Queens College, City University of New York*
Christine Hong, *University of California, Santa Cruz*
Grace Hong, *University of California, Los Angeles*
Ruth Y. Hsu, *University of Hawai'i, Mānoa*
Lynn Mie Itagaki, *University of Missouri*
T. Christine Jespersen, *Western Colorado University*
Wen Jin, *East China Normal University*
Betty Nobue Kano, *San Francisco State University*
Ikue Kina, *University of the Ryukyus*
Nataliya Krynytska, *Poltava V. G. Korolenko National Pedagogical University*
Hervé-Pierre Lambert, *Ministère Education Nationale France / Université Paris Nanterre*
Josephine Lee, *University of Minnesota, Twin Cities*
Long Le-Khac, *Washington University in St. Louis*
Anastasia Lin, *University of North Georgia*
Dorothea Löbbermann, *Humboldt University of Berlin*
Jessica Lewis Luck, *California State University, San Bernardino*
Rie Makino, *Nihon University*
J. Edward Mallot, *Arizona State University*
Ana María Manzanas-Calvo, *University of Salamanca*
Leah Milne, *University of Indianapolis*
Sudarat Musikawong, *Siena College*
Sarah Nolan, *University of Nevada, Reno*
Rory Ong, *Washington State University*
David J. Plante, *Western Colorado University*
T. V. Reed, *Washington State University / York University*

Caroline Rody, *University of Virginia*
Emilio Sauri, *University of Massachusetts, Boston*
Silvia Schultermandl, *University of Graz*
Jelena Sesnic, *University of Zagreb*
Rone Shavers, *College of Saint Rose*
Jolie A. Sheffer, *Bowling Green State University*
Carol Siegel, *Washington State University, Vancouver*
Begoña Simal-González, *Universidade da Coruña*
Stephen Hong Sohn, *University of California, Riverside*
John Streamas, *Washington State University*
Aya Tanaka, *New York University*
Pamela Thoma, *Washington State University*
Lai Ying Yu, *Tufts University*
Xiaojing Zhou, *University of the Pacific*

WORKS CITED

Adachi, Nobuko. "A Historical and Contemporary View of Brazilian Migration." *Migration and Immigration: A Global View*, edited by Maura I. Toro-Morn and Marixsa Alicea, Greenwood, 2004, pp. 19–34.

Adams, Rachel. "The Ends of America, the Ends of Postmodernism." *Twentieth Century Literature*, vol. 53, no. 3, Fall 2007, pp. 248–72.

Adiga, Aravind. *The White Tiger.* Free Press, 2009.

Aidoo, Ama Ata. *Our Sister Killjoy; or, Reflections from a Black-Eyed Squint.* Longman, 1977.

Alaimo, Stacy. *Bodily Natures: Science, Environment, and the Material Self.* Indiana UP, 2010.

Alaimo, Stacy, and Susan Hekman, editors. *Material Feminisms.* Indiana UP, 2008.

Alameddine, Rabih. *I, the Divine: A Novel in First Chapters.* W. W. Norton, 2002.

Alarcon, Daniel. *Lost City Radio.* HarperCollins Publishers, 2007.

Alvarez, Julia. *Yo!* Algonquin Books of Chapel Hill, 1997.

Ammons, Elizabeth. *Brave New Words.* U of Iowa P, 2010.

Amrith, Sunil S. *Migration and Diaspora in Modern Asia.* Cambridge UP, 2011.

Anderson, Benedict. *Imagined Communities.* Verso, 2006.

Anderson, Sherwood. *Winesburg, Ohio.* Dover ed., Dover Publications, 1996.

Andrade, Mário de. *Macunaíma, o herói sem nenhum caráter.* 1928. 2nd ed., Martins, 1955.

Ang, Ien. "Can One Say No to Chineseness: Pushing the Limits of the Diasporic Paradigm." *On Not Speaking Chinese: Living between Asia and the West*, by Ang, Routledge, 2001, pp. 37–51.

Anisfield, Nancy. "Godzilla/Gojiro: Evolution of the Nuclear Metaphor." *Journal of Popular Culture*, vol. 29, no. 3, 1995, pp. 53–62, doi.org/10.1111/j.0022-3840.1995.00053.x.

Anzaldúa, Gloria. *Borderlands/La Frontera: The New Mestiza.* 4th ed., Aunt Lute Books, 2012.

———. "From Borderlands/*La Frontera*: The New Mestiza." Leitch, pp. 2098–109.

Appadurai, Arjun. *Modernity At Large: Cultural Dimensions of Globalization.* U of Minnesota P, 1996.

Asher, Kiran. *Black and Green: Afro-Colombians, Development, and Nature in the Pacific Lowlands.* Duke UP, 2009.

Asian Women United of California, editors. *Making Waves: An Anthology of Writings by and about Asian American Women.* Beacon Press, 1989.

Asimov, Isaac. "True Love." *Being People: An Anthology for Non-Native Speakers of English*, edited by Thomas Kral, USIA, 1997, pp. 182–85.

Atanasoski, Neda, and Kalindi Vora. *Surrogate Humanity: Race, Robots, and the Politics of Technological Futures.* Duke UP, 2019.

Atwood, Margaret. *Negotiating with the Dead: A Writer on Writing*. Anchor Books, 2002.

———. *Oryx and Crake*. Anchor Books, 2004.

Augé, Marc. *Non-Places: Introduction to an Anthropology of Supermodernity*. Translated by John Howe, Verso, 1995.

———. *Oblivion*. Translated by Marjolijn de Jager, U of Minnesota P, 2004.

Bachelard, Gaston. *The Poetics of Space*. Translated by Maria Jolas, Beacon Press, 1994.

Backes, Evan, editor. *Displaced: Manzanar, 1942–1945: The Incarceration of Japanese Americans*. T. Adler Books, 2018.

Bahng, Aimee. "Extrapolating Transnational Arcs, Excavating Imperial Legacies: The Speculative Acts of Karen Tei Yamashita's *Through the Arc of the Rain Forest*." *MELUS: The Journal of the Society for the Study of the Multi-ethnic Literature of the United States*, vol. 33, no. 4, Winter 2008, pp. 123–44.

———. "Imperial Rubber: The Speculative Arcs of Karen Tei Yamashita's Futures." Bahng, *Migrant Futures*, pp. 25–50.

———. *Migrant Futures: Decolonizing Speculation in Financial Times*. Duke UP, 2018.

———. "Plasmodial Improprieties: Octavia E. Butler, Slime Molds, and Imagining a Femi-Queer Commons." *Queer Feminist Science Studies: A Reader*, edited by Cyd Cipolla et al., U of Washington P, 2017, pp. 310–26.

Bald, Vivek. *Bengali Harlem and the Lost Histories of South Asian America*. Harvard UP, 2012.

Bambillo, Marco, director. *Demolition Man*. Warner Bros. Pictures, 1993.

Barry, Peter. *Beginning Theory: An Introduction to Literary and Cultural Theory*. 2nd ed., Manchester UP, 2002.

Barthelme, Donald. "Indian Uprising." *The New Yorker*, 6 Mar. 1965, pp. 34–37.

Bary, Leslie. "Oswald de Andrade's 'Cannibalist Manifesto.'" *Latin American Literary Review*, vol. 19, no. 38, July 1991, pp. 35–37.

Baudrillard, Jean. Excerpt from *The Precession of Simulacra*. Leitch, pp. 1556–66.

Bautista, Veltisezar B. *The Filipino Americans: From 1763 to the Present: Their History, Culture, and Traditions*. Bookhaus, 1998.

Beck, Ulrich. *What Is Globalization?* Polity Press, 2000.

The Bedford / St. Martin's Texas Editorial Board, editor. *Texas Literature: A Case Study*. Bedford / St. Martin's, 2010.

Behdad, Ali. *A Forgetful Nation: On Immigration and Cultural Identity in the United States*. Duke UP, 2005.

Bender, Aimee. *An Invisible Sign of My Own*. Doubleday, 2000.

Bennett, Eric. *Workshops of Empire: Stegner, Engle, and American Creative Writing during the Cold War*. U of Iowa P, 2015.

Bennett, Jane. *Vibrant Matter: A Political Ecology of Things*. Duke UP, 2009.

Bernstein, Michael André. *Foregone Conclusions: Against Apocalyptic History*. U of California P, 1994.

"Betty, a Red Guard." Created by Choncy Shu, performances by Wylie Evan Huey and Goldie Chan, 2010. *Vimeo*, uploaded by Shu, 26 Apr. 2010, www.vimeo.com/11229669. Accessed 26 Oct. 2020.

The Big Sleep. Directed by Howard Hawks, Warner Bros. Pictures, 1946.

Birns, Nicholas. "An Incomplete Journey: Settlement and Power in *Brazil-Maru*." A. Robert Lee, pp. 90–104.

Blair, Sara. "Cultural Geography and the Place of the Literary." *American Literary History*, vol. 10, no. 3, Fall 1998, pp. 544–67.

Blyn, Robin. "Belonging to the Network: Neoliberalism and Postmodernism in *Tropic of Orange*." *MFS: Modern Fiction Studies*, vol. 62, no. 2, Summer 2016, pp. 191–216.

Bobis, Merlinda. "The Long Siesta as a Language Primer." *White Turtle: A Collection of Short Stories*, by Bobis, Spinifex Press, 1999, pp. 74–77.

Boltanski, Luc, and Eve Chaipello. *The New Spirit of Capitalism*. Verso, 2005.

Borges, Jorge Luis. *Borges on Writing*, edited by Norman Thomas di Giovanni et al., E. P. Dutton, 1972.

Bornstein, Kate. *Gender Outlaw: On Men, Women and the Rest of Us*. Routledge, 1994.

Boyle, T. C. *The Tortilla Curtain*. Penguin Books, 1996.

Brecher, Jeremy, and Tim Costello. *Global Village or Global Pillage: Economic Reconstruction from the Bottom Up*. South End Press, 1994.

Breines, Winifred. "Whose New Left?" *Journal of American History*, vol. 75, no. 2, Sept. 1988, pp. 528–45, doi.org/10.2307/1887869.

Brodkin, Karen. *How Jews Became White Folks and What That Says about Race in America*. Rutgers UP, 1998.

Brophy, Philip. "Monster Island: Godzilla and Japanese Sci-Fi/Horror/Fantasy." *Postcolonial Studies*, vol. 3, no. 1, 2000, pp. 39–42, doi.org/10.1080/13688790050001336.

Brown, Wendy. *Undoing the Demos: Neoliberalism's Stealth Revolution*. Zone Books, 2015.

Buell, Lawrence, et al. "Literature and Environment." *Annual Review of Environment and Resources*, vol. 36, 2011, pp. 417–40.

Butler, Judith. *Gender Trouble: Feminism and the Subversion of Identity*. Routledge, 1990.

Butler, Octavia E. *Parable of the Sower*. 1993. Reissued ed., Grand Central Publishing, 2019.

Bye Bye Brazil. Directed by Carlos Diegues, Carnaval Films, 1980.

Cahan, Richard, and Michael Williams. *Un-American: The Incarceration of Japanese Americans during World War II*. CityFiles Press, 2016.

Calvino, Italo. *If on a Winter's Night a Traveler*. Translated by William Weaver, Harcourt Brace Jovanovich, 1979.

———. *Six Memos for the Next Millennium*. Random House, 1988.

Carter, Angela. *Bloody Chamber*. Harper and Row, 1979.

Cat People. Directed by Jacques Tourneur, RKO Radio Pictures, 1942.

Chan, Jeffery Paul, et al., editors. *The Big Aiiieeeee! An Anthology of Chinese American and Japanese American Literature*. Meridian, 1991.

Chan, Sucheng. *Asian Americans: An Interpretive History*. Twayne, 1991.

Chesnutt, Charles W. The Conjure Woman *and Other Conjure Tales*, edited by Richard H. Brodhead, Duke UP, 1993.

———. *"The Wife of His Youth" and Other Stories of the Color Line*. U of Michigan P, 1968.

Cheung, King-Kok. "The Woman Warrior versus the Chinaman Pacific: Must a Chinese American Critic Choose between Feminism and Heroism?" *Conflicts in Feminism*, edited by Marianne Hirsch and Evelyn Fox Keller, Routledge, 1990, pp. 234–51.

Chin, Frank. "Come All Ye Asian American Writers of the Real and the Fake." *The Big Aiiieeeee! An Anthology of Chinese American and Japanese American Literature*, edited by Jeffery Paul Chan et al., Meridian, 1991, pp. 1–92.

———. *Donald Duk*. Coffee House Press, 1991.

Chin, Frank, and Jeffery Paul Chan. "Racist Love." *Seeing through Shuck*, edited by Richard Kostelanetz, Ballantine, 1972, pp. 65–79.

Chin, Frank, et al., editors. *Aiiieeeee! An Anthology of Asian-American Writers*. Howard UP, 1983.

Chiu, Monica. "Introduction: Visual Realities of Race." *Drawing New Color Lines: Transnational Asian American Graphic Narratives*, edited by Chiu, Hong Kong UP, 2014, pp. 1–24.

Choy, Curtis, director. *The Fall of the I-Hotel*. Chonk Moonhunter Productions, 1983.

———. *What's Wrong with Frank Chin?* Chonk Moonhunter Productions, 2005.

Chu, Patricia P. *Assimilating Asians: Gendered Strategies of Authorship in Asian America*. Duke UP, 2000.

———. "Authoring Subjects: Frank Chin and David Mura." Chu, *Assimilating Asians*, pp. 64–89.

Chua, Lawrence. *Gold by the Inch*. Grove Press, 1998.

Chuh, Kandice. *Imagine Otherwise: On Asian Americanist Critique*. Duke UP, 2003.

———. "Of Hemispheres and Other Spheres: Navigating Karen Tei Yamashita's Literary World." *American Literary History*, vol. 18, no. 3, Fall 2006, pp. 618–37, doi.org/10.1093/alh/ajl002.

Cisneros, Sandra. *The House on Mango Street*. 25th anniversary ed., Vintage Books, 1991.

———. *"Woman Hollering Creek" and Other Stories*. Bloomsbury, 1993.

Cixous, Hélène. *Three Steps on the Ladder of Writing*. Columbia UP, 1993.

Cohen, Ignacio Sánchez, et al. "Forced Migration, Climate Change, Mitigation and Adaptive Policies in Mexico: Some Functional Relationships." *International Migration*, vol. 51, no. 4, Aug. 2013, pp. 53–72.

Collins, Patricia Hill. *Black Feminist Thought: Knowledge, Consciousness, and the Politics of Empowerment*. 2nd ed., Routledge, 2000.

Columbo, Gary, et al. *Rereading America: Cultural Contexts for Critical Thinking and Writing*. 10th ed., Bedford / St. Martins, 2016.

Couser, G. Thomas. *Memoir: An Introduction*. Oxford UP, 2011.

Crawford, Chiyo. "From Desert to Dust to City Soot: Environmental Justice and Japanese American Internment in Karen Tei Yamashita's *Tropic of Orange*." *MELUS: The Journal of the Society for the Study of the Multi-ethnic Literature of the United States*, vol. 38, no. 3, Fall 2013, pp. 86–106.

Critchley, Simon. *Infinitely Demanding: Ethics of Commitment, Politics of Resistance*. Verso, 2007.

Crutzen, Paul, and Eugene Stoermer. "The Anthropocene." *Global Change Newsletter*, no. 41, May 2000, pp. 17–18.

Cruz, Denise. *Transpacific Femininities: The Making of the Modern Filipina*. Duke UP, 2012.

Davis, Mike. *City of Quartz: Excavating the Future in Los Angeles*. Verso, 2006.

Davis, Rocío G. *Relative Histories: Mediating History in Asian American Family Memoirs*. U of Hawai'i P, 2010.

Deleuze, Gilles. "Postscript on the Societies of Control" *October*, vol. 59, Winter 1992, pp. 3–7.

Delgado, Francisco. "Trespassing the U.S.-Mexico Border in Leslie Marmon Silko's *Almanac of the Dead* and Karen Tei Yamashita's *Tropic of Orange*." *CEA Critic: An Official Journal of the College English Association*, vol. 79, no. 2, July 2017, pp. 149–66.

DeLillo, Don. *Cosmopolis*. Scribner, 2004.

DeLoughrey, Elizabeth. "Satellite Planetarity and the Ends of the Earth." *Public Culture*, vol. 26, no. 2, Spring 2014, pp. 257–80.

DeLoughrey, Elizabeth, et al., editors. *Global Ecologies and the Environmental Humanities: Postcolonial Approaches*. Routledge, 2015.

De Loughry, Treasa. "Petromodernity, Petro-Finance and Plastic in Karen Tei Yamashita's *Through the Arc of the Rainforest*." *Journal of Postcolonial Writing*, vol. 53, no. 3, 2017, pp. 329–41.

Dephtereos, Andrew J. "Karen Tei Yamashita." *Asian American Literature: Reviews and Criticism of Works by American Writers of Asian Descent*, edited by Lawrence J. Trudeau, Gale, 1995, pp. 512–13.

Derrida, Jacques. "Hostipitality." Translated by Barry Stocker and Forbes Morlock. *Angelaki: Journal of the Theoretical Humanities*, vol. 5, no. 3, 2000, pp. 3–18.

Desai, Anita. "Winterscape." *"Diamond Dust" and Other Stories*, by Desai, Chatto and Windus, 2000, pp. 24–49.

Díaz, Junot. *The Brief Wondrous Life of Oscar Wao*. Riverhead Books, 2007.

Dick, Philip K. *The Man in the High Castle*. Gollanz, 1962.

Dillon, Sarah. *The Palimpsest: Literature, Criticism, Theory*. Continuum Books, 2007.

Dimock, Wai Chee. "The Planetary Dead: Margaret Fuller, Ancient Egypt, Italian Revolution." *Through Other Continents: American Literature across Deep Time*, by Dimock, Princeton UP, 2006, pp. 52–72.

Divakaruni, Chitra B. "Doors." *Arranged Marriage*, by Divakaruni, Anchor Books, 1995, pp. 184–202.

Duarte, Anselmo, director. *O Pagador de Promessas.* Cinidistri, 1962.

Du Bois, W. E. B. *The Souls of Black Folk.* Edited by Brent Hayes Edward, Oxford UP, 2008.

Duggan, Lisa. *The Twilight of Equality: Neoliberalism, Cultural Politics, and the Attack on Democracy.* Beacon Press, 2003.

Duncan, Patti. *Tell This Silence: Asian American Women Writers and the Politics of Speech.* U of Iowa P, 2003.

Duras, Marguerite. *Writing.* Lumen Editions, 1993.

Eco, Umberto. *Six Walks in the Fictional Woods.* Harcourt Brace, 1982.

Elias, Amy, and Christian Moraru, editors. *The Planetary Turn: Relationality and Geoaesthetics in the Twenty-First Century.* Northwestern UP, 2015.

The Enchanted Cottage. Directed by John Cromwell, RKO Radio Pictures, 1945.

Eng, Chris A. "Queer Genealogies of (Be)Longing: On the Thens and Theres of Asian America in Karen Tei Yamashita's *I Hotel.*" *Journal of Asian American Studies*, vol. 20, no. 3, Oct. 2017, pp. 345–72.

Eng, David L. "Queer/Asian American/Canons." *Teaching Asian America: Diversity and the Problem of Community*, edited by Lane Ryo Hirabayashi, Rowman and Littlefield, 1998, pp. 13–23.

———. *Racial Castration: Managing Masculinity in Asian America.* Duke UP, 2001.

Eng, David L., and Alice Y. Hom, editors. *Q and A: Queer in Asian America.* Temple UP, 1998.

Entin, Joseph. "Globalization, Migration, and Contemporary Working-Class Literature." *A History of American Working-Class Literature*, edited by Nicholas Coles and Paul Lauter, Cambridge UP, 2017, pp. 376–91.

Escobar, Arturo. *Territories of Difference: Place, Movements, Life, Redes.* Duke UP, 2008.

Espadas, Elizabeth. "Destination Brazil: Immigration in Works of Nélida Piñón and Karen Tei Yamashita." *MACLAS: Latin American Essays*, vol. 12, 1998, pp. 51–61.

Espiritu, Yen Le. *Asian American Panethnicity: Bridging Institutions and Identities.* Temple UP, 1992.

Feagin, Joe R., and Clairece Booher R. Feagin. *Racial and Ethnic Relations: Census Update.* 9th ed., Pearson, 2012.

Feng, Peter X. *Identities in Motion: Asian American Film and Video.* Duke UP, 2002.

Feng, Shuaizhang, et al. "Linkages among Climate Change, Crop Yields, and Mexico-US Cross-Border Migration." *PNAS*, vol. 107, no. 32, 10 Aug. 2010, pp. 14257–62.

Fielding, Tony. *Asian Migrations: Social and Geographical Mobilities in Southeast, East, and Northeast Asia.* Routledge, 2016.

Fishkin, Shelley Fisher. "Crossroads of Cultures: The Transnational Turn in American Studies—Presidential Address to the American Studies Association, November 12, 2004." *American Quarterly*, vol. 57, no. 1, 2005, pp. 17–57.

Fitzgerald, F. Scott. *The Great Gatsby*. Scribner, 2004.

Flood, Alison. "*The Brief Wondrous Life of Oscar Wao* Declared Twenty-First Century's Best Novel So Far." *The Guardian*, 20 Jan. 2015, www.theguardian.com/books/2015/jan/20/brief-wondrous-life-of-oscar-wao-novel-21st-century-best-junot-diaz.

Foer, Jonathan Safran. *Everything Is Illuminated*. Harper Perennial, 2003.

———. *Extremely Loud and Incredibly Close*. Mariner Books, 2005.

Foster, Laura. *Reinventing Hoodia: Peoples, Plants, and Patents in South Africa*. U of Washington P, 2017.

Foucault, Michel. *Archeology of Knowledge and the Discourse on Language*. Translated by A. M. Sheridan Smith, Pantheon Books, 1972.

"Frequently Asked Questions." *Thomas J. Watson Fellowship*, Thomas J. Watson Foundation, 2019, watson.foundation/fellowships/tj/faqs.

Friedman, Susan Stanford. *Mappings: Feminism and the Cultural Geographies of Encounter*. Princeton UP, 1998.

———. "Planetarity: Musing Modernist Studies." *Modernism/Modernity*, vol. 17, no. 3, Sept. 2010, pp. 471–99.

Friedman, Thomas L. *The Lexus and the Olive Tree*. Farrar, Straus and Giroux, 1999.

Fuentes, Carlos. *Diana: The Goddess Who Hunts Alone*. Translated by Alfred MacAdam, Farrar, Straus and Giroux, 1995.

Fung, Catherine. "'This Isn't Your Battle or Your Land': The Native American Occupation of Alcatraz in the Asian-American Political Imagination." *College Literature*, vol. 41, no. 1, Winter 2014, pp. 149–73.

Gaard, Greta Claire. *Critical Ecofeminism*. Lexington Books, 2017.

Gamber, John B. "'Dancing with Goblins in Plastic Jungles': History, Nikkei Transnationalism, and Romantic Environmentalism in *Through the Arc of the Rain Forest*." A. Robert Lee, pp. 39–58.

García, Cristina. *Monkey Hunting*. Reprint ed., Ballantine Books, 2014.

García Márquez, Gabriel. "A Very Old Man with Enormous Wings." Leaf Storm *and Other Stories*, by García Márquez, translated by Gregory Rabassa, Harper and Row, 1972, pp. 105–12.

Gardner, John. *The Art of Fiction*. Vintage Books, 1991.

———. *On Becoming a Novelist*. W. W. Norton, 1999.

Garland, Alex, director. *Annihilation*. Paramount Pictures, 2018.

George, Rosemary Marangoly. *The Politics of Home: Postcolonial Relocations and Twentieth-Century Fiction*. U of California P, 1996.

Giddens, Anthony. *The Consequences of Modernity*. Stanford UP, 1990.

Gilroy, Paul. *Postcolonial Melancholia*. Columbia UP, 2005.

Gómez-Peña, Guillermo. *The New World Border: Prophecies, Poems and Loqueras for the End of the Century*. City Lights, 1996.

Gotanda, Neil. "Multiculturalism and Racial Stratification." *Mapping Multiculturalism*, edited by Avery F. Gordon and Christopher Newfield, U of Minnesota P, 1996, pp. 238–52.

Grandin, Greg. *Fordlandia: The Rise and Fall of Henry Ford's Forgotten Jungle City.* Picador, 2010.

Graves, John. Excerpt from "Goodbye to a River." Bedford / St. Martin's Texas Editorial Board, p. 85.

Grewal, Inderpal. *Transnational America: Feminisms, Diasporas, Neoliberalisms.* Duke UP, 2005.

Grice, Helena. "Karen Tei Yamashita." *Dictionary of Literary Biography: Asian American Writers*, edited by Deborah L. Madsen, Bruccoli Clark Layman, 2005, pp. 338–42.

———. *Negotiating Identities: An Introduction to Asian American Women's Writing.* Manchester UP, 2002.

Grice, Helena, and Crystal Parikh. "Feminist and Queer Interventions into Asian America." Parikh and Kim, pp. 169–82.

Grimm, Henry. *The Chinese Must Go: A Farce in Four Acts.* A. L. Bancroft, 1879. *Online Archive of California*, oac.cdlib.org/ark:/13030/hb0m3n978s/?brand =oac4.

Guimarães, Roberto Pereira. *The Ecopolitics of Development in the Third World: Politics and Environment in Brazil.* L. Rienner, 1991.

Habal, Estella. *San Francisco's International Hotel: Mobilizing the Filipino American Community in the Anti-Eviction Movement.* Temple UP, 2007.

Hagedorn, Jessica, editor. *Charlie Chan Is Dead: An Anthology of Contemporary Asian American Fiction.* Penguin Books, 1993.

———, editor. *Charlie Chan Is Dead Two: At Home in the World: An Anthology of Contemporary Asian American Fiction.* Penguin Books, 2004.

———. *Dogeaters.* Pantheon Books, 1990.

Haggis, Paul, director. *Crash.* Bob Yari Productions, 2004.

Haraway, Donna Jeanne. *The Companion Species Manifesto: Dogs, People, and Significant Otherness.* Prickly Paradigm Press, 2003.

———, performer. "Donna Haraway Reads 'The National Geographic' on Primates." *Vimeo*, uploaded by Paper Tiger TV, 18 May 2017, vimeo.com/218047623.

———. "Manifesto for Cyborgs: Science, Technology, and Socialist Feminism in the 1980s." *Socialist Review*, no. 80, 1985, pp. 65–108.

———. "Situated Knowledges: The Science Question in Feminism and the Privilege of Partial Perspective." *Feminist Studies*, vol. 14, no. 3, Fall 1988, pp. 575–99.

Harbach, Chad. *MFA vs. NYC: The Two Cultures of American Fiction.* n+1 / Faber and Faber, 2014.

Hardt, Michael, and Antonio Negri. *Empire.* Harvard UP, 2000.

Harley, J. B. *The New Nature of Maps: Essays in the History of Cartography.* Johns Hopkins UP, 2002.

Harvey, David. *A Brief History of Neoliberalism.* Oxford UP, 2005.

———. *The Condition of Postmodernity: An Enquiry into the Origins of Cultural Change.* Blackwell Publishing, 1990.

———. *The Enigma of Capital and the Crises of Capitalism.* Oxford UP, 2010.

———. *Seventeen Contradictions and the End of Capitalism*. Oxford UP, 2014.

———. *Social Justice and the City*. U of Georgia P, 2009.

Heise, Ursula K. "Ecocriticism and the Transnational Turn in American Studies." *American Literary History*, vol. 20, nos. 1–2, Spring-Summer 2008, pp. 381–404.

———. "Globality, Difference, and the International Turn in Ecocriticism." *PMLA*, vol. 128, no. 3, May 2013, pp. 636–43.

———. "Local Rock and Global Plastic: World Ecology and the Experience of Place." *Comparative Literature Studies*, vol. 41, no. 1, 2004, pp. 126–52.

———. *Sense of Place and Sense of Planet: The Environmental Imagination of the Global*. Oxford UP, 2008.

Helton, Laura, et al. "The Question of Recovery: An Introduction." *Social Text*, vol. 33, no. 4, Dec. 2015, pp. 1–18.

Henry, Matthew S. "Nonhuman Narrators and Multinatural Worlds." *ISLE: Interdisciplinary Studies in Literature and the Environment*, vol. 25, no. 3, Summer 2018, pp. 566–83, doi.org/10.1093/isle/isx061.

Herzog, Werner, director. *Fitzcarraldo*. Werner Herzog Filmproduktion, 1982.

Higashide, Seiichi. *Adios to Tears: The Memoirs of a Japanese-Peruvian Internee in U.S. Concentration Camps*. U of Washington P, 2012.

Ho, Jennifer. *Racial Ambiguity in Asian American Culture*. Rutgers UP, 2015.

Hong, Grace Kyungwon, and Roderick A. Ferguson, editors. *Strange Affinities: The Gender and Sexual Politics of Comparative Racialization*. Duke UP, 2011.

Hong, Terry. "'Letters to Memory' Tells the Story of Author Karen Tei Yamashita's World War II Internment." *The Christian Science Monitor*, 13 Sept. 2017, www.csmonitor.com/Books/Book-Reviews/2017/0913/Letters-to-Memory-tells-the-story-of-author-Karen-Tei-Yamashita-s-World-War-II-internment.

hooks, bell. *Belonging: A Culture of Place*. Routledge, 2009.

———. *Outlaw Culture: Resisting Representations*. Routledge, 1994.

———. "Postmodern Blackness." Leitch, pp. 2509–16.

Hopkinson, Nalo. "An Interview with Nalo Hopkinson." Conducted by Dianne D. Glave. *Callaloo*, vol. 26, no. 1, 2003, pp. 146–59.

———. *Midnight Robber*. Grand Central Publishing, 2000.

Houston, Jeanne Wakatsuki, and James D. Houston. *Farewell to Manzanar: A True Story of Japanese American Experience during and after the World War II Internment*. Dell Laurel-Leaf, 1995.

Hsu, Ruth Y. "The Cartography of Justice and Truthful Refractions Found in Karen Tei Yamashita's *Tropic of Orange*." *Transnational Asian American Literature: Sites and Transits*, edited by Shirley Geok-Lin Lim et al., Temple UP, 2006, pp. 75–99.

———. "Rousseau and Emile in Karen Tei Yamashita's *Brazil-Maru*: The Intertexts of Colonies, Utopia, and Freedom." *De/Colonization in the Americas: Continuity and Change*, edited by Heidrun Mörtl et al., U of New Orleans P, forthcoming. Inter-American Studies.

Huang, Yunte. *Charlie Chan: The Untold Story of the Honorable Detective and His Rendezvous with American History*. W. W. Norton, 2010.

Hughes, Langston. *Short Stories*. Edited by Akiba Sullivan Harper, Hill and Wang, 1996.

Hunt, Alex. *The Geographical Imagination of Annie Proulx: Rethinking Regionalism*. Lexington Books, 2009.

Hwang, David Henry. *M. Butterfly*. Dramatists Play Service, 1988.

Ichioka, Yuji, et al., editors. *Before Internment: Essays in Prewar Japanese American History*. Stanford UP, 2006.

Imafuku, Ryuta. クレオール主義 [*Creole Shugi*]. Seidosha, 1994.

Inada, Lawson Fusao, editor. *Only What We Could Carry: The Japanese American Internment Experience*. Heyday Books / California Historical Society, 2000.

Ishi, Angelo. "Searching for Home, Wealth, Pride, and 'Class': Japanese Brazilians in the 'Land of Yen.'" Lesser, *Searching for Home Abroad*, pp. 75–102.

Ishizuka, Karen L. *Gidra, the Dissident Press and the Asian American Movement: 1969–1974*. 2015. U of California, Los Angeles, PhD dissertation.

———. *Serve the People: Making Asian America in the Long Sixties*. Verso, 2016.

Itagaki, Lynn Mie. *Civil Racism: The 1992 Los Angeles Rebellion and the Crisis of Racial Burnout*. U of Minnesota P, 2016.

———. "The Media Spectacle of Racial Disaster." Itagaki, *Civil Racism*, pp. 181–216.

Ivins, Molly. "Is Texas America?" Bedford / St. Martin's Texas Editorial Board, pp. 100–04.

———. "Texas on Everything." Bedford / St. Martin's Texas Editorial Board, pp. 17–28.

Izarra, Laura P. Z. "Theorising 'Teaching Back': Contemporary Literatures as a Socio-cultural Hologram." *Ensino de Língua Inglesa Através do Texto Literário*, organized by Izarra and Michela Rosa Di Candia, Associação Editorial Humanitas, 2007, pp. 73–87.

Jain, Shalini Rupesh. "Pigeons, Prayers, and Pollution: Recoding the Amazon Rain Forest in Karen Tei Yamashita's *Through the Arc of the Rain Forest*." *ARIEL: A Review of International English Literature*, vol. 47, no. 3, July 2016, pp. 67–93.

James, Henry. *Daisy Miller*. Harper and Brothers, 1906.

Jameson, Fredric. *Postmodernism; or, The Cultural Logic of Late Capitalism*. Verso, 1991.

"Japanese American Internment." *Encyclopedia Britannica*, 20 Sept. 2018, www.britannica.com/event/Japanese-American-internment.

Jay, Paul. *Global Matters: The Transnational Turn in Literary Studies*. Cornell UP, 2010.

Jen, Gish. *Mona in the Promised Land*. Alfred A. Knopf, 1996.

———. "Who's Irish?" *Who's Irish? Stories*, by Jen, Alfred A. Knopf, 1999, pp. 3–16.

Joo, Hee-Jung Serenity. "Flexible Chaos: Globalization and Race in Los Angeles Disaster Film and Fiction." *Lit: Literature Interpretation Theory*, vol. 23, no. 3, July 2012, pp. 246–66.

Juergensmeyer, Mark, editor. *Thinking Globally: A Global Studies Reader.* U of California P, 2014.

Kakuchi, Suvendrini. "Government Softens Stance on Humanities after Uproar." *University World News*, 22 Jan. 2016, www.universityworldnews.com/post.php?story=20160122155338974.

Kang, Laura Hyun Yi. "Generic Fixations: *Reading the Writing Self.*" *Compositional Subjects: Enfiguring Asian/American Women*, by Kang, Duke UP, 2002, pp. 29–70.

Kara, Esen. "Rewriting the City as an Oeuvre in Karen Tei Yamashita's *Tropic of Orange.*" *Interactions: Ege Journal of British and American Studies / Ege İngiliz ve Amerikan İncelemeleri Dergisi*, vol. 27, nos. 1–2, Spring-Fall 2018, pp. 75–87.

Kase, Yasuko. "Remapping L.A.: Spatio-temporal Rupture in *Tropic of Orange.*" *AALA Journal*, vol. 11, 2005, pp. 142–52.

Keith, Joseph. "Comparative Race Studies and Interracialisms." Parikh and Kim, pp. 183–96.

Keller, George Frederick. "'The Coming Man' 1881." *Thomas Nast Cartoons*, thomasnastcartoons.com/2014/04/03/the-coming-man-20-may-1881/. Accessed 29 Oct. 2020.

Kim, Claire Jean. "The Racial Triangulation of Asian Americans." *Politics and Society*, vol. 27, no. 1, Mar. 1999, pp. 105–38.

Kim, Daniel Y. *Writing Manhood in Black and Yellow: Ralph Ellison, Frank Chin, and the Literary Politics of Identity.* Stanford UP, 2005.

Kim, Elaine H. "Chinatown Cowboys and Warrior Women: Searching for a New Self-Image." *Asian American Literature: An Introduction to the Writings and Their Social Context*, Temple UP, 1982, pp. 173–213.

Kim, Jina. "Toward an Infrastructural Sublime: Narrating Interdependency in Karen Tei Yamashita's Los Angeles." *MELUS: The Journal of the Society for the Study of the Multi-ethnic Literature of the United States*, vol. 45, no. 2, Summer 2020, pp. 1–24.

Kincaid, Jamaica. *A Small Place.* Farrar, Straus and Giroux, 2000.

King, Laura Tanja. "Travelling without Moving: Navigating the Liminal Space between Memoir and Fiction." *New Writing*, vol. 12, no. 1, 2014, pp. 1–8, doi.org/10.1080/14790726.2014.956122.

Kingston, Maxine Hong. *China Men.* 1980. Alfred A. Knopf, 2005.

———. *Tripmaster Monkey: His Fake Book.* Alfred A. Knopf, 1989.

———. *The Woman Warrior: Memoir of a Girlhood among Ghosts.* 1976. Alfred A. Knopf, 2005.

Kogawa, Joy. *Obasan.* Anchor Books, 1993.

Korty, John, director. *Farewell to Manzanar.* NBC Universal Media, 2011.

Kundera, Milan. *The Art of the Novel.* Harper Perennial, 1988.

Kurosawa, Akira, director. *Rashomon.* Daiei Motion Picture Company, 1950.

LaLonde, Chris. "Did You Hear the One about . . . ? Humor in *Through the Arc of the Rain Forest* and *Brazil-Maru.*" A. Robert Lee, pp. 59–72.

Lamott, Anne. *Bird by Bird*. Anchor Books, 1994.

Latour, Bruno. *Politics of Nature: How to Bring the Sciences into Democracy*. Translated by Catherine Porter, Harvard UP, 2004.

———. *Reassembling the Social: An Introduction to Actor-Network-Theory*. Oxford UP, 2005.

Lee, A. Robert, editor. *Karen Tei Yamashita: Fictions of Magic and Memory*. U of Hawai'i P, 2018.

Lee, Chang-rae. *Native Speaker*. Riverhead Books, 1997.

Lee, Erika. *The Making of Asian America: A History*. Simon and Schuster, 2015.

———. "Orientalism in the Americas: A Hemispheric Approach to Asian-American History." *Journal of Asian American Studies*, vol. 8, no. 3, Oct. 2005, pp. 235–56.

Lee, Josephine. "Asian American Drama." Parikh and Kim, pp. 89–100.

———, editor. *The Oxford Encyclopedia of Asian American Literature and Culture*. Oxford UP, 2019, www.oxfordreference.com/.

———. *Performing Asian America: Race and Ethnicity on the Contemporary Stage*. Temple UP, 1997.

Lee, Josephine, et al., editors. *Asian American Plays for a New Generation*. Temple UP, 2011.

Lee, Rachel C. *The Americas of Asian American Literature: Gendered Fictions of Nation and Transnation*. Princeton UP, 1999.

———. "Asian American Cultural Production in Asian-Pacific Perspective." *Boundary 2: An International Journal of Literature and Culture*, vol. 26, no. 2, Summer 1999, pp. 231–54.

———. *The Exquisite Corpse of Asian America: Biopolitics, Biosociality, and Posthuman Ecologies*. New York UP, 2014.

———, editor. *The Routledge Companion to Asian American and Pacific Islander Literature*. Routledge, 2016.

Lee, Robert G. *Orientals: Asian Americans in Popular Culture*. Temple UP, 1999.

———. "*The Woman Warrior* as an Intervention in Asian American Historiography." *Approaches to Teaching Kingston's* The Woman Warrior, edited by Shirley Geok-lin Lim, Modern Language Association of America, 1991, pp. 52–63.

Lee, Shelley Sang-Hee. *A New History of Asian America*. Routledge, 2014.

Lee, Youngmin, and Kyonghwan Park. "Negotiating Hybridity: Transnational Reconstruction of Migrant Subjectivity in Koreatown, Los Angeles." *Journal of Cultural Geography*, vol. 25, no. 3, 2008, pp. 245–62.

Lefebvre, Henri. "The Right to the City." *Writings on Cities*, translated and edited by Eleonore Kofman and Elizabeth Lebas, Blackwell Publishing, 2000, pp. 63–184.

Leitch, Vincent B., editor. *The Norton Anthology of Theory and Criticism*. 2nd ed., W. W. Norton, 2010.

Lesser, Jeffrey. *A Discontented Diaspora: Japanese Brazilians and the Meaning of Ethnic Militancy, 1960–1980*. Duke UP, 2007.

———. "Japanese, Brazilians, Nikkei: A Short History of Identity Building and Homemaking." Lesser, *Searching for Home Abroad*, pp. 5–19.

———. *Searching for Home Abroad: Japanese Brazilians and Transnationalism*. Duke UP, 2003.

Lesser, Jeffrey, et al. "Why Asia and Latin America?" *Verge: Studies in Global Asias*, vol. 3, no. 2, Fall 2017, pp. 1–16.

Li, David Leiwei, editor. *Asian American Literature*. Edition Synapse, 2012. 4 vols.

———. *Imagining the Nation: Asian American Literature and Cultural Consent*. Stanford UP, 2000.

Li, Wenxin. "Gender Negotiations and the Asian American Literary Imagination." *Asian American Literary Studies*, edited by Guiyou Huang, Edinburgh UP, 2005, pp. 109–31.

Life and Debt. Directed by Stephanie Black, Tuff Gong Pictures, 2003.

Lim, Shirley Geok-lin, et al., editors. *The Forbidden Stitch: An Asian American Women's Anthology*. CALYX, 1993.

Lim, Shirley Geok-lin, et al., editors. *Transnational Asian American Literature: Sites and Transits*. Temple UP, 2006.

Lin, Anastasia. "Mapping Multiethnic Texts in the Literary Classroom: GIS and Karen Tei Yamashita's *Tropic of Orange*." *Teaching Space, Place, and Literature*, edited by Robert Tally, Jr., Routledge, 2018, pp. 40–48.

Ling, Huping, and Allan W. Austin, editors. *Asian American History and Culture: An Encyclopedia*. M. E. Sharpe, 2010.

Ling, Jinqi. *Across Meridians: History and Figuration in Karen Tei Yamashita's Transnational Novels*. Stanford UP, 2012.

———. *Narrating Nationalisms: Ideology and Form in Asian American Literature*. Oxford UP, 1998.

———. "Southward Migration: Empire Building and Transculturation in *Brazil-Maru*." J. Ling, *Across Meridians*, pp. 30–59.

———. "Subterranean Transnationality: Race, Affect, and Material Form in *Circle K Cycles*." J. Ling, *Across Meridians*, pp. 60–83.

Linmark, R. Zamora. *Leche*. Coffee House Press, 2011.

Lipsitz, George. *How Racism Takes Place*. Temple UP, 2011.

———. *The Possessive Investment in Whiteness: How White People Profit from Identity Politics*. Rev. and expanded ed., Temple UP, 2006.

Llosa, Mario Vargas. *Letters to a Young Novelist*. Picador, 1997.

Lone, Stewart. *The Japanese Community in Brazil, 1908–1940: Between Samurai and Carnival*. Palgrave Macmillan, 2001.

López-Calvo, Ignacio. "Seiichi Higashide's *Adiós to Tears*: Flexible Citizenship, American War Propaganda, and the Birth of Anti-Japanese Hysteria in Peru." *The Affinity of the Eye: Writing Nikkei in Peru*, by López-Calvo, U of Arizona P, 2013, pp. 33–66.

Lowe, Lisa. *Immigrant Acts: On Asian American Cultural Politics*. Duke UP, 1996.

———. *The Intimacies of Four Continents*. Duke UP, 2015.

Lugones, María. "Playfulness, 'World'-Travelling, and Loving Perception." *Hypatia: A Journal of Feminist Philosophy*, vol. 2, no. 2, Summer 1987, pp. 3–19.

Luna, Francisco Vidal, and Herbert S. Klein. *The Economic and Social History of Brazil since 1889*. Cambridge UP, 2014.

Lye, Colleen. *America's Asia: Racial Form and American Literature, 1893–1945*. Princeton UP, 2004.

Maeda, Daryl. *Rethinking the Asian American Movement*. Routledge, 2011.

Malcolm X. "Message to the Grass Roots." *Malcolm X Speaks: Selected Speeches and Statements*, edited with prefatory notes by George Breitman, Merit Publishers, 1965, pp. 4–17.

Mallot, J. Edward. "Signs Taken for Wonders, Wonders Taken for Dollar Signs: Karen Tei Yamashita and the Commodification of Miracle." *ARIEL: A Review of International English Literature*, vol. 35, nos. 3–4, July-Oct. 2004, pp. 115–37.

Manzanas-Calvo, Ana María. "'We the People of the International Hotel' and the Hotel State: Karen Tei Yamashita's *I Hotel*." *Hospitality in American Literature and Culture: Spaces, Bodies, Borders*, edited by Manzanas-Calvo and Jesús Benito Sanchez, Routledge, 2017, pp. 106–28.

Marshall, Kate. "What Are the Novels of the Anthropocene? American Fiction in Geological Time." *American Literary History*, vol. 27, no. 3, Fall 2015, pp. 523–38.

Marwick, Arthur. *The Sixties: Cultural Transformation in Britain, France, Italy, and the United States, c. 1958–c. 1974*. Oxford UP, 1998.

Marx, Karl, and Friedrich Engels. Excerpt from *Economic and Philosophic Manuscripts of 1844*. Leitch, pp. 651–55.

Matsumoto, Valerie. "Japanese American Women in the 1930s." *Asian Americans: An Encyclopedia of Social, Cultural, Economic, and Political History*, edited by Xiaojian Zhou and Edward J. W. Park, ABC-CLIO, 2013, pp. 605–08.

Maucione, Jessica. "Literary Ecology and the City: Re-placing Los Angeles in Karen Tei Yamashita's *Tropic of Orange*." *Toward a Literary Ecology: Places and Spaces in American Literature*, edited by Karen E. Waldron and Rob Friedman, Scarecrow Press, 2013, pp. 81–100.

"Maya Lin, Vietnam Veterans Memorial." *Khan Academy*, 2019, www.khanacademy.org/humanities/ap-art-history/global-contemporary/v/mayalin-vietnamvetmem. Accessed 11 Feb. 2021.

McCall, Leslie. "The Complexity of Intersectionality." *Signs: Journal of Women in Culture and Society*, vol. 30, no. 3, Spring 2005, pp. 1771–800.

McGurl, Mark. *The Program Era: Postwar Fiction and the Rise of Creative Writing*. Harvard UP, 2011.

McIntosh, Peggy. "White Privilege and Male Privilege." *The Teacher in American Society: A Critical Anthology*, edited by Eugene F. Provenzo, Sage Publications, 2010, pp. 83–92.

McLeod, John. *Beginning Postcolonialism*. 2nd ed., Manchester UP, 2010.

Meade, Teresa A. "Constructing a Nation of Free Laborers in the Nineteenth and Early Twentieth Centuries." *A Brief History of Brazil*, by Meade, Facts on File, 2004, pp. 95–118.

Melville, Herman. "Bartleby." Billy Budd *and* The Piazza Tales, by Melville, Dolphin Books, 1961, pp. 115–53.

Mermann-Jozwiak, Elisabeth. "Yamashita's Post-national Spaces: 'It All Comes Together in Los Angeles.'" *Canadian Review of American Studies*, vol. 41, no. 1, 2011, pp. 1–24.

Mezzadra, Sandro, and Brett Neilson. "Between Inclusion and Exclusion: On the Topology of Global Space and Borders." *Theory, Culture, and Society*, vol. 29, nos. 4–5, 2012, pp. 58–75.

Miller, Nancy K. "The Entangled Self: Genre Bondage in the Age of the Memoir." *PMLA*, vol. 122, no. 2, Mar. 2007, pp. 537–48, www.jstor.org/stable/25501720.

Moody, Kim. *Workers in a Lean World: Unions in the International Economy*. Verso, 1997.

Moretti, Franco. *Distant Reading*. Verso, 2013.

Morgan, Nina, et al., editors. *The Routledge Companion to Transnational American Studies*. Routledge, 2019.

Mori, Toshio. *"The Chauvinist" and Other Stories*. Asian American Studies Center of the U of California, Los Angeles, 1979.

———. *Yokohama, California*. 2nd ed., U of Washington P, 1985.

Morrison, Toni. *Beloved*. Alfred A. Knopf, 1987.

———. *The Origin of Others*. Harvard UP, 2017.

———. "Recitatif." *Call and Response: The Riverside Anthology of the African American Literary Tradition*, edited by Patricia Liggins Hill, Houghton Mifflin, pp. 1176–86.

Motohashi, Tetsuya. ポストコロニアリズム [*Posuto Koroniariuzumu*]. Iwanami Shoten, 2005.

Mughal-E-Azam. Directed by K. Asif, Thomsum Video, 1960.

Mukherjee, Bharati. The Middleman *and Other Stories*. Grove Press, 1988.

Muñoz, José Esteban. *Cruising Utopia: The Then and There of Queer Futurity*. New York UP, 2009.

Munro, Alice. "The Bear Came Over the Mountain." *The New Yorker*, 14 Oct. 2013, www.newyorker.com/magazine/2013/10/21/the-bear-came-over-the-mountain-2.

Mura, David. *Turning Japanese: Memoirs of a Sansei*. Anchor Books, 1992.

Murayama, Milton. *All I Asking for Is My Body*. U of Hawai'i P, 1988.

Myers, D. G. *The Elephants Teach: Creative Writing since 1880*. Prentice Hall, 1996.

Nakamura, Park, and Martha Wong. "Black Panthers and Yellow Power." *Giant Robot*, no. 10, Spring 1998, pp. 61–81.

Ng, Fae Myenne. *Bone*. Hachette, 2008.

Ng, Wendy L. *Japanese American Internment during World War II: A History and Reference Guide*. Greenwood Press, 2002.

Ngai, Mae M. *Impossible Subjects: Illegal Aliens and the Making of Modern America*. Princeton UP, 2014.

Nguyen, Viet Thanh. *Race and Resistance: Literature and Politics in Asian America*. Oxford UP, 2002.

———. *The Sympathizer*. Grove Press, 2016.

Ninh, erin Khuê. *Ingratitude: The Debt-Bound Daughter in Asian American Literature*. New York UP, 2011.

Nishida, Mieko. *Diaspora and Identity: Japanese Brazilians in Brazil and Japan*. U of Hawai'i P, 2018.

Nixon, Rob. *Slow Violence and the Environmentalism of the Poor*. Harvard UP, 2011.

Nye, Naomi Shihab. "Different Ways to Pray." *Poetry Foundation*, 2020, www.poetryfoundation.org/poems/48595/different-ways-to-pray.

Nyong'o, Tavia. *Afro-Fabulations: The Queer Drama of Black Life*. New York UP, 2018.

———. "Unburdening Representation." *The Black Scholar*, vol. 44, no. 2, Summer 2014, pp. 70–80.

O'Connor, William van. "Parody as Criticism." *College English*, vol. 25, no. 4, Jan. 1964, pp. 241–48, doi.org/10.2307/373569.

Oishi, Eve. "I-Hotel." Rachel C. Lee, *Routledge Companion*, pp. 132–43.

Okihiro, Gary. *Cane Fires: The Anti-Japanese Movement in Hawaii, 1865–1945*. Temple UP, 1991.

Okubo, Miné. *Citizen 13660*. U of Washington P, 1983.

Omatsu, Glenn. "'The Four Prisons' and the Movements of Liberation: Asian American Activism from the 1960s to the 1990s." *Asian American Studies: A Reader*, edited by Jean Yu-Wen Shen Wu and Min Song, Rutgers UP, 2000, pp. 164–96.

Omi, Michael. *Racial Formation in the United States: From the 1960s to the 1990s*. 1994. 3rd ed., Routledge, 2014.

On Strike! (at SF State). Created by Saul Rouda and David Dobkin. *DIVA*, San Francisco State U, diva.sfsu.edu/collections/sfbatv/bundles/201724.

On Strike! Ethnic Studies, 1969–1999. Directed by Irum Shiekh, Center for Asian American Media, 1999.

Palmer, Ryan. "Citrus Noir: Strange Fruit in Karen Tei Yamashita's *Tropic of Orange*." *Studia Neophilologica: A Journal of Germanic and Romance Languages and Literature*, vol. 88, supplement, 2016, pp. 96–106, doi.org/10.1080/00393274.2015.1100456.

Palumbo-Liu, David. *Asian/American: Historical Crossings of a Racial Frontier*. Stanford UP, 1999.

———. "Embedded Lives: The House of Fiction, the House of History." *Profession*, 2011, pp. 13–22.

Parikh, Crystal, and Daniel Y. Kim, editors. *The Cambridge Companion to Asian American Literature*. Cambridge UP, 2015. Cambridge Companions to Literature.

Park, Hyungji. "Toward a Definition of Diaspora Literature." Parikh and Kim, pp. 155–66.

Parreñas, Rhacel Salazar. *Servants of Globalization: Women, Migration, and Domestic Work*. Stanford UP, 2001.

Patell, Cyrus R. K. "Karen Tei Yamashita and the Cultivation of Cosmopolitan Virtue." A. Robert Lee, pp. 9–23.

Pease, Donald. *The New American Exceptionalism*. U of Minnesota P, 2009.

Peou, Sarith. *Corpse Watching*. Tinfish Press, 2007.

Pérez-Peña, Richard. "College Classes Use Arts to Brace for Climate Change." *The New York Times*, 31 Mar. 2014, www.nytimes.com/2014/04/01/education/using-the-arts-to-teach-how-to-prepare-for-climate-crisis.html.

Perot, Ross. "The Giant Sucking Sound." *Save Your Job, Save Our Country*, by Perot, Hyperion, 1993, pp. 41–55.

Pessoa, Fernando. *Always Astonished*. City Lights, 1988.

Petras, James F., and Henry Veltmeyer. *Extractive Imperialism in the Americas: Capitalism's New Frontier*. Brill, 2014.

Phillips, Kevin. *Wealth and Democracy: A Political History of the American Rich*. Broadway Books, 2003.

Phillips, Mary, and Nick Rumens, editors. *Contemporary Perspectives on Ecofeminism*. Routledge, 2016.

Piatti, Barbara, et al. "Literary Geography; or, How Cartographers Open Up a New Dimension for Literary Studies." Proceedings of the Twenty-Fourth International Cartographic Conference, 15–21 Nov. 2009, Santiago, Chile, icaci.org/files/documents/ICC_proceedings/ICC2009/html/nonref/24_1.pdf.

Ping, Wang. *Foreign Devil*. Coffee House Press, 1996.

Piñón, Nélida. *The Republic of Dreams*. Translated by Helen Lane, Alfred A. Knopf, 1989.

Plante, David J. *Sustainable Development and the North American Free Trade Agreement: A Polanyian Interpretation*. 2004. U of Utah, PhD Dissertation.

Poblete, Juan. *New Approaches to Latin American Studies: Culture and Power*. Routledge, 2018.

Pollin, Robert. *The Contours of Descent: U.S. Economic Fractures and the Landscape of Global Austerity*. Verso, 2003.

Pooch, Melanie U. "The Transcultural Novel and the Urban Complexity of Los Angeles: Narrative Transculturation and Karen Tei Yamashita's *Tropic of Orange*." *Cityscapes in the Americas and Beyond: Representations of Urban Complexity in Literature and Film*, edited by Jens Martin Gurr and Wilfried Raussert, Wissenschaftlicher Verlag Trier, 2011, pp. 85–97.

Prashad, Vijay. *Uncle Swami: South Asians in America Today*. New Press, 2012.

Primeau, Ronald. *Romance of the Road: The Literature of the American Highway*. Bowling Green State U Popular P, 1996.

Puig, Manuel. *Kiss of the Spider Woman*. Vintage Books, 1978.

Pynchon, Thomas. *The Crying of Lot 49*. Lippincott, 1966.

Radhakrishnan, R. "Ethnicity in an Age of Diaspora." *Theorizing Diaspora: A Reader*, edited by Jana Evans Braziel and Anita Mannur, Blackwell Publishing, 2003, pp. 119–31.

Ragain, Nathan. "(Re)Production Cycles: *Circle K Cycles*." A. Robert Lee, pp. 123–42.

———. "A Revolutionary Romance: Particularity and Universality in Karen Tei Yamashita's *I Hotel*." *MELUS: The Journal of the Society for the Study of the Multi-ethnic Literature of the United States*, vol. 38, no. 1, Spring 2013, pp. 137–54.

Rifkin, Mark. *Beyond Settler Time: Temporal Sovereignty and Indigenous Self-Determination*. Duke UP, 2017.

Robinson, Greg. "Writing the Internment." Parikh and Kim, pp. 45–58.

Rodriguez, Cristina M. "'Relentless Geography': Los Angeles' Imagined Cartographies in Karen Tei Yamashita's *Tropic of Orange*." *Asian American Literature: Discourses and Pedagogies*, vol. 8, 2017, pp. 104–30.

Rody, Caroline. "Impossible Voices: Ethnic Postmodern Narration in Toni Morrison's *Jazz* and Karen Tei Yamashita's *Through the Arc of the Rain Forest*." *Contemporary Literature*, vol. 41, no. 4, Winter 2000, pp. 618–41.

———. *The Interethnic Imagination: Roots and Passages in Contemporary Asian American Fiction*. Oxford UP, 2009.

———. "The Transnational Imagination: Karen Tei Yamashita's *Tropic of Orange*." *Asian North American Identities: Beyond the Hyphen*, edited by Eleanor Ty and Donald C. Goellnicht, Indiana UP, 2004, pp. 130–48.

Roh, David S., et al., editors. *Techno-Orientalism: Imagining Asia in Speculative Fiction, History, and Media*. Rutgers UP, 2015.

Rosello, Mireille. *Postcolonial Hospitality: The Immigrant as Guest*. Stanford UP, 2001.

Rosenwasser, David, and Jill Stephen. *Writing Analytically*. 7th ed., Wadsworth Publishing, 2016.

Roy, Deboleena. *Molecular Feminisms: Biology, Becomings, and Life in the Lab*. U of Washington P, 2018.

Rozelle, Lee. *Zombiescapes and Phantom Zones: Ecocriticism and the Liminal from* Invisible Man *to* The Walking Dead. U of Alabama P, 2016.

Rusert, Britt. *Fugitive Science: Empiricism and Freedom in Early African American Culture*. New York UP, 2017.

Rushdie, Salman. *Shalimar the Clown*. Random House, 2005.

"Ruth Benedict." *Encyclopedia Britannica*, 2020, www.britannica.com/biography/Ruth-Benedict.

Sadowski-Smith, Claudia. *Border Fictions: Globalization, Empire, and Writing at the Boundaries of the United States*. U of Virginia P, 2008.

———. "The U.S.-Mexico Borderlands Writes Back: Cross-Cultural Transnationalism in Contemporary U.S. Women of Color Fiction." *Arizona Quarterly: A Journal of American Literature, Culture, and Theory*, vol. 57, no. 1, Spring 2001, pp. 91–111.

Sadowski-Smith, Claudia, and Claire F. Fox. "Theorizing the Hemisphere: Inter-Americas Work at the Intersection of American, Canadian, and Latin American Studies." *Comparative American Studies: An International Journal*, vol. 2, no. 1, 2004, pp. 5–38.

Safran, William. "Diasporas in Modern Societies: Myth of Homeland and Return." *Migration, Diasporas, and Transnationalism*, edited by Steven Vertovec and Robin Cohen, Edward Elgar, 1999, pp. 364–80.

Sagan, Claire. "Ending the Anthropocene." *Public Books*, 22 Jan. 2019, www.publicbooks.org/ending-the-anthropocene/.

"San Francisco State Strike Collection." *DIVA*, San Francisco State U, diva.sfsu.edu/collections/sfbatv/2582.

Santos, Bienvenido N. "Immigration Blues." Hagedorn, *Charlie Chan Is Dead: An Anthology*, pp. 422–39.

Sassen, Saskia. *Globalization and Its Discontent: Essays on the New Mobility of People and Money*. New Press, 1998.

Saussy, Haun, editor. *Comparative Literature in an Age of Globalization*. Johns Hopkins UP, 2006.

Sayre, Robert F. "Autobiography and the Making of America." *Autobiography: Essays Theoretical and Critical*, edited by James Olney, Princeton UP, 1980, pp. 146–68.

Schalk, Sami. *Bodyminds Reimagined: (Dis)Ability, Race, and Gender in Black Women's Speculative Fiction*. Duke UP, 2018.

Schérer, René. *Zeus hospitalier: Éloge de l'hospitalité*. La Table Ronde, 2005.

Schlombs, Corinna. "'The IBM Family': American Welfare Capitalism, Labor, and Gender in Postwar Germany." *IEEE Annals of the History of Computing*, vol. 39, no. 4, Oct.-Dec. 2017, pp. 12–26.

Schlund-Vials, Cathy J., and Cynthia Wu. "Rethinking Embodiment and Hybridity: Mixed Race, Adoptee, and Disabled Subjectivities." Parikh and Kim, pp. 197–212.

Schlund-Vials, Cathy J., et al., editors. *Keywords for Asian American Studies*. New York UP, 2015. *Keywords*, keywords.nyupress.org/asian-american-studies/.

Scholte, Jan Aart. *Globalization: A Critical Introduction*. Oxford UP, 2005.

Schultermandl, Silvia. "Out of Line: Shifting Border Paradigms in Cooper, Morrison, and Yamashita." *Crossing Borders: Essays on Literature, Culture, and Society in Honor of Amritjit Singh*, edited by Tapan Basu and Tasneem Shahnaaz, Fairleigh Dickinson UP, 2017, pp. 3–16.

Schulze, Frederik. "Nation and Migration: German-Speaking and Japanese Immigrants in Brazil, 1850–1945." *Immigration and National Identities in Latin America*, edited by Nicola Foote and Michael Goebel, UP of Florida, 2014, pp. 115–38.

Scott, Ridley, director. *Blade Runner*. Warner Bros. Pictures, 1982.

Scott-Heron, Gil. "The Revolution Will Not Be Televised." *Small Talk at 125th and Lenox*, Flying Dutchman, 1970.

Segal, Lore Groszmann. *Her First American*. Alfred A. Knopf, 1985.

Serres, Michel. *The Parasite*. Translated by Lawrence R. Schehr, U of Minnesota P, 2007.

Sheffer, Jolie. *Understanding Karen Tei Yamashita*. U of South Carolina P, 2020.

Shimakawa, Karen. *National Abjection: The Asian American Body Onstage*. Duke UP, 2002.

Shimizu, Celine Parreñas. *The Hypersexuality of Race: Performing Asian/American Women on Screen and Scene*. Duke UP, 2007.

———. *Straightjacket Sexualities: Unbinding Asian American Manhoods in the Movies*. Stanford UP, 2012.

Showalter, Elaine. *Teaching Literature*. Blackwell Publishing, 2003.

Silko, Leslie Marmon. *Ceremony*. Viking Press, 1977.

———. "Lullaby." *Storyteller*, by Silko, Seaver Books, 1981, pp. 43–51.

Simal, Begoña. "The Junkyard in the Jungle: Transnational, Transnatural Nature in Karen Tei Yamashita's *Through the Arc of the Rain Forest*." *Journal of Transnational American Studies*, vol. 2, no. 1, 2010, escholarship.org/uc/item/4567j2n1.

———. "'The Waste of the Empire': Neocolonialism and Environmental Justice in Merlinda Bobis's 'The Long Siesta as a Language Primer.'" *Journal of Postcolonial Writing*, vol. 55, 2019, pp. 1–14.

Sirk, Douglas, director. *All That Heaven Allows*. Universal-International, 1955.

Slovic, Scott. "The Third Wave of Ecocriticism: North American Reflections on the Current Phase of the Discipline." *Ecozona: European Journal of Literature, Culture and Environment*, vol. 1, no. 1, Spring 2010, pp. 4–10, ecozona.eu/article/download/312/283.

Smith, Rachel Greenwald. *Affect and American Literature in the Age of Neoliberalism*. Cambridge UP, 2015.

Sohn, Stephen Hong. "Anime Wong: A Critical Afterword." Yamashita, *Anime Wong: Fictions*, pp. 357–79.

Soja, Edward. *Thirdspace: Journeys to Los Angeles and Other Real-and-Imagined Places*. Blackwell Publishing, 1996.

Solomon, Molly, reporter. "Once Lost, Internment Camp in Hawaii Now a National Monument." *Morning Edition*, NPR, 16 Mar. 2015. *NPR*, www.npr.org/sections/codeswitch/2015/03/16/393284680/in-hawaii-a-wwii-internment-camp-named-national-monument.

Song, Min Hyoung. "Asian American Literature within and beyond the Immigrant Narrative." Parikh and Kim, pp. 3–15.

———. *The Children of 1965: On Writing, and Not Writing, as an Asian American*. Duke UP, 2013.

Song, Min Hyoung, and Rajini Srikanth, editors. *Asian American Literature in Transition*. Cambridge UP, 2020. 4 vols.

Soyinka, Wole. "Telephone Conversation." *Modern Poetry from Africa*, edited by Gerald Moore and Ulli Beier, Penguin Books, 1963, p. 114.

Spade, Dean. *Normal Life: Administrative Violence, Critical Trans Politics, and the Limits of Law*. South End Press, 2011.

Spivak, Gayatri Chakravorty. "Can the Subaltern Speak?" *Marxism and the Interpretation of Culture*, edited by Cary Nelson and Lawrence Grossberg, Macmillan Education, 1988, pp. 271–313.

———. *A Critique of Postcolonial Reason: Toward a History of the Vanishing Present*. Harvard UP, 1999.

———. *Death of a Discipline*. Columbia UP, 2003.

———. *In Other Worlds: Essays in Cultural Politics*. Routledge, 2006.

Srikanth, Rajini., and Esther Yae Iwanaga. *Bold Words: A Century of Asian American Writing*. Rutgers UP, 2001.

Staszak, Jean-François. "Performing Race and Gender: The Exoticization of Josephine Baker and Anna May Wong." *Gender, Place and Culture*, vol. 22, no. 5, 2014, pp. 1–18, doi.org/10.1080/0966369X.2014.885885.

Steger, Manfred B. *Globalisms*. Rowman and Littlefield, 2009.

———. *Globalization: A Very Short Introduction*. Oxford UP, 2013.

Stepan, Nancy Leys. "Race and Gender: The Role of Analogy in Science." *Isis*, vol. 77, no. 2, June 1986, pp. 261–77.

Stockett, Kathryn. *The Help*. Amy Einhorn Books, 2009.

The Story of Stuff. Directed by Louis Fox, Free Range Studios, 2007, www.storyofstuff.org/movies/story-of-stuff.

Streeby, Shelley. *Imagining the Future of Climate Change: World-Making through Science Fiction and Activism*. U of California P, 2018.

Strugatsky, Arkady, and Boris Strugatsky. *Roadside Picnic*. Foreword by Ursula K. LeGuin, translated by Olena Bormashenko, Chicago Review Press, 2012.

Subramaniam, Banu. "The Aliens Have Landed! Reflections on the Rhetoric of Biological Invasions." *Meridians: Feminism, Race, Transnationalism*, vol. 2, no. 1, 2001, pp. 26–40.

———. *Ghost Stories for Darwin: The Science of Variation and the Politics of Diversity*. U of Illinois P, 2014.

Subramaniam, Banu, et al. "Feminism, Postcolonialism, Technoscience." *The Handbook of Science and Technology Studies*, edited by Clark Miller et al., MIT Press, 2017, pp. 407–33.

Sue, Derald Wing. "Racial Microaggressions in Everyday Life: Is Subtle Bias Harmless?" *Psychology Today*, 5 Oct. 2010, www.psychologytoday.com/blog/microaggressions-in-everyday-life/201010/racial-microaggressions-in-everyday-life.

Swanson, Philip, editor. *The Companion to Latin American Studies*. Routledge, 2014.

Sze, Julie. "From Environmental Justice Literature to the Literature of Environmental Justice." *The Environmental Justice Reader: Poetics, Politics, and Pedagogy*, edited by Joni Adamson et al., U of Arizona P, 2002, pp. 163–80.

———. "'Not by Politics Alone': Gender and Environmental Justice in Karen Tei Yamashita's *Tropic of Orange*." *Bucknell Review: A Scholarly Journal of Letters, Arts and Sciences*, vol. 44, no. 1, 2002, pp. 29–42.

———, editor. *Sustainability: Approaches to Environmental Justice and Social Power*. New York UP, 2018.

Tachiki, Amy, editor. *Roots: An Asian American Reader*. UCLA Asian American Studies Center, 1971.

TallBear, Kim. *Native American DNA: Tribal Belonging and the False Promise of Genetic Science*. U of Minnesota P, 2013.

Talusan, Grace. "Teaching with Collaborative Writing Projects: Creating an Online Reader's Guide to Karen Tei Yamashita's *I Hotel*." *Asian American Literature: Discourses and Pedagogies*, vol. 5, 2014, pp. 87–95, scholarworks.sjsu.edu/cgi/viewcontent.cgi?article=1059&context=aaldp.

Tateishi, John. *And Justice for All: An Oral History of the Japanese American Detention Camps*. U of Washington P, 1999.

Taylor, Alan, director. *Roadside Picnic*. Sony Pictures Television / WGN America, 2017.

Taylor, Diane. *The Archive and the Repertoire: Performing Cultural Memoire in the Americas*. Duke UP, 2003.

Taylor, Tate, director. *The Help*. Touchstone Home Entertainment, 2011.

Tenorio, Lysley. "Save the I-Hotel." *Monstress: Stories*, HarperCollins Publishers, 2012, pp. 161–94.

Thoma, Pamela. *Asian American Women's Popular Literature: Feminizing Genres and Neoliberal Belonging*. Temple UP, 2014.

———. "Of Beauty Pageants and Barbie: Theorizing Consumption in Asian American Transnational Feminism." *Genders: A Journal of the Arts, Humanities and Social Theory*, vol. 29, Apr. 1999, www.colorado.edu/gendersarchive1998-2013/1999/01/10/beauty-pageants-and-barbie-theorizing-consumption-asian-american-transnational-feminism.

Thompson, Kara. "Traffic Stops, Stopping Traffic: Race and Climate Change in the Age of Automobility." *Isle: Interdisciplinary Studies in Literature and Environment*, vol. 24, no. 1, Winter 2017, pp. 92–112.

"*Through the Arc of the Rain Forest* Summary and Study Guide." *Book Rags*, www.bookrags.com/studyguide-through-the-arc-of-the-rainforest/. Accessed 7 July 2017.

Tomlinson, John. *Globalization and Culture*. Polity Press, 1999.

Trexler, Adam. *Anthropocene Fictions: The Novel in a Time of Climate Change*. U of Virginia P, 2015.

Truong, Monique T. D. *The Book of Salt*. Houghton Mifflin, 2003.

Tsuda, Takeyuki. *Strangers in the Ethnic Homeland: Japanese Brazilian Return Migration in Transnational Perspective*. Columbia UP, 2003.

"The Turning Point" The San Francisco State '68 Strike. *YouTube*, uploaded by laborvideo, 8 Dec. 2014, www.youtube.com/watch?v=Qd6-P3kHRBY.

Tymoigne, Eric. "A Hard-Nosed Look at Worsening U.S. Household Finance." *Challenge*, vol. 50, no. 4, July-Aug. 2007, pp. 88–111.

Ullrich, J. K. "Environmental Hazards: Five Challenges on Writing Climate Fiction." *J. K. Ullrich—Fiction for Now*, 4 June 2015, jkullrich.com/2015/06/04/environmental-hazards-five-challenges-of-writing-climate-fiction-part-1/. Accessed 28 Jan. 2020.

VanderMeer, Jeff. *Annihilation*. Farrar, Straus and Giroux, 2014.

Vint, Sherryl. "Orange County: Global Networks in *Tropic of Orange*." *Science Fiction Studies*, vol. 39, no. 3, Nov. 2012, pp. 401–14.

Viramontes, Helena María. "The Cariboo Café." *The Moths and Other Stories*, by Viramontes, Arte Público Press, 1985, pp. 65–82.

Wald, Sarah D. "'Refusing to Halt': Mobility and the Quest for Spatial Justice in Helena María Viramontes's *Their Dogs Came with Them* and Karen Tei Yamashita's *Tropic of Orange*." *Western American Literature*, vol. 48, nos. 1–2, Spring-Summer 2013, pp. 70–89.

Wallace, Molly. "'A Bizarre Ecology': The Nature of Denatured Nature." *ISLE: Interdisciplinary Studies in Literature and the Environment*, vol. 7, no. 2, Summer 2000, pp. 137–53.

———. "Tropics of Globalization: Reading the New North America." *Symplokē: A Journal for the Intermingling of Literary, Cultural and Theoretical Scholarship*, vol. 9, nos. 1–2, 2001, pp. 145–60.

Walter, Benjamin. "Theses on the Philosophy of History." *Illuminations*, translated by Harry Zohn, edited and introduced by Hannah Arendt, Schocken Books, 1968, pp. 253–64.

Wang, Frances Kai-Hwa. "Agreement Reached in San Francisco Hunger Strike to Fund Ethnic Studies." *NBC News*, 12 May 2016, www.nbcnews.com/news/asian-america/agreement-reached-sfsu-hunger-strike-save-ethnic-studies-n572736.

Warf, Barney, and Santa Arias. "Introduction: The Reinsertion of Space in the Humanities and Social Sciences." *The Spatial Turn: Interdisciplinary Perspectives*, edited by Warf and Arias, Routledge, 2009, pp. 1–10.

The Water Margin. Directed by Chang Cheh, Shaw Brothers, 1972.

Wei, William. *The Asian American Movement*. Temple UP, 1993.

Weiner, Matthew, creator. *Mad Men*. Lionsgate Television, 2007–15.

"What's with the X in Latinx?" *YouTube*, uploaded by we are mitú, 2 Apr. 2017, www.youtube.com/watch?v=Tk10RAlqsMo. Accessed 13 June 2017.

Wiarda, Howard. *Democracy and Its Discontents: Development, Interdependence, and U.S. Policy in Latin America*. Rowman and Littlefield, 1995.

Williams, Raymond. "Dominant, Residual, and Emergent." *Marxism and Literature*, by Williams, Oxford UP, 1977, pp. 121–27.

Williams, Sherley Anne. *Dessa Rose*. W. Morrow, 1986.

Winterson, Jeanette. *Art Objects: Essays on Ecstasy and Effrontery*. Jonathan Cape, 1995.

Wong, Lily. "Dwelling Over China: Minor Transnationalisms in Karen Tei Yamashita's *I Hotel*." *American Quarterly*, vol. 69, no. 3, Sept. 2017, pp. 719–39.

Wong, Sau-ling Cynthia. "Denationalization Reconsidered: Asian American Cultural Criticism at a Theoretical Crossroads." *Amerasia Journal*, vol. 21, nos. 1–2, 1995, pp. 1–27.

———. *Reading Asian American Literature: From Necessity to Extravagance*. Princeton UP, 1993.

Woolf, Virginia. *To the Lighthouse*. Routledge, 1994.

Wray, L. Randall. "Minsky and the Global Financial Crisis." *Why Minsky Matters: An Introduction to the Work of a Maverick Economist*, by Wray, Princeton UP, 2016, pp. 137–61.

Wu, Ellen D. *The Color of Success: Asian Americans and the Origins of the Model Minority*. Princeton UP, 2014. Politics and Society in Modern America.

Yamamoto, Hisaye. *"Seventeen Syllables" and Other Stories*. Kitchen Table: Women of Color Press, 1998.

Yamanaka, Keiko. "Return Migration of Japanese-Brazilians to Japan: The Nikkeijin as Ethnic Minority and Political Construct." *Diaspora: A Journal of Transnational Studies*, vol. 5, no. 1, Spring 1996, pp. 65–97.

Yamashita, Karen Tei. "1968: Eye Hotel." Yamashita, *I Hotel*, pp. 1–113.

———. "1969: I Spy Hotel." Yamashita, *I Hotel*, pp. 117–89.

———. "1970: 'I' Hotel." Yamashita, *I Hotel*, pp. 193–220.

———. "1971: Aiiieeeee! Hotel." Yamashita, *I Hotel*, pp. 221–91.

———. "1972: Inter-National Hotel." Yamashita, *I Hotel*, pp. 293–369.

———. "1973: Int'l Hotel." Yamashita, *I Hotel*, pp. 371–420.

———. "1975: Internationale Hotel." Yamashita, *I Hotel*, pp. 491–531.

———. "1977: I-Hotel." Yamashita, *I Hotel*, pp. 577–605.

———. *Anime Wong: A CyberAsian Odyssey*. Yamashita, *Anime Wong: Fictions*, pp. 289–326.

———. *Anime Wong: Fictions of Performance*. Edited and with an afterword by Stephen Hong Sohn, Coffee House Press, 2014.

———. "Asaka-no-Miya." *Rafu Shimpo*, holiday ed., 20 Dec. 1979, pp. 8+.

———. "The Bath." *Amerasia Journal*, vol. 3, no. 1, 1975, pp. 137–52.

———. "Borges and I." *The Massachusetts Review*, edited by Jim Hicks, Summer 2012, pp. 209–14.

———. *Brazil-Maru*. Coffee House Press, 1992.

———. "Call Me Ishimaru." *Leviathan: A Journal of Melville Studies*, vol. 18, no. 1, Mar. 2016, pp. 62–91.

———. *Circle K Cycles*. Coffee House Press, 2001.

———. "'Colono:Scopy': DSM: Asian American Edition." *Open in Emergency: A Special Issue on Asian American Mental Health*, special issue of *Asian American Literary Review*, vol. 7, no. 2, Fall-Winter 2016, pp. 137–41.

———. "A Gentlemen's Agreement." *Review 72: Literature and Arts of the Americas*, vol. 39, no. 1, 2006, pp. 112–21.

———. *GiLArex (or Godzilla Comes to Little Tokyo)*. Yamashita, *Anime Wong: Fictions*, pp. 73–160.

———. *Hannah Kusoh: An American Butoh*. Yamashita, *Anime Wong: Fictions*, pp. 21–58.

———. *I Hotel*. Coffee House Press, 2010.

———. "Interlude: Circle K Rules." Lesser, *Searching for Home Abroad*, pp. 67–74.

———. Interview. Conducted by Ikue Kina, 15 Sept. 2016.

———. "Interview with Author Karen Tei Yamashita by Clint." Conducted by Clint Porte. *Reader's Guide to I-Hotel by Karen Tei Yamashita*, 10 Mar. 2011, ihotelguide.blogspot.co.at/p/interview-with-author-karen-tei.html. Accessed 15 Jan. 2021.

———. "An Interview with Karen Tei Yamashita." Conducted by Elizabeth P. Glixman. *Eclectica Magazine*, vol. 11, no. 4, Oct.-Nov. 2007, www.eclectica.org/v11n4/glixman_yamashita.html. Accessed 9 June 2017.

———. *Jan Ken Pon: A Dance Performance Idea*. Yamashita, *Anime Wong: Fictions*, pp. 327–53.

———. "Kiss of Kitty." *Asian American Literary Review*, vol. 7, no. 1, Spring 2016, pp. 116–22.

———. *Kusei: Endangered Species*. Yamashita, *Anime Wong: Fictions*, pp. 1–20.

———. "The Last Secretary." *2000andWhat? Stories about the Turn of the Millennium*, edited by David Gilbert and Karl Roeseler, Trip Street Press, 1996, pp. 191–201.

———. "The Latitude of the Fiction Writer: A Dialogue." Interview conducted by Ryuta Imafuku. *Café Creole*, www.cafecreole.net/archipelago/Karen_Dialogue.html. Accessed 24 June 2013.

———. *Letters to Memory*. Coffee House Press, 2017.

———. "Literature as Community: The Turtle, Imagination, and the Journey Home." *Asian American Literature: Rethinking the Canon*, special issue of *The Massachusetts Review*, edited by Cathy J. Schlund-Vials and Lawrence-Minh Bùi Davis, vol. 59, no. 4, Winter 2018, pp. 597–611.

———. "Madama B." Yamashita, *Anime Wong: Fictions*, pp. 59–71.

———. 熱帯雨林の彼方へ [*Nettai Urin no Kanata e*]. 1994. Translated by Kenji Kazama, reissued ed., Shinchosha, 2014.

———. *Noh Bozos*. Yamashita, *Anime Wong: Fictions*, pp. 199–260.

———. *Omen: An American Kabuki*. 1978. Karen Tei Yamashita Papers, Special Collections and Archives, University Library, U of California, Santa Cruz, MS 465.

———. "The Orange." *Chicago Review*, vol. 39, nos. 3–4, 1993, pp. 12–16.

———. "The Orange." *Los Angeles Times*, 30 June 1991, articles.latimes.com/1991-06-30/magazine/tm-2223_1_orange-tree. Accessed 13 June 2017.

———. *Sansei and Sensibility*. Coffee House Press, 2020.

———. *Siamese Twins and Mongoloids: Three Abstractions on Asian America*. Yamashita, *Anime Wong: Fictions*, pp. 261–88.

———. *Through the Arc of the Rain Forest*. Coffee House Press, 1990.

———. *Tokyo Carmen versus L.A. Carmen*. Yamashita, *Anime Wong: Fictions*, pp. 161–98.

———. *Tropic of Orange*. Coffee House Press, 1997.

———. "Tucano." *Rafu Shimpo*, holiday ed., 20 Dec. 1975, pp. 11+.

———. "Writing and Memory: Images of the Japanese Diaspora in Brazil." *Orientalism and Identity in Latin America: Fashioning Self and Other from the (Post)Colonial Margin*, edited by Erik Camayd-Freixas, U of Arizona P, 2013, pp. 217–29.

Yanagihara, Hanya. *The People in the Trees*. Anchor Books, 2014.

Yang, Gene Luen. *American Born Chinese*. Square Fish, 2008.

———. *Boxers and Saints*. First Second, 2013.

Yates, Julian. "Orange." *Prismatic Ecology: Ecotheory beyond Green*, edited by Jeffrey Jerome Cohen et al., U of Minnesota P, 2013, pp. 83–105.

Yogi, Stan. "Japanese American Literature." *An Interethnic Companion to Asian American Studies*, edited by King-Kok Cheung, Cambridge UP, 1997, pp. 125–55.

Yu, Lai Ying. "'Capturing the Spirit': Teaching Karen Tei Yamashita's *I Hotel*." *Asian American Literature: Discourses and Pedagogies*, vol. 5, 2014, pp. 61–86, scholarworks.sjsu.edu/cgi/viewcontent.cgi?article=1058&context=aaldp.

Zemeckis, Robert, director. *Forrest Gump*. Paramount Pictures, 1994.

Zhao, Xiaojian, and Edward J. W. Park, editors. *Asian Americans: An Encyclopedia of Social, Cultural, Economic, and Political History*. ABC-CLIO, 2013.

Zhou, Xiaojing. *Cities of Others: Reimagining Urban Spaces in Asian American Literature*. U of Washington P, 2014.

Zhou, Xiaojing, and Samina Najmi, editors. *Form and Transformation in Asian American Literature*. U of Washington P, 2005.

Zia, Helen. *Asian American Dreams: The Emergence of an American People*. Farrar, Straus and Giroux, 2000.

Zinsser, William. Introduction. *Inventing the Truth: The Art and Craft of Memoir*, edited by Zinsser, rev. and expanded ed., Houghton Mifflin, 1998, pp. 4–22.